BORDERLESS AFRICA

T0292800

/ AFRICAN
/ ARGUMENTS

African Arguments is a series of short books about contemporary Africa and the critical issues and debates surrounding the continent. The books are scholarly and engaged, substantive and topical. They focus on questions of justice, rights and citizenship; politics, protests and revolutions; the environment, land, oil and other resources; health and disease; economy: growth, aid, taxation, debt and capital flight; and both Africa's international relations and country case studies.

Managing Editor: Stephanie Kitchen

Series editors

Adam Branch
Alex de Waal
Alcinda Honwana
Ebenezer Obadare
Carlos Oya
Nicholas Westcott

FRANCIS MANGENI
ANDREW MOLD

Borderless Africa

*A Sceptic's Guide to the
Continental Free Trade Area*

OXFORD
UNIVERSITY PRESS

IAI   International African Institute

OXFORD
UNIVERSITY PRESS

Oxford University Press is a department of the
University of Oxford. It furthers the University's objective
of excellence in research, scholarship, and education
by publishing worldwide.

Oxford   New York

Auckland   Cape Town   Dar es Salaam   Hong Kong   Karachi
Kuala Lumpur   Madrid   Melbourne   Mexico City   Nairobi
New Delhi   Shanghai   Taipei   Toronto

With offices in
Argentina   Austria   Brazil   Chile   Czech Republic   France   Greece
Guatemala   Hungary   Italy   Japan   Poland   Portugal   Singapore
South Korea   Switzerland   Thailand   Turkey   Ukraine   Vietnam

Oxford is a registered trade mark of Oxford University Press
in the UK and certain other countries.

Published in the United States of America by
Oxford University Press
198 Madison Avenue, New York, NY 10016

Library of Congress Cataloging-in-Publication Data is available
Francis Mangeni and Andrew Mold.
Borderless Africa: A Sceptic's Guide to the Continental Free Trade Area.
ISBN: 9780197774168
Printed in the United Kingdom on acid-free paper

CONTENTS

CONTENTS

PART III

ACKNOWLEDGEMENTS

To begin with, we would like to stress that the opinions expressed in this book are entirely ours and must not be attributed to institutions we are or have been affiliated to, nor to any member state of such institutions, nor for that matter to any other institutions with which we are associated. In particular, the views expressed herein are those of the authors and do not necessarily reflect the views of the United Nations. Any errors or shortcomings are ours alone.

Having said this, a publication of this nature is inevitably a collaborative effort and ours has often benefited from the support of others. To them, we wish to convey our immense gratitude. Without attempting to list all of them, we would like to first mention Stephanie Kitchen, the Managing Editor of the African Arguments series, who has helped guide the book since its initial proposal, from a series of disparate ideas and draft chapters into a final manuscript. The team at Hurst Publishers, led by Alice Clarke, provided steadfast support in turning the manuscript into this book.

In the initial stages of researching this book, we counted on the inestimable help of some young and talented researchers, who assisted with background research and some of the more laborious tasks associated with writing a book of this nature. Special mention must go to Diana Owuor, as well as Lincoln Ngaboyisonga and Eunice Ishimwe. Martha Gedamu, at the library of the Economic Commission of Africa, did a wonderful job in providing some of the old texts and books on continental integration that lay in the repository of the institution's library.

ACKNOWLEDGEMENTS

We express our gratitude to the two anonymous reviewers of the initial draft of the manuscript. Their comments and suggestions were invaluable in the formative stages of this book. We thank also Axel Addy, Doyin Adedeji, Alan Hirsch, Adeyemi Dipeolu, Raphael Kaplinsky, Seth Gor, Melaku Desta, Rajneesh Narula, James Gathii, Karina Pacheco, David Luke, Jaime MacLeod and Christopher Onyango for reviewing individual chapters, with very helpful observations and pointers that enormously assisted our work.

We would also like to mention Astrid Haas of the African Development Bank; Marisella Ouma of the Central Bank of Kenya; Commissioner Albert M. Muchanga of the African Union; Issa Baluch, a former President of FIATA and founder and CEO of Swift Freight International; W. Gyude Moore, a Senior Policy Fellow with the Centre for Global Development and former Minister of Public Works of Liberia; Bruce Byiers of the European Centre for Development Policy Management; and Edem Adzogenu, co-founder of AfroChampions, for their encouraging comments on the manuscript.

Finally, we would like to thank all the attendees of the seminars and workshops across the continent where we have presented some of the ideas captured in this book, who have patiently (and often passionately) made their own views known. One thing that has struck us persistently is that while there are a wide range of opinions on the future of the continental project, the enthusiasm for achieving something akin to a 'Borderless Africa' is unwavering.

Francis Mangeni, Lusaka
Andrew Mold, Kigali
August 2023

TABLES AND FIGURES

TABLES AND FIGURES

TABLES AND FIGURES

1

MAKING THE CASE FOR THE AFCFTA

Introduction: What is the AfCFTA?

Signed in March 2018 by 44 countries at a summit of the African Union held in Kigali, Rwanda, the African Continental Free Trade Area (AfCFTA) came at a time when the rest of the world was losing faith in processes of economic integration and liberalisation. This was less than two years after the United Kingdom had voted to leave the European Union (EU), and also when President Trump—a populist nationalist and avowed anti-integrator—had ascended to power in the United States. Africa is very much swimming against the current with the AfCFTA. This book explains why the African continent is going against the grain: the motivations behind it and the potential of the agreement.

Since its inception at that historic meeting, there has been no escaping the media impact of the AfCFTA. Newspaper articles, academic papers, magazines and television programmes across the continent have been filled with references to the AfCFTA, even if some people have struggled to remember the rather difficult acronym. There has undoubtedly been a lot of hyperbole around the agreement, with terms being bandied around like 'game changer',[1] 'unique' and 'once-in-a-lifetime opportunity'. While accepting that some of the rhetoric around the AfCFTA is overblown, this book argues that the economic case for the AfCFTA is irrefutable.[2]

If this is the case, the reader may ask, why then the title of this book? While we believe that the economic arguments are compelling, there is an underlying degree of scepticism emanating from certain quarters both within and outside the continent. That scepticism needs to be addressed and contested robustly. The audience for this book is essentially policymakers and academics, particularly those who still maintain a (healthy) scepticism towards such a bold pan-African initiative. But it is also hoped that the arguments will be accessible to a wider audience.

The AfCFTA is very much a home-grown solution to a long-standing problem, namely the fragmented and balkanised nature of the African economy. How those borders came about in the first place is a topic which will be explained in Chapter 2. In our view, a lack of regional integration on the continent is very much what economists call a 'binding constraint' on the economic development of the continent.[3] The AfCFTA represents a strategic way forward that will remove that binding constraint while helping to catalyse the adoption of better policies across many areas.

Pointedly, the AfCFTA is not, as its name would seem to suggest, simply a free trade area. Rather, it is a project of 'deep integration', in that at its core are many components that go beyond the simple elimination of tariffs to include measures that tackle all the major impediments to greater cross-border trade and investment. These include policies to harmonise product standards, the adoption of a common approach to intellectual property rights, and the creation of mutually agreed competition rules. It would have been better and more accurately termed the African Continental Market, with the added advantage that it would have made for a more memorable acronym.[4]

Crucially, as the title of this book insinuates, the AfCFTA is accompanied by a protocol on the free movement of people. We argue in this book that this is *not* additional to the agreement, but is instead at its core. As in the EU (where it is considered one of the four fundamental freedoms of the single market),[5] the right to live and work in another member state of the African Union is essential to the whole project—with the added advantage that its principal beneficiaries will be Africa's youth. Removing the impediments for African citizens to travel, do business or study in another African country will be central to the process of continental integration under the AfCFTA.

The AfCFTA is an idea whose time has come. Past efforts at regional integration on the African continent are often perceived as having failed—an idea that we dispute repeatedly in this book (see, inter alia, Chapters 3 and 8). Yet it is true that a lot of earlier integrational projects hit macroeconomic and political headwinds. That may no longer be true. The global economy is currently undergoing some profound shifts which are propitious for the success of the AfCFTA.

For one thing, the Covid-19 pandemic and the war in Ukraine have reminded policymakers and companies of the fragility of contemporary means of organising economic activity.[6] In the face of growing protectionism and rising disputes between the main players in the global economy—that is, the United States, the EU and China—the existing configuration of economic activity no longer seems optimal. A space is thus opening up for the African continent to pursue a regional solution to its long-standing problems of economic, political and social development.

On a more profound level, the global economy is in the throes of casting aside one 'techno-economic paradigm'[7]—based on Fordist-type scale economies, the pre-eminence of global value chains (GVCs) and the remarkable degree of concentration of economic power caused by the 'big business revolution'[8]—and embracing a new, as yet uncertain one. But it is clear that it will coalesce around a different set of imperatives, including greater economic resilience and the building of a green economy, facilitated by the ongoing ICT revolution and a fourth industrial revolution.[9] The frenzied period during the 1980s and 1990s which some authors termed 'deep globalisation'[10]—marked by an unrelenting increase in transcontinental flows of trade, capital and people—may also be coming to an end. Arguably, there has never been a more propitious moment for Africa to launch a programme to promote the development of regional value chains and create a strong continental market.

The structure of the agreement in a nutshell

As we will explain in Chapters 2 and 3, the AfCFTA is far from a new idea. It should be seen as part and parcel of a long process of continental integration, stretching all the way back to the founding of the Organisation of African Unity in 1963. Negotiations on the AfCFTA began on 15 June 2015, at the 25th Ordinary Summit of the African Union Heads of State and Government. Despite their technical intricacy, the subsequent texts[11] were concluded in less than three years. By the June 2018 Summit of the African Union Assembly—just three months after the initial signing of the agreement in Kigali in March of that same year—further instruments had been negotiated and added to the agreement.[12] Admittedly, there was a subsequent slowing down of progress due to the Covid-19 pandemic, both in terms of the pace of the ratifications and the conclusion of negotiations in some areas like the rules of origin.[13] But it still represents stellar progress compared with the snail's pace of negotiations in most comparable international agreements.

Only those countries that have ratified the AfCFTA are bound by the new rules and will enjoy the benefits related to enhanced market access in goods and services.[14] Nevertheless, progress on that score has also been impressive, with 47 of the 54 member states having ratified the agreement by July 2023. The legal structure of the agreement is laid out in Table 1.1. The spirit of the agreement is easily summarised. According to Article 4, for purposes of fulfilling and realising its objectives, African Union member states have committed to:

- Progressively eliminate tariffs and non-tariff barriers (NTBs) to trade in goods;
- Progressively liberalise trade in services;
- Cooperate on investment, intellectual property rights and competition policies;
- Cooperate on all trade-related areas between state parties;
- Cooperate on customs matters and the implementation of trade-facilitation measures;
- Design a mechanism for the settlement of disputes concerning their rights and obligations; and
- Establish and maintain an institutional framework for the implementation and administration of the Continental Free Trade Area.

Table 1.1: Structure of the agreement establishing the African Continental Free Trade Area

Protocol on Trade in Goods	Annex 1 Schedules of Tariff Concessions
	Annex 2 Rules of Origin
	Annex 3 Customs Cooperation and Mutual Administrative Assistance
	Annex 4 Trade Facilitation
	Annex 5 Non-Tariff Barriers
	Annex 6 Technical Barriers to Trade
	Annex 7 Sanitary and Phytosanitary Measures
	Annex 8 Transit
	Annex 9 Trade Remedies
Protocol on Trade in Services	Schedules of Specific Commitments
	MFN Exemption
	Air Transport Services
	List of Priority Sectors
	Framework Document on Regulatory Cooperation
Protocol on Rules and Procedures on the Settlement of Disputes	Annex 1 Working Procedures of the Panel
	Annex 2 Expert Review
	Annex 3 Code of Conduct for Arbitrators and Panellists
Phases II and III Negotiations	Protocol on Investment
	Protocol on Competition Policy
	Protocol on Intellectual Property Rights
	Protocol on Digital Trade
	Protocol on Women and Youth in Trade

Sources: AUC, ECA, AfDB (2019); authors' elaboration.

The first task and most urgent is the elimination of the tariffs on intra-African goods trade. Tariff reductions should have started on 1 January 2021, but things were delayed by both the disruption caused by Covid-19 and the failure to conclude the negotiations on the rules of origin, which constitute the regulatory 'passport' for goods to benefit from the AfCFTA tariff reductions. While the initial objective is to liberalise 90% of tariff lines, countries are also allowed to implement reductions over a longer period in the case of 'sensitive goods'. Only 3% of tariff lines can be excluded completely from the tariff reductions (Table 1.2).[15] This basically implies that, by 2035, tariffs on intra-African goods will have been eliminated on 97% of all tariff lines.

The AfCFTA is not confined to merchandise goods, however. Service trade is also slated for liberalisation. Negotiations on this issue were undertaken on the basis of a 'positive list',[16] starting with five main sub-sectors (business services [including areas such as accounting, legal and ICT-related services], financial services, communication, transportation, and tourism). Those negotiations began in June 2018 and have now been concluded for the majority of countries. Protocols on Competition, Intellectual Property and Investment have also been concluded. However, there are still some outstanding issues to be negotiated to complete the legal framework for the AfCFTA—on Digital Trade and Women and Youth in Trade—which, at the time of writing, are close to being finalised. As such, the AfCFTA amounts to a comprehensive and 'deep' trade agreement.

All in all, this constitutes quite a substantial 'to-do' list for member states and the newly formed AfCFTA Secretariat (which was established in March 2020 in Accra, Ghana), and all within quite a tight timeframe for a regional agreement of such ambition. One challenge has been the innate and instinctive conservatism of African trade negotiators; this has its roots in recent history, whereby African trade negotiators have often been pitted against economically much more powerful trading partners like the United States and the EU. Success in such negotiations has often been considered to consist in conceding the minimum amount of effective liberalisation. Needless to say, the AfCFTA negotiations need to be approached in a different, more generous, spirit to enable the maximum amount of opening to greater cross-border trade and investment between African member states.

Table 1.2: Schedule of tariff liberalisation envisaged under the AfCFTA

		Tariff reductions		
		For non-sensitive products (90%)	For sensitive products (7%)	For excluded products (3%)
Country classification	Developing countries	Fully liberalised over 5 years (linear cut)	Fully liberalised over 10 years (linear cut)	No cut
	Least developed countries[17]	Fully liberalised over 10 years (linear cut)	Fully liberalised over 13 years (linear cut)	No cut

Sources: AUC, ECA, AfDB (2019).

Some observers take all this as evidence that the continent is not yet ready for the AfCFTA.[18] However, it is often not realised the extent to which building a regional market is a long-term project. For instance, the reduction in transaction costs involved in border formalities are often more serious hindrances to trade than customs duties. Eliminating these costs can be a complex process; for example, although the European Economic Community (EEC) was formed in 1957, more than three decades later the average truck carrying produce from one European member state to another still had to present 40 different administrative papers to be able to cross the borders. It took until the mid-1990s to get close to the ideal of having 'invisible borders' where such paperwork was no longer necessary.[19]

Africa does not have the luxury of that kind of timeline—nor can it afford, for instance, the lull in activity that characterised the first three decades of existence of the Association of Southeast Asian Nations (ASEAN) in Southeast Asia.[20] There is a feeling of urgency to getting the AfCFTA fully operational. To some extent, the credibility of the AfCFTA itself relies on making rapid progress and proving the cynics wrong.

A groundswell of popular support—but also some underlying concerns

The late Thandika Mkandawire often complained that a weakness of the continent's agenda for regional integration was that it was a purely top-down process:

> There is a very deep commitment to the continent ... if you walked up to most Africans and told them that they now belonged to the United States of Africa, they wouldn't be upset, because pan-African-ism has a positive emotional resonance. Unfortunately, there are no institutions translating that emotional commitment to the continent into regional integration.[21]

Despite this, a telephone poll of over 1,000 citizens from across the continent undertaken in November 2018 by the Rockefeller Foundation suggests that this may not be the case in this instance, as 77% of those interviewed supported the AfCFTA in principle.[22] In a more recent opinion poll among 800 private sector players, 68% of the respondents welcomed the AfCFTA, arguing it would be either very positive or positive for their businesses. Just 4% thought it might have a negative impact.[23]

Support for the AfCFTA is not only from Africa's political elite then—but it would also be wrong to take popular support for granted. Successful implementation of the AfCFTA will require political will as well as the buy-in of ordinary Africans whose labour, capital and knowledge will form the lifeblood of the continental market. Although in this book we stress that they will be among the principal beneficiaries, young people still seem largely unaware of the initiative, with approximately half of the responders in a recent poll saying they had no knowledge of the AfCFTA.[24] According to a series of Afrobarometer surveys conducted in 18 African countries in late 2019 and 2020, sizeable proportions of the population—more than half in some countries—were sceptical of opening their borders to businesses and products from other countries or regions, preferring that their government protect domestic producers.[25] However, at the same time, most also complained that crossing international borders in their region for work or trade was unduly difficult.[26] A majority supported the free movement of people and wanted their governments to allow foreign-owned retail shops.

It is important to put such views into their proper perspective. When the broad level of support for greater economic 'openness' is compared globally, it is much higher in Africa than in many other parts of the world—particularly some high-income countries which are supposed to be the cheerleaders of a more liberal global economic order. A Pew Research Center poll conducted in 2014, for instance, revealed that, when asked what they thought of growing trade and business ties between their country and other countries, 28% of Americans answered 'somewhat bad' or 'very bad'. The corresponding figures for the East African countries of Kenya, Uganda and Tanzania were just 11, 9 and 8%, respectively.

Perhaps a more pertinent comparison for the AfCFTA is with public opinion during the period of negotiations on the North American Free Trade Agreement (NAFTA). When this historic agreement was being ratified in the US Congress, a Gallup Poll conducted in November 1993, in the heat of the battle for congressional ratification, found that 46% of the public openly opposed NAFTA.[27] Yet NAFTA was implemented regardless. As the Rockefeller poll cited earlier suggests, such high figures of opposition would be unimaginable to the Pan-African project of the AfCFTA. So, if we step back a little, we see that Mkandawire was essentially right in affirming that levels of support for regional integration on the continent are high to start with. The challenge will be putting these beliefs into practice.

Why this book?

Faithful to the title of the book series African Arguments, this book tries to lay out the political economic case for the rapid implementation of the AfCFTA. What it does not do is provide a comprehensive description of all the AfCFTA legislation nor all the operational aspects. It is rather an 'argumentative' book, in the sense that it lays out all the reasons why the continent needs the AfCFTA in the first place. In other words, the book is more about the 'why' of the AfCFTA, rather than the 'how'. In that sense, it is meant as a complement to a lot of literature and reports already written on some of the more technical aspects of the agreement.[28]

Although we touch on the political economy of the agreement on multiple occasions, in essence the book does not pitch its arguments at the political level. Within the African continent, those arguments have broadly been won, as shown by the broad consensus in the signing and ratification of the agreement. Our book is focused principally on the economic arguments—arguments which are compelling both from the point of view of economic theory and, more crucially, empirical evidence.

That said, it is important to remind ourselves of the extent to which regional integration is always in some fundamental sense a political rather than economic project.[29] This has been the case with the EU, which was established explicitly to avoid further conflict on the European continent, and it has also been the case for most other regional agreements too, both in Africa and elsewhere. In West Africa, for instance, the Economic Community of West African States (ECOWAS) very much came to the forefront because of its peace and security dimensions. Similarly, the Southern African Development Coordination Conference (SADCC—the predecessor of today's Southern African Development Community [SADC]) is a good example of a reasonably successful regional integration effort whose purpose was mainly political, not economic (in this instance, beating apartheid).[30] In sum, we cannot neglect the underlying political economy of regional integration. While there is hardly a political leader on the African continent who does not adopt the language of Pan-Africanism, those words often remain relegated to the level of rhetoric. Moving Pan-African sentiment to action is one of the major challenges to implementing the AfCFTA.

In the same spirit, this book also provides a critique of both the opponents of the AfCFTA and those that unquestioningly embrace it. There are a number of specific points on which we depart with the consensus opinion[31] on the AfCFTA:

1. We argue that the extent of intra-African trade is seriously underreported, and its economic significance is already much greater than commonly appreciated, even before the AfCFTA is implemented. This is good news for the continental project, as there is a solid base upon which to build (Chapter 8).

2. There is currently an excessive emphasis on the role of small and medium-sized enterprises (SMEs) and small-scale, cross-border

traders. The AfCFTA is an opportunity to upscale economic activities on the continent—an opportunity that is too good to be missed (Chapters 9 and 13).

3. More efforts and initiatives are needed to promote intra-African foreign direct investment (FDI), which will be a major driver of increasing trade and investment linkages for the continent (Chapter 10).

4. Far from being an appendage to the agreement, the Free Movement Protocol is necessarily at the core of what the AfCFTA is trying to achieve. In other words, a greater intensity of intra-African trade and investment will only be achieved by facilitating the movement of people—and the principal beneficiaries of this will be young people (Chapter 12).

5. As part of its efforts to assist economic and social development on the continent, the international community could better focus its support in ways that help and not hinder the implementation of the AfCFTA (Chapter 13).

6. Finally, and perhaps most crucially, there is a need to avoid over-burdening the AfCFTA with unrealistic expectations. It cannot be the solution to all of the continent's developmental challenges (Chapter 14).

This last point leads us to make some observations about what the AfCFTA is not. Firstly, despite what is claimed in many publications on the AfCFTA, it is not essentially a vehicle through which to achieve high environmental and labour standards, gender parity and equity goals, etc. These are all laudable—nay, fundamental—objectives, but we argue these are best achieved by action at the national level. National governments will still be responsible for meeting the bulk of the developmental expectations, and they should be held to account if they fail to do so. To be sure, the AfCFTA will create pressure to achieve a degree of harmonisation of approach if a 'race to the bottom' is to be avoided—countries undercutting each other by not imposing health-and-safety standards, or by allowing companies to pollute indiscriminately. Yet there are risks here.

Ha-Joon Chang has written extensively on the dangers of developing countries being compelled to adopt labour, environmental and product standards which were, in the first place, never applied when high-income countries themselves were in the early stages of their own economic development, and in the second place, could end up being unrealistic, stringent and undermining the competitiveness of developing countries.[32] The beauty of the AfCFTA is precisely that it allows African countries to fix standards and norms that are more appropriate to their level of development. However, discussions in this area inevitably gravitate towards 'global standards' and 'norms'. This constitutes a risk for the success of the agreement, overburdened with too many peripheral objectives unrelated to its core objective of increasing intra-African trade and investment.

Secondly, the AfCFTA is not by any stretch of the imagination a 'neoliberal' project simply aimed at promoting more international trade. Yes, it is designed to increase trade, investment, and promote the harmonisation of trading and business rules and standards among African countries. But that goal is fully consistent with measures to increase the degree of integration of African countries, both individually and collectively, with the rest of the world. Moreover, while the AfCFTA remains a free trade area, member states will still be allowed to set their own tariff rates on imports from outside of the continent and will also be able to adopt their own policies towards foreign investment (although they will be encouraged to treat intra-African investment favourably). As such, the key term in relation to AfCFTA is 'selective integration'. That in no way makes it an endorsement of neoliberalism (unless one clings to the belief that all processes of regional integration are neoliberal in nature).

Finally, the AfCFTA is not a 'magic wand' to tackle economic shocks like the recovery from Covid-19. One of the frustrating things about current discussions on the AfCFTA is that many proponents make it sound like the benefits will materialise very rapidly. They won't. Processes of deep regional integration, even once they are fully agreed and have enjoyed broad popular support (as we will argue is the case of the AfCFTA), take time to implement. However, we do argue that over time the positive economic impacts will ripple across the whole of the continental economy and make it far more resilient.

An overview of the book

This book is divided in three parts. Part I (Chapters 2–7) explains how Africa's economic engagement with the rest of the world over recent decades has not delivered the promised benefits. Hence, there is a need for a new strategic approach, as embodied in the AfCFTA. Chapter 2 starts by providing a brief historical overview of what the continental economy looked like prior to the imposition of colonial borders, and goes on to summarise the intellectual and political battles in post-independence Africa to establish a more unified continent. Chapter 3 delves into a brief discussion of the trials and tribulations in the professional career of Nigerian economist Adebayo Adedeji—a man who could be rightly considered as one of the scholarly fathers of the AfCFTA. The chapter briefly summarizes his intellectual contributions and insights into how to achieve greater economic integration and unity on the African continent. It also highlights some of the work of the Malawian economist Thandika Mkandawire and the light his work threw on some of the fundamental challenges to achieving greater continental integration.

Chapter 4 describes Africa's trade performance from a long-term perspective, and explains why the lack of economic diversification and heavy dependence on commodity exports (an unfortunate legacy of the continent's colonial past) has ultimately undermined Africa's developmental aspirations. Chapter 5 reviews the evidence into why, contrary to a lot of contemporary literature, industrialisation and manufacturing are still key to the continent's economic growth and development. The fact that a large share of intra-African trade is already composed of manufactured and processed goods provides support for the idea that, to achieve economic diversification and move away from the dependence on commodities, the regional AfCFTA route is the one that should be pursued most vigorously. Finally, the chapter also discusses why, for the majority of countries on the continent, 'leap-frogging' into services is not a viable strategy for long-term growth and development.

Chapter 6 looks into the preferential trading agreements with high income countries—such as the Everything But Arms (EBA) agreement with the EU, or the Africa Growth and Opportunity Act

(AGOA) with the United States, and explains why these agreements have not achieved their ostensible objectives of helping the continent to expand their exports and diversify their economies. The chapter also looks at the more recent preferential scheme with China and discusses why trading relations with China have similarly failed to turn the situation around. The concluding chapter of Part I discusses the continent's troubled relationship with the global trading system, analysing both its formal governance (through the WTO) and informal governance (through the growth of global value chains).

Part II makes the broader political economic case in favour of rapid AfCFTA implementation. Chapter 8 argues that intra-African trade already has greater economic significance than commonly believed. Indeed, by some metrics, parts of Africa display a stronger degree of trade integration than comparable regions elsewhere in the world. The chapter ends by arguing that, as AfCFTA implementation begins, it is time to change the narrative and to start to 'talk up' intra-African trade. Chapter 9 explains the main economic benefits of the AfCFTA from the perspective of facilitating economies of scale and scope, of incentivising greater manufacturing trade, and the benefits from liberalised intra-African trade and investment in the services and agricultural sectors.

Chapter 10 doubles down on these points and argues that the expansion of intra-African trade will depend to a large extent on success in boosting cross-border investment. One of the principal drivers of trade, both globally and on the African continent, is FDI. Yet a lot of the focus on discussions of AfCFTA implementation have hitherto been focused on SMEs and informal cross-border traders. While recognising that there is traditionally a fair amount of hostility to FDI on the continent (partly tied up with its association with colonial exploitation), this chapter contends that, as long as the right regulatory framework is in place, greater intra-regional FDI would greatly increase competition and accelerate the emergence of intra-regional value chains. If that dynamism can be harnessed for the sake of deepening regional economic integration, it would go a long way towards increasing the level of economic interaction between African economies.

Chapter 11 observes that, in making the case for the AfCFTA, many numbers are bandied around regarding the impact of the agreement, but they are often not consistent and are contingent on a whole host of assumptions. There is understandably a huge demand for quantifying the impact of the agreement, for determining which sectors will be most benefited, what the costs of implementation may be (for instance, in terms of tariff revenue foregone by the reduction of intra-African tariffs), and which countries will gain the most and which, conversely, might not benefit at all. In this chapter, the reader is taken through a crash course in understanding how to contextualise the results of quantitative studies and appreciate both their strengths and limitations.

Chapter 12 discusses one of the most contentious parts of the package: the Free Movement Protocol. While acknowledging the reticence of some member states to fully endorse this Protocol, the chapter makes the case that liberalising the movement of people is essential for attaining the long-term goals of the AfCFTA. A greater mobility of labour across the continent will help address skill shortages, contribute to a faster rate of economic growth and reduce unemployment. It is going to be a boon for Africa's young people in particular, who are increasingly well qualified but often unable to find gainful employment in their own countries. The chapter argues that the political obstacles to the implementation of the Free Movement Protocol can be overcome, provided there are certain safeguards and that the implementation is gradual.

Part III takes a broader look at the way forward for the AfCFTA. Chapter 13 discusses what external partners should do to support the AfCFTA. In general, the donor community has expressed their backing for the AfCFTA. However, their actions have not always been compatible with the expressed goal. In particular, there has been a flurry of offers of signing free trade agreements with African member states. This risks undermining the coherence of the AfCFTA agreement. Against this backdrop, the chapter stresses the importance of development partners adopting the principal of 'doing no harm' and avoiding taking measures that destabilise the agreement. The chapter also explains that the donors should focus their support on the fundamental issues and/or measures that will increase cross-border trade, investment and the free movement of people, rather than distracting attention towards more peripheral considerations or objectives the agreement is ill-equipped to tackle.

Finally, Chapter 14 summarises some of the main issues raised in previous chapters and discusses some potential impediments to the full implementation of the AfCFTA. The chapter starts by arguing the case for bold regional leadership from the continent's larger economies. With the right political will, these hub economies could drive the whole process of continental integration. The chapter identifies the principal supporters and detractors of implementation, and argues that, amidst a pronounced shift in the global economy towards a new paradigm, the emergent Africa needs to be based on a very different developmental model from the past. The AfCFTA must embody that future.

PART I

2

THE HISTORICAL ANTECEDENTS

Introduction

This chapter provides a brief account of the historical antecedents to the AfCFTA. Africa accounts for 17% of the global population, but just 2.5% of global exports. Many people assume that the marginalisation of the continent from global trade is a permanent characteristic of African economies, and for this reason they doubt that the AfCFTA project will work. Yet historically, there has been nothing lacking on the continent in terms of acumen for seeking out economic opportunities through commerce. This chapter begins with a brief discussion about the vibrancy of trade on the continent in the pre-colonial period. Addressing the title of this book, the chapter then turns to how the continent's existing borders came into being in the first place during the notorious 'Scramble for Africa' of the late nineteenth century. A brief overview follows regarding the political struggles since independence to overcome the constraints of the colonial borders and strive for greater African unity. The chapter ends with a discussion about the appearance of the regional economic communities, which should rightly be considered as the 'building blocks' of the AfCFTA.

A continent of consummate traders

Africa has a long history of trading within and outside the continent. Historically, much of this trade predates trading networks that developed elsewhere.[1] In Phoenician times, Berber middlemen took gold and ivory to Europe mainly through two trails across the Sahara—westward from Morocco through Mauritania and southward from the Fezzan of the Garamantes to the Middle Niger and Lake Chad. In India, Hindu brides bedecked themselves with the carved ivory of Kenya and Tanganyika. Chinese officials travelled to court in rickshaws decorated with the same material.

In the nineteenth century, the Sokoto Caliphate in West Africa was an example of a regional economy spanning many 'countries'. John Iliffe noted that Kano's central position within the 'Sokoto common market' made its textile finishing industry 'the most capitalised in tropical Africa ... economies of scale enabled Hausa cloth to destroy Borno's textile industry, capture the Timbuktu market, outsell local textiles a thousand kilometres away and find outlets as distant as Egypt and Brazil.'[2] Research has revealed that cowrie shells (which acted as currency in West Africa) imported via Saharan caravans and European ships were not used to lubricate external trade; rather, they were used as currencies to facilitate intra-African trade.[3]

Yet historically, outsiders have tended to downplay the economic vibrancy of pre-colonial Africa. When and where there are instances of industriousness and trade, it is usually ascribed to external activity. For instance, when Great Zimbabwe—a magnificent construction which experienced its heyday between the twelfth and sixteenth centuries—was first discovered, European 'historians' stressed the links that it had with the outside world, pejoratively considering that it could not have solely been the product of indigenous effort and expertise. The importance of internal African trade for Great Zimbabwe, by contrast, was downplayed. This was highly misleading: the few foreign goods found, like Arabian and Persian glass beads, were scattered across the excavations, suggesting the inhabitants did not value them highly. The presence of copper ingots similar to those found in Congo and Zambia today, and metal gongs akin to those found across West and Central Africa, all imply that Great Zimbabwe was at the heart of an African network of trade.[4]

This story is not just about the vibrancy of pre-colonial trade. Africa also had a lot more experience with industrial production than is often believed. Proto-industrial activities have deep roots, as testi-fied by indigenous markets for textiles, ironware, ceramics, furniture, weapons, mats, baskets, soap, washing and cooking gear. The smelted iron of East Africa even acquired an international reputation. Collecting reports of Africa in twelfth-century India, al-Idrisi reported that while the best steel came from India, East African iron was supplied 'to all the lands of India … [and] at a good price—because it is most superior in quality and most malleable.'[5]

Regrettably, in the colonial period Africa also experienced a large-scale erosion of these proto-industrial roots. For instance, British, Indian, Japanese and Chinese textile imports in the early twentieth century effectively curtailed the evolution of the existing indigenous textile industry. There was a brief period of manufacturing expansion under import substitution industrialisation in the early years of independence, but it was short-lived, and the gains, with the notable exception of South Africa, evaporated in the crisis of the late twentieth century. Even in periods of structurally declining terms of trade for commodities (e.g. 1880–1940), Africa's specialisation in primary export commodities thus deepened further.[6] We take up these points further in Chapters 4 and 5.

The birth of the borders

Prior to the colonial era, hard geographical borders did not characterise states in Africa, with rulers having only loose control over territory and the movement of people.[7] To be sure, there were powerful kingdoms, such as the Ashanti in modern-day Ghana, or the Buganda in Uganda in East Africa, or the Zulu in Southern Africa—but they were not defined by the kind of boundaries that became prevalent in the Western world. Indeed, the late Cambridge historian Geoffrey Hawthorn liked to say that one of the enduring lessons that pre-colonial Africa had given to the world was how mankind could live in relative harmony, side by side, without the need for the Westphalian nation state, delineated by hard borders.

That was all to change at the Berlin Conference of 1884/5, when the colonial powers divided up Africa among themselves, creating territorial borders based on their de facto zones of control. These boundaries arbitrarily separated regions with long-standing ethnic ties

and often without clear geographical separators.[8] Moussa Faki
Mahamat, the chairperson of the African Union Commission, once
observed that the map of Africa looks like a shattered or broken mirror. Yet these bizarre borders have remained the basis for national
boundaries ever since the end of colonialism.

The historic injustice of the division of the African continent by the
European powers at the Berlin Conference in 1884/5 is beautifully
described in a recent book by Dipo Faloyin.[9] In it, he describes the
absurdity of the borders that were drawn up. No Africans were present at that infamous meeting; if they had been, Faloyin points out,
they would have surely pointed to the illogicality of drawing random
straight lines on an inaccurate map, and would have warned of the
long-term internal frictions that would inevitably take generations
and generations to untangle from their cursed roots:

> Perhaps African representatives would have chosen to identify on the
> map which communities spoke which languages and worshipped
> which gods. Some though might have gone into how dangerous it
> could be to run a border through proud, ancient kingdoms and cul-
> tures, and how forcing disparate ethnic groups to live under a single
> banner might make government of these wholly invented nations
> somewhat complicated. Perhaps a discussion might have broken out
> about what constituted civilised and uncivilised, savages and cultured,
> the developed and undeveloped world .... Perhaps .... But it didn't
> happen. And it was by design ....[10]

The boundaries of modern-day Africa are thus purely a construct of
the colonial period. Often bizarre boundaries split communities in
two or bound previously antagonist communities together in unhappy
marriages. In the Horn of Africa, for instance, Somalis were split into
French Somaliland, British Somalia, Italian Somalia, Ethiopian
Somalia, and the Somali region of northern Kenya.[11] Similarly, the
Afar people of Ethiopia were divided amongst Ethiopia, Eritrea and
Djibouti, and the Anyua and Nuer were split between Ethiopia and
what is now South Sudan.[12]

The most egregious examples were when the colonial powers
decided to draw straight lines, like the Caprivi Strip in Namibia. In
fact, 80% of African borders follow latitudinal and longitudinal lines,
more than in any other part of the world. A study by Alesina et al.

tried to assess econometrically whether these artificial states, defined by the predominance of straight-line borders and the erratic separation of ethnic groups, were more prone to political and economic instability.[13] Their findings confirmed that these countries tend to have greater economic problems and political violence. One of the most pronounced negative economic impacts was the way in which traditional trade routes were cut because commerce with people outside one's colony was forbidden. This is a point we take up further in Chapter 4.

Pan-African struggles

Undoing that mess has been an African aspiration ever since. Pan-Africanism as a political movement can be traced back to 1900, when Sylvester Williams of Trinidad organised the first Pan-African congress in London. Subsequent congresses all called for equal treatment for people of African descent, but concerns initially focused on welfare of subjugated peoples rather than on decolonisation per se.[14]

A significant departure occurred in the aftermath of the Second World War with the Pan-African Congress held in Manchester in October 1945. The European colonial powers were clearly much debilitated economically by the conflict, and the status quo was no longer going to be sustainable. Moreover, during the Second World War, the United States had voiced, in no uncertain terms, that it was no longer prepared to turn a blind eye to colonial excess and called for European countries to respect the wishes of colonised peoples to exercise the right of self-determination. The congress seized the opportunity of the moment by demanding an immediate decolonisation in Africa.[15] The independence of India in 1947 gave further impetus to African desires for a rapid process of decolonialisation. South of the Sahara, Ghana was first, attaining its independence in March 1957, to be followed in October 1958 by Guinea. From then on, it was only a matter of time for the house of cards to fall. And for much of the continent, African independence arrived at a speed that not even the key protagonists expected. By the end of 1966, 40 countries had become independent.[16]

During this period, Pan-Africanism gradually moved back to Africa and became an ideology of governments and no longer one driven by civil society. However, the transition was not an easy one. Disagreements quickly arose between the leaders of the newly independent countries about which approach to take towards achieving greater economic and political cooperation. A historic battle was waged for the soul of Pan-Africanism between a 'radical' Casablanca minority bloc led by Kwame Nkrumah (and also including Guinea, Mali, Egypt, Algeria and Morocco) and the majority of more conservative African states, grouped in the Brazzaville and Monrovia blocs, whose leaders favoured a more gradualist approach to continental unity.

In essence, the disputes boiled down to a familiar story of arguments as to whether politics should lead the process or economics.[17] In one corner, Nkrumah called for the rapid establishment of a 'United States of Africa', in which countries would pool their sovereignty in the areas of economics, security and foreign policy as a way of achieving industrialisation. The Ghanaian leader envisaged a continental authority to oversee integrated planning and transport systems and advocated the building of a vast road and railway network, a rapid increase in air links, and a massive upgrading of continental ports. Nkrumah regarded the association agreement between francophone African countries and the French-led European Common Market as 'collective colonialism' designed to make Africa a permanent supplier of primary products for European markets. He called instead for the establishment of an African Common Market, with a single currency and a common policy for intra-African and extra-continental trade.

In the other corner, a diametrically opposed vision of Pan-African cooperation was endorsed by the Senegalese president Léopold Senghor. While he supported cooperation on economic, financial, cultural, technical and scientific issues, he advocated for pursuing a minimalist agenda on political cooperation. Where Nkrumah urged Africa to harness its own resources, Senghor promoted a pragmatic use of European—in this case, French—financial resources and scientific knowledge to promote socio-economic development.[18]

Such views left many francophone leaders seemingly championing a subservient system of Françafrique which left them vulnerable to the charge of neo-colonialism.[19] Many aligned themselves with French policies in multilateral forums, even on issues involving the liberation of Algeria. However, the battle lines in this ideological conflict were not neatly divided between francophones and anglophones. So, for instance, the Senegalese scholar and scientist Cheikh Anta Diop shared Nkrumah's view that rapid political federation was a prerequisite for continental economic integration.[20] Faced by implacable opposition of the French authorities,[21] and bolstered by the solidarity provided by Nkrumah post-independence, Guinea's new president Ahmed Sékou Touré was also a committed member of the Casablanca Group.

There was, however, a third faction: the arguably more pragmatic perspective promoted by the Monrovia group, often operating under Nigerian leadership. Within this bloc, it was the Tanzanian president Julius Nyerere who offered the most cogent intellectual opposition to Nkrumah in calling for a more gradualist approach to regional integration on the continent. He argued in favour of using sub-regional bodies such as East Africa's British-inherited federal institutions as building blocks, before federating with a larger continental group: 'African unity is at present merely an emotion born of a history of colonialism and oppression. It has to be strengthened and expressed in economic and political forms before it can really have a positive effect on the future.'[22]

Like Nkrumah, Nyerere also advocated a federal 'United States of Africa' as a final goal, although he stressed—unlike the impatient Nkrumah—the need to convince newly sovereign countries, through persuasion, to take the necessary steps for integration willingly, and argued that they be allowed to travel at their own pace.[23] Nyerere thus urged an approach of what in more contemporary terms would be called 'variable geometry' in which different forms and speeds of integration would occur in different sub-regions. In East Africa, he focused on a federation of Tanzania, Kenya and Uganda as a first step towards attaining a United States of Africa.

In 1963, as these debates played out, a conference was called in Addis Ababa to draw up a charter for the founding of the Organisation of African Unity (OAU). By that stage, there were 32 independent African nations involved in the negotiations, whereas in 1958 there had been just ten—a sign of the rapid accelerating pace of decolonisation. Arguments in Addis for a continental union government— the Casablanca Group's position—did not receive the support of African leaders, and Kwame Nkrumah cast the lone vote in favour.

Leaders of the other factions openly voiced suspicion that Nkrumah had designs of self-aggrandisement, wanting to become president of Africa to their detriment. Uppermost in the minds of the new leaders was securing the existing boundaries and stabilising the internal political situation—a reasonable prioritisation given efforts by some of the former colonial powers to destabilise the new states through the support of rebel groups and, in the worst of cases, through political assassinations.

Almost all African countries acquiesced to the existing colonial borders when signing the Charter of the OAU in 1964. Only Somalia and Morocco did not accept the borders, and while Ghana and Togo raised some objections on their boundary that splits the Ewe, the border did not change.[24] President Philibert Tsiranana of Malagasy (now Madagascar) summed up the mood well:

> It is no longer possible, nor desirable, to modify the boundaries of Nations, on the pretext of racial, religious or linguistic criteria .... Indeed, should we take race, religion or language as the criteria for setting our boundaries, a few States in Africa would be blotted out from the map.[25]

The resulting OAU is commonly viewed as a failure. Yet these criticisms were not based on its actual goals, but on expectations the organisation had never sought to fulfil in the first place. Indeed, on its own terms, what the framers of the charter set out to achieve was a resounding success. They wanted non-interference, and they got it. They defeated programmes for supranational institutions to check betrayal of the national good and so survived on eliminating or disarming institutions for proper governance. Even the Secretary-General was not made a cogent institution because members did not want a super head of state who might do things of which they did not approve. They merely approved an administrative secretary with no executive authority.[26]

Later, as the OAU evolved into the African Union in 2002, the goals became bolder and focused more on economic development as well as governance and peacebuilding.[27] But by that time, the objectives of continental integration had been fixed. This is a story to which we will return in Chapter 3.

The emergence of Africa's regional economic communities

While the OAU deserves some credit for its firm and consistent commitment to decolonisation and the anti-apartheid struggles in Southern Africa, its establishment in 1963 clearly did not satisfy all demands for greater continental integration. For some, its deference to the past colonial borders was most problematic. For others, its sheer conservatism in dealing with the many challenges confronting the newly independent countries represented a serious limitation. And it was restricted by design—the OAU's founding charter rendered its executive and administrative branches ineffective by according them only limited powers. Resolutions of the OAU assembly were not legally binding and the body lacked implementation mechanisms.[28]

Unsurprisingly, the absence of practical progress of Pan-Africanism at the continental level meant governments increasingly resorted to sub-regional agreements with their neighbouring countries. At the risk of simplifying a complex sequence of events, there were basically two phases in the formation of regional economic communities. The first phase started with a flurry of initiatives in the early years of independence. One early example was the West African Customs Union (UDAO), established in June 1959 by Côte d'Ivoire, Senegal, Dahomey, Mauritania, Niger, Mali and Upper Volta. For various reasons, this agreement did not thrive, and it was disbanded in May 1970.[29] Among the anglophone countries of West Africa, independence was quickly followed by a degree of economic disintegration: the former British dependencies established separate central banks and replaced their common West African pound with national currencies (the leone in Sierra Leone, the cedi in Ghana, and the Nigerian pound in Nigeria). Likewise, the regional airline which operated in the four anglophone countries—West African Airways—was disbanded. Even research was affected, with joint research programmes abandoned in favour of national research institutions. As Adedeji lamented at the time, 'One striking feature of the past decade has been the inability of the anglophone and francophone West African countries to break the language and cultural barriers and to form effective economic groupings which cut across them.'[30]

27

East Africa was not spared the disintegrative wave. The East African Community (EAC) was formed in 1967 between Kenya, Uganda and Tanzania, only to fall apart in 1977 due to both political clashes and resentment over what was perceived as an unfair share of the economic benefits towards the most powerful country in the bloc, Kenya.[31] The result of the failures of this period was that, instead of coming closer together, a lot of African countries ended up parting company.

The second wave of regional integration on the continent started against a backdrop of the austerity imposed during the structural adjustment programmes (SAPs) of the 1980s and 1990s.[32] The spending cutbacks ushered in under the SAPs had resulted in a severe weakening of the state as an agent of economic performance and management of countries. In the face of the onslaught against state institutions, African countries sought solace in regional solutions to their economic travails through the establishment of a number of new regional economic communities (Table 2.1).[33] The newly formed regional economic communities (RECs) aimed to establish free trade areas, customs unions, common markets and economic unions in line with the Lagos Plan of Action and the Abuja Treaty. Each REC had its own focus: the Common Market for Eastern and Southern Africa (COMESA) focused on trade facilitation and supporting institutions, ECOWAS emphasised peace and security, Intergovernmental Authority on Development (IGAD) addressed drought and desertification, and SADC prioritised infrastructure and industrialisation (it also worked towards political liberation to complete the decolonisation struggle). These efforts contributed to the development of best practices and priorities at the continental level.[34]

To be sure, the progress of the new wave of RECs was uneven, with some being more successful than others. For example, not all member states of COMESA signed up for tariff liberalisation and NTBs remained a significant issue. A major reason for the slow or failed implementation of many regional projects was a lack of financial resources. While African member states have been criticised for not committing enough resources to finance regional projects, sometimes these resources were simply not available in the first place. Notably, it is alleged that ECOWAS has been more successful in fulfilling some of its objectives due to its better financing mechanism through the Community Levy Protocol of 1996.[35]

Table 2.1: Africa's eight 'approved' regional economic communities

Name	Abbreviation	Year of formation	Current number of members	Intra-group trade (USD billions), 2021
Arab Maghreb Union	AMU	1989	5	3.2
The Community of Sahel-Saharan States	CEN-SAD	1998	29	18.1
Common Market for Eastern and Southern Africa	COMESA	1994	21	15.1
East African Community	EAC	1967/2000	7	4.3
Economic Community of Central African States	ECCAS	1983	11	1.5
Economic Community of West African States	ECOWAS	1975	15	10.7
Intergovernmental Authority on Development	IGAD	1986	8	5.7
Southern African Development Community	SADC	1992	16	24.5

Sources: Authors' elaboration, from official sources and UNCTADStat (2023).

The multiplicity of regional economic communities in Africa also started to become an issue among the continent's political leadership. In July 2006, the African Union adopted a decision recognising the eight RECs in Table 2.1, but placing a moratorium prohibiting the formation of new ones. However, that decision did not stop individual states from joining as many existing regional bodies as they pleased, and it continues to be a popular option, with Tunisia joining COMESA in July 2018 and the Democratic Republic of the Congo (DRC) joining the EAC in March 2022. The latter was followed in June the same year by an announcement by the president of Somalia, Hasan Sheik Mohamud, at the Arusha Head of States Summit that his country intended to apply for EAC membership. Even Ethiopia has reputedly been mulling over the possibility of requesting membership of the EAC. Clearly, the regional approach continues to be extremely popular.

Another major recent development in Africa's regional architecture has been the formation of the Tripartite Free Trade Area (TFTA), which was negotiated between COMESA, the EAC, and SADC from 2012 to 2015. The implications in economic terms for the countries involved were potentially enormous—the TFTA involves almost half (26) of the countries on the continent, spanning the whole Eastern side from the Cape to the North African coast.[36] However, at the present juncture, there are some lingering doubts about when or whether the agreement will come into force because of the slow pace of ratification. Having been opened for signature in June 2015, as of February 2023, the TFTA had been ratified by only ten of its 26 signatories. A total of 14 ratifications are required for the agreement to enter into force. Yet in a significant way, the TFTA set a precedent for the AfCFTA by providing a valuable foundation for the negotiations through its working documents and draft legal instruments. Additionally, the experience of negotiating the agreement proved extremely useful during the AfCFTA negotiations.

Conclusions

The objective of this chapter has been to provide an overview of some of the historical antecedents to the AfCFTA. The truth is that Africa has had millennial traditions of engaging in long-distance trading relations—and this is without even touching on the cruel way in which it was thrust into the system of the transatlantic slave trade in the sixteenth and seventeenth centuries. Yet the vibrancy of intra-African trade was truncated by the imposition of colonial boundaries in the nineteenth century. It was a legacy that has proved difficult to throw off. Although Pan-Africanism as a political movement has been deeply engrained in the collective psyche, in economic terms the newly independent countries struggled to revive intra-African trade. Nonetheless, in this chapter we have outlined some of the positive contributions that the continent's regional economic communities have made to the continental integration. They are, in the words of David Luke and Jaime MacLeod, 'the uncelebrated heroes of the effort to establish and utilise common arrangements for cross-border trade and related regional initiatives'.[37]

However, in the 1980s and 1990s, existing regional integration efforts had to confront the headwinds of a severe economic downturn on the continent, precipitated in part by domestic factors, but also due to adverse external conditions and externally imposed Structural Adjustment Programmes (SAPs). As a reaction, at the foundation of the AfCFTA are the Lagos Plan of Action of 1980 and the Abuja Treaty of 1991. That is a story that we shall tell in the next chapter, through the optic of two historic thinkers on continental integration, Adebajo Adedeji and Thandika Mkandawire.

3

THE INTELLECTUAL UNDERPINNINGS
OF THE AFCFTA

Introduction

Successful projects of regional integration have many intellectual parents (the failures, as Kennedy once reputedly remarked after the 1961 Bay of Pigs fiasco, tend to be orphans). For the EU, this role has often been ascribed to Jean Monnet, but others (e.g., Robert Schuman or Walter Hallstein) could also claim parenthood. In Africa, there are equally many people who could claim parenthood to the idea of the AfCFTA.[1] Pan-Africanism has been a widely and deeply held sentiment for over a hundred years, and the pantheon of Pan-Africanists is a long and venerable one, including Kwame Nkrumah, Leopold Senghor, Amílcar Lopes da Costa Cabral and Julius Nyerere, to name but a few.

However, those early contributions were (understandably) usually framed within the context of the anti-colonial struggle. Practically minded contributions on how to achieve economic integration were rather thinner on the ground.[2] Yet once the archives are opened, and the reader has reviewed past debates, there is a realisation that many of the arguments on continental integration have played out before. Drawing on this existing pool of knowledge and experience will be vital, we argue, if the AfCFTA is to succeed in its goals.

This chapter provides a discussion and brief background of two African intellectuals—Adebayo Adedeji and Thandika Mkandawire—

who could rightly be considered as scholarly parents of the AfCFTA project. Their writings certainly influenced the shape of the debate on continental integration, whilst their personal histories also perfectly illustrate some of the previous triumphs, contradictions and disappointments of Pan-Africanism. Chapter 3 briefly summarises their individual intellectual contributions into how to achieve economic integration and unity on the African continent. Sadly, between 2018 and 2020, both passed away. However, such is the depth of their insights that their influence will undoubtedly endure.

Adebayo Adedeji (1930–2018)

A long road was travelled to get to the African Union Summit of March 2018 in Kigali, Rwanda, when the AfCFTA was signed. The story of post-independence integration is a rich one but also rather frustrating, full of drama and setbacks.[3] For the purposes of simplification, it can be divided into three overlapping phases.[4] The first period of regional integration occurred during decolonisation in the 1960s, when integration was perceived to be closely linked with achieving and preserving independence. The OAU, created in 1963, operated with a mandate to promote independence. As noted in the previous chapter, the second phase of regional integration occurred from the 1970s, with regional organisations created either to promote economic integration or to solve regional problems (for example, the goal of combating colonial and white-minority rule in South Africa led to the establishment of the Southern African Development Community). The third phase of Africa's integration started with the Abuja Treaty of 1991, followed by the Sirte Declaration of 1999, both of which envisioned the creation of an African Economic Community and the creation of the African Union (built from the ashes of the OAU).

In every one of these stages, Professor Adebayo Adedeji was an active participant and was what might now be vulgarly called a 'thought-leader'. He played an integral role in attempts to turn the Pan-African ideal into practice, and to turn regional integration into a political economic and social reality on the continent. Professor Adekeye Adebajo, who has published extensively on the legacy of Adedeji, expressly compares the vision and impact of Jean Monnet and Adebayo Adedeji, regarded respectively as the fathers of regional integration in Europe and Africa.[5] Certainly, a number of interesting parallels exist between the two men, despite their different backgrounds: they both assisted in reconstructing their respective economies after destructive wars (the Second World War [1939–45] for Monnet and the Nigerian Civil War [1967–70] for Adedeji); they both had distinguished careers in the civil service, devoted considerable energy to regional integration and were ultimately frustrated in their quests to unite Europe and Africa, respectively.[6]

In consonance with the title of this book, in every one of the steps that Professor Adedeji took during his career—as a minister in the Nigerian government, as the longest-serving executive secretary of the United Nations Economic Commission for Africa (ECA), and thereafter as a passionate advocate for continental integration—he issued warnings about the potential barriers to achieving a borderless Africa. Many of those warnings are still pertinent. Professor Adedeji was always outspoken. As one of his successors at the helm of the ECA (and in some respects very much Adedeji's intellectual 'alter ego'), K. Y. Amoako said:

> Adedeji was strident and unapologetic in his views that Africa should not be beholden to excessive western conditions in exchange for relief and assistance, and this earned him a lot of respect among fellow Africans. Over time, he grew close to the heads of state and governments, becoming an influential voice to many. He was vocal and highly visible and he was the face of ECA during the creation of the Lagos Plan of Action, an important effort to strengthen African unity and ownership.[7]

Born in 1930 in Ijebu-Ode, Ogun State, Nigeria, into a farming family, he began his university education at the University College of Ibadan, and proceeded to the University of London the following year, obtaining a BSc in Economics in 1958 and a PhD in 1967. Thereafter followed a tenure as a professor of public administration in Nigeria, at the University of Ife-Ife, where he trained public servants. As the director of the Institute of Public Administration, the Institute quickly emerged as one of the major centres of development and administrative studies in Africa, with high national and international standing in both academic and professional circles.[8]

In October 1971, at the age of 40, Adedeji was appointed as Nigeria's Federal Commissioner (Minister) for Economic Development and Reconstruction. It was, in many senses, a baptism of fire, as he had the responsibility of overseeing the country's difficult post-war reconstruction efforts after the tragic Biafran War of 1967–70, which had resulted in a million deaths and led to the destruction of much infrastructure, especially in the east of the country. Adedeji was involved in crafting and implementing the country's Five-Year Development Plan that called for rapid industrialisation and resulted in the building of infrastructure across the country.[9]

It was during this time that Adedeji also turned his attention to regional integration in West Africa. He is widely (and rightly) regarded as 'the Father of ECOWAS'. He had previously outlined his vision for regional integration in West Africa in an academic article published in the *Journal of Modern African Studies* in 1970, in which he identified six priority areas: building a regional road network; creating a regional airline; establishing regional infrastructure to facilitate trade and investment; facilitating the free movement of people, goods, and services; establishing a clearing and payments union; and abolishing foreign exchange controls.[10] While serving as Nigeria's Minister of Economic Planning, Adedeji 'midwifed' the creation of ECOWAS through intensive shuttle diplomacy. As an astute practitioner of public policy and an artful statesman, 'he exerted his influence on the design of ECOWAS and successfully navigated it through the policymaking labyrinths of the 16 West African countries'.[11]

In 1975, Adedeji then took over the leadership of the ECA, a part of the UN Secretariat, and one of five regional commissions globally.[12] When he arrived in Addis Ababa to start his new assignment, the institution had had just two previous executive secretaries. At the institution's inaugural meeting back in December 1958, the then Secretary-General of the United Nations (the ill-fated Dag Hammarskjöld, who was later to lose his life in the Congo) implored ECA to give priority to economic cooperation and regional integration.[13] It was a commitment that Adedeji was intent on delivering upon.

The considerable opposition to the establishment of Pan-African institutions like ECA in the late 1950s is often not appreciated. The idea of collaboration among the newly independent states of the continent was an anathema for the former colonial powers. The ECA had been established to tackle a wide range of issues: economic integration, industrialisation; transportation; commodity price stabilisation and other price stabilisation; human capacity development; social aspects and financing of development; and improving statistical data and research in Africa. But at its very first meeting, held in Addis Ababa in December 1958, issues of regional cooperation were already high on the agenda. The colonial powers—France, the UK and Portugal— were not amused, as the exercise of their control over their colonies depended largely on keeping African countries isolated and dependent on the metropolis.[14] As Richard Jolly, a notable British development economist who worked at ECA in its formative years, noted:

> ECA's early years were dominated by political battles against colonialism, racism, and apartheid and preoccupied with the development problems of collective self-reliance, indigenous development, and regional economic integration. Unfortunately, the rapidity with which African countries became independent produced, paradoxically, a negative impact on African solidarity. Independence reinforced boundaries established by the colonial powers and gave new leaders a vested interest in maintaining them.[15]

Adedeji's sixteen-year tenure became the organisation's longest and, arguably, most dynamic: he converted the ECA into a Pan-African platform to continue his efforts to promote economic integration, leading to the creation of the Preferential Trade Area for Eastern and Southern African States in 1981 (which became COMESA in 1994) and the Economic Community of Central African States (ECCAS) in 1983.[16]

The Lagos Plan of Action versus the Berg Report

Adedeji's first foray into trying to change the prevailing mindset on international development was to lead the development of a 'Revised Framework of Principles for the Implementation of the New International Economic Order' in 1976. This provided the theoretical foundation for the subsequent Monrovia Strategy of 1979 and the Lagos Plan of Action of 1980. The focus of these two reports—produced with teams of African economists at the ECA and in consultation with African policymakers—reflected Adedeji's core intellectual concern with the concepts of regional integration, economic decolonisation and self-reliance.[17]

During his tenure, the ideological conflicts—described by Adedeji as 'battles for the African mind'—were legendary. Adedeji's most bruising intellectual battles were with the World Bank and the International Monetary Fund (IMF). In one corner was the dogma of structural adjustment guided by the World Bank's Berg Report (1981)—essentially policies designed to open African economies to free trade and free markets, as desired by the industrial countries. In the other corner, the Lagos Plan of Action, which could, in many ways, be considered as the 'grandfather' of the AfCFTA. According to Amoako:

> Adedeji was passionate about Africa, but he was obstinate. When told that the Bank Report [the Berg Report] wasn't meant to undercut the Lagos plan and that African governments, via their executive directors to the Bank, had asked for it themselves, Adedeji didn't believe it to be the fact. He said it was an insult to be told otherwise.[18]

The Lagos Plan of Action identified seven strategic sectors for Africa's development: food and agriculture; industry; natural resources; human resources; transport and communications; trade and finance; and energy. The end goal would be the creation of an African Common Market culminating in an African Economic Community.[19] As a blueprint, however, the Lagos Plan of Action was excessively vague for many people. Adedeji himself admitted as much in a speech made at the University of Ife-Ife in March 1984.

> I must confess that … the Plan has meant many things to many people and organizations. To some, it is a plan to be costed to the last Kobo,[20] just as national development plans are costed. To others, it is a political economy document with long-term objectives. To us who participated in the formulation and adoption of this seminal document … a serious and sympathetic reading of the Lagos Plan of Action and associated documents will leave no doubt that [it] has short, medium, and long-term aspects and that it has more to do with *how* things should be done than a national development plan.[21]

Against a backdrop of rising neoliberalism in the United States and United Kingdom, by contrast, the Berg Report attributed blame for Africa's economic woes primarily to African governments themselves, most notably due to poor governance and state failure. The report advocated for a reduced role for the government and unfettered markets to allocate resources. It called for eliminating state subsidies and price control for wages and imports. It denied there was a role for industrial policy and rejected the import substitution strategies that many African countries had been pursuing (with admittedly mixed results), arguing that they should instead return to a focus on export-oriented agriculture and raw material exports, as they had done under colonialism. In sum, the Berg Report was, in essence, a manifesto for non-integration.[22] And although Africa was not the only developing region reeling under the harsh conditionalities imposed by the Bretton Woods institutions due to a heavy dependence on their loans, the Berg Report ushered in the era of SAPs which resulted in a considerable reduction in the policy space open to African governments to develop their own set of priorities.

Understandably, most African policymakers reacted extremely negatively to the propositions contained in the Berg Report. In February 1982, a meeting of African foreign ministers proclaimed that the report's 'glaring arrogant paternalism would cost Africans the independence to set their own goals.' In April of the same year, ECA's annual Conference of Ministers concluded with a declaration dismissing the Berg Report and reiterating that Africa's official goals and objectives should remain as identified in the Lagos Plan of Action.[23]

The ideological battles raged over most of the 1980s and beyond, morphing in the 1990s into new areas, such as the policies of the triumphalist 'Washington Consensus' and the IMF's poverty reduction strategies. While the World Bank did eventually concede its initial policy positions, as articulated in the Berg Report, had been too extreme (as reflected in a series of half-hearted mea culpa reports published in the 1990s and early 2000s),[24] by then the damage had been done, and the ability of the African states had been so compromised that they were unable to act upon the core propositions of the Lagos Plan of Action even if they had wanted to. In any case, despite Adedeji's fervent opposition, the intellectual battles were ultimately won by the Bretton Woods institutions, operating overwhelmingly in the interests of the industrial countries, and backed up by their overwhelming economic and voting power.[25]

As a blueprint for continental integration, however, it is also worth recognising the limitations of the Lagos Plan of Action. Critics have argued that it lacked a practical mechanism for achieving its objectives, as well as a timetable and a detailed assessment of the costs for implementing these ideas. The Lagos Plan of Action also failed to provide quantitative linkages between sectors and sub-sectors. Adedeji's own calls for increasing self-reliance were criticised as vague and impractical. Moreover, some critics regarded efforts to delink Africa from the global economy as foolhardy.[26] In sum, some of the proposals contained in the Lagos Plan of Action were touchingly idealistic, but unlikely to see the light of day. One such proposal was the creation of an African Monetary Fund. Adedeji laid out the case meticulously for this:

> [The existing financial] structures had been designed principally to serve the interests of the colonial powers and were used as conduits for channelling investments and other resources from the metropolitan powers to the colonial territories and vice versa or among the colonial possessions. As such, they were not designed to promote the social and economic development of the colonies and territories .... The Lagos Plan of Action ... called for the restructuring and reorientation of the African monetary and financial policies at the national, subregional and regional levels ... to make them more responsive to the expressed needs and current problems of African countries, as well as to enable African countries to absorb shocks emanating from disruptions in the international economic changes .... One of the most important of such institutions to be established is the African Monetary Fund.[27]

Certainly, had the Lagos Plan of Action been adopted, it would have had more legitimacy from African governments than the externally imposed policies during the period of structural adjustment. Moreover, many of the Plan's elements of domestically driven priorities and growth mirrored policies followed in parts of Asia—often with spectacular results. In perhaps a key lesson for the AfCFTA, it has been speculated that if only the Lagos Plan of Action had received support from the international financial institutions (IFIs) and donors, it may have led to a more dynamic period for African development.[28]

But its flaws may have been more fundamental. Some of the criticisms reflected the fact that the Lagos Plan of Action was a political consensus document adopted by all of Africa's leaders. While the Plan was accepted by the OAU, it was ultimately left to gather dust on the shelves of African development ministries, as the continent lacked both the resources to pay for it and the mechanisms to ensure its implementation. Mkandawire astutely remarked that the 'Lagos Plan of Action assumed that member states were planned economies, which they were not.'[29] Correctly, K. Y. Amoako observed: 'As an example of Pan-African unity and recognition of severity of its economic problems, the Lagos plan was admirable. As a viable economic recovery framework for Africa, it fell short.'[30]

The angst is sadly palpable during this period in the writing of influential African thinkers about the continent's economic and political vulnerability.[31] It was a period of soul-searching and reflected the frustration with being unable to put into action an Africa-led initiative of social and economic development. By 1993, Adedeji himself was lamenting:

> Unfortunately, this persistence in adopting resolutions and blueprints has not been matched by an equal stubbornness in translating them [into] international policies and action. The debt crisis and the collapse of prices on international commodity markets—soaring debt-servicing obligations thus striking concurrently with sharply falling commodity earnings—made the search for foreign aid and debt relief the consuming passion of most African governments. As both were conditional on the adoption of a structural adjustment program the leverage of the IMF and the World Bank to determine the direction of national social economic policies became overwhelming, all the more so when donor after donor introduced the same criterion for bilateral assistance. Country after country thus deserted Africa's indigenous strategy in favour of the one propounded as good for Africa by the Bretton Woods institutions.[32]

Needless to say, it is crucial for the AfCFTA to avoid a similar fate. Some elements in the contemporary contextual background are admittedly worrying. In the 2020s, debt levels have risen sharply, and not all the winds are currently blowing in favour of the continental project. We will return to these points in the closing chapter of this book.

The Abuja Treaty—Adedeji has the last word?

In the long run, however, many of the ideas of Professor Adedeji have been revindicated. Eleven years after the Lagos Plan of Action, African leaders agreed in Abuja, Nigeria, in 1991, to establish an African Common Market by 2023. The African Economic Community (AEC) was to be established progressively in six stages over 34 years from 1994 to 2028. The first three phases focus on the creation and strengthening of RECs,[33] which were to serve as the building blocks for the AEC.[34] The second three stages involve the forming of regional free trade areas (which require free movement of goods) and customs unions by 2017, merging into a continental customs union by 2019 (which requires a common external tariff and commercial policy as well as a common customs law), in turn transforming that union into the continental common market by 2023 (which requires free movement of goods, services, labour and capital), and, finally, forming a continental economic union by 2028. Albeit behind the scheduled 2011 deadline, the AfCFTA (which is also part of the African Union Agenda 2063) coincides with the fourth and fifth stages (Table 3.1).[35]

Thus, although they may sometimes go into hibernation for prolonged periods, good ideas have a habit of resurrecting themselves. In January 2008, already nearly in his eighties, Professor Adedeji chaired a high-level panel at the 10th Ordinary Session of the African Union held in Addis Ababa. The committee comprised 12 heads of state and discussed how to accelerate the implementation of the continental goals. They recommended the following actions: to establish the free movement of peoples across borders as contained in both the Abuja Treaty and the African Union Constitutive Act; to develop transcontinental and interregional infrastructures; to encourage the emergence of multinational African firms as accelerators of African integration; and to quickly establish the continental financial institutions identified in Article 9 of the constitutive act of the African Union, notably the African Central Bank, the African Monetary Fund and the African Investment Bank. The panel also recommended fast-tracking the move towards an African Common Market and the African Economic Community.[36] These recommendations form the bedrock of the AfCFTA—the negotiations for which were launched between 2015 and 2018.

Table 3.1: The stages for forming the African Economic Community

Stage	No. of years	Period	Key activities	REC level	Continental role	Remarks
1	5	1994–99	– Strengthen existing RECs – Establish RECs in regions without	Yes	Yes	Complete 8 RECs have been recognised, rather than the 5 envisaged (one for each region under Article 1(d))
2	8	1999–2007	– Stabilise tariffs and NTBs – Adopt a continental time-table for removal of tariffs and NTBs to REC and intra-community trade and establishment of a continental common external tariff – Sectoral integration at REC and community levels – Coordination and harmonisa-tion of RECs	Yes	Yes	Not done

3	10	2007–17	– Form REC FTAs and customs unions on the basis of the continental timetable for removal of tariff barriers and NTBs	Yes	Yes	Partly—EAC is a customs union and a common market, ECOWAS is a customs union, COMESA and SADC are FTAs
4	2	2017–19	– Coordinate and harmonise REC tariff and non-tariff systems – Form the continental customs union through adopting a continental common external tariff	Yes	Yes	Missed
5	4	2019–23	– Form the African Common Market through common policies, free movement of persons and rights of establishment and residence, and constituting resources for the community	Yes	Yes	Pending—a key priority for the period 2023 to 2028

6	5	2023–28	– Consolidation of the African Common Market – Integration of all sectors – Setting up the financial institutions – Set up the Pan-African Parliament – Coordinate and harmonise the RECs – Establish African multinational enterprises in all sectors – Setting up executive organs	Yes	Yes	Pending—a key priority for the period 2023 to 2028

Source: Article 6, Abuja Treaty (OAU 1991); authors' elaboration.

S. K. B. Asante, the renowned Ghanaian political economist who wrote a book on Adedeji's development strategies in 1991, described him as an 'African Cassandra': a visionary prophet who saw the future clearly, but whose prophesies often went unheeded until it was too late.[37] Such a judgement was perhaps precipitous—with the AfCFTA, Professor Adedeji may well have the last word.

Thandika Mkandawire (1940–2020)

Thandika Mkandawire was born in 1940 and raised in southern Africa. A native of Malawi, the family moved between Malawi, Zambia and Zimbabwe whilst he was a boy. His political conscious-ness arose in the twilight years of British colonialism. As a young student and activist in the United States in the 1960s, at the height of the civil rights movement, he immediately saw the intricate con-nections between the civil rights movement and Africa's own strug-gles for emancipation. This, as the Malawian economic historian Professor Zeleza noted, 'nurtured his profound respect and appre-ciation of African American society, culture, and contributions, which was a bedrock of his Pan-Africanism in the tradition of Kwame Nkrumah and others'.[38]

Mkandawire started his career as a journalist, but later switched to economics. He studied economics at Ohio State University and the University of Stockholm. He taught at several universities, including the London School of Economics and Political Science. He also had a distinguished research career, serving as the executive secretary of the Council for the Development of Social Science Research in Africa and as director of the United Nations Research Institute for Social Development.

In the tradition of all original thinkers, Mkandawire was an intel-lectual maverick who enjoyed turning orthodox opinions on their head. He encouraged 'lateral thinking' on all the major development issues facing the continent. Students and contemporaries of his testi-fied to his intellectual playfulness. As Gumede noted:

> Mkandawire has walked his own path in thinking about development in Africa. Interestingly, he cannot be compartmentalised or catego-rised into any existing school of thought, although he could easily be

confused for a heterodox economist. He has described himself as a
Pan-Africanist; not as an Economist or Political Economist or any
other academic inclination.[39]

It is probably fair to say that his ideas about Pan-Africanism were
shaped by two defining moments on the African continent—one was
the period of decolonisation, and the other was the period of structural adjustment in the 1980s and 1990s. Up until he spent some time
in the late 1960s in Ecuador, Mkandawire equated colonisation and
imperialism almost exclusively with the former European empires,
and, like a lot of his African contemporaries, he felt that the United
States, having fought for its own independence from Great Britain,
was not tainted by such ideologies. However, his experience in Latin
America led him to understand that US interventionism in other parts
of the developing world could also be extremely pernicious and
undermine national and regional autonomy. Mkandawire became
opposed to a unipolar world in which any one country could have a
disproportionate influence on the global system. He saw that smaller
developing countries could only thrive in a system in which there
were diverse centres of power in the world, and for this reason he
welcomed the growing influence of China and other emerging economies on the African continent.[40]

Like Adedeji, Mkandawire became a ferocious critique of the IFIs
that imposed these policies, and the Berg Report (1981) that provided
its intellectual scaffolding, noting that 'the World Bank gave us zero
growth. Someone once said, "we asked for bread and they gave us a
stone"'.[41] In Mkandawire and Soludo's 1998 joint publication, the
two authors document extensively the negative impacts of the SAPs
on African economies and society.[42]

It was reputedly Professor Adedeji who had first coined the term
'lost decades' to describe those years, but Mkandawire took it upon
himself to remind people of the extent to which the SAP period had
caused lasting damage to the African continent and its institutions.[43]
Indeed, he felt that the phrase 'lost decades' didn't adequately reflect
the scale of economic decline nor the long-lasting nature of its impact
and should instead be called 'the Great African Depression'.[44] The
economic impoverishment of the SAP period made its effects felt
through many channels, severely undermining the capacity of the

47

state and pauperising the African middle classes that had emerged since independence. Mkandawire insisted that the economic, philosophical and ideological repercussions of the 'Great African Depression' were still being felt three decades later.[45]

Despite this, Mkandawire was not a pessimist by nature. In a seminal paper on African economic development, John Sender, a professor at the School of Oriental and African Studies in London, complained that research and writing on the continent was overwhelming tinged with negativism and condescension.[46] Mkandawire's thinking was of the same ilk. This particularly came across in his writings and speeches on regional integration. He was insistent that the achievements of African regional integration had been given 'a bad rap'. He observed, for instance, that there was a persistent 'talking down' of the economic significance of intra-African trade, and efforts at deepening regional integration was frowned upon. Yet as he noted in one presentation:

> Given our levels of development and infrastructure, we are probably trading as much as you could expect. If you look at the levels of intra-African trade, and if you control for other variables such as level of industrialization or infrastructure, level of diversification within member states, we are doing as well as we can. It's perhaps therefore not the fault of the regional technocrats that we are not doing better, when comparing ourselves to other parts of the world.[47]

Another manifestation of negative attitudes towards regional integration efforts on the continent invoked what became known as the 'spaghetti bowl phenomenon'[48] whereby African states frequently belong to multiple regional economic communities, as if they were hedging their bets as to which was most likely to prosper.[49] Many economists have rallied against the apparent illogical nature of the spaghetti bowl and have made disdainful pronouncements about its consequences. Yet Mkandawire was insistent that there was an underlying rationale for the proliferation of regional agreements on the African continent:

> If you look very carefully, there is logic behind the madness. The logic being partly the political origins of member states. Member states in Africa have many identities, which we have to deal with. If you are Francophone, you are Francophone, you cannot ignore the peculiari-

ties of your origins. So in trying to manage their multiple identities, these states end up joining all kinds of integration groups.[50]

Echoing economists like Krugman[51] and Rodrik,[52] Mkandawire was also insistent that there was often too much focus on trade as a vector of economic growth and development:

> If you understand trade as not just marketing, selling, buying goods, but selling things to acquire technology—then you don't have to think that everything you produce is going to be traded globally. You can start thinking about how to use your home market for your own development, rather than allowing foreign companies and *Bottom of the Pyramid* schemes to capture all the gains of providing goods for Africans. So, I would hope that Africans would say, yes, we are looking for these external opportunities, but we just must resolve a lot that is still within our control. Ultimately how the outside world reacts to you will depend on how much leverage they have over you.[53]

In another instance of defending Africa's track record on regional integration, Mkandawire stressed the immense geographical scale of the challenge being 'akin to trying to [combine] the United States, India, China, Western Europe, Japan and more—they all fit into the African continent. So when you say "integrate Africa", you are saying integrate US, China, India, France.'[54]

While acknowledging the groundswell of popular support for regional integration on the continent, Mkandawire frequently expressed regret about the extent to which the African project had been built from above, rather than from below, noting that the preamble of the African Union says something along the lines of 'we, the heads of state', rather than saying 'we, the African people', leaving no room for appeal against member states 'mishandling' African people.[55] Indeed, Mkandawire went further and suggested that there was an underlying incompatibility between authoritarian governance structures which were commonplace in much of Africa and regional integration which 'leads to problems of the legitimacy of [the] whole regional integration project. When you have national structures that are authoritarian, the Pan-Africanism of the population finds no room for expression'.[56] He noted, for instance, that there had never been a referendum on the continent to consult on whether the country should join or exit a regional arrangement. Britain's vote for 'Brexit' in 2016 'brutally signalled that European construction is not immune to disintegrative effects'.[57] But while the choice taken by the British electorate was something he would not have approved of, Mkandawire would have agreed with their right to choose to do so.

Underlying his critique of the 'top-down' approach to regional integration on the continent was the constant tension that had existed since independence between Pan-Africanism and what he called (borrowing from Cambridge professor Gabriel Palma's seminal article on the Chilean state)[58] 'the discrete charm of African nationalism'. He noted how regional integration in Africa had hitherto been very 'state-centric'. And that, according to Mkandawire, was problematic, because the rise of neoliberal thinking not only damaged African economies, but also discredited African states as forces for development:

> It's the state that sees itself as the guardian of national interest. Given the centrality of the state, we have to understand the weakness of the African state as an actor in the project of regional integration. The very nature of statehood has certain imperatives, and we may not like those imperatives, but they are things that we have to worry about when we talk about regional integration.[59]

Yet, while state-building has often entailed a degree of what could be labelled 'hyper-nationalism',[60] Mkandawire stressed how, for the majority of the continent's citizens, a common African identity was foremost in their minds. He conceded that reconciling the legitimate different national interests could be a challenge, but that these could be dealt with through redistributive schemes using taxes at the regional level:

> [T]here is another element which we must bear in mind, which has been important in the European case: a notion of solidarity which, in fact, was at the heart of Pan-Africanism. We must rekindle the idea of solidarity. We must think of ourselves as a continent where we diverse nations and peoples share certain common objectives and that in certain cases some may have to pay more than others.[61]

This notion of collective solidarity carried over to his thinking on how to prepare African bureaucrats for the task at hand. He rhetorically asked whether a cadre of 'Afrocrats' (i.e. technocrats who are competent and driven by a Pan-African vision) existed and, if so, what motivated them?

Is it a commitment to the Pan-African ideal, or is it just another job in an international organisation? We have to deal with the question of how our regional bureaucracies are constituted, what their political agendas are and what their political perceptions of the project they are working on are.[62]

How to build a civil service loyal to the continental project was at the forefront of his thinking. Mkandawire very much stressed that regional integration constituted a diplomatic move by nation states that needed to be quintessentially African-driven and African-funded. Relying on outsider donors to help finance African integration was not an option. The fact that the African Union, by its own admission,[63] is currently not financed in a predictable, sustainable, equitable or accountable manner, and is heavily dependent on donor funding to run its programmes and operations, was something that was deeply troubling to Mkandawire. The situation is further compounded by the fact that more than 40% of member states do not even pay their yearly contributions to the institution. Notwithstanding recent efforts to put funding on a more sustainable footing,[64] member states only contributed approximately 27% of the spend budget in 2017.[65] Reflecting the high degree of dependence on external financing, almost thirty traditional and emerging donors provide money, technical assistance and in-kind donations. Even so, the biggest single contributor to the African Union budget remains the EU. Together with the bilateral programmes of a number of its member states, the EU is the prime funder and backer of both peace-keeping operations and of the AUC's programme budget. This dependence on Europe for financing and technical support was deeply problematic for Mkandawire:

[T]he very bizarre situation in which Europe is training Africans on how to negotiate with Europe. Of course, they will train you on how to lose! You don't see Chinese being trained on how to negotiate with Europe! It's not a question [of] evil intention of these Eurocrats; they are amazingly consistent on European interests. It can be a trivial thing, but once it's on the European agenda, they will pursue it consistently. [For instance] you could say 'why worry about Tobacco? Tobacco, for Europe, is nothing'. But if one-member state pushes the agenda, they will pursue it to the end.[66]

This struck at the core of concerns that outsiders would not fund and promote intra-African integration without undermining the integrity of its decision-making processes. Precisely for this reason, it was fundamentally important to Mkandawire that Africa develop its own cadre of civil servants that would loyally serve the interests of the continent:

> We should reflect on the expectation that outsiders will happily join us in weakening them—which is essentially what that story is. We're trying to strengthen ourselves, and in so doing, we are undermining other people's presence in Africa. I don't see why they would push for that.[67]

He contrasted this situation with the most developed countries, where the production of their bureaucracies is a matter of central interest. European civil servants, for instance, are mostly the products of a few elite universities (the majority have studied at either the College of Europe, Free University of Brussels, Catholic University of Leuven, Sapienza University in Rome or the London School of Economics).[68] By contrast, Mkandawire considered the lack of a common education and training highly disruptive to developing a collective vision on the African continent:

> In Africa, at the national level, we have all been trained at all kinds of universities ... there are BA's [sic] from USA, UK, France, Russia, China, America, national institutions, etc. They have no appreciation for each other's degrees, and yet they are running the same civil service. And that is not very smart, because just as we have failed to create coherent national bureaucracies, we are having the same problem in our regional institutions.[69]

To this problem, Mkandawire had a solution:

> I would suggest that the AU identify one or two universities where all their bureaucrats must spend 3 or 4 months before they join the African Union or undergo regular retooling, to create a coherent story for them and mutual understanding and mutual appreciation. You have to create a bureaucracy; they don't make themselves—they are created for the purposes of whoever needs them.[70]

It can be appreciated from this short summary that Mkandawire's work still has an enormous amount to offer in terms of its perceptiveness about how to achieve greater continental integration. Mkandawire liked to turn received wisdom on its head and was never hesitant to confront entrenched ideas. His passing just as the AfCFTA had begun to be implemented was a great loss for the continent, for his advice was always eminently practical in nature. In the final instance, though, Mkandawire stressed the extent to which regional integration was first and foremost a political construct:

> Bureaucrats, both national and regional, say that we must depoliticize the debate around regional integration. But regional integration *is* a political project. When it functions at all, it functions as a political project .... I would argue that in fact some of the strongest unifying factors are non-economic. And even within Africa, the strong motive of SADC was not economic; it was the liberation struggle, which has remained in many ways symbolically important in tying this region together. One of ECOWAS' most important roles in the region of West Africa has been building and maintenance of peace in the region.[71]

Mkandawire thus insisted that it was important to find ways of exploiting these non-economic motivations for regional integration— if the focus was exclusively on economics, in most cases it would undermine its political underpinnings.

Conclusions

In the end, President Julius Nyerere's words, uttered in 1963, proved to be prescient:

> Nothing short of a United States of Africa should be accepted as our ultimate destiny. This does not mean that we must—or that we could—achieve the goal tomorrow, in one step. We must progress towards it as and when we can, either by all African decisions or by steps towards unity in different areas of Africa. Although the goal must be clear, it would, however, be wrong to think in detail of the shape of government in a United Africa. This will be affected by the road we have to travel to get there, as well as by the demands made on a state by world affairs at the relevant time. But this lack of clarity should not stop us now.[72]

The road to the AfCFTA has indeed been paved with setbacks and false starts—a case of two-steps forward, one step back. But in this it is no different than other processes of deep integration like ASEAN or the EU. In moving the agenda forward, this chapter has stressed the importance of being cognisant of the wisdom expressed in the writings and speeches of leading African intellectuals, highlighting the contributions of Adedeji and Mkandawire. In making the case for the AfCFTA, there is no point in reinventing the wheel—after all, a lot of arguments have played out in previous efforts of regional integration on the continent.

Let us conclude this chapter with two pieces of advice that emanate loud and clear from re-reading that existing body of work. Firstly, African governments increasingly see their legitimacy based on achieving a superior economic performance. The AfCFTA will thus have strong support if—and only if—it sustains those ambitions for a better performance, in terms of economic growth and employment creation. One element in achieving that support, we argue, is by championing initiatives like the Free Movement Protocol (see Chapter 12), as well as more modest measures like regulating mobile roaming charges, liberating the intra-continental air market, and tackling the lack of consumer protection (Chapters 9 and 14). Policymakers need to be mindful that tangible benefits on the ground are required if the AfCFTA is to maintain popular support.

Secondly, in the past, top-down approaches to regional integration on the continent have floundered. Hence the importance of adopting more inclusive approaches to achieving sustainable economic development on the continent. In the words of Mkandawire:

> It is necessary that Pan-Africanism is, once again, turned into an ideology of a social movement, this time more anchored in democratic politics than before. There has never been a viable federation of dictators. A new Pan-Africanism must be democratically anchored and based on notions of solidarity and collective self-reliance.[73]

The words mirrored very much the sentiment of Professor Adedeji, as expressed during a speech he made at the University of Ibadan in the early 1980s:

> A development strategy based on ... four main pillars—self-reliance, self-sustainment, the democratization of the development process and the fair and just distribution of the fruit of development—calls for a complete departure from the past .... It puts domestic markets, including subregional and regional markets, rather than external foreign markets at the heart of the development effort. And when it

emphasizes indigenous factor inputs, it means African scientists and technologists, African entrepreneurs, indigenous market analysts and distributors and indigenous technology. In the new development strategy, external trade is seen as being mainly supplementary in character and not constituting the heart of our development effort.[74]

These points may seem clear, but achieving them is far from straight-forward. An ambitious agenda indeed. The question is: can the AfCFTA deliver?

4

THE HEART OF THE MATTER

A LACK OF ECONOMIC DIVERSIFICATION

Introduction

Chapter 3 provided an overview of the historic battle of ideas that preceded the AfCFTA. Although things have progressed rapidly since the AfCFTA's inception in 2015, the antecedents for continental integration were clearly tortuous. Chapters 4–7 explain why the AfCFTA is needed, focusing on the structural weakness in the way African economies have hitherto integrated into the global economy.

The view that Africa's trade performance has been dismal ever since independence is commonplace. That perception of 'Afro-export pessimism' is behind a lot of the anti-AfCFTA sentiment that was noted in Chapter 1—a feeling that little can be done to turn things around, and that all Africa can do is to continue to plough the same metaphorical furrow and hope that things suddenly come right. Yet if the AfCFTA is being proposed as the solution to many of the continent's economic problems, it is important to have a clear understanding of what these problems are in the first place. To counter such arguments, then, it is necessary to understand and evaluate how we got to where we are today. This chapter will argue that there are many misconceptions and ideas that are just plain wrong about Africa's trade performance.

The chapter begins with a discussion of trends and features of Africa's export performance during what we term the 'Great Trade Collapse' of the 1980s and 1990s, and then explains how commodity dependence has also undermined the aggregate performance of the sector. The chapter then steps back to explain how this pattern of specialisation of commodities is an inheritance from the colonial period. The following section discusses how there was a subsequent period of recovery in Africa's export performance starting in the late 1990s, due essentially to a combination of improving international prices for commodity exports and a new rush on the part of Western countries and China to exploit Africa's natural riches. There was a widespread belief at the time that this new 'commodity super-cycle' could result in a turnaround for the fortunes of commodity-dependent economies in Africa and elsewhere. However, we show that those hopes were largely misplaced and conclude that economic diversification must remain a priority for African policymakers. As will be explained more fully in Part 2, the AfCFTA provides a unique opportunity to achieve that goal.

The Great Trade Collapse of the 1980s and 1990s

It is well-established that Africa as a continent has been gradually marginalised from global trade. Africa's share of global exports declined from around 5% of the global total in the 1970s, to just over 2% in 2020 (see Figure 4.1). Notably, the fastest decline in the continent's share of global trade occurred in the 1980s and 1990s, when Africa suffered its 'lost decades' (see Chapter 3). According to a World Bank study, Africa's export collapse incurred 'cumulative terms of trade losses in 1970–97 representing almost 120% of GDP, a massive and persistent drain of purchasing power'.[1] The nature, scale and drivers of Africa's trade 'collapse' in the 1980s and 1990s were much debated in the literature at the time.[2] Some economists presented deeply pessimistic assessments, with Sachs and Warner[3] or Collier and Gunning,[4] for instance, portraying Africa's trade performance as having been an unmitigated disaster.

Others, however, presented a more nuanced interpretation. Using a gravity model specification, Rodrik arrived at the conclusion that when other variables affecting trade were controlled for (such as location and per capita income), 'there is little evidence that trade policies have repressed trade volumes below cross-national benchmarks'.[5] Likewise, Helleiner[6] stressed that Africa's marginalisation from the global economy was not due to poor trade performance per se, but rather because of a wider 'development failure', given that, in the aftermath of the debt crisis and harsh structural adjustment programmes, the African economy contracted sharply during this period.[7]

Figure 4.1: Africa's total and share of global exports (current prices) (1957–99)

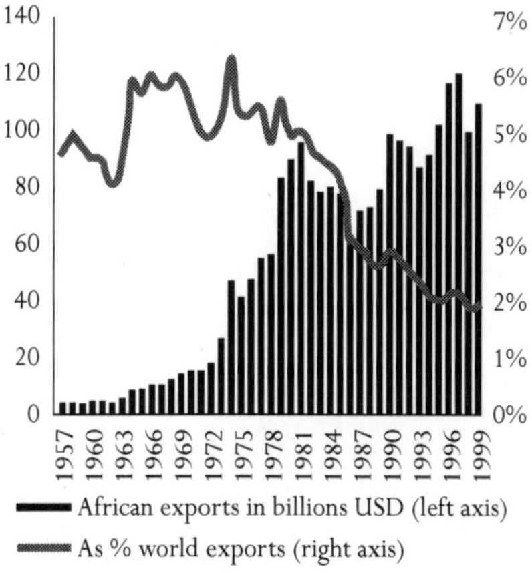

Figure 4.2: Growth of world exports (constant prices) (1913–2014)*

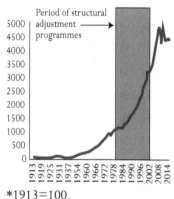

African exports in billions USD (left axis)

As % world exports (right axis)

Source: Calculated from IMF DOTS (2023).

*1913=100.

Source: Federico and Tena-Junguito (2017), cited in Ortiz-Ospina and Beltekian (2018).

Such narratives were supported by the fact that there was no sense in which Africa was systematically 'under-trading'. As revealed in Figure 4.1, the continent's export performance was certainly disappointing in the 1980s and 1990s, but even after the two decades of economic collapse (as discussed in Chapter 2), average export-to-GDP ratios in 1999 were still significantly higher than the global average (22.2% versus 18.1%), and comparable with those of Asia and Western Europe (Figure 4.3). In consonance with this narrative, econometric studies have confirmed that, once per capita income and other structural characteristics are controlled for, Africa could even

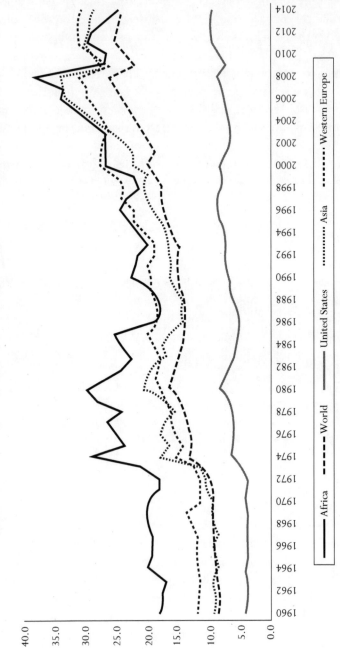

Figure 4.3: Merchandise exports as percentage of GDP (1960–2014)

Source: Fouquin and Hugot (2016), cited in Ortiz-Ospina et al. (2018).

have been considered to be overtrading during this period compared with other developing regions.[8]

Why then the persistent perception of a poor performance in terms of Africa's share of global trade? Quite simply, exports did not keep pace with the rapid growth in trade elsewhere in the world, coinciding with a period of sharp acceleration (see Figure 4.2), and hence the continent's share of global exports declined.[9] Indeed, at the time, it became habitual to compare Africa's trade performance unfavourably with Asia's, whose share of global trade rose rapidly from a low of 8% in 1970 to around 36% of total global merchandise exports by the early 2000s (compared with a decline for the African continent over the same period from around 5% to just under 2%). But what the continent experienced during the lost decades was not so much a collapse in its export performance but rather its growth performance, as was discussed in Chapter 3.

Were African governments to blame for this failure? The answer to that question is not straightforward. Contrary to many suppositions, African development strategies were not at the time inward-looking in a simplistic autarkic or 'hostile-to-trade' manner; as such, the continent's low share in world trade cannot simply be attributed to such policies.[10] Most economists subscribed Africa's poor performance to the lack of diversification in its export portfolio—and in particular an excessive dependence on primary commodity exports.[11] From a simple numerical point of view, this was clearly the case. Whereas in 1955, commodities represented 54% of global merchandise trade, 40 years later that share had collapsed to just 22%. Manufactured goods, meanwhile, enjoyed a much more dynamic rate of growth, and went up from 45% to 74% of global trade.[12] Clearly, to specialise in primary commodities represented an uphill struggle, and the countries that moved into manufacturing were able to catch the tailwinds of global trade growth. Taken in isolation, the exhortation to increase exports, under the notorious SAPs, might have made sense—but what about collectively? All countries expanding their exports at the same time was inevitably going to lead to lower prices and a commodity crash.[13] Indeed, such was the scale of the commodity price collapse that John Iliffe declared that by the mid-1990s 'tropical Africa's share of world trade probably fell to its lowest point in a thousand years'.[14]

More profoundly, perhaps, the continent's burgeoning trade deficits during this period also reflect the extent to which the continent failed to implement effective import substitution policies in the 1960s and 1970s—that is, the gradual replacement of manufactured imports with equivalent domestically produced products—particularly compared with Southeast Asia.[15] Indeed, one of the most outstanding features of Southeast Asia's economic success in the 1960s and 1970s was the combination of both 'export-promotion' with 'import-substitution' policies. They were in no sense polar opposites, and in fact, as we shall argue later, most successful development strategies of economic diversification have blended these approaches.

The commodity curse and what it has meant for Africa

There are swathes of literature on the 'commodity curse' and how an excessive dependence on primary production may condemn countries to a place on the lowest rung of the development ladder.[16] Yet it may surprise the reader to learn that, until the end of the Second World War, it was generally assumed that the terms of trade would move in favour of commodities—that is to say, that the prices of commodities would rise over time, relative to the price of manufactured goods. Colonial development policy (if that is the right term, because generally their economic development was hardly a priority of the colonial powers—the best most colonies could hope for was 'benign neglect') believed that increasing commodity exports towards the metropolis was the only route to raising incomes.

That orthodox view was challenged in 1950 by the writings of two pioneering development economists: Raúl Prebisch and Hans Singer.[17] Drawing on emerging empirical evidence on the character of the United Kingdom's trade, they uncovered a long-term trend for the prices of commodities to fall relative to those of manufactures.[18] In layperson's terms, this basically means that commodity exporters have had to export higher and higher volumes of commodities in exchange for the same amount of manufactured goods or services (in other words, their 'terms of trade' have declined). As an illustration, in the mid-1980s, the Tanzanian Minister of Finance and Planning Kigoma Malima complained that whereas in

1973 his country needed to export no more than 5.4 tons of tea in order to purchase one tractor, because of the decline in tea prices, by 1983 the same tractor required them to export almost twice that amount (10.1 tons of tea).[19]

To explore all the drivers of these trends would take us on an intellectual detour, but essentially it is tied up with the fact that the share of expenditure on commodities proportionately declines as incomes rise, whereas demand for manufactured goods rises as people become wealthier. There is also a sociological dimension to the arguments. Prebisch and Singer stressed that whereas workers in the developed 'North' were already better organised in terms of having union representation, in the developing world unions were almost unheard of or still brutally suppressed by colonial authorities. Thus, whereas productivity gains in the North were more likely to lead to higher wages, in the South no such pressure existed, and hence productivity gains were more likely to manifest themselves in lower prices. A further element in play was the fact that some tropical commodities were increasingly susceptible to being replaced by synthetic substitutes, placing further downward pressure on prices. For instance, the process of producing synthetic rubber was refined and commercialised in the 1920s–30s, and ended up replacing the more expensive natural product, bankrupting rubber-producing countries like Liberia.[20] In textiles, nylon substituted for silk, hemp and sisal; saccharine and beet substituted for sugar; aluminium replaced pig-iron, and so on. The impact on prices was brutal.

Although the Prebisch–Singer hypothesis was not without controversy, most subsequent studies broadly supported their conclusion about a secular decline in the terms of trade of commodity-producing countries.[21] Notwithstanding two short-lived commodity price booms in the early 1950s and early 1970s (precipitated by the Korean War[22] and the Arab-Israeli conflict, respectively), the prices of commodities fell relative to those of manufactures in the long term.[23]

For Africa, the impact of deteriorating and volatile terms of trade has been particularly pernicious and arguably felt more keenly compared to other parts of the developing world. For developing countries as a group, the loss was calculated at about USD 5 billion a year from 1981–85, accelerating to USD 55 billion a year from 1989–91, and totalling USD 350 billion for the whole period 1980–92.[24] The net barter terms of trade for sub-Saharan Africa fell by as much as 50% between 1980 and 1998.[25] In other words, by the end of the millennium, African economies were having to export double the amount of the same commodity to attain the same income they would have got for that commodity in 1980. They were running to stand still.[26]

Africa's terms of trade deteriorated sharply from the mid-1970s. Copper prices fell by three-quarters during the next decade, devastating the economies of Zaire (now the Democratic Republic of Congo) and Zambia, while many new mining ventures elsewhere collapsed. Agricultural export prices followed suit in the late 1970s and were still at historically low levels in the early 1990s.[27] To take one example of the economic consequences of this shift in prices against African exports, coffee exports at the end of the 1990s were reportedly of such a low value that smallholder farmers could barely get enough revenue to cover the costs of feeding their families, let alone being able to pay school fees for their children's education.[28] Deprivation also impacted heavily on cotton farmers in West Africa in the 1990s as prices hit historic lows. For some countries, the impact of declining terms of trade were particularly perverse. Tanzania's overall terms of trade for goods dropped by nearly 40% from 1987 to 2001. The agricultural terms of trade declined by even more (around 50%), and the result was that poverty reduction went into reverse despite rising average per capita incomes.[29]

Policy changes implemented during the application of abhorred SAPs compounded these tremendous challenges in international markets. The SAPs were supposed to improve external performance, but through the imposed liberalisations (i.e. the reduction of tariffs and removal of quantitative constraints) all they really achieved was an increase in imports and a minimal improvement in export levels.[30] The economic impacts that this had on Africa's incipient manufacturing industry was catastrophic. The scale of this shakeout in terms of manufacturing capacity and employment is well documented by Buffie:[31]

- In Sierra Leone, Zambia, Zaire, Uganda, Tanzania and Sudan liberalisation in the 1980s brought a tremendous surge in consumer imports and sharp cutbacks in foreign exchange available for purchases of intermediate inputs and capital goods. The effects on industrial output and employment were devastating. In Uganda for example, the capacity utilisation rate in the industrial sector languished at 22% while consumer imports claimed 40 to 60% of total foreign exchange.

- Similar problems plagued liberalisation attempts in Nigeria. The average capacity utilisation rate in manufacturing fell to just 20–30% and harsh adverse effects on employment and real wages provoked partial policy reversals in 1990, 1992, and 1994.
- Senegal experienced large job losses following a two-stage liberalisation program that reduced the average effective rate of protection from 165% in 1985 to 90% in 1988 and by the early 1990s had eliminated one-third of all manufacturing jobs.
- In Côte d'Ivoire, the chemical, textile, shoe and automobile assembly industries virtually collapsed after tariffs were abruptly lowered by 40% in 1986.
- Manufacturing output and employment initially grew rapidly in Ghana after liberalisation in 1983, bolstered by aid from the World Bank which increased access to imported inputs. But when the liberalisation spread to consumer imports, large swaths of the manufacturing sector succumbed to import competition and employment in the sector plunged from 78,700 in 1987 to 28,000 in 1993.
- Following trade liberalisation in 1990, formal sector job growth slowed to a trickle in Zimbabwe and the unemployment rate jumped from 10 to 20%. Adjustment in the 1990s was also difficult for much of the manufacturing sector in Mozambique, Cameroon, Tanzania, Malawi and Zambia. Import competition precipitated sharp contractions in output and employment in the short run with many firms closing down operations entirely.[32]

For the agricultural sector, the results were equally ruinous. Pressure was placed upon African countries to abolish their marketing boards on the grounds that they distorted price incentives in the agricultural sector and had been used to 'plunder agriculture'. As a result, by the early 1990s, 16 marketing boards covering cash crops in 23 countries had given up their monopoly positions or had been eliminated.[33] No matter that the high-income countries retained their own institutional arrangements to maintain price stability and provide support to their own farmers. Although sometimes corrupt or inefficient, Africa's marketing boards did provide important information and facilities such as credit and extension services to farmers. They also mobilised the respective country's market power in selling the crop for export.

Nonetheless, their elimination left farmers vulnerable to the full force of price shocks in commodity markets and undermined export performance. A study by Boratav,[34] surveying evidence on 20 sub-Saharan countries, found that deregulation had not been associated with improvements in real producer prices or in the terms of trade. Similarly, in an authoritative account of trends in the cocoa market, Ul Haque documented the decline in cocoa prices subsequent to liberalisation.[35] In such circumstances, regardless of trends in international prices, a poor supply-side response on the part of African farmers and producers was less surprising.[36]

The negative effect on producing countries of the long-term decline in prices for their commodity exports was compounded by considerable price volatility, with large and frequent fluctuations throughout the 1980s and 1990s. One long-term study into the declining terms of trade between 1862 and 1999 confirmed that it was volatility more than a predictable and stable decline in commodity prices that was most damaging to producers.[37] Moreover, because of the portfolio of its commodity exports, terms of trade volatility was significantly higher for Africa than for other less developed economies.[38] In some extreme cases, commodity prices varied by more than 100% on a year-to-year basis, affecting government budgets, employment, profitability and a country's foreign exchange reserves.[39] Such was the impact of this uncertainty that it was very difficult for governments to plan their long-term development expenditures.

The Asian experience of exporting to the global market, by contrast, was quite different. By being able to rapidly shift production into light manufacturing, Asian countries experienced a trend of improving terms of trade. For instance, Taiwan, which in the 1990s increased its share of manufactured goods in total exports to over 90%, saw an improvement in its terms of trade by 27% between 1980 and 1996 (recall that over a similar period, Tanzania experienced a 40% decline). The exact reasons why Asia was able to diversify while Africa was not would take us on an excessively long detour, but most analysts argue that it was due to a combination of fortuitous geopolitical circumstances, sustained efforts to improve technological capacity, and a more pragmatic application of industrial policy.[40] It also successfully combined export promotion with a degree of import substitution in key sectors, a strategy which helped reduce pressures on the balance of payments. Asia's experience also illustrates that trade openness can work well for industrialisation and transformation, but only when complemented by strategic action by the state.[41] For both complex geopolitical reasons[42] (which gave Asian states a larger margin of policy space) and because the state had been battered by SAPs (see Chapter 3), regrettably African economies were unable to follow suit.

A historical interlude

It is pertinent to step back and ask where Africa's excessive dependence on commodities came from. And the answer is relatively straightforward: it is clearly an inheritance from the colonial period. Under colonial rule, Africa was often seen by Europeans as little more than a source of these raw materials, foodstuffs and tropical beverages like coffee, tea and cocoa. The mineral wealth of the continent had long been known in Western Europe. Thirteenth-century Malian leader Mansa Musa was reputedly the richest man to have ever lived due to the country's abundance of gold, and stories abounded of his wealth after he visited Cairo and flaunted his affluence. The rumours of precious metals and diamonds (the mythical 'King Solomon's Mines') was one of the key motivators behind the exploration and colonisation of the continent in the nineteenth century, and it did not take the first European settlers long to discover the diamond deposits of Botswana and South Africa, or the gold of the Ashanti in present-day Ghana. European colonisation of Africa set up extractive institutions focused on transferring resources to the metropole, which is one of the principal reasons why a large share of African infrastructure still connects the hinterland with the coast, but often fails to integrate economies among themselves.[43]

It is a legacy which the continent is still trying to shake off—with one recent analysis of two mega-infrastructure corridors currently under development in East Africa (the Lamu Port-South Sudan-Ethiopia Transport Corridor project in Kenya and the Central Corridor in Tanzania) claiming that 'the current resurgence of state-led territorial design in East Africa owes just as much to spatial visions and territorial logics of early colonial administrators as it does to national development and spatial planning initiatives in the independence era'.[44] In such circumstances, it is hardly surprising that in some cases trade did not produce, as it might otherwise do, positive effects on development, but instead retarded economic growth.[45]

As for agricultural commodities, the story is a little different, but the end result was more or less the same. In areas where the climate was more temperate and white settlement more feasible (for example, the Kenyan Highlands, South Africa, or the plains of Zimbabwe), the best farmlands were taken over by the white settlers, and African people were reduced to working for minimal wages on the large plantations. Where there was a shortage of indigenous labour, the colonialists imported indentured labour—a practice little better than slavery—from elsewhere, principally from the Indian subcontinent. In other parts of the continent, the model of exploitation was different, with local indigenous farmers being co-opted into abandoning their traditional crops and planting the commodities demanded by the colonial metropolis.

In either case, the end result was similar, namely an excessive dependence on cash crops and mineral exports. The search for new markets amidst a global Great Depression in the early 1880s was a widespread concern that spurred on imperialism in the African continent. Modern scientific techniques were introduced into colonial territories that led to the production of minerals and cash crops including cocoa, coffee, palm oil, rubber, cotton, phosphates, diamonds, gold and tobacco. African economies were thus structured—as the economies in the Caribbean and the Americas had been two centuries earlier—to produce crops to meet European consumer needs. This both increased the dependence of African economies on metropolitan economies and, in many cases, negatively impacted on the ability of African populations to produce their own food. As

Adebajo notes, 'Africans imbibed Western consumption patterns without acquiring Western production methods'.[46] Escaping from that structural legacy is one of the prime objectives of the AfCFTA.

Yet Africa's exports have remained stubbornly concentrated in fuels, ores and metals. The value of the export of these products fluctuates substantially with their prices but has accounted for no less than 60% of Africa's exports in any year since at least 1995, and as much as 89% at its relative height in 2008.[47] As an illustration of its endurance, by the end of the 1990s, the three main tropical beverages destined for European markets—tea, coffee and cocoa—were still responsible for one-third of all agricultural exports, and even by the 2020s, they still accounted for a quarter of the total.[48]

In an authoritative review of the developmental record of the British in their tropical colonies from 1850–1960, Havinden and Meredith conclude that while British colonialism did not prevent *all* growth, it had serious limitations: 'The major economic failing was the structural imbalance which created colonial economies which were excessively dependent on the export of a narrow range of unprocessed primary commodities, and which experienced deteriorating terms of trade as a result'.[49]

Moreover, Britain did little to stimulate secondary industries and was not prepared to invest sufficiently to generate real growth in its colonies. Although as much as 30% of Europe's savings became available for overseas investment by 1914, almost all of it went to white settler regions, such as Australia, the United States, Canada, and New Zealand. Africa and Asia got just USD 11 per capita compared with USD 131 per capita in the European offshoots. A 1938 study by Frankel remains the only attempt at a comprehensive count of foreign investment in colonial sub-Saharan Africa.[50] The fact that nearly 45% of the total was public investment (that is, grants and loans from the imperial metropoles) underlines the paucity of foreign private investment outside the mining industries of South Africa, Zimbabwe and the Copper Belt of Central Africa (Zambia and the Belgian Congo).[51]

Investment in human capital was even more derisible. The first technical college in the Gold Coast (Ghana) opened in 1951, just six years before independence. In Portuguese Angola and Mozambique, just 86 Africans were attending secondary-level technical schools in the mid-1950s, and just two had become engineers by 1961. At independence, British colonies in tropical Africa had only 150 graduates in agronomy and the French colonies had only four. As a result, living standards rose very slowly, as did the provision of social and welfare services. In Egypt, per capita income actually fell by roughly 20% between 1900 and 1945. Nigeria's per capita income toward the end of British occupation in 1963 was officially estimated at £2, which was low even for the time. As Amsden notes, the British Empire is best remembered as a place where 'the sun never sets and wages never rise'.[52]

French colonialism had essentially similar effects, with the added negative dimension that its neo-mercantilist trade policies towards its colonial possessions heavily influenced European trade policy with developing countries in Africa.[53] The first European Community (EC) trade and development policy towards former colonies was adopted in 1975 in Lomé, the capital of Togo; and while it did agree to increase foreign aid and allow the export of goods duty-free to Europe, it was only under the provision that those exports did not compete directly with European goods. What one hand giveth, the other taketh away. Maintaining 'imperial preference' was very much at the heart of such policies and, subconsciously or not, it is a policy that still persists (see Chapters 5 and 13). For example, although the language has changed, the UK government's post-Brexit trade policy is cloaked in the idea of revitalising the trading links with the former colonial countries (the 'Commonwealth') and retaining a 'privileged' trading relationship.

One key question is why Asia managed to diversify, but Africa did not. Both had to contend with their colonial past. The question is of course rather simplistic, because Asia, like Africa, is not a homogenous entity and there has been a great deal of variety to its developmental experience. Once again, to deal with this issue in any depth would take us beyond the scope of this book.[54] But, apart from the geopolitical situation, one reason why parts of Asia diversified out of primary commodity production and thrived was the existence of a regional hegemon with prior experience of manufacturing: Japan.

Japan emerged from a self-imposed feudal seclusion to industrial prowess surprisingly rapidly at the end of the nineteenth century, and although its economic progress suffered the tremendous upheaval of defeat and destruction of the Second World War, its post-war recovery—crucially with US backing[55]—was astonishing, to such an extent that by the mid-1980s, Japan's economic vitality was considered a major threat to US hegemony. Japan's rapid economic recovery between the 1950s and 1980s ended up providing the necessary impetus to what the Japanese economist Kaname Akmasutu called the 'flying geese' phenomenon of industrialisation towards the rest of the region.[56]

The textile sector is illustrative of this sequence of industrialisation. In the post-war period, Japan's prowess in manufacturing quickly recovered, focusing initially on labour-intensive manufacturers. But as the country recovered and per capita incomes rose, Japan slowly displaced its production towards other less-developed Asian economies. This was partly the consequence of trade policies of the West. For instance, once the United States started to experience surging textile imports from Japan, it changed the rules and imposed voluntary export restraints. However, as is often the case in economics, the policy ended up having the unforeseen consequence of Japanese manufacturers trying to evade the controls by investing outside the country in other Southeast Asian economies (initially, Taiwan, Singapore and South Korea). These countries subsequently saw a surge in their own exports to the US market, while Japan itself upgraded into synthetic fabrics and clothing.[57] Meanwhile, the second-tier locations started to cascade their know-how to other locations. For instance, in the late 1970s, one of the first investors to produce garments for export in Bangladesh was Daewoo Corporation of Korea. At that time, the South Asian country had no modern industry. By the early 2000s, the industry was generating more than USD 12 billion in export revenue. By 2019, Bangladesh's textile and clothing exports had risen to USD 43 billion compared with just USD 18 billion for the whole of the African continent.[58] This pattern of transferring manufacturing capacity and know-how to other locations in Asia (primarily through foreign investment) occurred in many other sectors. Thus, for instance, Japanese investment in its automobile parts sector helped Thailand overtake the United States as the world's main producer of one-ton pickup trucks.[59] And as a consequence of this flying-geese pattern of investment, intra-regional trade flourished in Southeast Asia in a way unlike anywhere else in the world.

Sadly for the continent, Africa lacked a country capable of playing a similar role.[60] South Africa was sufficiently industrialised and developed, but because of its abhorrent apartheid regime, it was economically isolated from the rest of the continent through sanctions. Without a regional hegemon to help promote the transfer of capital (in the form of FDI) and technology, African countries struggled to integrate into the global economy at the time when it was most propitious to do so (i.e. when demand for manufactured goods in Western markets was not yet saturated and before the incredible rise of the Chinese economy, which largely changed the panorama for manufacturing elsewhere).

The commodity super-cycle to the rescue?

So far, so bad. But the story has an important twist. In the early 2000s, commodity prices started to revive strongly. Strong demand from emerging economies, particularly China, led to the start of a spectacular boom in commodity prices, particularly for the precious metals needed as inputs into manufacturing processes. Suddenly, the financial media started talking of a 'commodity super-cycle'—an unprecedented and allegedly sustained increase in commodity prices.[61] The pessimistic narrative about the prospects of commodity exporters in Africa and elsewhere suddenly shifted to almost unbounded optimism. Even when the global financial crisis hit in 2008–09, commodity prices proved to be quite resilient—something quite unusual in the history of global recessions. (Commodity prices are usually one of the first things to be hit.) The reason being that the Chinese economic juggernaut was barely impacted by the financial crisis, and its voracious demand for primary products continued unabated, thereby acting as an important shock absorber for commodity exporters.

As a consequence, the African share of global trade climbed back up to over 3% just prior to the global financial crisis of 2008–09. Around this time, in their fervour for securing access particularly to precious minerals and fuels, multinational investors also started to see Africa in a new light and investment into the sector rebounded. In the oil sector, for instance, there was a flurry of exploratory activity on the continent, and new fields were rapidly opening up. It was around this time that countries such as Angola, Chad, Gabon, Equatorial Guinea and Sudan started to become significant oil producers for the first time.[62]

Moreover, there were some strategic reasons why the continent was favoured by 'big oil', including the fact that the development of African oil fields reduced dependence on the Middle East, the high quality of African crude, the fact that the new producers were not Organization of the Petroleum Exporting Countries (OPEC) members, and the lack of experience of African states in striking a hard bargain with the multinationals in terms of the share of profits.[63] Chinese, European and American firms all competed to secure lucrative contracts. European and American companies often looked on jealously as Chinese state-owned firms started to carve out a major niche in the mineral and oil sectors.

There was thus a remarkable degree of renewed interest in Africa as a source of commodities at around this time. Illustrative of the economic consequences, Angola was selling around USD 68 billion of oil annually at its peak—around double official development assistance to sub-Saharan Africa at that time. Yet no one would have noticed: the endless discussions around development finance and overseas development assistance distracted attention from where the real sources of revenue were coming from, and the uses to which those revenues were being put.

There was another phenomenon at work in the early 2000s that compounded this trend towards rising export revenues. Studies started to show that it was now the turn of manufacturing prices to suffer a decline in their terms of trade. This was precipitated by what Harvard economist Richard Freeman termed the 'great doubling', when the global workforce effectively doubled in size due to the simultaneous collapse of Soviet communism, China's movement toward market capitalism, and India's decision to undertake market reforms and enter the global trading system.[64] The world's total labour force grew from approximately 2.3 billion in 1990 to 3.4 billion in 2017. More dramatically, the number of workers in exporting industries across the globe quadrupled between 1980 and 2003.[65]

This led to enormous downward pressure on the prices of labour-intensive manufactured goods. This was best illustrated in sectors where global competition was intense, such as the textile sector. One study showed that unit prices in clothing declined by nearly 50% in just one year (2004–05), when the final restraints on the global clothing trade were removed under the elimination of the Multi-Fibre Arrangement.[66]

Around this time, buoyed by the upward swing of commodity prices, a number of studies were published that purported to show that dependence on commodities was not a 'curse'. For instance, using an econometric analysis of time series data, Lederman and Maloney concluded that there was a mildly positive correlation between dependence on natural resources and GDP growth.[67] Other authors stressed the economic history of countries such as Norway and Sweden to show that there has often been a positive synergy between commodities production and manufacturing. The settler economies of countries like Argentina, Australia, Canada, New Zealand and the United States were also cited as evidence that high levels of income per capita could be attained on the back of exploiting natural resources, leading one group of authors to conclude:

> There is thus no strong causal link between commodity dependence per se and the underdevelopment of the industrial sector. Indeed, what is frequently interpreted as a manufacturing sector weakened by a commodities specialisation may in fact simply reflect a commodities' specialisation in economies with no or little history of industrial development.[68]

This ignores the fact that the settler economies generally had quite a different development trajectory, with large uninhabited cultivable areas, privileged trading relations with the metropolis, and were often dependent on the subjugation or annihilation of indigenous populations.[69] It was neither a model that was replicable nor desirable from a socio-economic perspective. In any case, as Figure 4.4 makes clear, the gains in export revenues were not sustained, with Africa's share in global trade falling again from around 2013, as commodity prices weakened.

Moreover, the fleeting improvement in Africa's global share of trade was driven largely by improved prices for the continent's

Figure 4.4: Africa's total and share of global exports (2000–20)*

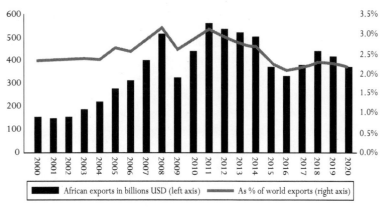

* At current prices and exchange rates.
Source: Calculated from IMF DOTS (2023).

exports, not because of expanding volumes of exports, which only improved weakly over the course of the 2000s.[70] One reason for the poor supply-side response to higher prices was the oligopolistic nature of a lot of commodity markets, whereby it was the middlemen traders who were skimming off an important part of the profits from rising prices. During the course of the 2000s, large trading companies made spectacularly lucrative trades. In the decade from 2001–11, Vitol, Glencore and Cargill—the world's largest oil, metal and agricultural trading houses, respectively—enjoyed a combined net income of USD 76.3 billion. That was ten times the profits the traders were generating in the 1990s and more than either Apple or Coca-Cola made over the same period.[71]

In the end, however, the 'super-cyclists'—like most who claim that each new high price cycle is structurally different from ones in the past and will be sustained indefinitely—proved to be naïve. The commodity price boom started to peter out in the mid-2010s, led by a collapse of oil prices and followed by minerals and other commodities. The budgets of oil-producing nations came under particular pressure, and there was a marked divestment in the African mining industry. Presciently, Nobel Prize-winning economist Angus Deaton said: 'Rising commodity prices will not solve Africa's poverty; rather, only an end to tropical poverty will bring increases in commodity prices.'[72]

The literature has also shown that commodity dependence is associated with poor governance and low social development. For instance, it is often alleged that a higher share of fuel and mineral exports tends to have a negative effect on the quality of both institutions and on governance.[73] Mineral wealth is often seen as particularly subject to this commodity curse. Ownership of minerals is often concentrated, so that the benefits of the export income are not widely spread and mining results in a particularly unequal distribution of income.[74]

Moreover, commodity dependence has been linked to both lower social development[75] and lower human development.[76] Crucially, from an economic perspective, a higher share of commodities in exports is linked to lower levels of export diversification[77] and lower aggregate labour productivity.[78]

More granular analysis of export performance on the African continent seems to confirm the broad hypothesis about the dangers of an excessive dependence on commodity exports. Using an augmented production function approach involving 64 developing countries for 1960–80, Ghanaian professor August Fosu found that high shares of commodity exports had little or no impact on economic growth, whereas manufactured exports did exert a positive and significant impact on the pace of growth.[79] Similarly, in a later study based on 76 developing countries over 1967–86, Fosu estimated a near-zero effect of primary exports on the non-export sector, suggesting that there is little or no spill-over effect on the rest of the economy.[80] Reviewing a large number of studies on export composition and growth on the African continent, Fosu concluded that 'taken together … the above studies imply the desirability of pursuing policies that alter endowments in order to achieve export diversification and concomitant economic growth'.[81]

Nor should we be naïve either of the considerable difficulties of leveraging oil or mineral wealth to pursue other agendas. Many countries across the continent dream of 'adding value' to their commodity exports, but these plans rarely bear fruit. Granted, in recent years, some countries have had a degree of success in increasing their earnings from their commodity exports.[82] Contracts have been renegotiated with more favourable terms for some African countries (for example, in Tanzania). But the pernicious nature of the global oil and mining industries on the political economy of the continent should not be underestimated. Echoing sentiments made earlier by Collier,[83] Cramer et al. observe that:

> Natural resources offer 'easy money' to greedy governments, gener-ating a large flow of royalties into the state budget from highly con-centrated sources. A government in this position need not bother with the politically difficult and administratively challenging business of taxing the population and providing public goods in return. With less connection to the population and given the scope for resource rents to become something of a 'honey pot' attracting all manner of rival claimants, this is a potential recipe for corruption, extreme inequalities, and violent conflict.[84]

In many countries, the extractive capacity of the state had collapsed during the period of structural adjustment, and so states were no longer able to capture the new rents of the commodity boom. Mkandawire[85] makes the stark comparison between Zambia and Chile, two major copper producers. Chile was making USD 35 billion of revenues annually out of the copper boom in the 2000s, while Zambia made just USD 200 million. Under the recovery, hardly any industrialisation took place because the capacity for it had gone. Although Zambia accumulated additional reserves during the surge in prices, the country did not have capacity for investing in the long term, as there were no institutions for financing long-term projects.

The fact that, more recently, countries like Ghana, with ostensibly better governance, have experienced a significant deterioration in their economic performance since the inflow of oil money, suggests that such concerns are still warranted. Since the discovery of oil in 2007, there has been a pronounced deterioration of Ghana's fiscal and monetary discipline over this period, resulting in rising debt, a weak-ening of the external balance, and a fall in public investment.[86] The resource curse is still alive and kicking.

Conclusions

All the available evidence points almost unambiguously in the same direction: economic diversification should remain a primary objective of African policymakers. Unfortunately for the continent, there is compelling evidence that it is extremely difficult to escape this 'commodity trap'. A recent report by the United Nations Conference on Trade and Development (UNCTAD) found that, under current conditions, it would take the average commodity-dependent country 190 years to reduce by half the difference between its current share of commodities in total merchandise exports and that of the average non-commodity-dependent country.[87] As we shall argue in Part 2, for a host of reasons, the AfCFTA provides a unique opportunity to improve the chances of escaping commodity dependence—but it is the kind of opportunity that only comes around once. We argue that the continent needs to seize it with both hands.

5

THE FLIP SIDE OF COMMODITY DEPENDENCE

THE MANUFACTURING DEFICIT

Introduction

The material world of goods, buildings, roads and infrastructure surrounds us more than at any other time in economic history. Yet judging by the comments of some academics, you would think we live in a post-industrial world. The debate about whether we inhabit a post-industrial society goes back a long way; in fact, Daniel Bell started these discussions five decades ago.[1] More recently, authors like Rodrik have questioned whether, regardless of its desirability, the traditional path to raising per capita incomes through industrialisation is still an option. It is argued by some that insofar as China and Asia will continue to be the world's dominant factory for the near future, and technological change (automation, 3D printing, etc.) may be returning competitive advantages back to high-income countries, there is less scope for developing countries to significantly expand manufacturing.[2] An important stylised fact in this regard is that developing countries appear to be moving into services at a faster rate than was observed in previous periods and prematurely deindustrialising as a result.[3]

These observations easily give way to some erroneous ideas about priorities for economic development, such as the possibility to 'leap-

79

frog' the manufacturing stage of development altogether and move out of commodities production and straight into the high-value added-service sector. All this has enormous pertinence for discussions on the value proposition of the AfCFTA, because it is largely believed that the manufacturing and industrial sectors will be the principal beneficiaries of the agreement (see Chapter 11).

In this chapter, we will tackle this question by reviewing the evidence regarding the primacy of the role of manufacturing, which, despite dramatic changes in the global economy, remains surprisingly robust. We start by explaining the arguments that 'manufacturing still matters', and then move to a discussion on whether 'leap-frogging' manufacturing into services is a feasible strategy for the majority of African economies (spoiler alert—it is not). Finally, we highlight evidence regarding the (largely unexpected) recent revival in the African manufacturing sector. This, we argue, provides a promising foundation on which the AfCFTA can build.

Why manufacturing still matters

Different positions exist on the importance and role of manufacturing in development. The traditional view (as reflected in the work of Helleiner et al.;[4] Kuznets,[5] etc.) was that all countries undergo a structural transformation of their economies from agriculture to manufacturing/industry and then towards services. And there was an associated belief that, for that transition to happen, governments needed to take an active role in creating the right conditions for the emergence of new industries. In other words, there was a fundamental place for 'industrial policies'.

In the 1980s and 1990s, during the period of structural adjustment, those ideas were generally abandoned in favour of the proposition that the market would lead the way, and that the sectoral composition of GDP would resolve itself.[6] In the end, that didn't happen: despite being compelled to adopt a more laissez-faire stance towards economic development, the majority of African countries either remained stubbornly dependent on agriculture and commodity exports, or experienced a sharp increase in low value-added-service and informal sector activities.

Figure 5.1a: Employment shares in a stylised industrialisation process

Figure 5.1b: Employment shares in Africa (1991–2021)

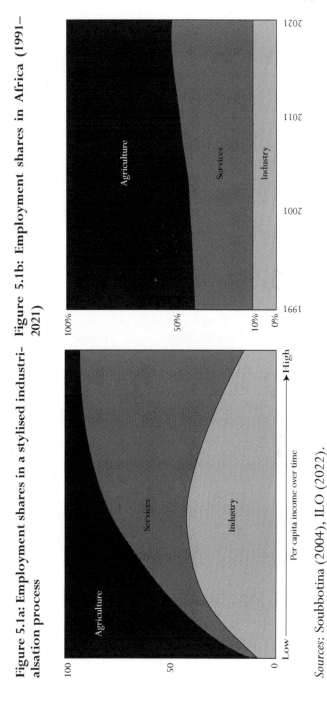

Sources: Soubbotina (2004), ILO (2022).

A visual illustration of the failure of the continent to produce much in the way of meaningful structural change over the past few decades is shown in Figures 5.1a and 5.1b. The panel on the left shows the 'idealised' distribution of employment between agricultural, industrial and services sectors over time. Economies start their development trajectory with an overwhelming dependence on the agricultural sector, but as incomes per capita rise, this is gradually supplanted by industrial employment. Then, as per capita incomes rise higher still, employment shifts increasingly towards the services sectors. The panel on the right, by contrast, reveals a remarkable degree of continuity in the share of employment between the three sectors on the African continent, with industry's contribution either stagnant or even having fallen (Figure 5.1b). The pattern is at least partially explained by the fact that more than one quarter of African countries had not even exceeded their per capita income value of 1970 by 2020.

More recently, however, the idea of the importance of manufacturing has reasserted itself in academic and policy circles.[7] There has been a renewed recognition that, without at least a minimum level of industrialisation and manufacturing, rapid productivity growth and development will remain elusive. Some of the writings on this subject are becoming increasingly alarmist. Rowden, for instance, claims that most of Africa has missed the boat in terms of opportunities to use this period of renewed economic growth to finance and fuel industri-

Figure 5.2: Africa's merchandise trade balance with the world as a percentage of GDP (1970–2021)*

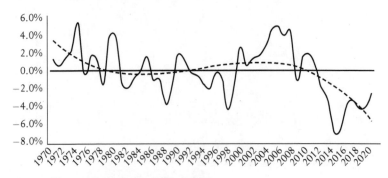

* Dotted line is the polynomial trend line.
Source: Computed from UNCTADStat (2023).

alisation.[8] The writings of Rodrik also tend to concur, noting that Africa's growth over the last 10–15 years has not been driven by export-led manufacturing.[9]

That is certainly the case for most countries on the continent, many of which sustain large trade and current account deficits—deficits that, as we shall see, are very much driven by large net imports of manufactured goods. In consonance with our narrative in the previous section, the commodity super-cycle did provide some macro-economic relief, with a sharp improvement in the aggregate trade balance for the continent at the turn of the century, but this quickly deteriorated again after the global financial crisis and, worryingly, since the mid-2010s, has turned decisively negative again.

It needs stressing the extent to which this temporary improvement in the continent's merchandise trade balance was concentrated only on the trade performance of a select number of countries (Figure 5.2). For instance, by the end of the period 2000–08, when Africa as a whole enjoyed a trade surplus due to the commodity boom, just 16 out of 55 countries registered a trade surplus and only 13 had a current account surplus. Most of these countries with either a trade or current account surplus were resource-rich countries (e.g. Algeria, Angola, Equatorial Guinea, Gabon, Nigeria). Indeed, the extent to which the trade of African countries is dominated by a small number of major economies is remarkable, with the five largest exporters, between 2016 and 2020, exporting more than the next 49 African countries combined. This includes South Africa, Nigeria, Algeria, Angola, and Egypt—countries either 'blessed' with hydrocarbons or having achieved a degree of industrialisation.[10]

Against this backdrop, it will not surprise the reader to discover that it is the manufacturing sector that is driving the large trade deficits on the continent. Table 5.1 shows the trade balances in East Africa (as representative of a more general problem on the continent), broken down by sub-sector and expressed as a percentage of GDP. The results are striking. It is inescapable that the trade deficits have principally been driven by net imports in manufacturing. Tragically for the region, some countries have also become net importers of food, reflecting the weakness in productivity in traditional agriculture, and most countries are also heavily dependent on fuel imports. A few countries are significant net mineral exporters (particularly DRC), and most register balanced trade in agricultural commodities. However, there is no escaping the fact that an improved trade performance revolves principally around strengthening the capacity and competitiveness of manufacturing.

Table 5.1: Trade balance for East African countries by sector as a percentage of GDP (2021)

	Ores & Minerals	Food Items	Agric. Raw Material	Fuels	Manufactures
Burundi	2%	−3%	0%	−4%	−18%
Comoros	0%	−6%	0%	−1%	−13%
DRC	33%	−2%	0%	0%	−6%
Djibouti	6%	−4%	−3%	9%	−28%
Eritrea	11%	−10%	2%	−1%	−26%
Ethiopia	0%	0%	0%	−2%	−11%
Kenya	0%	0%	1%	−2%	−10%
Madagascar	6%	2%	0%	−5%	−15%
Rwanda	4%	−1%	0%	−2%	−14%
Seychelles	−1%	1%	−3%	−4%	−46%
Somalia	2%	−4%	0%	0%	−8%
South Sudan	0%	−8%	0%	10%	−17%
Tanzania	4%	2%	0%	−2%	−9%
Uganda	0%	2%	0%	−2%	−10%

Source: Calculated from UNCTADStat (2023).

Chronic and increasing trade deficits can be interpreted in different ways. Trade deficits can be evidence that domestic firms suffer from low productivity and cannot compete with foreign firms. This not only limits the capacity of exports but also constrains the development of import-competing industries, which in turn increases import dependence and thus unemployment and poverty.[11] There is a converse story, however, whereby trade deficits can also result from a country investing in physical capital (through imports of intermediate goods) and building productive capacity, which has the potential of boosting employment and reducing poverty, provided the investments are effective and allocated to job-creating activities. Some take this as far as almost a fetishism for higher imports, as a sign of a healthy economy that is growing rapidly. According to Cramer et al.:

> To some extent, it may be possible to limit the rate of growth of luxury consumer goods imports, but it is impossible to successfully sustain rapid development if imported capital and intermediate goods dry up. The building of the Grand Ethiopian Renaissance Dam, the Kandadji Dam in Niger, and the infrastructure renewal programme in Côte d'Ivoire are all associated with sharp spikes in imports.[12]

It is certainly true that capital goods make up a significant proportion of African countries' imports; according to World Bank data, between about a quarter and a third of total goods imports in 2019.[13] These capital goods can, in principle, provide a very significant boost to long-term economic growth. The import of consumer goods, however, explains by far the largest share of total imports—and ultimately that resultant trade deficits need financing. Moreover, as the example of East Africa shows, it is the weakness in local manufacturing that is driving these deficits (Table 5.1).

It is an interesting but under-researched empirical question as to which segments of society are driving these deficits. Take, for example, the admittedly extreme case of South Sudan. Through their humanitarian assistance and development programmes, the presence of the international community is manifest in the country, and they are largely import-dependent (usually doing so free of tariffs, depriving the state of any income from their voracious demand for imports). But the wealthy South Sudanese (of which there is a small but significant minority) are clearly responsible for a large share of the imports, too—particularly in luxury items like 4x4 vehicles and other fast-moving consumables (goods like air conditioners, TVs, refrigerators, washing machines—what Amsden described as 'typical balance-of-payments busters').[14] This pattern is probably reproduced

85

across many countries on the continent, with the bulk of imports often being made by the top quintile of the population. What one can be sure of is that, beyond some seriously food-insecure countries, the poorest segments of society in Africa usually have a very low propensity to import.

Beyond these distributional issues, there is another concern about large structural (as opposed to temporary) trade imbalances, and that is their macroeconomic consequence. It is no use wishing away the challenge of financing large and sustained trade deficits. A lack of access to foreign exchange has been a historic challenge even for some high-income countries and has resulted in them being subjected to the usual IMF conditionalities.[15] For many African countries, having to accept such conditionalities is commonplace. As of June 2022, 19 countries have programmes with the IMF in place,[16] and it is something that often significantly diminishes their policy space.[17]

Arguably more serious still from a macroeconomic point of view, many countries across Africa are running up against what Thirlwall coined as the 'balance of payments constraint', whereby the economy cannot grow faster without engendering an un-financeable and unsustainable widening of the current account deficit.[18] Notwithstanding the assertions of Cramer et al., there have been a number of studies that have confirmed the existence of such balance-of-payment constraints in African countries.[19]

The scale of the manufacturing deficit

All this suggests that manufacturing still matters—there is no direct golden path for Africa to a post-industrial heaven. In an important book on the prospects for industrial development on the African continent, Newman et al. make some pertinent comparisons with other 'benchmark countries'[20]—a comparison that really drives home the scale of the manufacturing deficit on the continent (Table 5.2).

The manufacturing value-added and the labour shares in low-income African countries are about half of the benchmark values. The share of manufacturing in GDP is less than half of the average for all developing countries. Manufacturing output per capita is about 10% of the global developing country average. Even Mauritius and South

Table 5.2: Africa's manufacturing deficit compared with benchmark middle-income countries

	Value-added share (%)			Labour share (%)		
	Agriculture	Manufacturing	Services	Agriculture	Manufacturing	Services
Benchmark middle-income country	21.7	21.9	44.2	45.2	11.6	36.6
Africa low-income	27.8	11.1	49.3	63.1	6.6	25.2
Africa middle-income country	4.8	17.1	67.2	8.6	16.8	62.7

Notes: Benchmark countries as described below:

Africa low-income sample: Ethiopia, Malawi, Ghana, Kenya, Madagascar, Mozambique, Senegal, Tanzania.

Africa middle-income sample: Mauritius, South Africa.

Sources: Adapted from Newman et al. (2016), based on 2010 data.

Africa—middle-income countries and arguably among Africa's two most successful industrialisers—fall short of the benchmark in terms of the share of manufacturing value-added in GDP. This reflects the scale of the region's 'manufacturing deficit' relative to other developing countries. Newman et al. find that the manufacturing sector in Africa is on average six times more productive than agriculture.[21] Another study reports that the gap is even larger—ten times higher than in agriculture.[22] Because of low employment growth in manufacturing, Africa's structural transformation from low-productivity, often subsistence agriculture has principally been towards low-productivity, urban-based services in the informal sector. The economic cost of this has been high. It is a process that has thus generally been growth-reducing rather than growth-enhancing. According to one estimate, income per capita could have been two and a half times larger in Malawi and Kenya if physical and human capital were sufficiently reallocated to the higher-productivity industrial sector.[23]

Particularly worrying is the weak aggregate trade performance of the manufacturing sector, with per capita manufactured exports at around just 10% of the developing country average. Moreover, there is little evidence that the complexity of African exports (measured as the diversity of products) or the quality of exported goods (derived from price differences within specific product categories) have been improving over the past two decades.[24] This has a major economic cost, as a large body of evidence documents the presence of significant export productivity premiums, whereby manufacturing exporters outperform their non-exporting counterparts.[25] For example, evidence from Côte d'Ivoire, Ethiopia and Tanzania provides strong support for the proposition that increased trade exposure significantly raises plant-level total factor productivity.[26]

Finally, a simple econometric test of the proposition that manufacturing influences the prospects for long-term economic growth and development was performed by Amsden.[27] She found that 75% of the variation in manufacturing output per capita in 1994 could be explained by variations in per capita manufacturing output in 1950. This was a powerful finding and suggested that success in manufacturing is dependent ('path-dependent') on past success in manufacturing. In other words, you cannot simply achieve success without any prior track record or experience. Arguably, it is where the poor economic legacy of European colonialisation (as discussed in Chapter 4) weighs most heavily on the African continent. It is also where the continent's experience parts company with that of South Korea, which was colonised by the Japanese between 1910 and 1945, and, despite its brutality, brought a level of industrial development.

And yet, as noted at the beginning of this section, some authors have suggested that the continent may have missed the proverbial boat in terms of achieving an acceptable degree of industrialisation. Due to underlying changes in the global economy, it is argued, the window of opportunity has now closed and the continent is undergoing a process of relative deindustrialisation. Others highlight the difficulties the continent has had in integrating into GVCs.[28] These authors tend to stress that the 'traditional' path of economic growth and development may be less applicable to lower-income countries today than it was in the past. Insofar as China and Asia will continue to be the world's dominant factory for the near future, technological change (automation, additive manufacturing, etc.), combined with policy pressures on multinational firms to re-shore or near-shore production, may imply less scope for developing countries to significantly expand manufacturing.[29]

Is leapfrogging manufacturing into services feasible?

Does this matter? Some recent research has emphasised the importance of diversification into non-manufacturing activities for the creation of jobs in Africa.[30] It is maintained that in the modern global economy, countries are no longer pre-destined to slavishly following a single path to development and high incomes; furthermore, it is argued that it is absurd for countries to invest excessive amounts of resources in 'a mad rush towards industrialisation' when many opportunities now exist to 'leap-frog' that stage of development and move straight into higher value-added activities in the service sector. Thanks to revolutions in transport and technologies, traditional services like tourism, health and education services, newer services like e-commerce, digitally enabled business, as well as non-traditional industries 'without smokestacks', such as horticulture and agro-processing, are argued to have the great potential to drive job creation. It is certainly true that many developing countries are moving into services at a faster rate than previously.[31] Services are certainly heterogeneous in terms of skill intensity, tradability and scope for productivity growth, and some services offer scope for the type of productivity dynamics that have characterised manufacturing.[32]

Arguments that services can play a role similar to that played by the manufacturing sector in the past are based on the view that the nature of services is changing dramatically, due in part to the changes occurring in the organisation of international production, the reduction in transport costs and opportunities offered by new technologies. Many services activities are (increasingly) tradeable, have experienced high productivity growth, and can achieve economies of scale.[33] Within services, shifts in resource allocation are a driver of productivity growth in the same way as in goods-producing sectors. One commonly cited study finds that average productivity growth in services is similar to that in other sectors.[34] Some services offer great scope for the type of productivity dynamics that have characterised manufacturing, others do not.

To some extent, the debate about services versus manufacturing is a semantic and definitional one. Many manufacturing activities are services-intensive, and the 'servicification' of manufacturing has been increasing over time. Conversely, a lot of services depend on manufactured inputs and machinery—be it computer hardware, telecom infrastructure, aeroplanes, lorries etc.[35] Many of the high-productivity services that are supposed to be replacing manufacturing—such as finance, transport and business services (e.g. management consulting, engineering, design)—cannot exist without the manufacturing sector, because it is their main customer.[36] And some services only look 'new' because they used to be provided in-house by manufacturing companies (and thus counted as output of the manufacturing sector) but are now supplied by firms specialising in those services (and thus counted as outputs of the service sector).

The idea of 'leapfrogging' manufacturing and moving directly into services holds particular appeal in countries that are landlocked and face high import and export duties; countries where it is often deemed that manufacturing industries will generally be uncompetitive. Adding to these arguments are doubts over whether the type of export-led manufacturing strategies used successfully in the past are still feasible, given the backdrop of rising competition from the Asian Giants and other low-cost producers (particularly in Southeast Asia).[37] All these concerns coalesce around discussions over 'premature deindustrialisation', and the generally hostile attitude of the donor community towards industrial policy measures in developing countries, as well as the diminished policy space resulting from World Trade Organization (WTO) rules and other trade treaties.[38] In sum, in a lot of writing on the prospects for industrialisation on the African continent, there is a pervasive feeling that the proverbial 'window of opportunity' has closed, and pursuing a service-oriented agenda is the only way forward.

The question is, however, whether a services-centric economic development strategy could, as an alternative strategy, generate sufficient employment creation and productivity growth needed for sustainable development of low-income countries in Africa and elsewhere.[39] In dealing with this question, the first thing to note is that there is a real sense in which the decline in the importance of the manufacturing sector globally is exaggerated. In an important but overlooked paper, Haraguchi et al. note that, in aggregate, the size of manufacturing value-added produced in developing countries as a whole has not changed since 1990—indeed, by some measures, it has mildly increased.[40] What *has* happened is a change in the economic geography of global manufacturing, with a rapid concentration of manufacturing in a small number of 'successful diversifiers' (e.g. Bangladesh, Brazil, China, Türkiye, Vietnam) as well as countries now considered to be high-income economies (e.g. South Korea, Taiwan and Singapore).

Does this mean that the opportunities and policy space available for manufacturing development have changed? Trade liberalisation and the increasing role GVCs play in manufacturing production and trade have certainly intensified price competition among countries and given distinct advantages to certain countries with economies of scale and agglomeration. India's growing global dominance in exports of medical equipment and pharmaceuticals, or China's dominance in electronics and computers, or apparel and clothing are examples of this degree of concentration. One example is that 60% of the world's buttons are now produced in a single location—a town in China called Qiatou specialised in the production of buttons.[41] There are similar towns dedicated to the production of underwear. These are economies of agglomeration on a scale that has never been seen before. The Asian Giants cast a big shadow on the global economy. It would seem to suggest there is a new imperative for African countries to work at scale if they are to have any chance of recapturing a share of manufacturing in their domestic and regional economies, let alone in global export markets. As we explain in Chapter 9, the AfCFTA will provide such an opportunity for upscaling.

Another reason to doubt the ability to 'leap-frog' manufacturing directly into services is the relatively low tradability of services. Yes, it is true that, through technological innovation, some services have become more tradeable over time. For example, it is now possible for some business services to be provided at a distance in a way that would have been impossible several decades ago. Handy reports the example of a UK-based mall using security guards based in Lagos to supervise the security cameras.[42] None of this, however, is arguably substantive enough to fundamentally change the need for exports of merchandise goods to deal with the balance-of-payments challenges. Moreover, services have remained at around 20–25% of global exports for the last two and a half decades—and are substantially lower for African countries (see Figure 5.3).[43] Subsequently, services can make a difference to the overall trade balance; however, aside from the smallest economies, they are unlikely to be able to generate sufficient revenues to compensate for the continent's weakness in manufacturing.

Perhaps most compelling of all is the abundant evidence that the manufacturing sector has an inherently faster productivity growth than the services sector. In a classic text on the pre-eminence of the manufacturing sector in being the 'engine' of productivity growth, John Cornwall stressed the benefits deriving from the sector's ability to achieve higher levels of capital accumulation, economies of scale and technological progress relative to the agricultural and services sectors.[44]

Cornwall's arguments have proven to be surprisingly robust over time. For instance, Marconi et al. examine the 'engine of growth'

Figure 5.3: Share of services in total exports for the world and Africa (1990–2021)

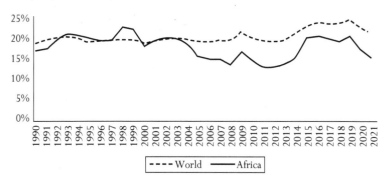

Source: Calculated from UNCTADStat (2023).

hypothesis using an econometric model of dynamic panel data for a sample of 63 countries for the period 1990–2011.[45] The results confirm that higher increases in manufacturing output leads to both faster GDP and manufacturing productivity growth, with particularly notable effects in low and lower middle-income countries. Similarly, Szirmai and Verspagen econometrically tested the relationships between the value-added share of manufacturing and growth of GDP per capita using a panel of 92 countries over the period 1950–2005, and used the same methodology for the service sector.[46] Their results showed that manufacturing acted as an engine of growth for low- and some middle-income countries, but only if they had a sufficient level of human capital—a finding that underpins the importance of education in being able to absorb technologies.[47] Pointedly, such growth engine features were not found in the service sector. There is some evidence that parts of the service sector do have positive characteristics as a spur to economic growth.[48] However, the balance of evidence seems to suggest that manufacturing sector growth drives services sector growth, not the other way around.[49] And it is also the case that manufacturing is still responsible for the bulk of technological innovation. Even in countries like the US and the UK, where manufacturing accounts for only around 10% of economic output, 60–70% of research and development (R&D) is conducted by the manufacturing sector; the figure is 80–90% in more manufacturing-oriented economies like Germany or South Korea.[50]

Where structural change in Africa has bypassed the manufacturing sector, the consequences have generally been reduced productivity and economic growth. McMillan and Headey, for example, found that between 1990 and 2005, the movement of labour into service sectors (including tourism, trade and others) saw labour moving 'from high to low-productivity activities and reducing Africa's growth by 1.3 percentage points per annum on average'.[51] Throughout the world, the quality of jobs in manufacturing also tends to be better than in agriculture and most service sub-sectors. Between 2002 and 2012, only 5.4% of those in Africa defined as 'working poor' (i.e. with an income that is insufficient to pull them out of poverty) were employed in industry, compared with 16.4% in the service sector and 78.2% in agriculture.[52]

Industry is the pre-eminent destination sector at early stages of development because it is a high-productivity sector capable of absorbing large numbers of moderately skilled workers.[53] Indeed, Newman et al. calculate that between 1950 and 2006 about half of the catch-up to advanced economy levels of output per worker which developing countries managed was explained simply by rising productivity within industry combined with the shift of workers out of agriculture.[54] In another study using manufacturing establishment data for Chile, Colombia, India and the United States, Hallak and Sivadasan show that exporters sell higher-quality products, charge higher prices, pay higher input prices and higher wages, and use capital more intensively.[55] This adds to the evidence that, by providing new opportunities for increasing manufactured exports, trade integration under the AfCFTA may facilitate technological upgrading.[56]

The (unexpected) revival of African manufacturing

The current dominant narrative about African manufacturing is that it is failing and that the continent is de-industrialising. But fortunately, there is growing evidence of a revival in the fortunes of African manufacturing, building a base upon which the AfCFTA can thrive. The long decline in manufacturing's share of GDP since the period of structural adjustment has bottomed out, and for sub-Saharan Africa it now stands at around 12% of GDP (having dipped below 10% around the time of the global financial crisis of 2008–09). For the continent as a whole, far from languishing, the sector's output is up 91% in real terms since 2000.[57] Between 2000 and 2015, manufacturing achieved an average annual growth rate of more than 5% per year, faster than in the rest of the world. Though admittedly starting at a lower level, that growth is impressive, especially after adjusting for income and population. Some countries, such as Nigeria and Angola, have experienced an increase in output of over 10% per year. Southern Africa appears to be the only sub-Saharan region to have experienced deindustrialisation, with a falling share of manufacturing in GDP.[58]

A further encouraging sign is that the share of the workforce in sub-Saharan Africa employed in manufacturing has started rising again, from 7.2% of the total in 2010 to 8.4% in 2019.[59] For example, Côte d'Ivoire created about 24,000 manufacturing jobs between 2003 and 2014, and Ethiopia added 128,000 manufacturing jobs over the 1996–2016 period.[60] In North Africa, Morocco's automotive sector alone created 67,000 jobs between 2004 and 2015, and multiplied its export revenue by a factor of 12 from USD 400 million in 2004 to USD 5 billion in 2015.[61] Again, the only African economies where the absolute level of employment in manufacturing declined between 2004 and 2014 were Mauritius and South Africa.[62] This revival suggests an improvement in the fortunes of manufacturing, contradicting the pessimistic narrative of an unstoppable downwards slide.[63]

We should also be encouraged by the fact that, while manufacturing firms across Africa generally perform worse than firms in other regions in terms of productivity levels and growth rates,[64] these weaknesses may not prove insurmountable. Research by Harrison et al. suggests that, once the disadvantages of geography, infrastructure, political competition and the business environment are controlled for, African manufacturing firms actually exhibit a conditional advantage in productivity compared with non-African firms.[65] This is especially true in low-tech manufacturing. These findings suggest that there is no inherent 'curse' that hinders the development of African manufacturing and that African firms should be able to thrive, given the right opportunities and measures to address the infrastructure deficits and unpredictable business environments. The AfCFTA provides one such opportunity.

Above all, the long-term preconditions for industrial success may be changing. Not only can the manufacturing sector leverage the large and burgeoning consumer markets across the continent (see Chapter 9), but certain fundamental dynamics are shifting in favour of industrialisation. Despite a lot of evidence to the contrary, economists and economic historians still like to measure a country's or region's 'comparative advantage' by measuring 'resource ratios'—the relative abundance of one factor of production (e.g. land) versus another (e.g. labour force or capital). From here, it is deduced that a country, region or even continent should 'specialise' in producing goods in which it is relatively 'factor-rich'. Traditionally, because of its geographic enormity (China, Europe, the United States and India could fit into the map of the continent, and still have space to spare), Africa is considered 'land-rich' and with a sparse population. But because of demographic pressures, and the prospect that Africa will soon overtake India and China in terms of population, there is a perception that Africa is shifting towards 'labour abundance'. In the words of one economic historian, 'Africa's resource ratios have changed radically in recent decades, towards labour abundance plus much greater human capital formation. This greatly increases the chance that industrialization, initially labour-intensive, can take off in at least some African economies, with state support'.[66]

As highlighted by John Sender in a seminal article published in 1999 that provides a wealth of empirical evidence to counter the arguments of Afro-pessimists, one of the biggest achievements of the post-independence governments was the rapid expansion of formal education at all levels.[67] In the period since Sender wrote that article, adult literacy has continued to improve on the continent, reaching around 70% in 2019, but with much higher levels prevailing in both Northern and Southern Africa.[68] Although this is low compared with contemporary Asia, it is well above the threshold for countries successfully industrialising in the past. To be sure, there are numerous question marks regarding the quality of education that prevails on the continent. But in the context of cheaper and better-educated labour, the prospect of labour-intensive manufacturing taking off in Africa becomes much more realistic.[69]

Conclusions

In this chapter, we argued that there needs to be a rapid transition out of commodity production into higher-productivity activities. While this does include some service sub-sectors, this cannot be achieved while neglecting the manufacturing sector. Building a more resilient manufacturing sector is a necessary but not sufficient condition to overcome the macroeconomic constraints on growth on the continent: it is the way to improve the trade balance, hasten job creation and accelerate technological acquisition and transfer. Even the landlocked countries, which may consider themselves at a competitive disadvantage, need a minimum level of manufacturing if their economies are going to be resilient and provide the ecosystem around which tertiary firms will thrive.

Against this backdrop, the claim that Africa has 'nothing to trade' is often heard:[70] one argument commonly voiced is that there is a need for a prolonged period of investment in productive capacities before contemplating deeper continental integration. These concerns are understandable, but misplaced. Economies evolve through 'growth on the margin'—that is, in response to new market opportunities. Without that spur to growth, there is no real incentive to invest in the first place. It is imperative, therefore, to provide the incentives to expand manufacturing; in Hirschman's expression, to create the conditions for 'unbalanced growth'.[71] Within the remit of the AfCFTA, those incentives include the elimination of tariffs and reduction of NTBs on intra-African trade. And they are powerful stimulants if pursued aggressively and unrelentingly. The potential of the agreement to spur structural diversification will thus depend to a considerable extent on whether member countries embrace industrialisation as a path to sustainable economic growth.[72]

Yet the AfCFTA will not automatically accelerate industrialisation on the continent. At the moment, the AfCFTA does not have any specific programme governing industrial policy.[73] Strong arguments have been made in favour of the adoption of regional industrial policies that would help create the conditions to allow for scale economies and complementarities that can drive more production, processing, and high-value exports.[74] We will return to these points in Chapters 9 and 14.

6

WEAKNESSES OF AFRICA'S CURRENT PATTERNS OF INTEGRATION INTO THE GLOBAL ECONOMY

Introduction

In the past, African countries have tried hard to increase their exports and diversify their economies by focusing on high-income markets. Yet despite being granted preferential trading terms since the early 1970s, this strategy has largely been unsuccessful. The multilateral trading system (aka the General Agreement on Tariffs and Trade [GATT]/WTO) has also largely failed to meet the high expectations in terms of providing a framework for African countries to gain better market access.

This chapter starts by looking at the shifting geography of African trade, noting the decline of the share of trade with the continent's traditional trading partners in Europe, and the rise in 'South–South' trade. The next section explores the strategic implications of this shift. We then look at the failings of African countries to integrate into the global economy under preferential market access schemes to high-income economies. Although on the face of it generous, the shortcomings of these agreements are highlighted. The chapter also explores the nature of the rapidly evolving trading relationship with China, and notes that while it has some positive characteristics, it too suffers from a similar structural defect (in the sense that it is dominated by commodity exports in exchange for manufactured imports). Moreover, the competitive threat posed by manufactured imports from China to Africa's ambitions to industrialise has proven to be a real one, as confirmed in multiple studies. Against this backdrop, we conclude with a discussion of a few interesting proposals to strengthen preferential market access but discard these proposals as broadly unrealistic.

The shifting economic geography of African trade

Over the last two decades, the African continent has experienced a sea change in its trading relations with the rest of the world. Trade flows with advanced economies, which represented close to 80% of exports in 2000, slumped in the wake of the global financial crisis. Back in 2000, the EU was the destination for nearly half (46%) of all Africa's exports and 43% of its imports. The United States too was a major export destination, accounting for 17% of the total. Fast forward two decades and a remarkable shift has occurred (Figure 6.1).[1]

Reflecting the country's rapid ascent as the world's largest economy,[2] China has become Africa's largest single-country trading partner in terms of both exports and imports, responsible for 17% of exports and one fifth (20%) of all imports in 2019. Other developing country trading partners have also risen to prominence. For example, since 2005, India has become the largest export destination for Ghana, Nigeria and Tanzania; Pakistan has been the top destination for Kenya's exports (principally its tea).[3] Meanwhile, new trade partnerships have been forged with emerging markets such as Brazil, Indonesia, Russia and Türkiye.[4]

To be sure, as a regional block, the EU does remain the single largest trading partner at the continental level. But there is a lot of regional variation: while West and North Africa are still highly dependent on the European market, Southern, Central and Eastern Africa now have much lower levels of dependence. It also needs to be born in mind that the EU has expanded from just 15 members in 1995 to 27 members in 2021, an expansion that does not seem to have halted the decline of its share of trade on the continent. The EU is not the only trading partner in decline on the continent. Notwithstanding AGOA and major oil investments since the early 2000s (see Chapter 4),

Figure 6.1: Africa's main trading partners in 2000 and 2021

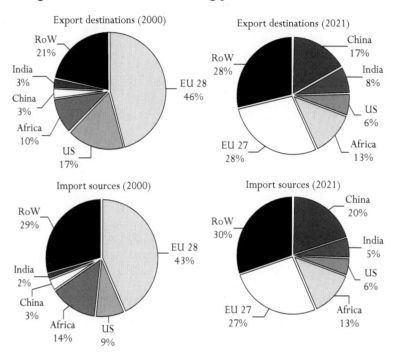

Export destinations (2000)

RoW 21%
India 3%
China 3%
Africa 10%
US 17%
EU 28 46%

Export destinations (2021)

China 17%
RoW 28%
India 8%
US 6%
EU 27 28%
Africa 13%

Import sources (2000)

RoW 29%
India 2%
China 3%
Africa 14%
US 9%
EU 28 43%

Import sources (2021)

China 20%
RoW 30%
India 5%
US 6%
EU 27 27%
Africa 13%

Source: Calculated from UNCTADStat (2023).

the United States has also seen its share of African exports decline from 17% to just 6% over the same period and has now been overtaken by India as an export destination.

One might have hoped that these geographic shifts would have helped the composition of African trade towards a more diversified trading pattern. But, on the contrary, they seem to have compounded the central problem of the excessive dependence on commodities described in Chapter 4. The structure of China's trade with the continent, in particular, very much replicates the 'North–South' pattern of trade that has prevailed with Europe and North America since independence, with an ever-widening trade imbalance in China's favour: crude oil, mineral ores, tobacco and wood contribute over 90% of China's imports from Africa, which is in sharp contrast to its more diversified export to Africa, largely consisting of value-added goods.

Bilateral trade between the two trading partners stood at more than USD 170 billion in 2022, according to IMF DoTs data. Standard Bank has forecast that the associated widening trade imbalance that started in 2015 could become unsustainable. More than 40 African countries currently run a trade deficit with China, and for some, such as Kenya, it is huge. The largest volume of China–Africa trade is with South Africa (which is also the largest African investor in China), while trade with the DRC, Mozambique and Zambia is growing most rapidly.[5] In economic development terms, however, trading relations with China are little better than those with the West—to the extent that the continent's exports are almost exclusively comprised of commodity exports and imports of manufactured goods, the one caveat here being that a significant share of those manufactured imports are capital goods and intermediate inputs which China produces competitively.

Hard strategic choices for the continent

Yet despite these remarkable shifts in trading patterns, policymakers on the continent often behave as if the old dynamics are still in play. A great deal of political capital and effort is expended in negotiating trading agreements with high-income economies. For most countries on the African continent, it is true that those economies remain important trading partners. But the trend is clear. From a strategic point of view, this raises a lot of questions. According to compelling economic research, we now know that the bulk of global trade growth (nearly two thirds) is not through exporting higher volumes of the same products, nor indeed through exporting higher-priced products of higher quality, but through moving into new products—in other words, economic diversification.[6]

We also know that over the last two and a half decades, the overall growth performance of high-income economies has been sluggish versus the average for low- and middle-income economies (Figure 6.2). Medium-term growth prospects for US and European economies range from moderate to bleak.[7] A gradual but long-term decline has been observed in both productivity growth and investment rates in high-income economies since the 1990s, a trend accelerated after the global financial crisis in 2008.[8]

Figure 6.2: Developing and developed countries' GDP growth (1980–2027*)

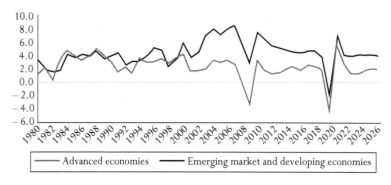

* Forecasts from 2023. *Source*: IMF (2023).

It is worth noting that the faster growth in the low- and middle-income economies over the period prior to the Covid-19 pandemic was not due just to the 'China effect', but also a notable improvement in the economic performance of many other developing economies in Asia and Africa (though, pointedly, not so much in the western hemisphere—another region that is still heavily dependent on commodity exports).[9] However, whether that performance can be sustained post-pandemic is currently a matter of conjecture.[10]

The geographic shifts in economic growth are accompanied by marked changes in consumption spending. Over the last decade or so, China in particular has been making efforts to incentivise greater consumption spending so as to reduce its reliance on investment as the main driver of its economic growth. Consumption spending by China's middle class alone was on track to pass that of the EU by 2027; India's consumption growth is on a similar trajectory.[11]

On the African continent, too, much of the economic growth seen over the last two decades has been consumption-driven.[12] While Africa's total consumer spending is comparatively small, accounting for 5.5% of global spending in 2019, the rate of change is rapid, and it is expected that spending in Africa will increase by USD 1.8 trillion in the next decade, measured in purchasing power parities. That is nearly double South America's projected growth (USD 1 trillion) and not so far short of growth in Europe's total consumer spending (USD 2.6 trillion).[13]

This raises the question of whether it is better strategically for African firms and farmers to target markets in larger, higher-income countries as destinations for their exports, or the faster-growing but often smaller markets of other developing countries. The traditional high-income export markets certainly have an impressive concentration of global buying power, but are also markets which are growing more slowly, and are highly competitive and heavily saturated, with many other potential sources of supply. This implies that if African exporters are to establish a stronger foothold in these traditional markets, it usually has to be at the expense of an existing supplier. It means, in effect, that African firms become locked in direct competition with other developing country suppliers if they are to win a larger market share. Given the pressures of the global marketplace, that is quite a tall order, particularly when those competitors are large Asian economies with considerable advantages of economies of scale and scope.

An alternative strategy would be to focus on the much smaller but more dynamic markets closer to home—specifically, other African countries. Export growth generally occurs most successfully at the margin; in other words, when exporting to a rapidly expanding market. We will elucidate on this point in the following sections which also explain why, despite receiving 'preferential' market access, exporting to the high-income countries has not broadly achieved the high hopes expected from it.

The disappointing performance of exports to high-income economies under preferential market access schemes

The irony of this relative decline in the role of traditional trading partners is that Africa has had preferential market access since the early 1970s. The first preferential access scheme, known as the Generalised System of Preferences (GSP), came into effect in the EC and Japan in 1971, Canada in 1974 and the United States in 1976. There are important contrasts between the functioning of these different schemes: the US's GSP excluded certain developing countries and certain so-called 'sensitive products', whereas the EC scheme was more comprehensive in its coverage but put stricter limits on the amount of an individual product that could be imported under preferential conditions. One characteristic that all these schemes had, however, was that they applied strict 'rules of origin' which required that exports be substantially produced within the beneficiary country to qualify.[14]

From the perspective of African countries, preferential market access has generally been thought to be valuable on two basic counts.[15] Firstly, because of its direct link to productive activities, it is often argued that 'trade is better than aid', a slogan whose origins can be traced back to the first meeting of UNCTAD, held in Geneva in 1964. A second reason for the popularity of market preferences from an African perspective is that they embody the idea of 'special and differential treatment' for developing countries. Many developing countries view preferential schemes as superior policy instruments because they do not require reciprocity (such as a reduction in tariffs or trade barriers) by the recipient country. This is due to the belief that their productive capacities may not be strong enough to compete on a 'level playing field' with producers in industrialised countries.[16]

Yet despite their popularity, there is a fundamental problem with preferential market access—and that is that events have overtaken matters. The prime motivating factor behind the original schemes was to provide an impetus to economic diversification. Preferential market access made sense in a world in which industrial tariffs were high, and so the margin of the preference was large. That was indeed the case in the 1960s and 1970s, when tariff protection to high-income markets was still extraordinarily high, particularly in specific sectors like textiles, steel, shipping, etc.

However, since the early 1970s, weighted applied tariffs have come down sharply (Figure 6.3), and industrial tariffs have come down even more dramatically. In a world where the average tariff on industrial goods is in the region of 3–4%, the cost advantage provided by preferential access to exporters in developing countries is now often negligible.[17] One study confirmed this by evaluating the trade impact of replacing the GSP scheme with standard most favoured nation (MFN) tariff rates. The trade effects were quite small, with

Figure 6.3: Average weighted applied tariffs (1948–2016)

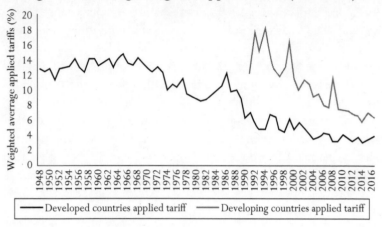

Source: World Bank (2020a).

only South Asia suffering an appreciable loss of exports (-1.58%), while for sub-Saharan Africa it was under 1% (-0.75%). The effects were also concentrated in a small number of sectors, particularly textiles and processed agriculture.[18]

In fact, the only areas where preferential market access is still of value are in sectors which continue to be highly protected (for instance, particular sub-sectors of the agriculture sector such as horticulture or seasonal exports like citrus fruits or flowers). But this adds to the irony of preferential market access, as now the only significant incentive provided by market access is for developing countries to continue specialising precisely in agriculture, compounding existing specialisation in primary production. One result of this is that fresh fruit, flower and vegetable exports to Europe have replaced traditional tea and coffee exports on parts of the African continent[19]—hardly what was originally intended with regards to goals of diversification.

Nonetheless, some economists praise the developmental potential of such exports.[20] Cramer et al. note, for instance, that much agro-industry is more labour-intensive than a great deal of the manufacturing industry located in export-processing zones or industrial parks. In Ethiopia, for example, despite being a relatively new 'industry', the total number of workers employed by agribusiness in floriculture was, by 2012, reportedly already considerably larger than total employment in the manufacture of textiles or in the basic metal and engineering industries. In Kenya, meanwhile, 125,000 workers were employed in the cut-flower sector in 2015, which was about three times the number of people employed in textiles, and 20 times larger than the number of people employed in the motor vehicles sub-sector.

However, there are still a number of objections that can be raised to such specialisation. Firstly, these sectors tend to be highly vulnerable to the misuse of phytosanitary standards—which have on frequent occasions in the past been used to limit exports from African countries.[21] Secondly, these new sectors are usually characterised by low wages and poor working conditions, with studies showing particularly noxious conditions in sectors like floriculture.[22] Thirdly, the traditional complaints made about cash crops diverting the best land away from food production towards serving foreign markets are often still valid, particularly in the more land-constrained parts of the continent (there is, however, some ambiguous evidence on this point).[23]

Finally, there is little hope of accelerating economic innovation through the development of these sectors, as they are sectors which typically will not provide many spill-overs or impetus to broader diversification except in a few peripheral sectors like packaging or for agricultural inputs. In sum, some new areas of specialisation provide opportunities for income-generating activities, but have limited long-run development potential, and expose African countries to the vagaries of exporting to fickle markets in high-income countries. To drive home the point, we briefly review the evidence of specific schemes of preferential market access towards the US, EU and—relatively speaking, much understudied—Chinese markets.

The case of AGOA

More than two decades after it was passed by the US Congress in 2000, the AGOA still lies at the heart of US–African engagement on trade. AGOA provides 39 countries with tariff-free access to the US market for products ranging from oil and agricultural goods to textiles and handicrafts. In 2015, AGOA was extended to 2025 (although there is considerable concern now about what comes after AGOA; see Chapter 12). In addition to the duty-free, quota-free access for about 5,000 product lines under the US Generalised System of Preferences, AGOA-eligible countries are granted preferential access to an additional 1,800 product lines.[24]

A pivotal provision of AGOA is the 'apparel' provision. While garments are excluded from the GSP, sub-Saharan countries qualify for AGOA preferences subject to a special apparel visa system and specific rules of origin.[25] However, duty-free access to the US market for apparel exports is not automatic when AGOA eligibility is granted, and countries need to be specifically declared eligible for the apparel provision. African apparel made from fabric made in another beneficiary African country is acceptable on the condition that it is derived from US yarn and not exceeding an applicable percentage.[26] AGOA also makes provision for a more relaxed rule of origin for less-developed countries: duty-free access was granted to their apparel irrespective of origin of fabric used to produce it, in line with a 'single transformation' requirement.[27]

Despite the stylised facts regarding a secular decline in the importance of the United States as an export destination, access to the US market—still the world's largest economy when measured at market exchange rates—clearly retains a lot of strategic importance for many African countries. However, it is also true that non-reciprocal market access offered under AGOA during these past two decades has not led to the kind of results that were expected. While a good thing in principle, for a variety of reasons it has rendered disappointing outcomes and has not led to a notably stronger export performance nor more diversified economies in African beneficiary countries.[28] The design of the preferential agreement is partly to blame, with strict rules of origin and unnecessarily tough phytosanitary and product standards. But so too has been the lacklustre response of African firms to the new opportunities opened up. As noted by one exhaustive review of the evidence: 'AGOA has had a positive impact on apparel exports from a small number of Sub-Saharan African LDCs [least developed countries]. Outside of the apparel sector there is little or no evidence of AGOA induced gains in any other sectors for LDCs'.[29]

Other studies have concurred with this negative evaluation. Early studies by Mueller,[30] Seyoum[31] and Nilsson[32] found that AGOA had had no significant impact on overall exports from sub-Saharan Africa. More pointedly, AGOA has not helped Africa to diversify its export basket, with energy commodities still constituting the bulk of AGOA-eligible countries' exports to the United States.[33] Between 2013 and 2015, there was a significant decline—more than 25%—in AGOA exports to the United States, mainly because of the massive decline in commodity prices.[34] A dissenting view is presented by Cook and Jones, who suggest that AGOA has contributed to export diversification, specifically through its apparel provision.[35] Countries that are eligible for the AGOA apparel provision not only export more apparel products, but also export more non-apparel products to the United States. To be frank, however, there is no need to go to excessive lengths to review the technical studies on this topic—a simple inspection of the data tells the story well (Figure 6.4).

We already commented on how the share of African exports to the US market had collapsed from 17% to just 6% between 2000 and 2019. That in itself is damning enough; in such a context, it would be hard to argue that AGOA has had a strong, positive impact on trading relations between Africa and the United States. Figure 6.4 reveals the extent to which African exports to the US market under AGOA boomed in the early 2000s, but subsequently fell sharply in the aftermath of the global financial crisis of 2008–09. The strong apparent correlation between global oil prices and the subsequent downward trend in African exports to the US market is particularly revealing—and reflects the fact that 80% of exports under AGOA have been oil. It is no coincidence that the top LDC exporter to the US is Angola (accounting for around 47% of total imports under AGOA).

Why such a poor overall performance? One Achilles heel of AGOA (and other similar agreements) is its impermanence: it is concessional, and can therefore be suspended or simply not renewed.[36] In this sense, the United States itself is vulnerable to the accusation that it has used AGOA more as a tool of economic diplomacy than of development. The recent suspension of Rwanda from certain provisions of AGOA because of a disagreement over its policy to reduce the imports of second-hand clothing is illustrative.[37] But it is not the only

Figure 6.4: US imports from Africa under AGOA (2000–19)

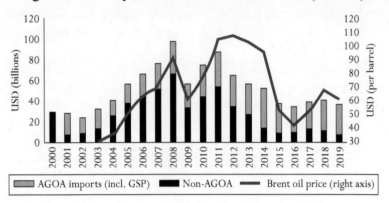

Sources: Calculated from UNCTADStat (2023); AGOA.info.

case. Madagascar, for instance, was suspended from AGOA in 2010; Ethiopia, Guinea and Mali in 2022; and Kenya has been threatened in the past with suspension due to alleged rules-of-origin violations in its textile sector.

Regardless of the circumstances around suspensions of preferential market access,[38] these examples do highlight its temporary nature. For the business community, this makes it particularly difficult to take a long-term view and invest in a beneficiary sector when it is uncertain whether the preferential market access will still exist in a year or two's time. Under the recent Trump administration,[39] the whole survival of AGOA was put in question. There is even talk of replacing it in 2025 with reciprocal bilateral free trade agreements—something which does not bode well with regard to the impetus for more cohesive and deeper integration under the AfCFTA.

Trade relations with the EU

Evaluations on the effectiveness of the EU's preferential market access schemes tend to depend on which literature you choose to read. If, for instance, you start with Davies and Nilsson[40] or Gasiorek and López González,[41] you will find a generally positive appreciation of the EU's EBA and GSP. Davies and Nilsson, for example, compare the EBA very favourably to the AGOA scheme, and their econometric results suggest that the EU trade policy vis-à-vis LDCs leads to 1.8 times more imports than US trade policy vis-à-vis LDCs when holding other factors constant.[42]

The EU's non-reciprocal trade preferences purportedly aim at (i) increasing export volumes for developing countries, thereby boosting their export earnings, and (ii) facilitating export diversification.[43] Evidence from some research[44] points to a degree of progress in achieving the first goal. The European Commission itself finds robust positive effects of the EU's GSP preferences and EBA programme on developing countries' exports, with LDCs benefiting the most.[45]

Nevertheless, problems remain with this narrative. For the African continent, it is clear that in value terms, exports to the EU have expanded considerably since 2000, more than doubling from around USD 58 billion to USD 157 billion in 2021. However, that is not the whole story. Firstly, as Davies and Nilsson themselves concede, the top LDC exporters to the EU are Bangladesh (31.6% of total imports from LDCs), followed by Angola and Equatorial Guinea.[46] For these countries, the main exported goods are either mineral fuels (Angola and Equatorial Guinea) or clothing (Bangladesh). This in itself should ring alarm bells about the limited economic impact for most beneficiary countries and does not differ very much from the AGOA experience in this respect.

Secondly, other econometric studies provide much more sobering results. Using a structural gravity model,[47] Cipollina et al. find a 'minor impact of EU preferential trade policies trade flows'.[48] Similar results were also found by Gradeva and Martínez-Zarzoso.[49] Empirical findings take on a particularly negative tone when African countries (rather than the broader group of African, Caribbean and Pacific [ACP] countries) are singled out in the analysis.[50]

Thirdly, contrary to their stated goals, the EU's unilateral trade preferences also appear to have an adverse impact on export diversification. Research suggests that ACP preferences granted during 1989–2007 (Lomé IV-Cotonou) may have actually resulted in increased specialisation.[51] The proportion of manufactured goods exported by the beneficiaries was extremely small and showed little or no improvement. Most exports were concentrated in fuels and to

a lesser extent ores and metals, reinforcing the view that trade preferences had failed to promote manufactured exports and export diversification, especially for LDCs in Africa.[52]

Rather than stress, as Manchin does,[53] that it has been the fault of
African countries themselves that they have 'not taken advantage' of
the enhanced market access provided to them, a more compelling
reason for the lack of results is that the tariff structure of the EU no
longer favours branching out into new sectors in manufacturing. We
already mentioned the broad impact of 'preference erosion'.
Table 6.1 shows the average weighted tariff rates specifically on
manufacturing goods, which have clearly come down significantly
since the early 1990s and now stand at just 4.1% for exporters in
developing economies and 2.3% for those in developed economies.
This, in itself, means that preferential market access barely makes any
difference now, and unit cost differences are likely to play a far more
fundamental role in export success to the EU market.

Table 6.1: EU tariffs on manufactured goods (5-year averages, weighted)
(1990–2019)

Region	1990–94	1995–99	2000–04	2005–09	2010–14	2015–19
Developing regions	9.0	6.1	4.7	4.2	4.1	4.1
Developed regions	6.3	4.3	2.6	2.4	2.3	2.3

Source: UNCTADStat (2023).

Even the LDCs outside of the African continent which have managed to successfully expand their exports to Europe over the last two
decades (e.g. Bangladesh and Cambodia) have generally done so
through one niche sector, such as textiles and clothing exports. It has
not been a broad-based phenomenon. In fact, the most successful
developing country to improve its access to the European market
over this time period was China, which managed to expand its exports
to the EU in a spectacular fashion after joining the WTO in 2000.[54]
Whether Africa is in a position to be able to compete with the low

unit costs of Chinese manufacturing, particularly in the saturated markets of the US and Europe, is another bone of contention—and there are a number of studies which give rise to some pessimism on this point.[55]

Rising competition is not the only explanation for the failure of European preferential access to achieve its goals on the African continent. Tariff escalation—the practice of imposing higher tariffs on finished or semi-processed goods, as against raw materials—has been a long-standing complaint on the part of developing countries, and is seen as undermining efforts towards economic diversification. Although the literature generally concedes that this is less of a problem than it was several decades ago, there remains a pronounced tendency to impose higher tariffs on processed goods. EU tariffs are still five times higher on semi-processed goods and six times higher on processed goods.[56]

Another major challenge are rules of origin: the 'passport' enabling goods to take advantage of preferential market access duty-free, as long as they qualify as 'originating' from the beneficiary country. Rules of origin are necessary to avoid third-party countries from taking advantage of reduced preferential tariffs by disguising their origin. An example would be legitimate concerns raised by Nigeria about the trans-shipment of Chinese or Indian goods through Niger to take advantage of ECOWAS tariff liberalisation. Yet research suggests that the excessively strict rules of origin of EU schemes appear to have a negative effect on both utilisation rates and total aggregated trade flows. The costs of compliance often act as a trade barrier and can even outweigh the benefits of the tariff reduction.[57]

Also problematic according to the research has been the application of sanitary and phytosanitary standards, which represent another 'hurdle to pass' before the product can gain access to the EU market.[58] Anecdotal examples of problems confronted by African exporters underpin such findings. In the 1990s, for instance, Uganda built up considerable exports of Nile perch caught in Lake Victoria to the EU market. However, the exporting firms became victims of their own success when the EU banned the imports under phytosanitary grounds, ostensibly related to the fact that some cases of cholera had been reported in the region surrounding Lake Victoria. The case was made that this presented a health risk, on spurious scientific grounds that the fish could pick up cholera from the water and pass it on to consumers. In reality, the cause of the action was reportedly related to complaints from Spain about the rise of fish imports into the EU from Uganda (Spain has the largest fishing fleet in the EU).[59] Similar difficulties have been encountered with South African citrus fruit and Kenyan green beans.[60]

Phytosanitary standards and technical barriers to trade have thus become one of the new preferred ways to protect domestic markets. Complying with such standards can be extremely costly. For instance, the quality certification costs to meet International Organization for Standardization standards are fairly onerous. The industry certification rate is USD 850/day, and the time required for certification ranges from two days for an enterprise with 6–10 personnel up to 10 days for 276–425 personnel. Certifying environmental management standards likewise ranges from 3.5 days to 15 days, respectively.[61] In some cases, such measures would appear to be applied without proportionality. One example is the application by the EU of bovine spongiform encephalopathy (commonly referred to as BSE) regulations to African countries in which the disease has never been diagnosed.[62] In principle, the WTO is there precisely to rectify such conflicts but, as we will see in the following chapter, developing countries have generally struggled to get redress through these mechanisms.

There is a final irony to all this—precisely because of the extremely low use of fertilisers and pesticides, which currently stands at about 1% of the level that is commonplace in the EU or the US, African crops are usually nutritious and low in toxins.[63] Yet, there is independent evidence to suggest that most European-produced fruit and vegetables would fail their own phytosanitary controls if domestic production was subjected to the same high standards of control as imports from the African continent and elsewhere. According to a nine-year analysis of nearly 100,000 popular homegrown fruit samples in Europe by the Pesticide Action Network of Europe, for instance, 87% of pears in Belgium and 85% of those in Portugal were contaminated by at least one toxic pesticide. Close to a third of all fruits sampled were tainted by hazardous substances in 2019.[64] With a less protectionist approach to its own agriculture, Europe and other high-income countries could indeed source a lot of their food from the land-abundant countries on the African continent, serving much the same role that Argentina or New Zealand did in the early twentieth century. A few African countries have managed to penetrate the European agricultural and horticultural markets—Kenya in cut flowers, Botswana in beef, for instance. But without the certainties of being able to sell their produce unhindered by excessive regulation, it would be naïve to think that this kind of strategy can be generalised.

Finally, there is potentially a new threat on the horizon for African exporters to the European market—and that comes in the form of a proposed set of environmental controls. As part of a plan to decarbonise its economy by 2050, the EU is considering the introduction of a carbon border adjustment mechanism. However, a recent UNCTAD study confirmed that while the scheme might help reduce CO_2 emissions, the reduction represents only a tiny percentage of global CO_2 emissions.[65] Moreover, if the controls are implemented, European trade will favour countries where industrial production is already relatively carbon-efficient, which tends to be developed countries. The carbon border adjustment mechanism thus represents another potential tool in the armoury of policy instruments that restrict trade in their favour.[66]

Engagement with China

Although the literature has focused on the economic impact of AGOA and the EBA, China also has a preferential market access scheme. China first granted preferential market access for 190 products from designated African LDCs in 2005 and more than doubled the product coverage three years later, offering an average preference margin of 10.4%. In principle, nations exporting primary products and simple manufactures such as sesame seeds, cocoa, beans, leather and cobalt stand to gain from the Chinese trade preference scheme.[67]

Nevertheless, the scheme suffers the same kind of limitations that we described above for the cases of the preferential market access schemes of the United States and the EU, namely;

i) The benefits of freer access to the Chinese market are offset by competition from other LDCs enjoying the same preferences;

ii) Non-tariff measures imposed by China to safeguard health, environment and national security often undermine any preference margins.[68]

Notwithstanding the Chinese claim that the preferences were 'tailored to Africa's existing export capacity', the economic impacts of the scheme have been modest and more symbolic in nature: using a simple 'implicit transfer' calculation, according to one study, the economic value of the scheme was estimated to be just USD 10 million per year, spread across 30 beneficiary countries.[69]

This sentiment is echoed in a study by Co and Dimova,[70] who found that while the Chinese preferential programme led to a degree of export diversification for some beneficiaries, it did not enhance export competitiveness of African exports on the Chinese market. These findings are not surprising considering that the additional duty-free products only represent 1.2% of African exports to China, and the bulk of African exports (90%; in particular oil and minerals) already entered China duty-free before the scheme was implemented.[71]

Yet, there is no denying the dramatic increase in bilateral trade between Africa and China over the last two decades. Unsurprisingly, this has sparked the interest of many scholars, keen to understand its impact on the continent's growth. Busse et al.[72] report that African economies exporting natural resources have generally benefited from positive terms of trade effects from the growth in Sino-African trade, but other economies have experienced losses, due to the closure of domestic firms as a result of low-priced competition from Chinese imports. Baliamoune-Lutz[73] studies the growth effects of Sino-African trade by analysing separately imports and exports, finding some modest support for the hypothesis that African trade with China is growth-enhancing.

There is some evidence therefore that China's trade has on balance exerted a positive influence on the continent. It is certainly a differential impact, however, with some countries benefiting more directly (through higher prices for their commodities) while others have found themselves flooded by imports which have either knocked out domestic producers or undermined opportunities in third party markets elsewhere in the world. The regional textile industry is a good example of a victim of this kind of import competition. Economic liberalisation policies in the 1980s and 1990s had already led to factory closures and large-scale job losses. In Ghana, for instance, employment in the sector declined by 80% from 1975 to 2000; in Zambia, it fell from 25,000 to below 10,000 in 2002; and Nigeria's 200,000-strong workforce has all but disappeared.[74] But the dominant position of China in global apparel and garment manufacture after the elimination of the Multi-Fibre Agreement in 2005 meant that there was no reprieve for the sector, and as collateral damage, even African exports of garments to the United States market suffered.[75]

This import competition needs to be offset against the growth-enhancing impact of China on the cost of capital goods—that is, machinery and hardware that makes the production of goods possible—with one study estimating that Chinese prowess in the production of capital goods has made them more affordable, reducing their price by around one third.[76]

Partial confirmation of this hypothesis of a broadly positive impact comes from Mullings and Mahabir.[77] Using panel data for the period 1990–2009, they look at the causal factors driving the recent turn-around in Africa's growth, disaggregating the separate growth impacts of Africa's bilateral trade with China, Europe and America. Among the three major bilateral partners, only Africa's bilateral trade with China has been a relatively important factor spurring growth on the continent and especially so in resource-rich, oil-producing, and non-landlocked countries. However, the debatable point is the extent to which greater engagement with China over the last two decades has failed to catalyse economic diversification on the continent, and hence has not helped make growth and development any more sustainable than in the past. Indeed, on some levels, it has actually undermined productive capacities on the continent, through surging imports of consumer goods which have knocked domestic and regional producers out of the market. This pernicious side to China's engagement on the continent should not be overlooked.

Conclusions

The objective of this chapter has been to show how trading relations with both its traditional trading partners in Europe and America and with China have proved problematic for the African continent. Despite initial good intentions, preferential market access has not delivered on its promise. It has become, in the words of one recent World Bank study, 'a double-edged sword; although they may encourage exports when the schemes are more liberal, they may also restrict domestic value addition and [limit] the links to domestic industries by encouraging imports of low-cost intermediate inputs'.[78] Some econometric analysis has purported to show that such schemes have had beneficial impacts. But looked at it in its entirety, the evidence simply does not support the contention that preferential market access has achieved its objectives. Even for countries that have had some measure of success in cultivating export niches, these schemes have oftentimes created new vulnerabilities.

Collier summed up the evidence accurately but with characteristic bluntness:

> These schemes don't work. This is not because they are a bad idea but because the devil is in the details and the details are wrong, probably deliberately—such schemes were designed not to be effective but to appease lobbies. AGOA got adopted because sixty thousand African Americans sent letters to their congressional representatives supporting it.[79]

Against this backdrop, the belief that simply by doubling down, or with more effort on the African side, these schemes will produce better results next time seems at best like wishful thinking. One book by a group of well-known economists (Newman et al.)[80] acknowledges that most of the existing preferential schemes are neither well designed nor effective and argues that the multiplicity of schemes is at the heart of the problem, leading to a needless source of complexity.

However, their solution is less than convincing. They call, rather unrealistically, for the EU and the United States to harmonise and liberalise their individual preference schemes for Africa, the Economic Partnership Agreement (EPA) and the AGOA, respectively.[81] To be fair, this had in fact been the original intention in the 1960s—to have a single GSP for all developing countries. That GSP does still exist, in fact, but it is overlain by a series of other 'enhanced' preferential agreements. The political economy of such measures, and the very strong leverage over developing countries in Africa (and elsewhere) that such schemes can confer to the preference-granting countries, means there is no incentive for the high-income countries to do so. In addition, while Chinese engagement on the continent has broadly had a positive growth impact, its own preferential market access scheme seems to be even more ineffective in providing a boost to Africa's diversified exports than the EU and US schemes. Like Newman et al., Collier puts forward a similarly unrealistic proposal—a period of protection for African countries from Asian imports. He identified one of the right problems confronting the continent's economies, but the political reality is that this is not going to happen.[82]

If bilateral arrangements have failed to deliver, what of the multilateral approaches to trading relations? Has Africa fared better in multilateral fora where, in principle, policies are made on a more democratic, transparent basis? That is the subject of the discussion in the following chapter.

7

AFRICA'S TRIALS AND TRIBULATIONS WITH GLOBAL TRADE GOVERNANCE

Introduction

In the mid-1990s, the WTO emerged as a key organ of the governance and management of the globalising world economy. In principle, it is the most democratic of global institutions—the only one beyond the General Assembly of the UN where the principle of 'one country, one vote' is followed. And, for the first time in its history, it currently has an African Director-General, Dr Ngozi Okonjo-Iweala of Nigeria. Yet, as observed by the trade economist Ademola Oyejide (a fellow Nigerian), over two decades ago, 'the WTO remains the international institution in which the African voice is, perhaps, least heard'.[1] This chapter will discuss the limitations and frustrations for African countries in terms of reaping benefits from WTO agreements.

The chapter will also look briefly at the more informal, but according to some voices more insidious, form of governance of trade through GVCs. Starting with the seminal contributions by Gereffi,[2] this area of work has spawned an enormous amount of literature in recent years, but in essence comes down to the power of lead firms at the head of GVCs to determine production networks and the distribution of 'rents'. Again, with some noticeable exceptions, the

conclusion is that this form of informal governance of the global trading system has not led to outcomes favourable to Africa's development aspirations either. In the words of Gibbon and Ponte,[3] the
continent has become trapped in a situation where it is more often
than not 'trading down', rather than 'trading up'.

The birth of the global trading system

To understand the marginalisation of Africa in global systems of trade
governance, it is important to take a step back. At the founding of the
General Agreement on Tariffs and Trade—the WTO's predecessor—in 1948, only one African country (South Africa) was among
the 23 original contracting parties (now called 'members'). The
GATT was established in 1948 in order to boost post-war economic
recovery and create a more liberal global trade regime than the one
that had prevailed during the inter-war period, when the combined
effect of a severe financial crash and protectionist trade policies had
compounded the global economic recession.[4] In the initial years of the
GATT's existence, for the bulk of its membership (comprised largely
of high-income industrial economies) the goal of the GATT was to
liberalise trade in industrial products while ensuring that liberalisation
did not adversely impact their commitment to other post-war political goals such as maintaining low levels of unemployment.

However, by the 1960s and 1970s, many developing countries—
some recently freed from colonial rule—also became members of the
GATT in their own right.[5] By 1994, there were 128 GATT signatories, of which 35 were African. This gradually caused a profound shift
in the interests represented at the GATT. These countries sought to
use the WTO to gain preferential market access consistent with their
development needs. However, the shift in the composition of the
GATT also led to a situation where developing countries' demands
started to conflict with the trading interests of the industrialised
nations that had initially formed the GATT.[6]

The initial objective of the GATT was a general desire to not
return to the pre-war situation of high tariff barriers and protectionism, but to embrace a more liberalised and rules-based global economic order. Nominally, parties to the agreement consented to

enforce three principles in promoting and regulating trade and set-tling trade disputes:

- **Predictability, transparency and reduction of trade bar-riers:** Tariffs were to be progressively lowered through rounds of negotiations, and non-tariff barriers were to be gradually replaced with tariffs (tariffication). Quantitative restrictions and unfair trade practices, such as voluntary export restraints, dumping and subsidies, were to be prohibited or at least limited/sanctioned. And a requirement was made on member states to notify and make public all trade-related measures.
- **Non-discrimination:** All signatories of the GATT agreed to give MFN status to products from other members. That is to say, any favourable trade conditions granted to one party had to be generalised to all GATT signatories so that everyone would receive exactly the same treatment.
- **Reciprocity:** Multilateral talks negotiated mutually applied tariff reductions.

These principles informed eight rounds of negotiations under the GATT.[7] Although the direction of causality between economic and trade growth is disputed (as is the relationship between tariff reductions and trade growth), the establishment of the GATT certainly coincided with a spectacular rise in global trade. From 1950 to 1995, the volume of trade in real terms grew by a factor of 15, much faster than the growth of global GDP (which only expanded by a factor of 6).[8]

Yet tariff reductions under the GATT had largely been confined to industrial products,[9] and, bowing to pressure from some of its most powerful members, the agreement contained numerous qualifica-tions, exemptions and 'escape hatches', including: 'voluntary' export restraints against successful foreign exporters (e.g. US constraints on Japanese car exports); quotas on textile and clothing imports (through the Multi-Fibre Agreement);[10] agricultural subsidies; and anti-dump-ing duties.[11]

This framework sowed the seeds of future confrontation: while many developed nations resisted agricultural trade liberalisation, developing nations opposed tariff cuts on manufactures.[12] The latter group of countries were assisted in this goal by the establishment, under Part IV of the GATT, of 'Special and Differential Treatment', which allowed (at the complete discretion of a developed country member) for a waiver in the reciprocity requirement. This meant that when developed countries extended preferential market access to developing countries, developing countries were not expected to make any corresponding tariff reductions in return for the concessions. Not all that glitters is gold, however: in practice, most of the concessions were often made on products that were of little interest to developing countries, and usually were granted subject to restrictive conditionalities.[13] As a consequence, as explained in Chapter 6, they have largely fallen short of their developmental promise.

Crucially from an African perspective, very little was done to liberalise trade in agricultural products, and by 1997, agricultural exports had shrunk from its pre-First World War predominance to stabilise at around just 10% of world trade.[14] More worrying still, as tariffs fell to low and even insignificant levels by the end of the 1980s, the most powerful member states resorted more frequently to GATT loopholes that permitted voluntary export restraints, quantitative restrictions, and 'negotiated offsets' to protect domestic producers.[15] By the beginning of the 1990s, it became apparent that the global trading system was in need of a thorough overhaul.

The GATT's successor, the WTO, embodied a different ethos. It was, in the words of Alice Amsden, a much more 'hawkish' organisation.[16] While the underlying objective of trade governance was to achieve economic welfare for all members, according to Schwartz,[17] the birth of the WTO also reflected:

> US desires to open up markets which the post-war consensus had left closed in the name of employment and macroeconomic stability, and to secure profitability for firms producing intangible goods protected by patents, copyright, and brands. Declining US competitiveness in consumer goods manufacturing through the 1980s created political pressures in the United States to open up markets elsewhere for highly competitive US agricultural and services exports.[18]

With the support of other high-income economies (particularly the EU), negotiations thereafter shifted to a new set of issues related to transparency in government procurement, trade facilitation, competition and investment ('the Singapore issues'); and also matters related to Intellectual Property ('TRIPS')—issues in which high-income countries clearly had vested interests to promote and protect.[19] Nevertheless, the new WTO immediately ran into problems. The first WTO round collapsed in the face of the 1999 riots in Seattle. Resurrected as the Doha Round in 2001, these talks collapsed during the 2008 global financial crisis. In the face of the insistence of high-income countries on pursuing the controversial 'Singapore issues', the African position at the time became increasingly insistent on the need to first significantly reduce agricultural subsidies in high-income countries and improve market access in agricultural products. It is not, perhaps, coincidental that during the Doha Round of WTO negotiations in Cancun in September 2003, such was the rift in positions on the Singapore issues that it was Kenya that was the first country to abandon the negotiations.[20]

The organisation was thus unable to make progress on its core mandate on determining the rules that govern international trade. Indeed, in the three decades since the Uruguay Round, the WTO's only major success in multilateral trade negotiations has been the conclusion of the Trade Facilitation Agreement, which came into force in 2017.[21] Moreover, as the United States has gradually lost ground in its global competitiveness in merchandise trade, its attitudes have become increasingly ambivalent to the organisation, as was apparent during the administration of Donald Trump from 2017 to 2021.[22]

For developing countries, especially those in Africa, it is hardly surprising then that faith in the WTO gradually waned. As one observer put it:

> The markets of the bottom billion are so tiny that even if their governments were prepared to reduce trade barriers, this would not confer any bargaining power on them. If the U.S. government decides that the political gains from protecting cotton growers outweigh the political cost of making American taxpayers finance a hugely expensive farm bill, the offer of better access to the market in Chad is not going to make much difference. So far, the WTO has functioned badly. The present round of trade negotiations was termed a "development round," but such labels really have no possibility of content in an organization designed for bargaining .... Trade negotiators are there to get the best deal for their own country, defined in terms of the least opening of the home market for the maximum opening of others. The countries of the bottom billion joined the WTO hoping

125

to receive transfers in some shape or form, just as they do in the other international organizations such as the World Bank, the IMF, and the United Nations. But the WTO is simply not set up to do this. As long as it is merely a marketplace for bargaining, the bottom billion have no place in it. Their only possibility of power is to threaten the legitimacy of the whole organization.[23]

African perspectives on multilateral processes

For African countries, the experience of engaging with the WTO has often proven frustrating. Agriculture had been a stumbling block in the final GATT round in Uruguay, when African and other developing countries tried to flex their muscles with regard to the opening of the sector, in exchange for further liberalisation in areas of industrial goods and services. Some concessions were made, but they were more cosmetic than of substance. For more than 50 years, global trade negotiations reduced tariffs on the manufacturing and industrial sectors in which developed economies led the world, while sectors such as agriculture, textiles and clothing—where low-cost developing countries have the comparative advantage—were heavily protected and subsidised by rich industrialised countries.[24] For example, despite reforms in the way the subsidies are provided (so as to limit the extent to which they could be accused of adopting unfair trade-distorting measures),[25] the United States and the EU each give more than USD 235 billion dollars in agricultural subsidies annually,[26] undermining the comparative advantage that some developing countries enjoy in agricultural trade.

Agriculture remains a major component of Africa's economy, fluctuating at around 18% of GDP on average over several decades, and representing a much higher share in Africa's poorer economies. As such:

Africans [tend to] obsess about access to agricultural markets in the developed world, particularly Europe. For decades, no meeting on trade in Africa would start without reference to the extent to which agriculture in the EU benefits from large subsidies, as well as the regulatory hurdles in Europe that effectively bar most agricultural imports.[27]

However, one should not by any means think that agricultural protectionism is exclusively a European phenomenon: Japan, for instance, has some of the highest agricultural tariffs in the world, and the United States provides massive subsidies to its farmers, most of which go to large producers of corn (maize), soybeans, wheat, rice and cotton. If we take, for instance, the case of cotton, one important aggravating factor for African producers is the extent to which the United States has subsidised its own cotton farmers, thereby distorting the world cotton market, deflating international prices and enabling American farmers to maintain their position as the largest exporter of cotton. World cotton prices are reduced by an estimated 10% due to the effect of US subsidies.[28] The WTO has twice judged US subsidies to be illegal, but each time the US government has failed to act. The United States is not alone in such practices. In 2009–10, China overtook the United States as the largest dispenser of cotton subsidies; it is also the world's largest importer of cotton, accounting for 36% of all imports (followed by Bangladesh, Turkey, Indonesia and Vietnam), and holds half the world's stockpile.

Yet according to an analysis by the Centre for Trade and Sustainable Development (2013), Chinese trade regulations negatively affect African cotton farmers:

[China] imposes import duties from 5 percent up to 40 percent on cotton imported outside of the annual 894,000-ton import quota related to WTO obligations. If China were to allow entry of African cotton free of duty, such cotton would therefore gain some competitiveness versus other origins of cotton.

Against this backdrop, one could legitimately question the extent to which Africa has a 'comparative advantage' in agriculture at all. Yes, the continent has a huge agricultural potential and Africa has the largest tracts of uncultivated arable land in the world. But outside of Kenya, Morocco, South Africa, and a few other specific parts of the continent, very few countries have commercial agriculture on a major scale. Most African agriculture is characterised by small-holding, subsistence production—it is not commercialised and, pointedly, not competitive on global markets.

As Cilliers notes:

Access to agricultural markets outside Africa has served as an effective lightning rod to divert attention from other, more important matters relating to trade, namely, schemes that would incentivise value-added

exports, low-end manufacturing and the beneficiation of the continent's vast mineral exports.[29]

Adding to the disappointing outcomes, decision-making processes
themselves within the WTO came to be dominated by its richest
members: namely the United States, the European Union, Canada
and Japan (referred to as the 'Quad'), just as in the old GATT.[30]
Resolutions on important issues were often made without broad-
based consultation with the entire WTO membership and the domestic constituencies of member countries.

In such circumstances, African countries have frequently struggled
to have their voices heard. The various dimensions of participation in
the WTO process pose significant challenges for African and other
developing countries.[31] Many of the poorest countries are not even
represented in Geneva, where decisions are made. Even countries
that have representation in Geneva are stretched too thinly to attend
the thousands of formal and informal meetings, symposia, workshops
and seminars held under the auspices of WTO bodies to negotiate or
discuss new or existing trade rules or disputes about the application
and interpretation of the rules.[32] Most tellingly, until 2022, Tunisia
was the only African country ever to have filed a dispute as a com-
plainant. This concerned a case against Morocco on anti-dumping
measures on school exercise books. In July 2022, South Africa filed a
complaint against EU phytosanitary requirements on its fruit exports.
On the respondent side, only three African countries (Egypt,
Morocco and South Africa) have been sued, being subject to a total of
13 disputes. Most of these disputes concerned anti-dumping claims
and were resolved in the consultation phase. Unsurprisingly, the
three African countries that have been subject to disputes are among
the largest economies on the continent.[33]

Jawara and Kwa[34] and Tandon[35] highlight some of the tactics
deployed to inhibit developing countries from negotiating more
favourable rules or to prevent them from challenging unfair pre-
existing ones, such as those which prevail in the agricultural sector.
These tactics include 'divide and rule' strategies against coalitions
opposed to the interests of developed countries, by arm twisting
countries and pressuring delegations to the agenda of the Quad countries, and drafting texts which ignore the views of developing coun-

tries. Ministerial meetings are held over the space of a few days, with the result that 'the negotiations are conducted in a pressure-cooker atmosphere'. Powerful WTO members like the United States and the EU have also used their development assistance and preferential trading programmes as a 'carrot and stick' to prevail upon developing countries with objections to their agendas.

Although unrelated to WTO processes, one recent example of this kind of bilateral pressure was the suspension of Rwanda from certain provisions of AGOA because of the country's insistence on implementing a high tariff regime on the import of second-hand clothing.[36] The policy reflected concerns that second-hand clothing was decimating the regional manufacturing of clothing and textiles—a once vibrant sector had been reduced to a shadow of its former self, mostly because of the inability of the region to compete against the extremely low unit prices of imports from China and India, but also because of the surge of second-hand clothing since the 1990s.[37] In principle, the EAC had decided to implement the more restrictive policy as a bloc, but the US placed pressure on countries bilaterally to rescind the measure to restrict second-hand clothing. Kenya was relatively easy to convince about the error of its ways, as it was successfully exporting around USD 450 million a year to the US market, but Rwanda had much less at stake, as its total exports under AGOA textile provisions did not amount to more than USD 2 million. Rwanda rightly stood up to the bilateral pressure and implemented the high-tariff policy on second-hand clothing, but the flood of these goods continued unabated into the regional market. As a result, the US largely achieved its objectives through a policy of 'divide and rule'.

Some economists additionally argue that membership of the WTO seriously constrains developing countries from adopting industrial policy, considered by many as central to efforts to achieve economic diversification.[38] Synthesising a large number of country case studies, Ghanaian trade economist Professor Augustin Fosu bemoans:

> ... many of the developed countries were able to employ consistently the leverage of government in the economy, including the use of government subsidies and more freely available technological ideas. Under WTO, however, this political space has now been severely limited, via particularly the TRIMs and TRIPs agreements ....

Unfortunately, the measures may be severely constraining, especially
for low-income and least-developed countries....[39]

This view is not universally accepted, however. The late MIT professor Alice Amsden[40] wrote a paper suggesting that, on the margins,
there are still many policy levers that developing countries can still
use, a point also made by other development economists.[41] The problem, however, is that realpolitik gets in the way. It is not that African
countries are completely powerless to act, but their margins of
manoeuvre are far more constrained than in the case of high-income
countries or larger developing countries elsewhere in the world like
India, China or Brazil, which have the critical mass and diplomatic
skills to protect their own interests.

What the empirical studies say

In the final analysis, all of this discussion may be somewhat academic.
There is fairly compelling evidence that the multilateral trading system—the GATT and WTO—has not contributed as much to the
phenomenal expansion of global trade over the last 70 years as many
observers assume. Despite impressions to the contrary, that growth
has often been led within regions and not between them.[42] Again, this
contributes a further argument in favour of prioritising regional integration through the AfCFTA.

The point is driven home by trade simulations undertaken around
the time of the formation of the WTO. Computable general equilibrium (CGE) models were used to estimate the welfare gains from the
trade liberalisation achieved under the Uruguay Round. In principle,
these models were rolled out in order to make the case for further
tariff cuts. The Organisation for Economic Co-operation and
Development (OECD) predicted welfare gains to the order of USD
200 billion, approximately a third of which would accrue to developing countries. Yet according to subsequent estimates, 70% of the
gains from the Uruguay Round went to the developed countries;
more importantly, the remaining 30% were captured by a small number of large export-oriented developing countries. Indeed, within the
first six years of the Uruguay Round (1995–2001), it was estimated
that Africa (excluding North Africa) would be worse off by USD 1.2

billion.[43] In one study, Francois summarises three of the major CGE studies of the Uruguay Round, all of which predicted losses for Africa.[44] One principal reason for these losses is the deterioration in the terms of trade for African countries following liberalisation. A second reason is that the reduction in industrialised country subsidies embodied in the Uruguay Round would lead to higher prices for food imports to the region.[45]

Just to test the proposition that further global trade liberalisation might not benefit the African continent in the way the supporters of the multilateral system insisted, Fosu and Mold tried out an extreme scenario, using the Global Trade Analysis Project's (GTAP) method of removing all remaining tariffs on global trade.[46] Not only were the global gains relatively small (USD 94.25 billion, or 0.3% of global GDP), but Africa (excluding North Africa) would gain just USD 259 million, equivalent to an insignificant 0.08% of regional GDP. What's more, these results hinged on the inclusion of South Africa. Excluding South Africa, the welfare result is a loss for the region of USD 579 million.[47] As the redoubtable Harvard professor Jeffrey Sachs later put it:

> When huge gains are attributed to trade reforms (hundreds of billions of dollars per year), we need to look at the fine print: almost all of those gains accrue to the richest countries and the middle-income countries, not the poorest countries, and especially not the poorest countries in Africa. How, after all, could trade alone enable isolated rural villages in Africa to meet their basic needs?[48]

Global value chains: The new informal governance of trade

Building principally on the initial insights of Gereffi,[49] the expansive literature on 'global value chains' has its origins in an earlier body of work entitled 'global commodity chain' analysis.[50] But it has morphed into an all-encompassing framework for analysing global trade. A joint programme between the WTO and the OECD estimated that around 75% of global trade occurs within GVCs.[51] Arguably, as a framework it has more power in explaining cases of 'export success' and 'export failure' than analysis of the formal trading system through the GATT/WTO.

131

The key insights of GVCs from the perspective of Africa are two-fold. Firstly, GVCs have been becoming increasingly fragmented, as lead companies (usually based in high-income economies) have out-sourced production towards (selected) parts of the developing world. This raises the hope that, through joining such value chains, African countries could break into the elusive high-income markets (although the distinct possibility also exists that it could compound the margin-alisation of Africa from global trade flows, depending on the decisions of the 'lead firms').

Which takes us to the second major insight from Gereffi's frame-work, and that is each value chain has a form of 'governance', which can either be 'producer-driven' or 'buyer-driven'. Producer-driven chains are usually found in sectors with high technological and capi-tal requirements, such as automobiles, aircraft and electrical machinery, where capital and proprietary know-how are the main entry barriers to lead firm status. In such chains, producers tend to keep control of capital-intensive operations and subcontract more labour-intensive functions. Buyer-driven chains are found in more labour-intensive sectors, such as garments, shoes and horticultural produce, where market information, product design and market-ing/advertising costs set the entry barriers. In these chains, produc-tion functions are usually outsourced, and key actors concentrate on branding, design and marketing.[52]

Pointedly, both types of GVCs have usually involved a shift in power towards the multinational companies that sit at the top of the pyramid. For instance, in the food and horticultural sectors, GVCs are increasingly dominated by retail giants who pose very stringent demands on quality, traceability, timeliness and even 'social respon-sibility' that only a minority of dynamic farmers can meet.[53] So, as if the stringent rules for exporting under preferential schemes like the EBA and AGOA were not sufficient enough, private companies now impose another layer of compliance.

Some believe the dominance of GVCs is a positive development for the African continent. For countries with a limited existing manu-facturing or service export basis and a large pool of labour, they argue that GVCs can provide a golden opportunity: by specialising in a specific segment of a production chain, each participating country can generate a portion of the goods' or services' value added, even if that means that a lower share of the value added of exports is captured locally.[54]

The alternative view is that, given the power dynamics of GVCs, the position of the African continent in the global trading system has been further compromised. The participation rate in manufacturing GVCs in sub-Saharan Africa is greater than 40%, which indicates that a significant share of the region's trade occurs along value chains.[55] However, sub-Saharan Africa's participation in GVCs is more pronounced in forward integration compared with backward integration, a reflection of the fact that most of the region's integration into GVCs is dominated by exports of primary products, not by diversified products.

Lead firms govern global supply chains by establishing and imposing a range of requirements upon supplier firms—including product specifications, production conditions, delivery times and, most significantly, prices. Lead firms have concentrated increasingly upon their 'core competencies'—areas where they possess or can establish a competitive advantage and where they can establish powerful relations over supplier firms. These strategies enable lead firms to outsource risks, costs of production and supply.[56]

A consequence of lead firms' concentration on core competencies has been a 'cascade effect' across industrial sectors, generating intense pressure upon first- and then second-tier suppliers to merge, acquire and themselves follow multinational enterprises' strategies: large firms now stand at the centre of a vast network of outsourced businesses which are highly dependent on the core systems integrators for their survival. The systems integrators possess the technology and brand name which indirectly provides sales to the supplier firms. They are therefore able to ensure that they obtain the lion's share of the profits.[57]

Crucially, the figures confirm this has been the case. Since the 1980s there has been a widespread increase in firms' profits. In 134 countries, the average global markup increased by 46% between 1980 and 2016, with the largest increases accruing to the largest firms in Europe and North America and across a broad range of economic sectors.[58]

By contrast, evidence suggests that developing countries at the bottom of the value chain are being squeezed. In Ethiopia, for instance, firms that buy inputs abroad and sell their final products in the external market have lower markups than other types of firms. And the more intensely a firm is integrated into a GVC (measured as the share of the export value added and imported inputs in total sales), the lower its markup.[59] In South Africa, markups charged by manufacturing exporters are on average significantly lower than those charged by non-exporters.[60] The risk that firms from developing countries experience limited profits after becoming suppliers for global firms mirrors the rise in profits in developed countries.

There is also evidence that GVC participation can increase the precariousness of employment. A case study in Ghana and Côte d'Ivoire on participation in the pineapple and cocoa value chains found that, even when GVC participation benefits successful farmers (e.g. through improved growing processes, higher yields, and higher incomes), it is also associated with an increase in the hiring of casual labour, as well as displacement of farmers from land because of their low bargaining positions and lack of knowledge on their rights to land ownership. Research has similarly documented the growing use of casual and seasonal contract labour both on farms and in packhouses in South Africa (fruit exports) and Kenya (fresh vegetable exports).[61]

Against this backdrop, it is thus not surprising to find that a number of recent studies have found that only middle- and high-income countries benefit, on aggregate, from participating in GVCs, while the benefits are minimal for small countries or less-advanced economies.[62] This is explainable by the way the value chains are governed and the degree of control and power asymmetries along them.[63] Lead firms may exert their market power by specifying the rules of production: if local suppliers are characterised by weak capabilities and operate within weak national innovation systems, production modalities may be dictated by the leading actor of the global value chain.[64]

In view of all this, it is pertinent to ask whether the rise of GVCs has facilitated or made it even more difficult for African countries to integrate into the global trading system on terms which are beneficial for their long-term development. African countries still generally find themselves at the start of their integration process into GVCs. At 15% of exports, the share of foreign value added embedded in the production of exports is low and has barely increased since the mid-1990s.[65]

Achieving economic diversification appears to be as challenging as ever. An example are the attempts of West African countries to add value to their cocoa exports. Collectively, Africa accounts for 75% of the world's production of cocoa beans and 20% of total grinding.[66] But the multinational companies at the apex of the chocolate value chain retain a tight control over sourcing and intermediate processing, in order to pursue strategies of product differentiation and to meet quality and traceability requirements. The sector is also characterised by an oligopolistic market structure, whereby upstream producers—especially those that are geographically disperse and lack the support of strong farmer-based organisations—derive relatively small benefits from their participation in the value chain, while manufacturers and retailers capture the bulk of value added.[67] This situation is compounded by a worldwide chocolate consumption that is still dominated by mature developed country markets, notwithstanding the greater dynamism of emerging markets. As a result, companies prefer to locate processing plants near large destination markets, or at least in areas with good infrastructure and logistics, disadvantaging African countries whose trade costs are significantly higher than their competitors.[68]

Building regional value chains is of strategic significance for African countries. Low-income markets are not only less certification-intensive, but also less sensitive to product quality (price is the dominant competitive attribute in these markets). Opportunities for African producers arise partly as a consequence of the low preference for quality and certification in the final markets, and partly because demand characteristics are often similar in the exporting and importing economies, providing fewer requirements for market intelligence and product adaptation.[69] They are also the more rapidly growing markets—smaller, but more dynamic, where there are greater chances of export success compared with the saturated markets of high-income economies. As an illustration, returning to the example of cocoa, although intra-African exports of cocoa and related products are dwarfed by the exports to higher-income countries—on average USD 7.8 billion per year, compared with USD 170 million in the 2015–17 period—the latter's composition is centred primarily on higher-value added products, with chocolate accounting for nearly 60% of the total.

Conclusions

This chapter has documented how the multilateral trading system has broadly failed to deliver on its promises for the African continent. With the rules-based trading system at an impasse, it is not surprising that the trend in recent years has been towards regional agreements and the emergence of so-called 'plurilateral negotiating structures', which allow some countries to agree on specific issues beyond WTO rules, but which are insufficiently inclusive to be called multilateral agreements.[70] Mkandawire, as usual, put things correctly:

> We haven't benefited from this free trade world. In fact, there were all these calculations by the World Bank and everybody—the world will benefit by however many billions of dollars from the Uruguay Round—except for Africa. So, obviously, these free arrangements don't help us .... If they decide that they are going to allow some protectionism—in a framework where every region could have some industrial policy—then there is no problem. This is what happened after World War II and that was the era when most Third World countries grew fastest, in terms of industrialization. Only if Africa is required to open, while others are allowed to close—then we are in trouble.[71]

During the last round of negotiations under the GATT (the Uruguay Round), several analysts[72] suggested that African countries had failed to unite and act in a coordinated fashion, and that their general lack of success could be attributed, at least in part, to the failure to harmonise their negotiating agenda and strategies.[73] Achieving a greater degree of coordination so as to be able to better resist the 'divide and rule' strategies of more powerful trading partners documented in this chapter has been a long-standing aspiration of the African continent, and in principle is something that can best be achieved once a continental market is established under the AfCFTA.

The second part of this chapter has looked at Africa's flawed integration into GVCs. Although it is always possible to point to exceptional cases, the rising power of the apex companies in these value chains has not benefited the continent in terms of achieving its goals of economic diversification. One author claims that, such is the intensity in reducing costs and downward pressure on prices, the 'empirical evidence suggests that, contrary to optimistic claims, these GVCs generate new forms of worker poverty ... such chains should be renamed and re-theorised as Global Poverty Chains'.[74]   We thus conclude the case elaborated in Part I of this book that the status quo is no longer sustainable for the African continent. Part II of this book presents the positive case for priming continental integration, under the AfCFTA, rather than continue to plough the same strategic furrow as in the past. We beg the indulgence of the reader, as in places the arguments that follow are quite technical. But we believe that the case supporting the AfCFTA is broadly incontrovertible.

PART II

8

THE ECONOMIC SIGNIFICANCE
OF INTRA-AFRICAN TRADE

GETTING THE NARRATIVE RIGHT

Introduction[1]

If mainstream narratives are to be believed, the starting point for the AfCFTA is less than auspicious. Intra-African trade is widely perceived as extremely low, an argument made ad nauseum in both academic and policymaking circles.[2] Barely a presentation is made on the AfCFTA which does not start by lamenting how intra-regional trade in Africa is far below the averages of other continents.[3] This leads many observers to doubt the capacity of intra-African trade to turn around the economic fortunes of the continent. For instance, in an otherwise evidence-led and generally optimistic assessment of African economic development, one recent book claims:

> Despite decades of negotiations and agreements within subregions and Regional Economic Communities in Africa, intra-African trade remains a tiny proportion of the continent's overall trade .... Greater intra-African trade may be rhetorically appealing on grounds of economic nationalism or South–South solidarity, [but] as a blueprint for accelerated development it is a fantasy.[4]

Contrary to such views, this chapter argues that intra-African trade has greater economic significance than is commonly believed, even prior to the implementation of the AfCFTA.

To the layperson, it might seem strange to argue over such a proposition; surely, it could be contended, the statistics on the scale of intra-African trade are not debatable? However, this chapter argues that the measurement of the extent of intra-African trade is affected not only by statistical errors, but also by a series of cognitive biases and omissions of the kind spelled out by Rosling et al.[5] In addition, economists themselves are often surprisingly poor at gauging the relative importance of magnitudes and do not always perceive the full extent of the limitations of many statistics that they use on a daily basis.[6] Rectifying these misconceptions matters because it affects our judgement about the prospects for continental integration.

Some stylised facts of intra-African trade

Historically, African peoples have been consummate traders, with much of that commerce predating trading networks that developed elsewhere.[7] During colonial times, however, intra-continental trade was truncated as a result of several factors, including the balkanised nature of respective colonies, each colony's trading system being oriented towards bilateral trade with their colonising country,[8] and the fact that Arabic-speaking, francophone, lusophone and anglophone economies barely interacted with each other.[9]

At the beginning of decolonisation in the late 1950s, intra-continental trade stood at just 3% of total African trade (Figure 8.1). It then gained in intensity during the early years of independence before falling back during the 'lost decades' of the 1970s and 1980s. In the 1990s, intra-continental trade experienced a gradual recovery, but suffered a setback in the early 2000s because of the strong performance of commodity exports (the 'commodity super-cycle' discussed in Chapter 4), as oil and mineral exports to destinations outside the continent rose. Indeed, the broad trends in intra-African trade shown in Figure 8.1 need to be contextualised against broader shifts in the value of total exports, which clearly have been strongly correlated with commodity prices (Figure 8.2).[10]

As stressed in the introduction to this chapter, the African continent is frequently compared in a poor light vis-à-vis other continents in terms of the extent of intra-regional trade. At first sight, this seems a correct assessment (Figure 8.3).

Figure 8.1: Intra-African trade as a percentage of total trade (1957–2020)

Source: Calculated from IMF DOTS (2023).

Figure 8.2: Correlation between African export growth and shifts in commodity prices (1996–2020)

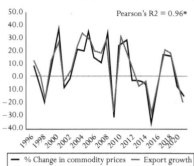

*Measures the degree of correlation: 1=perfect correlation, 0=no correlation. Based on current prices.

Source: Calculated from UNCTADStat (2023).

Figure 8.3: Intra-regional trade (imports and exports) as a percentage of total trade (2019)

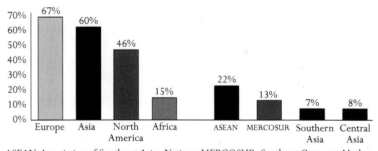

ASEAN, Association of Southeast Asian Nations; MERCOSUR, Southern Common Market.

Source: Calculated from UNCTADStat (2023).

However, such comparisons are misleading. To arrive at a fair assessment, we should look at the level of intra-regional trade from different optics. If, for instance, we focus on sub-regional groupings, other continents' intra-regional trade shares are suddenly not so impressive. Thus, compared with the Asian average, Central and

Southern Asia are relatively less prosperous regions with less industrialised and diversified economies, and hence register levels of intra-
regional trade that are around half those for the African continent.

In resource-rich MERCOSUR (Argentina, Brazil, Paraguay and
Uruguay), the level of intra-regional trade is actually lower than the
African continental average—the logical consequence when the two
largest economies in the bloc are highly dependent on their commodity exports to the rest of the world. Asia's largest regional bloc,
ASEAN, has a somewhat higher level of intra-regional trade than the
African continent, but includes countries with highly diverging levels
of income, economic diversification and economic integration into
the global economy. Less than 10% of Vietnam's trade, for example,
is currently with other ASEAN member states. Evidently, our perceptions about the intensity of intra-regional trade are very much tied
up with how a 'region' is defined. Asia's high level of intra-regional
trade, for instance, is fundamentally a function of the fact that the
continent accounts for nearly 60% of humanity and nearly half of
global GDP;[11] all other things being equal, the larger a 'region' and
the more economic activity it encompasses, the higher the level of
'intra-regional' trade.

Africa's intra-regional trade performance can be gauged by other
metrics too, bringing the continent out in a more favourable light.
For instance, Table 8.1 shows how the share of intra-regional trade
within distinct economic/political groupings has changed over
time.[12] This data again gives some reasons for optimism, with several
African regional economic communities being among the regional
groupings where intra-regional trade has increased the most over the
last two decades.[13] This is clearly not the face of stagnant or declining
intra-African trade. Ironically, given the way the EU is always cited
as an exemplary instance of high intra-regional trade intensity, its
share has barely changed since the mid-1990s. Indeed, even this
modest increase can be attributed to the rapid expansion in EU
membership since the late 1990s, when membership rose from 15
to a peak of 28 member states just prior to Brexit; if we keep constant the membership at the beginning of the period (the EU-15),
the intra-regional intensity of EU trade actually declined, proving
again that intra-regional trade shares are largely dependent on how

Figure 8.4: Intra-regional trade shares (%) by selected regional groupings (1996–2020)

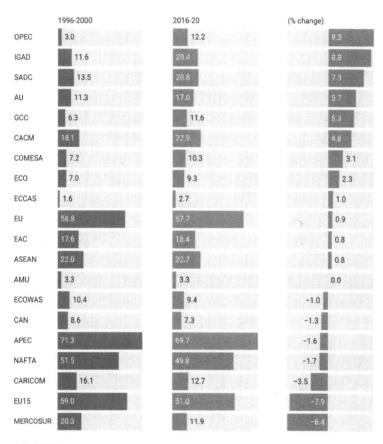

Created with Datawrapper

Note: Regional blocs are ordered by 1996–2020 percentage change.

AMU, Arab Maghreb Union; APEC, Asia-Pacific Economic Cooperation; ASEAN, Association of Southeast Asian Nations; CACM, Central American Common Market; CAN, Andean Community; CARICOM, Caribbean Community; COMESA, Common Market for Eastern and Southern Africa; EAC, East African Community; ECCAS, Econ. Community of Central African States; ECOWAS, Econ. Com. of West African States; EU, European Union; EU15, European Union 1995–2004; GCC, Cooperation Council for Arab States of the Gulf; IGAD, Intergovernmental Authority on Development; MERCOSUR, Southern Common Market; NAFTA, North American Free Trade Agreement; OPEC, Organization of Petroleum Exporting Countries; SADC, Southern African Development Community.

Source: Calculated from UNCTADStat (2023).

the regional bloc is defined. Moreover, it is worth noting that intra-European trade was already at a relatively high level even prior to the signing of the Treaty of Rome in 1957. In 1956, intra-European trade stood at 45% of total trade; it rose quickly until 1966, reaching 56%, but thereafter stagnated for nearly two decades, only surpassing 60% in 1991. MERCOSUR, and Latin America in general, display the worst performance, with sharp declines in their intra-regional trade since the mid-1990s.

To drive the point home, Africa's relatively robust performance comes through just as clearly when trade data are broken down by geographic rather than political regions (Table 8.2). While Central Africa is thus ranked the least economically integrated sub-region in the world (from the perspective of the level of intra-regional trade), Central America, Central Asia and Southern Asia do not fare much better. Although Latin American sub-regions display a larger share of intra-regional trade overall, the continent performs poorly compared with some African sub-regions (Central, Northern and Western Africa). It is no coincidence that the three best performing sub-regions (Eastern Asia, Western Europe and North America) are economically the most developed regions. However, when broken down by geographic sub-region, the performance by Europe no longer looks so impressive either: Southern Europe is barely more integrated than East Africa.

Table 8.1: Share of intra-regional trade (%) by geographic sub-region (1996–2020)

Region	1996–2000	2016–20
Central Africa	1.6	2.4
Central America	3.1	4.2
Northern Africa	3.6	5.1
Central Asia	9.5	6.7
Southern Asia	5.2	9.0

Western Africa	10.7	9.5
Caribbean	8.4	12.2
Southern Africa	6.5	13.6
Latin America and Caribbean	19.3	15.7
East Africa	12.9	16.1
Southern Europe	16.3	16.4
South America	25.2	16.8
Western Asia	8.6	18.0
Northern Europe	22.4	20.5
Eastern Europe	24.1	20.8
Southeast Asia	22.0	22.8
Northern America	37.8	30.2
Western Europe	36.1	33.4
Eastern Asia	33.8	35.2

Data ordered by 2016–20 average.
Source: Calculated from UNCTADStat (2023).

To summarise, we have seen that conclusions on intra-regional trade shares are partly contingent on how a 'region' is defined. This section has also highlighted the fact that over the last 25 years, different regional blocs have experienced markedly different trajectories regarding their shares of intra-regional trade. Trade in some regional blocs has prospered, whereas in others it has dwindled. But what is clear is that Africa is far from being an outlier in terms of the underlying dynamics and trends. In fact, some Africa regional economic communities have done well in expanding the level of intra-regional trade. The question remains, therefore: why do analysts[14] continue to talk down intra-African trade?

Why is the economic significance of intra-African trade underestimated?

The true economic significance of intra-African trade is distorted by a number of additional factors. Firstly, some of Africa's largest economies are less oriented towards the continental market: as such, the average of intra-regional trade is dragged down by the continent's larger economies—especially Egypt, Nigeria, and (to a lesser extent) South Africa (Figure 8.4).[15] The explanation for the low dependence on the African market varies for each of these cases: Egypt has long-standing market access agreements with the EU, and has prioritised the markets of its northern neighbours across the Mediterranean Sea in the past; Nigeria's lower dependence on intra-continental trade reflects the country's oil wealth; for South Africa, there are historical reasons related to its apartheid economy, making its economy less dependent on its regional neighbours' markets than would otherwise have been the case. As noted in a recent AU report,[16] Algeria, Egypt and Nigeria collectively represent about half of Africa's total GDP, but account together for only 11% of continental trade. In contrast, many smaller African economies (particularly the landlocked ones) have significantly higher levels of dependence on intra-regional trade than the continental average, particularly in Southern Africa.

A second reason why intra-African trade is frequently underestimated is that continental averages are distorted by large-scale commodity exports of a small but significant minority of countries. Africa finds itself possessing a high proportion of global mineral reserves (e.g. 60% of manganese and cobalt; 75% of phosphates and diamonds; 80% of chrome and as much as 85% of platinum) and is responsible for nearly 10% of global oil and gas production.[17] As is common for resource-rich regions,[18] the bulk of the continent's natural resources are destined for markets outside the continent, dragging down the share of intra-continental exports.

Angola is a case in point: oil comprises more than 90% of its exports, nearly all of which is destined for the United States. Strip out those extra-regional commodity exports and suddenly the importance of intra-African exports for Angola jumps to around three quarters of the country's total exports.[19] It also needs remembering that while the continent is rightly regarded as 'resource-rich', this is not true for

Figure 8.5: Average intra-African trade as a share of total trade (2019–21)

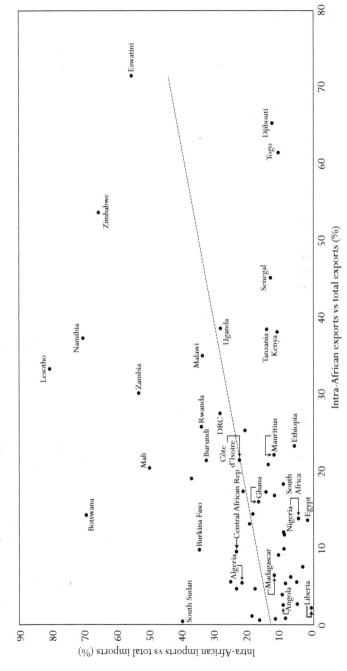

Source: UNCTADStat (2023).

many African countries, with about one third being net commodity importers (not exporters).[20] As a corollary of this, this latter group of countries tend to have a higher dependence on the continental market than the main commodity exporters.

A final reason for the systematic under-appreciation of intra-African trade is the scale of informal cross-border transactions which are not captured in official statistics. We turn to this topic next.

Informal cross-border trade—measuring its economic significance

It is well recognised that a lot of African borders are extremely porous; indeed, their sheer length often inhibits tight controls.[21] While informal cross-border trade (ICBT) is a global phenomenon, studies tend to concur that it is more widespread on the African continent than in other developing regions.[22] Almost all informal trade is, by definition, intra-continental because it happens in goods between neighbouring countries and its prevalence means the real extent of intra-regional trade is much higher than can be gleaned from official trade data alone. One group of authors claim, for instance, that 'informal cross border trade generates nearly USD 18 billion annually and accounts for over two-thirds of the trade flows in some African countries.'[23] ICBT is most intensive in smaller landlocked countries. Summarising the existing studies, Harding concludes that by omitting informal trade, intra-African trade is systematically under-reported by anything between 11% and 40%.[24] Other authors put this tally even higher, at nearly half of formal sector trade.[25] Therefore, an assessment of regional trade cannot be complete without capturing ICBT.[26]

Some interesting studies have been undertaken across the continent into ICBT. One thing that stands out from that literature is the heterogeneous nature of ICBT. For instance, in the Horn of Africa, ICBT focuses on livestock, traded from Ethiopia, Kenya and Somalia to regional markets and the Middle East. The export of livestock from Somalia to the Middle East is one of the largest live animal trades globally, with annual exports close to USD 1 billion.[27] Nairobi purchases about 450,000 cattle annually, with Somalia and Ethiopia supplying 75,000 and 40,000 respectively.[28]

In West Africa, by contrast, a lot of ICBT comprises 'entrepôt trade', where imported goods are informally re-exported from countries with few trade barriers into more highly protected markets. This leads to distortions in official trade statistics in the region. In an ICBT data collection exercise carried out between June 2013 and May 2014, the Nigerian Central Bank estimated that more than 70% of the USD 655 million of informal imports that entered the country in that period consisted of 're-exports' of goods originating from countries other than Nigeria's immediate neighbours. Similarly, in Central Africa, Cameroon's informal trade consists of exports and re-exports of manufactured goods to Chad and Nigeria, and imports of manufactured goods. INS-Cameroon estimated that at least 7–10% of traders surveyed in 2013 had no intention of declaring their goods at the border.

North Africa has scarce data on the scale of ICBT but studies show it is a deeply embedded sociocultural practice, often connected with the nomadic lifestyles of indigenous Bedouin. The most comprehensive estimate of the overall scale and scope of ICBT in the North Africa region is provided by Ayadi et al., who used mirror statistics, field observations and interviews with customs officials and cross-border traders to assess ICBT flows between Tunisia and two of its neighbours, Libya and Algeria.[29] They estimated that informal trade accounted for less than 10% of Tunisia's total imports in 2013 but played a significant role in bilateral trade with Libya and Algeria, as well as in certain sectors. Fuel was responsible for the lion's share of informal imports into Tunisia, though other major categories included apples, bananas, textiles, clothes, bedsheets, shoes, carpets, kitchenware, household electrical goods, white goods (refrigerators, air conditioners) and car tyres.

In the Great Lakes Region, the Democratic Republic of Congo is a major focal point for ICBT. Due to rapid population growth and constraints to domestic production, the country runs large trade deficits with most of its neighbours and a significant proportion of these imports are procured from neighbouring countries through small-scale cross-border traders. In Uganda and Rwanda, survey data shows that ICBT accounts for a significant percentage of total exports— around 16–20% in the former case, and as much as 34% in the latter. In Southern Africa, ICBT is estimated to contribute between 30–40% of total intra-SADC trade, standing at an impressive USD 17.6 billion per year.[30] In some places it far exceeds formal trade. For example,

at the Mwami/Mchinji border between Zambia and Malawi it is estimated that ICBT surpasses formal trade by 70%.[31]

Finally, in discussions about ICBT, the gender aspect is often
stressed. Certainly, women traders are highly visible in a lot of cross-
border activity. It is estimated, for example, that the share of women
traders in West Africa is anywhere between 70–90% of all small-scale
traders. An informal cross-border trade survey conducted on the
Abidjan-Lagos corridor in West Africa found that women traders
conducted 61% of all such transactions.[32] Notably, North Africa is the
only region where ICBT is largely dominated by men.[33]

As can be garnered from the above discussion, informal trade is not
an unmitigated blessing. It has become idealised by parts of the donor
community as 'plucky little traders' that defy the constraints imposed
by unjust border officials. It is certainly extremely important, as a
survivalist strategy, for many border communities given how few
other economic opportunities often exist.[34] Yet a significant share of
transactions are associated with simple arbitrage—traders buying
goods cheaply in one market to sell them in another. With that in
mind, to some degree ICBT may actually decline with the elimination
of tariff and NTBs, as the AfCFTA leads to a convergence of prices
across borders and the reduction in the arbitrage incentive.

Recalculating the true extent of intra-African trade

Bearing in mind all the errors of perception discussed above, what
would constitute a more accurate picture regarding intra-African
trade? Table 8.3 provides some proximate calculations, distinguishing
between landlocked countries, oil exporters and other resource-
intensive countries,[35] which try to compensate for the aforementioned
biases and omissions. It provides a quite different picture of the economic significance of intra-African trade to the standard narrative.

Consistent with the arguments in the preceding section, the breakdown in Table 8.3 demonstrates how data are distorted by high levels
of commodity exports of a few countries. For instance, Africa's nine oil
exporters only sent 8% of their total exports to other African countries
in 2019, compared with 22% when we exclude the major oil exporters.
The dependence on the African market for the continent's landlocked

Figure 8.6: Re-estimating the share of intra-African exports in total exports

	Intra-African exports (USD, billions)	Total exports (USD, billions)	Intra-African (%)	With ICBT at 30%	With ICBT at 50%
Oil exporters*	14.4	178.0	8%	10%	
African average	80.3	482.1	17%	22%	25%
Africa (excl. oil exporters)	66.0	302.2	22%	28%	33%
Other resource-intensive	40.2	160.2	25%	33%	38%
Landlocked countries	11.2	40.1	28%	36%	42%

Created with Datawrapper

* Definitions of typology provided in the Annex (p. 157). Trade data based on 2019 values.

Source: Authors' computations from UNCTADStat (2023).

countries is three and half times higher, at 28%. Adding 30% to account for informal cross-border trade (an arbitrary figure, but well within the range of Harding's aforementioned estimates) gives us an intra-African trade figure of 28.4% as a continental average (versus 16.7% using formal sector trade data for the 55 economies of the continent). Results of surveys suggest that ICBT could be as high as 50% of formal trade for smaller, landlocked economies. Applying this higher figure, the average share of intra-African trade relative to extra-African trade for landlocked countries becomes 42%. These approximations serve to give us a better grasp of the magnitude of intra-African trade relative to the official trade figures commonly in circulation.[36]

Conclusions

This chapter has had a simple objective: to correct the standard narrative that intra-African trade is an aberration, and that it is structurally lower than in other parts of the world. The chapter has shown that pessimistic claims about the potential of intra-African trade do not stand much scrutiny; in fact, in many parts of the continent, intra-African trade is already vibrant and rising. This provides a promising starting point from which to launch the AfCFTA. For African countries, it is no longer a case of fighting against an inherent tendency to not trade with each other, but rather to leverage trends that are already well established.

The evident potential of intra-continental integration for Africa begs the question: why are popular perceptions of intra-African trade so negative? An easy response to this question is that the story has gained gravitas simply through repetition, and few economists have taken the time to verify the figures. A more convoluted argument is that some parties might have a vested interest in promoting the continued dependence of the African economy on higher-income countries, and therefore underplay the viability of the intra-African economy.[37]

Regardless of the roots of the misconceptions over the economic significance of intra-African trade, the correction of stylised facts described in this chapter has an important implication at a time when trading under the AfCFTA has already begun. The impression of sluggish intra-African trade is wrong: across most of the continent, it represents a high share of total African trade and is usually the more dynamic—and certainly the more diversified—component of a typical African country's exports. This disarms the excessively simplistic but widespread myth that African countries have nothing to trade with each other.

ANNEX Table—Classification of African Countries

Oil exporters	Other resource-intensive	Landlocked
Angola, Cameroon, Chad, Democratic Republic of the Congo, Equatorial Guinea, Nigeria, South Sudan, Libya, Algeria	Botswana, Burkina Faso, Central African Republic, Democratic Republic of Congo, Ghana, Guinea, Liberia, Mali, Namibia, Niger, Sierra Leone, South Africa, Tanzania, Zambia, Zimbabwe	Botswana, Burundi, Central Africa, Chad, Lesotho, Malawi, Mali, Niger, Zimbabwe, Rwanda, Swaziland, Uganda, Burkina Faso, Zambia, Ethiopia, South Sudan

Source: Classification according to IMF (2019b).

9

THE PROMISE OF THE AFCFTA

THE ECONOMIC CASE FOR ESTABLISHING
A CONTINENTAL MARKET

Introduction

The previous chapters have explained why the current international trading system does not work in Africa's favour, and why, despite popular impressions to the contrary, intra-African trade already has major economic significance for the vast majority of countries on the continent. Although the importance of non-economic objectives in regional integration is not to be gainsaid, this chapter makes the case in favour of rapid implementation of the AfCFTA on economic grounds. Accelerating the structural transformation of the African economy is essential to put growth on the continent on a more sustainable footing, and the chapter stresses that the best strategic route to achieve this goal is through both greater intra-African trade and investment. We touch on the latter point in Chapter 11.

Above all, the AfCFTA provides a unique opportunity to scale up economic activities so that firms are better able to compete on regional and global markets. The chapter also provides a discussion of the necessity of adopting policies to 'recapture the continental market'—which is essentially a modern variant on much maligned 'import substitution policies'. Finally, the chapter discusses the potential under the AfCFTA for greater intra-African agricultural trade.

Market size and persistence of scale economies

A lot of analyses on the African economy belittle its size. A few decades ago, it was commonplace for reports to start with the observation that the whole of the African economy was 'only a little larger than that of Belgium'.[1] After two decades of sustained demographic and economic growth, the situation has changed: at just shy of 3 trillion USD in 2022, collectively Africa's economy is currently the seventh largest in the world. When measured in purchasing power parities (PPPs) (i.e. reflecting better purchasing power of individual currencies in their domestic economies), the scale of readjustment is substantial: measured in such a way, the African economy reaches over USD 8.3 trillion, behind only China, the United States and India.[2]

The corresponding size of the consumer market is also impressive. According to World Bank data, again measured in PPPs, total consumer spending in Africa totalled USD 3.6 trillion in 2019, and is projected to reach USD 5.3 trillion by 2030. In absolute terms, that increase of 1.7 trillion USD will be nearly double that in South America and not much lower than the forecasted increase for Europe (USD 1 trillion and 2.6 trillion, respectively).[3] The takeaway from this is that we frequently underestimate the real market potential of the African continent.

Of course, it is not just a question of absolute market size, but purchasing power of individuals. Here, with the prevalence of low per capita incomes, the continent still confronts a major challenge. However, African countries frequently dominate the list of fastest growing economies in the world and nearly half of its people live in countries where economies have grown consistently over the past 20 years. Annual GDP growth in these primarily mid-size economies in East and West Africa has averaged more than 4 percent.[4] Moreover, on average, the income per capita of African cities is more than double the continental average, making them already attractive markets for many businesses.[5] Lagos now has a consumer market that is larger than Mumbai's, and the spending power displayed by continental households exceeds those observed in India and Russia.[6]

The emergence of a vibrant middle class in cities across the continent is well established in the literature. Whether someone is classified as 'middle-class' is of course a definitional issue, and depends, within each of these definitions, on the cut-off values used; Kharas[7] puts the figure at 114 million for the continent, while Roxborough[8] puts a much higher figure of 425 million people, with projections ranging from over half a billion by 2030 to 1.1 billion people by 2060.[9] By that time, the population of Africa will have surpassed that of both China and India combined. As a share of Africa's total economy, consumer spending is now the fastest-growing source of demand compared with government and business spending, and this trend is projected to continue through 2030.[10]

As a result of these trends, industries supplying Africa's consumer markets are expected to increase revenues rapidly. Given the still relatively low average purchasing power of African consumers, the greatest increase in household expenditure over the short term is likely to occur in the fast-moving consumer goods sector, comprising low-cost products with short shelf-lives that are constantly in high demand, with the largest benefits expected to accrue in food and beverages, housing, transportation, and hospitality and recreation.[11]

Market size matters for a whole host of reasons, but it is currently a highly fragmented market. This is where the balkanisation of the African economy hurts most. Because of its colonial heritage (see Chapter 2), Africa has much smaller countries in terms of population than other regions. The continent is split into 55 AU member states, with two thirds of the continent's economies having GDPs smaller than USD 20 billion. Moreover, close to one third of the countries are landlocked. Although population growth has been prodigious over recent decades, many countries still have extremely low population densities, particularly in the semi-arid parts of the continent. This limits the scope for labour specialisation.[12] It also makes it costly to construct and maintain the necessary infrastructure for goods to reach the market. One by-product of this is high costs of transport. Despite the vibrancy of cross-border trade in many commercial 'hotspots' on the continent,[13] poor market integration has hampered the use of trade for risk sharing;[14] for instance, by diminishing the amount of intra-regional trade in foodstuffs, regional food security is impaired. One of the challenges for the AfCFTA will be precisely to raise the provision of infrastructure to an intensity that will facilitate greater cross-border transactions.

There are other serious consequences stemming from smallness. Small economies are often perceived by investors as significantly riskier, thereby diminishing their ability to attract much-needed investment.[15] Indeed, one of the classic primary rationales for entering into a regional integration scheme in the first place is to escape from the constraints of a small domestic market. Repeated studies show that market size is an important determinant of being able to attract sufficient fixed investment.[16] It has even been hypothesised that small economies suffer from a slower rate of technological innovation, the argument running that the incidence of discoveries may be broadly proportional to the population, so that low-population societies will be less innovative.[17]

Crucially, some domestic markets on the continent are currently too small for producers to attain the minimum efficient scale of production, implying that large firms must operate in multiple jurisdictions to reap economies of scale. In some instances, a few large firms operate across countries by forming cartels to limit foreign competition in their jurisdictions and to exploit consumers. A case in point is that of the cement industry, where nine firms in Africa produce more than 50% of the cement, and anticompetitive practices have regional dimensions.[18]

Yet it is pertinent to ask whether this still matters. Some economists argue that being a small economy is no constraint in a globalised world.[19] It is certainly true that some small countries—cases like Singapore and pre-reunification Hong Kong come to mind—have done very well through their participation in global trade. Moreover, because of technological changes, the advantages conferred by size are often no longer decisive, and through the use of new technologies, small-scale production is increasingly viable. One of the most cogent analyses of these changes is Kaplinsky's recent book,[20] which describes the birth of a new 'techno-economic paradigm', marked by the death throes of mass production. The Fordist model of mass production, which was invented a century ago, is gradually being eclipsed by more flexible manufacturing practices, where economic scale is no longer so crucial, and more emphasis is placed on logistics, innovation and adaptability.[21]

Such arguments are compelling, but it may be premature to discount the advantages of scale. Schwartz highlights the way in which scale economies still drive the dynamics of different industries.[22] For instance, garment assembly tends to have low economies of scale, which enables dispersion to multiple locations and thus no risk of bidding up local wages.[23] By contrast, car production has high economies of scale—250,000 to 300,000 units for assembly and 400,000 units for engines—which inhibits dispersion to small markets. Design and R&D for a new model requires about 2 million units to attain maximum economies of scale, but the actual vehicles can be produced at different locations over multiple years. Scale is thus of critical importance in the automotive industry.[24] Unsurprisingly, companies like Volkswagen S.A. have been very explicit about their interest in setting up African regional production networks, but only once they are sure that barriers to intra-regional trade will be removed.

As another example, the electronics industry has scale economies similar to the vehicle industry, but in reverse: scale is greatest in components and lowest in assembly. Component production of dynamic random-access memories (memory chips), for example, requires a factory costing between USD 2–10 billion. But assembly can be done at individual workstations, much as in garment assembly.[25] Other sectors may enjoy inherent scale economies simply because of the laws of physics. For example, in the chemical sector or beer manufacturing, the ratio of volume to circumference in spherical containers is 1.6, providing an important impetus for important cost savings when production is on a larger scale.[26]

Against such a backdrop, simply by virtue of their size, large firms often benefit from a set of innate advantages.[27] These positively affect their direct costs of production in terms of what Chandler famously described as 'economies of scale and scope' (e.g. by larger production runs or by sharing certain fixed costs like marketing, product development and design, management serves across multiple products).[28]

But even in cases when scale economies like those described above are not technologically determined, the global concentration of R&D in large firms means that the spectrum of efficient technologies available for purchase is often in reality confined to larger and capital-intensive operations. The financial muscle of large firms also allows them to drive down the price of inputs, and to gain from privileged access to low-cost and long-term finance. Larger firms also tend to enjoy higher rates of capacity utilisation.[29] Finally, the ability to produce in large volumes facilitates feeding into value chains serving large and often global markets.[30]

Arguably, one of Africa's main developmental constraints is that it does not have enough large companies. Despite some notable corporate success stories,[31] Africa lags behind other emerging regions in hosting large companies. Outside South Africa, Africa's firms earn less than half the revenue of their emerging market peers as a proportion of GDP. Not a single African company—not even from South Africa—was featured in the 2022 Global Fortune 500. By comparison Brazil and India posted seven and nine companies on that list, respectively. China had 136, outpacing the United States with 124.[32] This structural feature of African economies is again partly attributable to the period of SAPs of the 1980s and 1990s, when many of the larger firms and industrial complexes were culled, deemed uncompetitive to global competition.[33]

Africa's lack of big companies matters for society because of the way in which these larger firms are the primary drivers of economic growth. They account for the bulk of R&D, pay better, and provide more stable jobs. In a memorable turn of phrase, Leke et al. describe big firms on the African continent as the 'baobabs of the business landscape': not only do they tower over the rest, but they also have deeper roots and longer lifespans. Known as the tree of life, the baobab produces highly nutritious fruit that sustains many communities.[34] It is this ecosystem of larger firms providing sustenance and shade within which smaller firms can grow and flourish which is so often missing in African economies.

Studies on specific countries on the African continent have confirmed the validity of this narrative. In Ethiopia, for instance, contrary to conventional wisdom, large firms create just as much employment as the myriad of smaller firms, who create more initial employment, but also lose more jobs because of the high attrition rates.[35] It is a finding repeated in other studies on the African continent: net job creation is driven by the larger firms.[36] Yet over the last two decades of relatively fast growth, things have been going in the wrong direction: there has been a rapid increase in the number of African manufacturing enterprises with less than 10 employees.[37] Meanwhile, while there is evidence of robust labour productivity growth in Africa's large firms, employment in such firms has not been growing.[38] We will come back to these points in Chapters 10 and 14. For now, suffice to say that the AfCFTA represents a unique opportunity for the continent to turn this state of affairs around and to upscale economic activities on the continent.

Intra-African trade as a motor of industrialisation and development

In the previous chapter, we explained that even prior to the implementation of the AfCFTA, intra-African trade is already more buoyant and has a greater economic significance than is commonly understood. Nevertheless, it has not always been that way. In the late 1950s, low levels of intra-African trade were another unfortunate inheritance from the period of colonisation. 'Imperial preference' and the heightened competitiveness and even hostility between francophone- and anglophone-administered countries (not to mention the lusophone countries, which had a peculiar world order of their own and, like Spain's control over Equatorial Guinea, were stuck in a time-warp) meant that neighbouring countries lived, in economic terms, with their backs to each other. And then of course there was the divide that existed between the Arabic-speaking countries of North Africa and the rest of the continent. In many parts of the continent, these divisions are still apparent; in West Africa, for instance, there remains a pronounced cleavage between francophone, lusophone and anglophone countries. The francophone countries also conserve a common currency linked to the euro, with their Central Bank reserves being deposited with the French Treasury—surely one of the most anachronistic manifestations of contemporary macroeconomic policy and something that arguably acts as a further barrier to economic integration in West and Central Africa.[39]

161

Thanks to advances in applied economic analysis, we now know a lot more about how individual countries can achieve success in expanding their exports. In a seminal paper, Hummels and Klenow showed that around 60% of trade growth is through the 'extensive margin' rather than the 'intensive margin'.[40] That is to say, the bulk of the growth of trade does not usually happen by exporting more of the same products, but rather by countries either moving into new product lines or improving the quality (and thus price) of existing products. In a study analysing exports from 64 developing countries to 29 developed countries between 1990 and 2005, Amurgo-Pacheco and Pierola distinguish between export growth along intensive margins—existing products to existing markets—and extensive markets involving diversification through either selling new products to existing markets, old products to new markets, and/or new products to new markets.[41] They conclude not only that developing countries with higher levels of export diversification tend to record higher economic growth rates, but that the extensive margin is the dominant force, accounting for 37% of export growth in sub-Saharan countries. In a similar study, Brenton and Newfarmer estimated this rate to be even higher, at 57% for African countries.[42] The message from this literature is pretty resounding—to prosper in trade, you must diversify.

In Chapter 6, we also noted the way in which Africa's trading patterns have shifted and that the old patterns of external dependency have largely been consigned to history. Everyone is aware of the phenomenal rise of China as a global trading partner—it is evident in shops and supermarkets across the world, and many countries in Africa now also display a marked reliance on imports from China. What is less remarked upon is the rapid shift in global trading patterns more generally—something influenced by the rise of China but far from wholly dependent on that country. Developing countries are becoming consistently more important as sources of world import growth, and the share of high-income countries in world imports has been steadily declining (Figure 9.1).[43]

Going forward, South–South trade will become particularly important as a source of export-led growth for developing countries, provided that policymakers remain committed to the progressive opening of those markets.[44]

Figure 9.1: The rising importance of South-South trade, 1840–2021

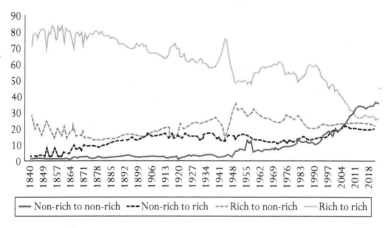

Non-rich to non-rich --- Non-rich to rich --- Rich to non-rich --- Rich to rich

Source: Mold (2023).

The change in global trading patterns raises some important strategic choices for developing countries in general, and African governments in particular. Figure 9.2 reveals that intra-African trade is far more diversified than extra-African trade. While manufactured exports represent just 19% of extra-African exports, that share rises to 44% for the African market. Moreover, that is a continental average; in more consolidated regional blocs like the EAC, manufacturing products account for as much as two thirds of all intra-regional transactions. Intra-African manufacturing trade also has a higher (and rising) share of medium and high technology goods than embodied in exports to the rest of the world (Figure 9.3).[45] The majority of the manufacturing exports end up in neighbouring countries because of proximity and lower transport costs.[46] An anecdotal example of this is Rwanda, which exports around 80% of its manufacturing exports to neighbouring DRC. In many countries across the continent, the bulk of their diversified exports are already destined for the continental market.

The conclusion is clear: if the continent wishes to prime technological upgrading and export diversification, the regional route is the most expedient one.

Figure 9.2: Sectoral distribution of African exports by destination as percentage of total (2019)

Figure 9.3: Share of medium and high technology goods in Africa's exports by destination (2005–16)

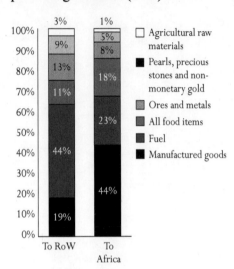

Legend:
- ☐ Agricultural raw materials
- ■ Pearls, precious stones and non-monetary gold
- ▨ Ores and metals
- ▤ All food items
- ▦ Fuel
- ■ Manufactured goods

Source: UNCTADStat (2023).

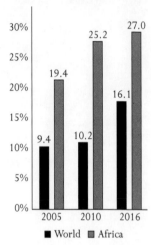

■ World   ▨ Africa

Source: UNCTAD (2019).

Recapturing the continental market

Import substitution industrialisation is a trade and economic policy that advocates for the gradual replacement of foreign imports with domestic production.[47] Ever since the period of structural adjustment, it has been getting a bad rap. This is despite the fact that the theoretical case against import substitution, as a part of a wider economic development strategy, is surprisingly weak.[48] As one renowned trade economist has noted:

> The failure of extreme protectionist policies does not establish that an export promotion strategy is superior to a moderate, intelligently formulated, program of import substitution. And contrary to the claims made by advocates of outward oriented policies, neither theory nor empirical evidence suggests there is likely to be a greater exploitation of scale economies, more rapid technological progress, less underemployment or faster capital accumulation under one strategy than the other.[49]

It is often claimed that African countries failed in their efforts to implement such strategies in the 1960s and 1970s and there are varying narratives about why.[50] Critics tended to denigrate the capacity of the state in Africa to act in a way that was conducive to making import substitution work in the way it did in Asian economies like South Korea, Taiwan, or later in China. One explanation put forward is that most of Africa was still, in relative terms, labour-scarce and labour costs remained high compared with Asia.[51]

Some observers also point to the fact that the import substitution industrialisation phase was shorter in duration in many African countries than in other regions, being undermined by the economic crises of the 1970s and the SAPs of the 1980s and 1990s (see Chapter 3).[52] In addition, African countries at independence were far behind the world technological frontier and lacked the skills endowments, especially in terms of experience in manufacturing compared with other developing regions.[53] As noted in Chapter 5, countries elsewhere in the developing world that had a stronger experience in manufacturing prior to the Second World War tended to be more successful in their subsequent industrialisation drives.[54]

However, a more fundamental reason for the perceived failures of import substitution in Africa during the 1960s and 1970s is tied up with the way strategies ignored the potential of the regional market. As noted by Mkandawire, much of the industrialisation that occurred at the time was either state-controlled or involved joint ventures with multinational corporations.[55] And it was premised on the ability to perform in the national market. As a consequence, these companies were quite happy with the position they held in the protected national market, undermining their economic imperatives for these business enterprises to lobby for regional integration.

In recent years, however, there has been a notable shift in the prevailing opinion on these matters.[56] Much to the chagrin of some old-school economists, import substitution is back, although in order to reduce the irritation of its erstwhile critics, it has been christened with a different name: 'recapturing the domestic market'.[57] And it is a strategy which is very much, in some shape or form, necessary at a continental level if the transition to an economic model based more on regional and continental markets is to thrive.

Two thirds of African imports currently consist of manufactured goods by value. Africa currently imports roughly one third of all the processed goods it consumes, compared with just 20% in ASEAN countries and 10% in the MERCOSUR trade bloc. Among manufactured products like cars and chemicals, 60% of Africa's supply is imported, a figure twice that of MERCOSUR. Even for goods which are extremely costly to transport, import dependency is often surprisingly high. For instance, the continent imports 15% of its cement needs.[58]

It is a reasonable proposition that many of the imported goods could be manufactured locally more easily and cheaply and thereby boost the value of intra-African trade.[59] For sophisticated capital goods, successfully undertaking such a policy would certainly be more challenging. But the range of low-to mid-tech goods susceptible to strategies of 'recapturing the domestic market' is large, with quick wins including items such as foodstuffs, clothing, beverages and cigarettes, rubber and plastics, some types of electronics, and non-metallic mineral products.[60] There are also ample opportunities for African distributors to target local suppliers and manufacturers more, something which would ultimately cut costs and boost profit margins while contributing to job creation and rising incomes.

One widely held myth is that productivity in African firms is so low that unit labour costs exceed those of competitors in the global market for low-end manufactures. It is thus concluded that manufacturing firms on the continent cannot effectively compete with imported goods from more efficient Asian producers. As noted in Chapter 5, there are reasons to doubt such sweeping claims. For instance, Harrison, Lin and Xu use the World Bank Enterprise Surveys (WBES) to understand the determinants of firm performance and behaviour in 32 African countries, focusing principally on manufacturing firms, and comparing their performance with the other 48 developing countries.[61] While their analysis of performance finds that African manufacturing firms suffer significant disadvantages across all performance measures (including productivity, labour productivity growth, sales growth, investment rates and export intensity), once they control econometrically for deficits in infrastructure, access to finance, and the political and business environment, African firms actually led in productivity levels and growth rates. After controlling for the political and business environment, the authors conclude that African manufacturing firms suffer no inherent disadvantage.[62]

Indeed, many of the elements commonly used to explain the underperformance of African firms were found to matter relatively little, namely geography, crime, domestic and international competition. In contrast, infrastructure and access to finance prove to be of paramount importance in explaining Africa's disadvantage relative to firms in countries of a similar income. In other words, African firms would be perfectly capable of competing on regional and international markets if policy focused strategically on removing some of the constraints.[63]

None of this is to suggest that a policy replacing imported products with goods made in Africa will be easy. Global value chains have placed tremendous downward pressures on prices, making it difficult for new entrants to compete in many sectors. But there are clever ways to kick-start the process, specifically by adopting what is called 'smart industrial policy'. For instance, having been vanquished by import competition, in Nigeria, a domestic cement industry was re-established by offering a four-year licence to import cement, on the condition that the licence holder invested in a domestic cement production plant. Today, Nigeria is a net exporter of cement and the deal created the richest African individual, Aliko Dangote.[64] In Rwanda, although companies like Uganda's Hima Cement Ltd. and Tanzania's Simba Cement PLC continue to dominate segments of the local market, efforts by the national cement manufacturer CIMERWA have been successful in capturing close to half the domestic market in recent years.[65] This is precisely the kind of intra-African competition that will ultimately lead to a more productive African economy.

Supermarkets are another potential catalyst for stimulating local food processing and light manufacturing industries. Although countries in Africa still rely more on alternative retail routes, such as wet markets and small traditional informal retailers, the expansion of supermarket chains have important implications for the participation and success of local suppliers. Some of those firms have explicit policies to source more of the products from local markets, although, again, it is an area where more regulatory pressure could be brought to bear.[66]

There is also the issue of recapturing segments of the capital goods market. The failure to maintain a strong industrial base in machinery and equipment is most evident in the declining competitiveness in the Southern African region. For example, South Africa's market share of machinery and equipment (particularly mining equipment) in Zambia fell from above 60% in 2002 to around 30% by 2019. This points to the need to build strong regional value chains for South Africa to regain the lost ground in machinery and equipment exports.[67]

Prioritising greater openness to intra-African imports

Ultimately, the success of a strategy to gradually 'recapture the continental market' is contingent on countries becoming more open to intra-African imports—and that requires a rapid removal of intra-African tariff and non-tariff barriers. Where there is a political will, this is perfectly achievable. Since 2004, for instance the EAC had resolved 234 of the 256 reported NTBs.[68] The AfCFTA is not simply an opportunity for member states to expand their export opportunities while remaining closed to greater intra-African imports, for the simple reason that every dollar of increased intra-regional exports must be matched by a dollar of intra-regional imports.

In this sense, countries with large negative trade balances with the continent (e.g. the Southern African countries neighbouring South Africa, Zambia, Ghana, Mali, Burkina Faso, South Sudan and Uganda) could all be considered 'good continental citizens', while those with large positive balances with the rest of the continent (particularly the three largest economies on the continent: Nigeria, South Africa, and Egypt) could do a great favour for AfCFTA implementation by opening up their economies more to imports from the rest of the continent (Figure 9.4). We will say more on this point in the concluding chapter. It should also be realised that while the AfCFTA will boost intra-regional trade, it will not necessarily have a significant effect on overall trade balances, except to the extent that, with the emergence of more regional value chains, greater investment and more allocative efficiency, Africa's firms will be more competitive and better able to compete on regional and global markets.

Finally, it is also crucial that there is not an exclusive focus on 'recapturing domestic markets'. Both import substitution and export promotion can be pursued simultaneously, with a pragmatic mix of

Figure 9.4: Net trading position on the continent (2021)

	Largest Net Exporters			Largest Net Importers		
1	South Africa		8,313	Botswana		-4,415
2	Egypt		3,968	Namibia		-3,377
3	Nigeria		2,388	Mali		-2,769
4	Djibouti		2,166	Zimbabwe		-2,333
5	Senegal		1,454	Zambia		-1,918
6	Ghana		1,196	Mozambique		-1,790
7	Kenya		907	Uganda		-1,718

Created with Datawrapper

Source: Calculated from UNCTADStat (2023).[69]

policies aimed at shifting resources from non-traded commodities to those that are tradeable. Under this strategy, the non-traded sectors are 'squeezed' of resources, allowing for a net increase in the production of both import replacements and exports.[70] Vietnam is an example of a country that has successfully diversified its economy over the last three decades using an industrial and trade policy that merged both import substitution measures and export subsidies to promote an export-driven growth strategy, supported by strong FDI.[71] With the implementation of the AfCFTA, African countries are now well-placed to adopt similar pragmatic trade strategies.

What about agriculture?

Agriculture is a relatively neglected topic in discussions on the potential of the AfCFTA, with most of the focus going on industrial and services sectors. This is a mistake for two principal reasons. Firstly, Nobel Prize-winning economist Arthur Lewis famously noted how 'it is not profitable to produce a growing volume of manufactures unless agricultural production is growing simultaneously. This is also why industrial and agrarian revolutions always go together, and why economies in which agriculture is stagnant do not show industrial development'.[72] Historical precedent shows that this is demonstrably the case.[73] Secondly, the AfCFTA represents an opportunity to catalyse greater agricultural trade and investment and, in so doing, improve food and nutrition security on the continent.

There are a lot of misconceptions about both the state of African agriculture and the degree of dependence on food trade.[74] One is the persistent claim that Africa is dependent on imports for large shares of the food it consumes—one report going so far as to claim that Africa imports 85% of its food (what it probably meant was that 85% of food imports come from outside the continent, which would have been quite correct).[75] Of course, with approximately half of continental employment being in the agricultural sector,[76] the truth is that the majority of food consumed on the continent is also produced on the continent.

It is also not quite accurate that Africa has become increasingly dependent on food imports over the last decade, as some claim.[77] The aggregate value of food imports for the continent has shadowed international food prices: they were correspondingly high in 2011–12, at around USD 90–92 billion, but fell back to just USD 74 billion in 2016. Thereafter, the big increase came in 2021–22, in the wake of rapidly rising food prices due to the Covid-19 crisis and, in early 2022, by the Ukraine war, with imports rising to a record USD 97.4 billion in 2021, representing a 22% increase in just one year. Nonetheless, the fact that even with rapidly growing demand driven by population growth and rising per capita incomes, the value of food imports has not inexorably risen over the past decade is in part a testimony to the region's success in expanding food production (it is not a widely recognised fact, but sub-Saharan Africa has experienced—albeit from a low base—the highest rate of agricultural production growth of any region of the world since 2000).[78]

This said, given its vast agricultural potential, it is obviously disappointing that Africa is still heavily dependent on imports for some basic foodstuffs, such as rice, cereals, vegetable oils, sugar, meat and dairy products. However, seen against a backdrop of an extraordinary degree of concentration in global food supply, it is perhaps not so surprising. For instance, just five countries (Thailand, Vietnam, India, the USA, and Pakistan) sell 77% of the world's rice, and five (the USA, France, Canada, Russia and Australia) supply 65% of the wheat. Only three nations (Brazil, the USA and Argentina) grow 86% of the world's soybeans (which in turn supply three quarters of its feed for farm animals). In just 18 years, the number of trade connections between the exporters and importers of wheat and rice has doubled; and roughly 40% of the world's population now rely on food from other nations.[79]

As a consequence, countries that once produced a little less or a little more than the food they needed are now polarising into super-importers and super-exporters. Some nations, especially in the Middle East, Central America and North Africa, rely on imports because they no longer have enough fertile land or water to grow their own crops. Others, such as the poorer countries of East Africa, might have enough land and water, but their yields are low, and their production is often undercut by cheap imports from countries with larger farms and generous government subsidies.[80]

In such a context, it is perhaps not so surprising to discover that around two thirds of African countries are net food importers (although most countries are relatively marginal net importers).[81] The bulk of continental food imports are accounted for by North Africa[82] and Nigeria (which alone is responsible for USD 7.9 billion of imports); Angola, DRC and Botswana are responsible for another USD 4.5 billion of imports (see Figure 9.4). Notably, there is also a worryingly high dependence on food imports in some of the Sahel countries and others being negatively impacted by climate change.[83]

Changing consumption patterns, linked to accelerating urbanisation, have affected the composition of demand for food, shifting it towards wheat and rice and away from traditional crops like cassava.[84] Most food imports are sourced from outside the continent (e.g. wheat, sunflower oil and dairy products from Europe; rice and palm oil from Asia; maize, poultry and beef from Latin America). Food is also relatively expensive in many parts of the continent, with one World Bank study finding that the retail prices of essential food items are at least 24% higher in African cities compared with other major cities around the world.[85]

Higher domestic prices are intimately tied up with difficulties in transporting and trading food. Estimates by FAO (2021) suggest that due to excessive sanitary and phytosanitary measures alone, domestic

Figure 9.5: Average net food trade balance (2019–21)

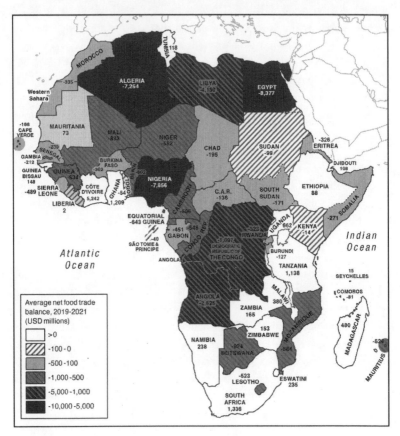

Source: Calculated from UNCTADStat (2023).

food prices in Africa (excluding North Africa) are 13% higher on average. Other NTBs, such as roadblocks, contribute to high domestic transportation costs, accounting for between 50% and 60% of marketing costs. Finally, dependence on extra-regional imports for food makes African countries vulnerable to disruptions in international logistics and distribution, as revealed during the Covid-19 pandemic. These vulnerabilities result in food shortages and raise food prices, particularly in countries that are highly dependent on food imports.[86]

Against this backdrop, promoting intra-regional food trade could help wean African countries off their overdependence on external agricultural markets and assist them in weathering future global agricultural shocks better. Building greater resilience is particularly important for the continent because of climate change. Africa is already affected more than any other region by climate change: large areas of Southern Africa and the Horn of Africa are subject to more frequent droughts, and Malawi, Ethiopia, Nigeria, Uganda, Mali, Mozambique are suffering heat stress. Catastrophic flooding is also rising in intensity (e.g. recently in South Sudan and Kenya).[87] The diversity of Africa's agriculture and climate provides major opportunities for regional trade, yet the proportion of African countries' food imports originating from other African countries is currently low on average (at about 20% over recent decades), with South Africa alone accounting for over one third of all intra-African food trade.

There are thus many potential benefits to expanding intra-African food markets, particularly in a post-Covid-19 world. Many of the same food crops are grown throughout large parts of Africa, yet clear differences between countries in climate and patterns of comparative advantage provide opportunities for regional trade. Using an analysis of revealed comparative advantage, Diao et al. identify 29 food commodities exported in significant quantities by some African countries alongside other countries that import significant quantities, providing the potential for intra-regional trade.[88] Greater regional trade could also help to smooth the impacts of extreme climatic events on production and prices, since production and rainfall are often weakly correlated even within regions.[89]

As in the manufacturing sector, there is also great potential for 'recapturing the domestic market' in some segments of the agricultural sector. For instance, rice from the Senegal River Valley is produced under irrigation and partial mechanisation at costs only slightly above those in Thailand (the world's leading exporter of rice). Senegal has made major progress in increasing yields to reach 3.6 tons per hectare nationally.[90] With relatively efficient milling and transportation, local rice could be competitive—even more so if aromatic rice varieties can be produced commercially.

Another opportunity arises in processed foods and beverages— such as pasta, sugar, animal feed, salt and wine. African countries currently import huge quantities of these products from Western

Europe and countries like Brazil. A surge in supermarkets across the continent offering 'Made in Africa' processed foods could target the continent's growing middle class. By relying on local, cross-border or regional food supply chains, these supermarkets could significantly reduce transport and logistics costs and, consequently, sell their processed foods at more affordable prices. A rapid and ambitious implementation of Africa's integration agenda could help capture the benefits of food trade with neighbouring economies while reducing the continent's exposure to global supply chain shocks.[91]

Effective implementation of the AfCFTA will thus be an important step in enabling African farmers and agribusinesses to increasingly meet the region's growing demand for food. The first, and possibly easiest, step is to remove tariffs on the bulk of intra-African agricultural trade. Although they are often not representative in agricultural produce (because of high tariff peaks and quotas in particular products), the weighted average of effectively applied agricultural tariffs for sub-Saharan Africa in 2019 was 9.54%, whereas the MFN weighted average tariff was 13.23%. Given this, the removal of tariffs on intra-African trade will have some impact, while still leaving a measure of protection from imports on outside the continent.[92]

The liberalisation will not apply to absolutely all agricultural products—during the tariff negotiations on goods, for reasons of domestic political economy, member states frequently resorted to ring-fencing some for agricultural products from liberalisation. However, member states need to be aware that the more they carve out niches of excluded products in particular sectors, the less continental trade will pick up.

A more challenging issue for the continent is dealing with the NTBs that plague intra-African food trade; that is, the phytosanitary standards and other certification standards that impede a lot of cross-border economic activity. Restrictive policies also cause quite serious distortions in regional trade in agricultural inputs. The cross-border movement of seeds and fertiliser is hampered by differences in certification and standards between countries and the resulting issues of checking compliance at the borders. A lack of agreement on common standards as well as mistrust in other countries' testing and certification capabilities often translates into duplicate procedures, which are inevitably associated with high costs. These duplicate procedures also raise revenue for certifying bodies, which creates an additional obstacle for removing them.[93] This really takes us to the essence of the AfCFTA—it is about agreeing and applying common standards.

To realise these opportunities for intra-African agricultural trade, African countries will also need to focus on improving agricultural productivity to compete effectively against low-cost imports from the international market. This will require greater investments in agricultural R&D and extension services, something that has been very much neglected in recent years.[94] As Professor Calestous Juma used to stress, these deficits are often best tackled with regional programmes.[95] For many crops, Africa's average yields are far below their potential: current maize yields reach only 20% of potential yields and even export-oriented cash crop yields reach only 30–50%.[96] Irrigation development in Africa, at less than 5% of cultivated area, lags behind every region of the world by far. Just three countries—Madagascar, South Sudan and South Africa—account for two thirds of the currently irrigated area. Total economically exploitable irrigation potential is estimated to be at least 39 million hectares, which is four times the current level.[97] Similarly, Africa's current use of fertilisers, at around 26 pounds per acre, is only a quarter of the world average. One company responding to that demand is Morocco-based OCP, which is poised to become a global leader in phosphate mining and fertiliser production. The company has made Africa its major growth market; in just one year, it managed to increase its exports to the rest of the continent by 70%.[98] Two South African giants—Sasol and AECI—are also well placed to take advantage of greater intra-regional trade in agricultural inputs.

Beyond the burgeoning demand for agricultural inputs, it is the agro-industrial sector that stands to gain the most from the continental agreement. As a share of total manufacturing, the value of agro-industries already accounts for as much as 50–60% in countries like Ethiopia, Ghana, Madagascar and Senegal. The empirical studies reviewed in Chapter 11 tend to all converge on the point that agro-processing will be the principal beneficiary from enhanced trading opportunities under the AfCFTA. Major African and international companies are now involved in food processing (including Nestlé,

Unilever, Tiger Brands and Tongaat Hulett), beverages (including Coca-Cola, InBev, Anheuser-Busch and SABMiller) and food services (including Compass Group, McDonald's, Anglovaal and Astral Foods), among others.[99] Through greater investment in downstream food processing, the AfCFTA has the potential to catalyse a significant reinvigoration of the agricultural sector.

Conclusions

This chapter has had a straightforward objective: to explain the economic case for implementation of the AfCFTA by focusing on manufacturing and agricultural trade. In most areas, the case is clear-cut and supported by a lot of empirical evidence. Greater intra-African trade and investment will make the continental economy more dynamic and resilient. But it does require a lot of pre-conditions to fulfil its potential. The AfCFTA is a necessary, yet not sufficient, condition for greater dynamism in intra-regional trade and investment. It is going to need effective implementation, and purposeful policies at the national and sub-regional levels to change things on the ground, including through the development of coordinated industrial policy. In Chapter 10, we discuss the rationale behind greater cross-border investment—a major vector through which the benefits will materialise. In Chapter 11, we review the quantitative studies on the benefits of the AfCFTA.

10

THE IMPORTANCE OF CATALYSING GREATER
CROSS-BORDER INVESTMENT

Introduction

As laid out in the previous chapter, the AfCFTA provides a unique opportunity to scale up economic activities so that firms are better able to compete on regional and global markets. Scaling up involves either the expansion of already existing domestic firms or attracting larger-scale investments from abroad. Both outcomes are likely as a consequence of creating a larger continental market. One dimension often missing in these discussions is how the AfCFTA will impact on inflows of FDI, both from within the continent and outside. Although FDI both to and within Africa has been relatively low compared with other regions, empirical evidence shows that joining a free trade area can boost FDI by a considerable amount.[1] By removing the 'small-market' constraint, the AfCFTA promises to change both the volume and composition of FDI inflows on the African continent, in terms of which sectors will receive more investment and where that invest-ment proceeds from.

This chapter argues that the expansion of intra-African trade will depend to a large extent on success in boosting cross-border invest-ment. FDI is one of the principal drivers of trade both globally and on the African continent. If that dynamism can be harnessed for the sake of deepening regional integration, it would go a long way towards increasing the level of interaction between African economies and accelerating the emergence of regional value chains.[2] Yet a lot of the focus on discussions of AfCFTA implementation has hitherto been on SMEs and informal cross-border traders. There is a general belief that 'large firms can take care of themselves'. This faith is misplaced. Because of both the strong link between FDI and trade, on the one hand, and the high share of trade linked to intra-firm trade (i.e. between affiliates of the same company group and their headquarters) on the other, one of the best hopes for greater volumes of trade on the continent is through high levels of cross-border FDI. More intra-regional FDI would greatly increase the chance of the emergence of intra-regional value-chains.

Much like the arguments expounded in the previous chapters on trade, intra-African FDI is more diversified than FDI from outside the continent (which, as we have noted in Chapter 6, is focused excessively on the mineral, oil and financial sectors). Again, like with the case for trade, the conclusion is that to accelerate structural diversification on the continent, the intra-African route is the way to go. This involves not only greater investment in the manufacturing sector, but also in a whole gamut of services sectors, as having a physical presence in the target market is the preferred mode of delivery for many services. Whether that is in telecommunications, tourism, transport or business services, this chapter argues that there are many lucrative opportunities for African investors ripe for the taking.

What—or who—are the drivers of cross-border trade in Africa?

It has become commonplace to associate the AfCFTA with increasing the opportunities for small-scale cross-border trade. The number of seminars, workshops and conferences held across the continent on this topic is quite astounding. In Chapter 8, we provided a lot of evidence that informal cross-border trade is extremely vibrant across the continent and, for the communities dependent on that trade, it is an important—indeed, in some cases vital—source of income. Yet it is not a contradiction to also stress that very few informal-sector firms engage in export, and when they do, they still sell most of their output to the local market, not the foreign one. For example, in South Africa, the median exporter only exports 4% of its output. South African exports are also highly concentrated, with a few 'super exporters' dominating the export bundle.[3] This relationship is not unique to South Africa. In Rwanda, for instance, one study estimated that 88% of total manufactured exports were made by the ten largest companies.[4] At a continental level, according to one study undertaken by UNIDO, the top 1% of trading firms on the continent accounted for over 75% of the total value of exports.[5]

The most recent World Bank Enterprise Surveys[6] confirm that small African firms tend not to engage in exporting at all (Figure 10.1): only 3% of small firms[7] in Tanzania export, for instance, compared with nearly 47% of large firms. We should not be surprised. The reality is that small firms rarely export, and for good reasons—it exposes them to risk and can be very costly to try to get a tenuous foothold on foreign markets. Encouraging them to do so may thus open them up to vulnerabilities much in the same way as providing credit to the most vulnerable households can push them further into poverty.[8]

Research confirms that firms that participate in international trade tend to be larger and more productive.[9] Moreover, as countries develop, a larger share of exports tends to come from the largest exporters. Average exporter size grows as countries get richer because allocative efficiency improves, with the most productive firms absorbing more resources and exporting more.[10]

There is, however, one caveat to this story. Small firms on the African continent tend to be more represented in regional trade. Data from the World Bank's Exporter Dynamics Database reveals that intra-African exports are less dominated by large firms than exports to the rest of the world.[11] But this partly reflects the dearth of larger companies on the continent noted in Chapter 9, something which puts African firms at a significant competitive disadvantage on global markets but may be less of a handicap in markets closer to home.

As noted in Chapter 7, the nature of international trade has changed dramatically over recent decades, with a sharp rise in the emergence of both global and regional value chains. Even though a lot

Figure 10.1: Propensity of firms to engage in exports, by firm size (% of all firms)

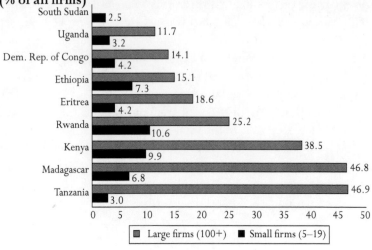

Source: World Bank Enterprise Surveys (2021).

of work is now outsourced to smaller companies, at the heart of these production networks are multinational corporations. According to a McKinsey analysis, 88 large multinationals operating in Africa have already built pan-African businesses with operations in more than 10 countries. Nearly a third of them are present in more than 20 countries, and on average the firms with the widest footprint have the largest revenues. For these multinationals, drawing a pan-African map has typically been a decades-long undertaking.[12] This is why having these firms on board in terms of implementing the AfCFTA is so crucial for its effectiveness.

The fundamental role of cross-border investment in regional integration

Foreign direct investment and its corollary—the activities of multinational firms—have an essential role to play in bringing about regional integration. Multinational firms are, by nature, integrators of cross-border trade in goods and services. It is estimated that up to 80% of global trade relates to transactions by multinational firms, and of these totals, half are intra-firm transactions (i.e. within affiliates and the parent of the same company).[13] They are, in effect, the hand-maidens of trade.

Multinationals account for about two thirds of global exports and are overrepresented in sectors where 'intangible assets'—such as patents, brands, trademarks or copyright—are the most relevant factor in competitiveness. For instance, they account for about 80% of exports in global innovation sectors such as automotive, pharmaceuticals and electronics, where intangibles can be deployed globally at low marginal cost (think, for instance, of developing a new drug or new smartphone technology).[14]

So how will the implementation of the AfCFTA affect cross-border investment? The answer to that question is partly contingent on how the recently negotiated Investment Protocol is rolled out. However, in theoretical terms, we can anticipate some outcomes.

Generally speaking, FDI to the African continent is dominated by two investment motivations: 'resource-seeking' and 'domestic mar-ket-seeking'.[15] The first type is easily understood in the context of an Africa rich in resources. The second type of investment has as its strategic objective the tapping into of the domestic market of the host economy. Market-seeking investment is often seen by economists as a substitute for trade; that is, instead of serving a particular market through exports, a company chooses to make an investment in the host economy and produce and sell the goods or services directly to customers. When tariff or other trade barriers are high, there is thus an incentive for firms to serve the markets directly through FDI; this is known in the literature as 'tariff-hopping FDI'. In the relatively closed economies of the 1960s and 1970s, much of the foreign invest-ment to the African continent was of this type. Before the instigation of the European single market in the 1990s, it was also a prominent feature of much FDI into Europe by American and Japanese firms.[16]

There is a third type of motivation however, and that is called 'efficiency-seeking' investment. This is where companies seek to take advantage of local factors like competitive labour costs or favourable tax regimes for the production of more complex goods or services, and invest in a particular location for the sole purpose of producing their goods or services most efficiently. This kind of firm is not investing because of local market conditions, but rather looking purely at the supply-side attractiveness of the location, with an eye to selling their goods or services on regional or global markets. This is the type of investment that is typically associated with the emergence of value chains, although, as discussed in Chapter 7, the continent is often marginalised from global value chains (with the one important proviso of being the ultimate supplier of the raw materials at the base of many sophisticated value chains, such as the cobalt and coltan which come from the DRC and are essential components in mobile telephones).

From the above discussion, we can make a number of conjectures about how the AfCFTA will change volume and geographic dispersion of FDI on the African continent. Firstly, a number of studies have confirmed that forming a regional bloc like the AfCFTA can have a negative effect on market-seeking FDI among countries party to the agreement.[17] That said, it seems reasonable to suppose that countries with low initial trade restrictions are less likely to host market-seeking FDI projects that might subsequently be withdrawn as trade barriers are reduced under the AfCFTA.[18] Secondly, the AfCFTA will facilitate the separation of activities spatially across countries in order to reduce costs. This may result in plants becoming specialised, and component specialisation or assembly operations being more widely dispersed amongst member countries. In other words, in principle it would raise the attractiveness of the continent to efficiency-seeking investment and facilitate the emergence of both regional value chains and the entry of more companies into global value chains.

Thirdly, resource-seeking FDI both from the continent and outside will continue—the scarcity of alternative sources of supply for mineral and energy products guarantees that. But as new investment flows towards the manufacturing and service industries in reaction to the opportunities opened up by the AfCFTA, the share of resource-seeking FDI in continental investment should decline over time. Finally, there is likely to be a differential impact between African-based firms and firms outside the continent. As we shall explain shortly, the former group will have some strategic advantages over the 'outsiders' because of their deeper knowledge of the African market. The latter must make the strategic choice between serving the

African market through exports or decide that the elimination of tariff barriers under the AfCFTA is sufficient to persuade them to convert themselves into 'insiders'.

This then is the theory. What about in practice? What does the existing body of research show?

Existing empirical studies into FDI, trade and regional integration

Both simulation work and econometric studies confirm the major role that FDI and multinationals play in promoting exports on the African continent, with one recent paper suggesting that, in the absence of FDI, exports for some African countries would decline very significantly—by as much as 40% or more.[19] Further confirmation is found in a paper by Mijiyawa that uses panel data for 53 African countries over the period 1970–2009 to estimate the effect of FDI inflows on the export of goods and services.[20] His results confirm that FDI has a positive and significant effect on exports (although we should stress that given the strong link between FDI and the extractive sector exports, such findings are not surprising).

We also know from the literature that the formation of regional blocs like the AfCFTA tends to boost FDI. Studies have found positive effects for specific agreements such as NAFTA,[21] the EU SMP,[22] and the China–ASEAN agreement.[23] In one recent study, Kox and Rojas-Romagosa[24] use a structural gravity model analysis to measure the effects of international agreements on bilateral FDI stocks and flows, finding that membership of a preferential trade agreement increases bilateral FDI stocks by about 30% on average.[25]

To date, as far as we are aware there are only two published empirical studies on the impact of the AfCFTA on FDI.[26] The first of these uses a gravity model approach to compare current greenfield FDI flows in Africa in 2018 to a counterfactual in which an African free trade area is in effect. Overall, they find that trade liberalisation under the AfCFTA will increase intra-Africa FDI by 14%, although with significant differences across countries.[27] Using a similar approach but with a vastly different outcome, Echandi et al. find a much larger increase of intra-Africa FDI once the AfCFTA is implemented of between 54–68%.[28] The rise in FDI from the rest of the world is even more impressive—between 86 and 122%, suggesting a promising response by external investors to the creation of the continental market. Europe is expected to account for the lion's share (60%) of increased FDI into Africa, followed by Asia and North America.[29] Whether or not figures of such large magnitudes are tenable is an interesting question. It is worth noting that the study forms part of a wider CGE exercise into the AfCFTA which also provided some improbably large figures of impact due to the inclusion in the simulations of large trade facilitation effects and an implausible 75% reduction in NTBs (see Chapter 11).

How much cross-border investment is there already?

In Part I of this book, we discussed how Africa became marginalised from global trade. For foreign investment (in the guise of FDI), the story has regrettably been a similar one (Figure 10.2). Indeed, the trajectory of the share of global FDI follows very closely the share of global trade: namely, a sharp decline beginning in the mid-1970s which bottomed out in the late 1990s, followed by a modest but uneven recovery in the 2000s. Clearly, Africa is just as marginalised as a destination for investment as it is in trade.[30]

Figure 10.2: Inward FDI inflows to Africa (1970–2021)

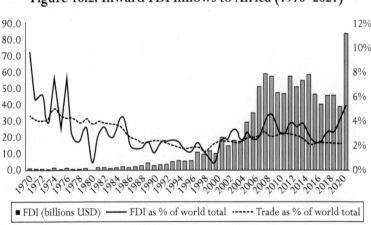

Sources: Calculated from UNCTADStat (2023); IMF DOTS (2023).

Figure 10.3: Shares of total outward FDI stock from Africa (2021)

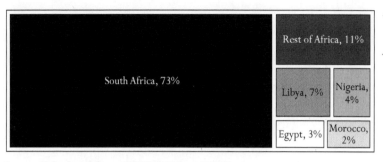

Source: Calculated from UNCTADStat (2023).

In terms of outward investment (i.e. where African firms are engaged in cross-border investment outside their country of origin), just five countries are responsible for 90% of the outward investment from Africa. One country in particular stands out—South Africa, accounting for nearly three quarters of the total (Figure 10.3). According to IMF data, South Africa had a stock of USD 33 billion in the rest of the continent in 2018, which implies that, of its total outward FDI stock of USD 246 billion in that same year, just 13% was destined for the African continent.[31] Again, this is where the AfCFTA should help improve the attractiveness of intra-African investment and encourage more South African firms to invest on the continent.

One complication with gauging how much African firms are currently engaged in outward investment is that Mauritius, as an offshore financial centre, distorts the true level of intra-African FDI. It may surprise people to learn, for instance, that in countries like Kenya and Rwanda, Mauritius is consistently one of the leading sources of FDI. But in reality, this is often investment from European, US or Asian firms simply taking advantage of the negligible tax liabilities of investing through Mauritius. For instance, a company like the Dutch alcoholic beverage company Heineken has extensive operations across the continent,[32] but that is usually all channelled through Mauritius. Thus, adjustments need to be made to the statistics: according to estimates by the World Bank, while the total inward FDI stock for the continent was valued at approximately USD 800 billion in 2018, as much as USD 300 billion could be attributed to FDI from Mauritius.

Discounting that amount, the World Bank's estimate was about USD 500 billion in 2018, or around 22% of continental GDP.[33]

What do we know specifically about the levels of intra-African investment? Theoretically, low intra-regional flows are to be expected to some extent—within Dunning's seminal framework, which provides a theoretical explanation of cross-border direct investment flows, low investments in firm-specific assets (as reflected in extremely low investments in R&D) do not translate into strong ownership advantages[34]—a necessary precondition for any FDI to take place. Put simply, prevailing productivity levels in Africa, as reflected in low per capita incomes, do not lend themselves to the development of ownership advantages, which are crucial to giving foreign firms a competitive edge; hence the capacity for regional firms to undertake FDI is relatively limited. That is reflected by the fact that, while Africa's share of global inward FDI stock is just 2.3%, its outward share is as low as 0.7%.[35]

Nonetheless, intra-Africa FDI—direct investment by firms in Africa into other countries in the region—has been increasing

Figure 10.4: Intra-African FDI stock: countries with more than USD 1 billion (2018)*

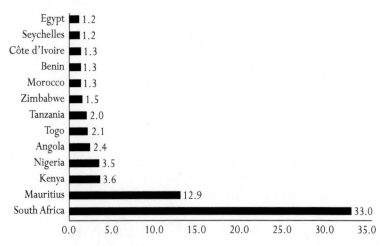

Source: IMF (2021b). * Only countries with an estimated outward FDI stock in excess of USD 1 billion.

steadily. By 2017, the stock of intra-Africa FDI hit an estimated high of USD 52 billion, or 11% of the region's total FDI stock. Southern Africa dominated, because of specifically South Africa, which is the main source of intra-Africa FDI, making up 60 to 70% of intra-Africa FDI stock in most years (Figure 10.4). But West Africa has recently emerged as another important source. Investment from Northern Africa has also increased in recent years, from less than 1% of Africa's FDI stock in 2002 to almost 6% in 2018. For individual African economies, intra-African investment takes on a particular importance. With the exception of South Africa, this is particularly the case of the regional 'anchor' economies (e.g. Nigeria, Kenya, Egypt, Morocco). For instance, in East Africa, Kenya invests over 90% of its outward investment flows on the continent. In the case of Nigeria, two thirds of all its outward investment is towards the rest of Africa.[36]

The incentives to greater intra-African investment

Since 2003, South–South FDI—that is, investment between developing countries—has been growing faster than North–South FDI, accounting for more than half of total FDI in some of the poorest countries.[37] Research suggests that South–South flows can bring more benefits than North–South ones to recipient countries. The scale of the 'technology gap' with South–South flows is often much smaller, implying a greater capacity of recipient countries to absorb these technologies. There is also some evidence that South–South FDI is superior with respect to the potential for upgrading exports into higher value-added goods and services. Notably, the positive marginal effect of additional investment is stronger in low-tech industries such as the processing of agricultural products or the textiles and apparel sector.[38] According to the research, efficiency-enhancing investment is a dominant motivation for South–South FDI which, as noted above, bodes well for assisting in raising productivity and creating regional value-chains.[39]

Some of these arguments apply equally to intra-African FDI. More intra-African investment under the AfCFTA could be beneficial from a number of other perspectives.

- *Better knowledge of regional markets:* Investors from the continent are likely to have a more intimate knowledge of regional markets and are more capable of navigating the cultural factors that can sometimes impede foreign investment from further afield. In other words, there is a greater cultural affinity which facilitates cross-border business.[40]
- *Greater employment-creating potential:* There is some evidence that intra-African FDI creates both more employment opportunities and greater technological transfer than extra-African FDI.[41]
- *Spur to economic diversification:* Much of the FDI received by the region from outside the continent has been in the natural resource sector. Intra-regional FDI, by contrast, has a more diverse portfolio.[42] Greater intra-African FDI could thus contribute very positively to the sectoral diversification of regional economies.
- *Scaling up:* As noted in Chapter 9, despite some notable corporate success stories, Africa lags behind other emerging regions in hosting large companies.[43] Outside South Africa, Africa's firms earn less than half the revenue of their emerging market peers as a proportion of GDP. No African company was featured in the 2022 Global Fortune 500.[44] Greater intra-African FDI could help consolidate existing businesses and scale up their activities.

This is where the implementation of the AfCFTA could have a decisive impact by encouraging greater intra-African investment. The Investment Protocol was approved by the AU Assembly in January 2023, and provides a number of incentives propitious to greater intra-African FDI, including guaranteeing national treatment to investors from other African countries.

It also promises to phase out by 2028 the extremely complex web of more than 170 intra-African investment treaties among African member states—and instead provide a more homogeneous treatment of FDI at the continental level. If it is effectively implemented, the Protocol could give a significant boost to regional FDI in manufacturing and services sectors, such as tourism, finance, communication, transport and retail.

One final point to stress is that, despite its low share of global FDI inflows, Africa is commonly considered one of the most attractive destinations in the world for investment capital.[45] Although global profitability of FDI appears to be falling,[46] there is an abundance of opportunities for achieving high rates of return on the continent. Average firm profitability in African countries is significantly higher (10–20%) compared to other emerging market and developing economies. Firm markups are also about 11% higher relative to other countries at a similar level of development, thereby implying a lower degree of competition in the region.[47] Some sectors, like banking or alcoholic beverages, are spectacularly profitable. From a social point of view, of course, such outcomes are highly undesirable—but this is where, by inducing greater investment, the AfCFTA can contribute to turning things round, improve the competitive environment and help drive prices down. According to van Beemen:

> There is so little competition that in a lot of [African] countries, one small bottle of beer is no cheaper—or even more expensive—than in Europe, while production costs are lower. Beer in Africa is almost 50% more profitable than anywhere else. Some markets, like Nigeria, are among the most lucrative in the world.[48]

To corroborate these observations, it is useful to analyse the list of top 250 companies in Africa, published each year by the magazine *African Business*. The survey focuses on companies which derive at least half their revenues on the continent, and which are accessible to African investors because they are listed on an African stock exchange. They are ranked by market capitalisation, and data are provided on both revenues and net income. This allows us to compute proximate measures of 'profitability' (expressed as net income as a share of total revenues).

The calculations confirm the narrative of major opportunities on the African continent, with an average level of profitability that is comparable with, for instance, US or UK markets.[49] Non-energy materials include mining but also highly profitable firms in the cement sector (e.g. the Nigerian companies BUA Cement and Dangote Cement, Ciments du Maroc, Tanzania Portland Cement, etc.) and fertilisers (e.g. the Egyptian firms Misr Fertilizers Production Company and Abu Qir Fertilizers and Chemicals). Remarkably, the financial sector accounts for nearly one third of total market capitalisation for the 250

Figure 10.5: Imputed profitability of the largest 165 African companies

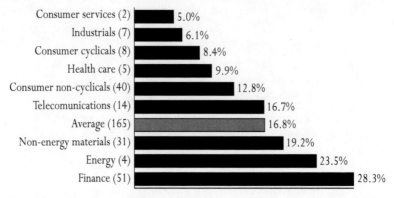

Note: The number of companies in each sector is given in parenthesis. Imputed profitability is calculated as the most recent reported income as a share of revenue for the 165 companies where both revenue and income data are provided.

Source: Authors' elaboration from African Business (2023).

companies. But telecoms, utilities and consumer goods industries also show very high rates of return on investment.

Lots of analysts qualify such figures by talking of the 'risk-premium' of investing on the continent. But this is often misjudged. Most African analysts share the opinion that the risks are exaggerated, and that there are many lucrative opportunities for investing on the continent. Moreover, notwithstanding the spate of military coups that occurred in 2023, perceptions of political risks in Africa have generally improved over the past decade among investors. According to one private consulting firm, 'African countries are now more stable and predictable places to live, work and build businesses'.[50]

Some anecdotal examples of intra-African investment

A number of the larger African players are already heavily investing in the rest of the continent. In the retail sector, for instance, South African supermarket chains have spread over Southern, East and West Africa. Four supermarket chains (Shoprite, Pick n Pay, Spar, Massmart) had 554 stores outside of South Africa by 2016. Their stores are still mainly supplied with products from South Africa, although local supply is steadily increasing. Some regional governments are pressurising the supermarket giants to expand domestic supply from local firms and farms. The expansion of these supermarket chains into the rest of Africa also creates the potential for regional supplier upgrading.[51]

Another example of a firm with a continental reach is the South African telecommunications giant MTN Group. By market capitalisation, it was the fourth-largest firm on the continent in 2022, after more than doubling its market capitalisation to USD 24.5 billion, up from USD 11.1 billion in 2021. The company raised finance by listing its operations in Nigeria, Ghana, Uganda, Rwanda and other countries, ploughing its investment into new networks, infrastructure and data centres. Pointedly, MTN Nigeria, Scancom (MTN Ghana) and MTN Uganda are all much more profitable than the parent operation in South Africa. The company's pan-continental vocation stems back to the late 1990s and early 2000s, when it was well placed to take advantage of a process of competitive liberalisation of the telecommunications sector throughout much of the continent that one author has described as the 'golden age of deregulation in sub-Saharan Africa'.[52]

At the other extreme of the continent, in North Africa, it seems reasonable to assume that deeper integration under the AfCFTA via the trade route is more challenging; the distances are enormous, and most trade must be conducted either via sea or air routes. Thus, for economic integration to take place between sub-Saharan and North Africa will tend to be more contingent on cross-border investment. There is evidence to show that is already happening. In 2017, for instance, it was estimated that Moroccan investment in Africa was USD 4.75 billion, up from USD 3.4 billion in 2016.[53] The African Development Bank estimated in 2016 that as much as 85% of Morocco's investment in that year was destined for the continent.[54] Its portfolio of investments is wide-ranging, in sectors including phosphates, banking, construction, telecoms and consumer goods such as home-grown textiles.[55]

An example of the dynamism of intra-African FDI in the services sector is the Moroccan-based company Saham Assurance's rapid growth from a small local firm into a leading African insurance company operating in 23 countries across the continent. Between 2005 and 2015, it increased its sales nearly tenfold to over USD 1 billion. The company had embarked on a bold strategy of buying stakes in existing insurance firms, overhauling the management and rapidly growing their sales. In East Africa, the company has already invested in Kenya, Rwanda and Madagascar.[56] Other Moroccan firms are investing heavily in Ethiopia, and there are plans for constructing a gas pipeline from Nigeria to Morocco.

Another example of an industry which is rapidly becoming Pan-African, again linked with Morocco, is fertiliser giant OCP. Morocco has 75% of global reserves of phosphate, and OCP is making investments in 16 African countries, including Nigeria, Ethiopia, and Rwanda, and has 12 subsidiaries.[57] The continent is endowed with sufficient resources to become both self-sufficient and a net exporting region for fertiliser. There is enormous potential for future fertiliser demand as a result of projected population growth and the need for food security.[58] As a case in point, under a partnership between Togo and the Nigerian Dangote Group, Togo processes phosphate before export to Nigeria (rather than exporting it in raw form). The output then becomes an input to the production of fertiliser in Nigeria, which would be both supplied to the domestic market and exported to the rest of the continental market.

One sector where the economic benefits from intra-African FDI have arguably been more questionable is cross-border banking. Research by Acha Leke et al. suggests that broad-based regional expansion has not always resulted in better performance in the banking sector. On average, banks with significant regional or Pan-African footprints have underperformed the 'national champions' focused on their home markets.[59] More thought is required on how to tackle the problems associated with the financial sector, for without this it will be difficult to foresee how the private sector will have the ability to respond to the opportunities presented by the AfCFTA. More will be said on this in Chapter 14.

A clear role for investors from outside the continent

Traditionally, there has been a lot of hostility towards foreign investment on the African continent. It is inevitably (and understandably) associated with the period of colonial exploitation.[60] However, at least among policymakers, attitudes have changed, and most countries now have policies in place to attract greater FDI.[61] Yet, as the example above of Pan-African banking suggests, FDI is certainly no magic bullet. Indeed, if you read the research carefully, there is a realisation that the benefits from FDI—technology transfer, more capital investment, employment creation and positive spill-overs onto the rest of the economy—are far from automatic and highly contingent on a host of pre-conditions (Box 10.1). Reaping benefits from the presence of FDI requires a strong institutional framework, good negotiating skills and a strategic approach to using foreign investment in a way that furthers the goals of the host country. Likewise, as the late Professor Raymond Vernon (one of the most astute observers of the strategies of multinational firms) once noted, there is an intrinsic conflict of interest between the multinational entity that wants to integrate its operations across borders, and the host country which wishes to have as much economic activity as possible to take place within its national boundaries.[62] Moreover, it is a power balance which has shifted in favour of the multinational corporations in recent decades; this is due in part to the rise of global value chains and the much wider options that multinational corporations have in terms of where to place their investments.[63]

Box 10.1: The ambiguous evidence on the impact of FDI and economic development

Based on a well-cited literature review, Elizabeth Asiedu[64] concluded that FDI in Africa had the following effects: (i) it had a (direct and an indirect) positive impact on domestic employment; (ii) it boosted wages; (iii) it fostered the transfer of technology; and (iv) it enhanced the productivity of the labour force. Was this the final word? No. The evidence is actually much more ambiguous.[65] Part of this reflects the sectoral distribution of FDI on the African continent—the excessive concentration on mining and oil sectors by external investors has led to numerous cases where there were 'enclaves' of FDI, with few or no linkages to the local economy. More broadly, however, studies that focus on FDI spill-overs in developing countries have often reported an insignificant or negative effect of FDI on productivity in host countries.[66] The studies that do tend to find positive effects are mostly focused on developed economies and high-technology industries.[67] Nor does it appear that there is any guarantee that greater FDI inflows will lead to a net addition to the capital stock, with one study finding that there was a significant 'crowding out' effect on domestic investment by FDI in Africa over the course of the 1990s.[68] Moreover, FDI almost inevitably has a long-term negative impact on the current account, as profit repatriation exceeds the size of the original investment, with investors understandably seeking to derive income from their investments.[69] Some studies suggest that any positive effects are contingent on a country reaching a certain level of economic development. For the poorest countries, this implies that there are few positive impacts from FDI.[70] Finally, as part of a coherent development strategy, it should be remembered that FDI is not the only option. For instance, policymakers in some East Asian countries consciously chose to tap foreign capital in ways other than FDI, drawing instead on a combination of debt financing, the building up of domestic companies, and various forms of technology transfer.[71]

That said, a cogent argument can still be made that FDI from outside the continent can have an extremely important role to play in constructing the continental market under the AfCFTA.

One common concern is that it will not be African firms that are the principal beneficiaries from AfCFTA, but companies from outside. While it is clearly important that African firms fully take advantage of the new opportunities arising of the the the AfCFTA—a sentiment reflected in projects like the AfroChampions Initiative[72]—the potential contribution of multinationals from outside Africa should not be gainsaid. For instance, in the construction of the European single market in the 1980s and 1990s, Mold shows how American firms integrated their activities between their different subsidiaries well in advance of the implementation of the EU SMP.[73] As far back as the late 1950s, American firms like Ford, IBM and Proctor & Gamble were already integrating their European operations by specialising activities in particular locations and by promoting intra-firm trade to a far greater extent than their European competitors.[74] As 'outsiders', they showed no allegiance to a particular geographic pattern of investment, but rather rationalised and integrated their activities on purely economic criteria, helping raise the levels of both intra-regional trade and investment. Crucially, the 'demonstration effect' paved the way for European companies to adopt similar strategies and, in the process, become more efficient and competitive on the global stage. There is no reason why a similar outcome cannot occur in Africa, with well-established firms from Europe, North America or China leading the way in terms of boldly integrating their cross-border operations and activities on the continent.

Getting foreign firms to treat Africa as a single market is a key challenge for the AfCFTA. Data available for US multinationals suggests that on average they still treat the African market as a fragmented one, with just 17% of sales being made on the continent to other African countries.[75] And yet, there are plenty of anecdotal examples of multinationals wanting to integrate their continental operations. More than 35 of the 50 largest packaged goods producers in the world are already tapping into Africa's rapidly growing consumer market. Of these corporations, one in three generates more than 5% of its global sales on the continent (and that figure is as high as 14% for Diageo and 10% for

Figure 10.6: US multinational sales by affiliates to countries other than host country (2019)*

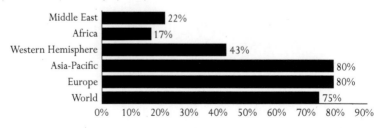

* Data are given as proportion of regions' third-country sales that are intra-regional.

Source: Davies and Markusen (2020).

Parmalat, for example)—evidence once again of the lucrative nature of segments of the African market.[76]

The automobile industry is a clear case of a sector that would dearly like to integrate its operations across the continent, but it is wary of doing so because it wants to see the continental market become a reality first. After Volkswagen established a car manufacturing plant in Rwanda, Peugeot and Opel established a plant to assemble up to 5,000 cars per year in Namibia.[77] Ghana too has attracted car-assembly plants from Nissan and Volkswagen. Ford SA has announced large investments in the rest of Southern Africa. Morocco has been extremely successful in developing its car industry, surpassing South Africa in terms of export values (worth USD 10 billion in 2019). And while the bulk of its exports (around 80%) is oriented towards Europe, it is increasingly selling cars to its domestic and regional markets, and has an eye on the West African market.[78]

Conclusions

This chapter began by highlighting the complementarities between FDI and trade. African firms need to be encouraged to spread their wings and make more investments in regional markets. The banking sector has managed to do it—and so too have other service-based sectors such as the hotel industry or the telecommunications sector. Although it is always possible to name exceptions, such as the breweries, what is lacking is the same Pan-African vigour from the manufacturing sectors. Africa's share of global outward FDI is currently low and reflects the weak firm-specific advantages that will differentiate African products from those imported from outside.

The chapter has also stressed that external investors have an important role to play in creating the continental market. It is what happened in Europe with regard to US and Japanese firms, and it is what can be expected to play out on the African continent. Guiding FDI towards industrial exports, the development of technological and marketing capabilities, and increasing local content continues to be a key challenge.[79] Under the Investment Protocol, we argue that there should be a preference for attracting greater intra-African investment. For one thing, the repatriated profits from such undertakings will remain on the continent. But it is also the way to drive the rapid growth of intra-continental trade.

Calls to provide the right environment for the emergence of more Pan-African businesses are not new. Professor Adedeji reminded people frequently that one of the commitments of the Lagos Plan of Action was 'the establishment of African multinational corporations and joint ventures as instruments of directed procurement, production, marketing, shipping and civil aviation, banking and insurance, consultancy and other critical services'.[80]

Finally, in much of the discussion on the importance of structural diversification in Africa, excessive focus is arguably placed on the role of external actors and SMEs, at the expense of attention to larger domestic and regional firms. The neglect of domestic diversified business groups (DBGs)[81] in policy circles is of particular concern because the interests of these firms are usually more closely aligned with the broader health of their host economies, rather than narrow sectoral interests. This failure is, as stressed by Behuria, a considerable oversight, since many of the largest African DBGs have grown through responding to domestic and regional demand within their country.[82] Against a backdrop of the urgency of implementing the AfCFTA, it is a neglect that needs redressing.

11

WHAT THE STUDIES SAY ON THE AFCFTA'S IMPACT—AND HOW TO INTERPRET THEM

Introduction

One of the main jobs of the professional economist is to quantify things. Policymakers and the general public often wish to know what the economic consequences will be of a certain policy if it is implemented.

For the AfCFTA in particular, there is a huge demand for quantifying the impact of the Agreement, explaining which sectors will benefit the most, what the costs of implementation may be (for instance, in terms of the amount of tariff revenue foregone), and which countries will gain the most (as well as which might not benefit as much). This is true of all trade agreements—for example, in the 1990s, the creation of NAFTA led to an enormous outpouring of studies by North American economists trying to understand the trade and distributional consequences of the agreement.[1]

It was also the case for the EU: many impact studies were conducted in anticipation of the implementation of the EU SMP, estimating the trade and sectoral impacts of the agreement.[2] But they did not always do a very good job of this, with their forecasts often being very wide of the mark.

In the African case, many numbers are bandied around regarding the impact of the AfCFTA, but those sets of numbers are often not consistent and are contingent on a whole host of different assumptions and data availability/quality. Contrary to what a lot of economic practitioners would like to admit, however well-grounded in its theoretical foundations, such modelling is often more of an art than a science. Modelling also has a political purpose, particularly with respect to trade negotiations; obviously, it strengthens the hand of a negotiating party when they have a set of numbers of their own to put on the table.

In this chapter, then, we will take the reader through a crash course of how to contextualise the results and appreciate both their strengths and limitations. Space does not allow a fully comprehensive explanation; that would require an encyclopaedic treatment of the topic, plus a strong background in quantitative economic analysis. However, we provide some references for the interested reader to follow up on the topic. It is nonetheless important to have at least an intuitive understanding of what the studies are saying with regard to the impact of the AfCFTA, and also to be able to understand where the limitations might lie. We beg the reader's indulgence if the terminology becomes rather jargon-laden.

The chapter critically reviews the quantitative studies estimating the benefits arising from implementation of the AfCFTA. We arrive at an agnostic conclusion with regard to the results of these studies. Alongside Rodrik, Banjeree and Duflo,[3] Mkandawire and Adedeji, we believe that many trade economists are guilty of overstating their case and often are not transparent about either the limitations of their calculations or the extent to which their results are subject to a whole range of caveats.[4] Nonetheless, despite these problems, we do have ample post-hoc evidence—which is often much more reliable—on the impact of other comparable regional schemes. We should rely much more on this kind of evidence as we develop our narratives on the benefits on the AfCFTA.

Ex-post econometric versus ex-ante simulation models

There are a number of methodologies for measuring the impact of forming a regional bloc like the AfCFTA, including *ex-post* econometric estimation (e.g. the gravity model) and *ex-ante* simulation models (either partial or general equilibrium approaches). *Ex-post* approaches use econometrics and historical data to conduct an analysis of the effects of past trade policy, under the supposition that useful lessons can be drawn for new policy initiatives like the AfCFTA, whereas *ex-ante* simulation involves simulating the effects of an antici-pated trade policy change (say, an elimination of tariffs on intra-African trade) onto a set of economic variables of interest. The results of trade policy analysis can, therefore, vary depending on the choice of model, the structure of the model and data.[5]

Most of the quantitative analyses of regional integration are carried out in the context of the Vinerian concept of net-trade creation. This stems from the premise that to measure the welfare impact of a regional agreement, it is first necessary to calculate if more trade is created between partner countries than the trade diverted away from third-party countries. Whether this is the best way to measure the benefits is contested in the literature. As far back as 1955, the Nobel Prize-winning economist James Meade noted that aggregate trade creation and trade diversion were insufficient to infer the welfare effects of a regional or preferential trade agreement.[6] In reality, it is necessary to compute the amount of trade creation and trade diver-sion by sector rather than in aggregate for the whole economy (as is the standard practice), and to then use the information on the sec-toral decline in import prices and the height of remaining trade bar-riers to evaluate the net benefits/costs. Yet the detail of information required for such calculations is too demanding for them to be car-ried out in practice.[7]

From a technical perspective, three broad approaches are usually used to model the economic impacts of regional trade agreements (RTAs):

- **Gravity econometric estimation models** are used for *ex-post* assessment of trade policy and are helpful for understanding both the drivers of trade and for assessing the effects of certain trade policies, such as membership of a regional bloc. They do so by 'explaining trade' as a function of some key variables such as dis-tance between markets, income per capita and the size of the respective economies. It is an approach which has been widely used, but whose theoretical underpinnings are actually quite weak, appealing as it does to Newtonian ideas of 'gravity'. Unlike CGE models, they are not usually used to predict the direct impact of forming a regional bloc, but they can provide useful evidence to gauge the potential trade effects.

- **Partial Equilibrium (PE) and Computable General Equilibrium (CGE)** are widely used in the *ex-ante* assessment of the future effect of trade policies. They involve computer-based simulations, which compute how the economy will look in the future as a consequence of a specified policy change. The choice between the two approaches depends on a number of factors. PE models are largely driven by the data that they are based on and only a relatively limited number of equations are considered in the simulations.[8] The PE models give the magnitude of the direct effects of the trade policy change, but assuming all other things remain unchanged or constant (the *ceteris paribus* condition), whereas CGE models take into account second-round effects such as inter-industry effects through changes in relative prices and corresponding macroeconomic adjustments. Under the CGE, a differentiation can be made between single- and multi-country models and between static and dynamic models (the latter being critical to capture the transition and its potential costs and benefits). In practical terms, the data requirements for PE are less demanding than for the CGE. This allows for greater precision in identifying key products and trading partners affected by a particular policy of trade liberalisation, but at the price of disregarding broader economic effects.[9]

Because of increasing computer capabilities, and also the stellar work of research groups like Purdue University's GTAP, and CEPII in Paris, which have painstakingly built up global databases, CGE modelling has become an increasingly popular tool for evaluating the impacts of trade reform. However, because the framework tends to be over the long term (which often abstracts from short-run realities of structural rigidities in developing countries, such as the inability to rapidly redeploy workers from one sector to another), some scholars (e.g. De Maio et al.;[10] Charlton and Stiglitz[11]) have argued that they are inappropriate for analysing the problems of the typical developing country. Despite the wealth of results that they provide, CGE models also rely on a large number of theoretical assumptions and have received considerable criticism—sometimes from unexpected quarters.[12] According to Panagariya:

> It is relatively easy to manipulate the structure of the model, functional forms and parameter values in these models to obtain one's desired results ... [for example] most modelers rely on the so-called Armington assumption according to which goods are assumed differentiated by the country of origin [and] the assumption plays a key role in determining the outcome .... It is [also] not uncommon to use Stone-Geary utility function or the linear expenditure system to represent demand. This greatly limits the possibilities of substitution. For instance, it can be shown that if the partner's product shows a high degree of substitutability with that of the outside country but low substitutability with the product of the home country ... an FTA is likely to be harmful.[13]

Another major drawback from the perspective of analysing African economic integration is that product categories for which there are initially no bilateral trade flows cannot be projected to become non-zero after the introduction of zero tariffs.[14] Given the limited number of products exported by the average African country, with a high concentration of total exports in commodities, it means, in effect, that CGE and PE modelling is a poor predictor of where countries are able to move into the export of new products. In other words, these methodologies are likely to significantly underestimate the emergence of trade in new sectors where there was none previously. In sum, although they can be 'tweaked' to reflect certain market characteristics, CGE models are not so good at capturing accurately the dynamic effects such as exploiting economies of scale, the gains from heightened competition, increased innovation, and the potential for more diversified economic activities.[15]

Beyond these limitations, and despite their apparent sophistication, there are some simple rules of thumb which help anticipate the results from both CGE and PE analysis. For the AfCFTA, the largest gains are likely to accrue to countries that:

• have initial import tariffs that are higher than in other countries (the trade effect being proportional to the scale of the tariff reductions);

- face higher initial export barriers in their trade with the rest of the continent (thus benefiting more from the enhanced market access under the AfCFTA); and
- already have relatively strong initial trade ties with other African countries, thereby minimising trade diversion with third parties.[16]

In any case, the more prudent modellers make it clear that these methodologies should only be used to give a sense of the order of magnitude that a change in policy can mean for economic welfare or trade, rather than pretend that they provide precise estimates.[17] Let us now turn to a summary of the results of some major studies using the different approaches.

Econometric studies measuring benefits from existing regional integration agreements

Until recently a lot of published research found that RTAs between developing countries (South–South agreements) had had a small or negligible impact on trade flows.[18] Partly as a consequence of such studies, pessimism on the prospects for African trade integration became commonplace. However, due to a series of methodological and econometric errors, this earlier generation of empirical studies did not always provide credible estimates.[19] More reliable statistical methods have since become available. In particular, a new econometric technique, using the improbably named Poisson Pseudo-Maximum-Likelihood (PPML) estimator[20] has become the workhorse of trade economists in modelling RTAs.

What has this new generation of studies revealed? Put simply, studies that use the PPML tend to produce results much more favourable to South–South regional integration. For instance, using data from 1981–2008, Macphee and Sattyanwat studied the impact of 12 different RTAs from various regions of Asia, Africa and the Americas on trade creation and trade diversion.[21] Of the three African RTAs included in the study (ECCAS, EAC and SADC), only ECCAS failed to have a net positive impact on trade creation.[22] Intra-SADC trade was estimated to have increased by a staggering 208% due to the formation of the RTA. Deme and Ndrianasy find that economic integration is welfare-improving and has a particularly robust trade-creation effect for the ECOWAS region, despite being economies with a low initial share of trade between each other.[23] Afesorgbor carried out a careful meta-analysis combining 14 previous studies covering the period from 1980–2006; and found that, on average, the formation of African regional blocs boosted bilateral trade by about 27–32%.[24]

Finally, based on a gravity model with bilateral goods trade data at the 1-digit industry level, a study by the IMF of the potential benefits stemming from the AfCFTA finds that intra-African trade would increase by about 16% (or USD 16 billion) with the elimination of tariffs on 90% of existing intra-regional trade flows.[25] Despite the relatively modest trade impact, the authors argue that improving trade logistics and addressing poor infrastructure could be up to four times more effective in boosting trade than tariff reductions alone. They also stress the importance of complementary policies to address non-tariff bottlenecks.[26]

Partial equilibrium studies

Although they are generally a less preferred option (now that increased computing power has facilitated the use of more complex CGE modelling),[27] in the past, PE models were extensively used in studies assessing the impact of the trade agreements on African economies.[28] A more recent example is an impact study on the AfCFTA conducted for COMESA.[29] That paper concluded that liberalising 90% of tariff lines under the AfCFTA would result in trade creation of about USD 521 million for COMESA countries, with a further USD 140 million being diverted away from the regional bloc. The authors calculate that about USD 319 million would be lost in tariff revenue. These magnitudes are not very impressive when bearing in mind that, according to the same study, intra-COMESA trade was worth USD 10.3 billion and total exports from COMESA member states were valued at USD 113.5 billion in 2018.

Another study undertaken by ECA/TMEA compares PE with CGE simulations on AfCFTA implementation for East African countries.[30] Like the study done on COMESA, the partial equilibrium simulations used the WITS-SMART model,[31] but in this case assuming full liberalisation of the tariffs on trade in goods.[32] Their results estimate that East Africa's intra-African trade would increase by around USD 737 million, translating into a 13% increase when compared to the exports of the base year. Although all countries in the region stand to benefit from the expansion of trade following the removal of the tariff barriers, the largest increases (in absolute amounts) in the value of exports accrue to Uganda, Kenya and Tanzania. In contrast, for some countries in the region, the changes in exports are quite trivial, but this partially reflects low levels of existing intra-African trade and, for the smaller countries, very low absolute values too. The increase in intra-African trade was most pronounced in the manufacturing sector, accounting for almost 40% (USD 235 million) of the total increase in the intra-African exports, followed by the agricultural sector (food and live animals) at 28% (USD 176 million).

CGE models—the current 'gold standard' of modelling

Over recent decades, CGE models have become the go-to tool for trade economists in terms of measuring the impact of trade agreements on signatory countries. Nonetheless, there are some a priori reasons why we should not expect large gains from simulations that restrict themselves to tariff liberalisation alone. As noted by Fosu and Mold, because of the strong trend towards preference erosion (see Chapter 7), simulations of trade liberalisation have tended to show a secular decline in the magnitudes of benefits.[33] A further consideration is that, contrary to popular opinion, average applied tariffs within Africa are already relatively low. In 2016, the simple average tariff on merchandise trade from Africa was just 5% while the MFN average tariff was 12.5%.[34] The benefits from the AfCFTA in the studies are further diminished because of the complex web of existing agreements produced by the overlapping membership of regional economic communities. In fact, the extent to which further tariff reductions under the AfCFTA are likely to produce welfare benefits is inversely proportional to the amount of intra-REC tariff liberalisation that has already taken place (Table 11.1).

Table 11.1: Applied tariffs (2016)

	Intra-regional	Effectively Applied	Most Favoured Nation (MFN)
Africa	**5.0**	**11.8**	**12.5**
AU-recognised regional economic communities			
AMU	5.0	8.9	14.0
COMESA	5.0	8.9	11.0
CEN-SAD	12.0	12.1	13.1
EAC	0.0	11.6	12.8
ECCAS	9.0	14.4	14.6
ECOWAS	11.0	12.4	12.2
SADC	4.0	7.7	9.2
IGAD	9.0	13.5	16.1
Other preferential trade agreements			
CEMAC	0.0	18.5	17.8
WAEMU	9.0	12.4	12.2
SACU	0.0	6.0	7.7
IOC	0.0	5.0	5.1

Data are in percentages.

* AHS, effectively applied tariff (simple average), MFN, most favoured nation-tariff (simple average). For IGAD the entries for AHS and MFN are 2016 for Kenya and Uganda, 2015 for Ethiopia and 2013 for Sudan.

Source: Abrego et al. (2019).

This means that, in effect, the AfCFTA only 'fills in the gaps' in the existing regional architecture. Thus, for instance, the EAC has already eliminated tariff barriers on intra-regional trade (although NTBs remain a significant challenge). As a consequence, if a model simulation removes all tariffs on intra-African trade, the results may be negligible for the groups of countries which have already removed their tariffs. That rule of thumb can sometimes be misleading, however. For example, membership of COMESA, which overlaps with several RECs in Southern, Central and East Africa, does not automatically imply that they are implementing the COMESA tariff reductions. As of August 2022, a number of countries (among them DRC and Ethiopia) were only applying the tariff reductions in part.

In principle, and to reiterate the point made above, the strength of the initial trade ties with other African countries matters: an economy that already trades considerably with other African countries (e.g. Namibia, Uganda) would be able to expand its market opportunities more easily than one that does not have extensive intra-African trade ties (e.g. Comoros, Liberia). In addition, as trade theory predicts, smaller countries tend to benefit more from positive changes in the terms of trade (i.e. the relative price of imports as opposed to exports). In contrast, larger economies generally see their terms of trade weaken, offsetting welfare gains from improved resource allocation.[35] This is precisely one of the strengths of CGE modelling: the ability to take into account these complex second-round effects.

To illustrate the differences of approach, let's look at a recent summary of CGE studies into the impact of the AfCFTA (Table 11.2). These studies are classified into three types: (1) those that model the elimination of intra-African trade tariffs under the AfCFTA; (2) those that try to also incorporate reductions in NTBs through accompanying measures such as the provision of better infrastructure, the harmonisation of rules of origin or product standards, etc.; and (3) studies that try to model the reduction of both tariffs and NTBs as well as additional trade facilitation measures (basically, factoring in larger investments to support the growth of trade).

In practice, there are also some further distinctions to draw. Some studies only focus on merchandise trade, for which there is good—if not perfect[36]—bilateral data. Others incorporate liberalisation within services. As we noted earlier, services comprise around 20% of total African trade, so clearly the topic is important and, under the terms of the agreement, services are subject to a gradual liberalisation (starting with five out of 12 main service sectors). However, the data on intra-African service trade is far patchier than for merchandise data. More subjective still is the way to measure 'tariff liberalisation' on services when in fact the restrictions on services trade are of a different nature and are often related to the regulatory environment. Tariff equivalents are used for modelling services, but it is a brave soul that puts their hands into the fire to defend the estimates of tariff equivalents in services, given their often intangible nature.

One final distinction to draw in these studies is that some use 'static' models (i.e. reflecting a simple on/off between the period before and after AfCFTA implementation) and others are more complex 'dynamic' models, taking into account the timeframe for the implementation of the agreement, and providing results which are based on speculative future values of GDP, trade, population and production. By nature, these dynamic models must include often 'heroic' assumptions regarding future trends in these macro-indicators, and it can become difficult to comprehend the magnitudes because of the need to frame them in constant prices of a base year.

The point about limited GDP and trade effects from tariff liberalisation alone is really driven home by Table 11.2, as not a single study leads us to believe that tariff liberalisation alone will result in major welfare benefits, in aggregate, from AfCFTA implementation. Furthermore, although intra-African trade rises significantly in all but one study,[37] the aggregate trade impacts are also relatively small. Taken literally, these studies do not provide a resounding endorsement of the AfCFTA: they all forecast gains, but the magnitudes in most cases are modest in macroeconomic terms. Seen in the correct perspective, this is comprehensible; it is a 'dirty secret' of the economics profession (to use one of Paul Krugman's favourite phrases)[38] that such CGE models generally predict limited gains to African economies from further tariff liberalisation. As noted in Chapter 7, Fosu and Mold showed, for instance, that many of the easier gains from trade liberalisation had been exhausted in earlier rounds of multilateral liberalisation.[39]

Hence it is unsurprising that studies have subsequently shifted the simulations towards including reductions of NTBs. NTBs in Africa remain high and prevalent, and represent a critical obstacle to trade.

Table 11.2: Summary of selected CGE simulations into the impact of AfCFTA

Source	Scenario for tariff and/or NTB removal	GDP gain	Intra-African trade	Total exports	Total imports
Removal of tariffs on intra-AfCFTA trade					
AfDB (2019)	Removal of all tariffs on intra-AfCFTA trade	0.10% (USD 2.8[†])	14.60% (USD 10.1[†])	1.00% (USD 5.8[†])	0.90% (USD 5.8[†])
Mevel and Karingi (2012)	Removal of all tariffs on intra-AfCFTA trade by 2017 + CET	0.20%	52.3%	4.00%	–
Jensen and Sandrey (2013)	Removal of all tariffs on intra-AfCFTA trade	0.70%	4.30%	3.11%	–
Saygili et al. (2018)	Removal of all tariffs on intra-AfCFTA trade	0.97%	32.80%	2.50%	1.80%
Abrego et al. (2019)	Removal of all import tariffs	0.037–0.053%[†]	–	–	–
World Bank (2020)	Gradual removal of 97% of tariffs on intra-AfCFTA trade	0.13% (USD 12.0[†])	21.76% (USD 131.0[†])	1.78% (USD 35.0[†])	2.31% (USD 41.0[†])

Removal of tariffs and NTBs on intra-AfCFTA trade					
AfDB (2019)	Removal of all tariffs on intra-AfCFTA trade; removal of NTBs	1.25% (USD 37.0†)	107.2% (USD 74.3†)	44.3% (USD 107.2†)	33.8% (USD 214.1†)
Jensen and Sandrey (2013)	Removal of all tariffs on intra-AfCFTA trade; 50% reduction in NTBs	1.60%	7.26%	6.28%	—
Abrego et al. (2019)	Removal of all tariffs; 35% reduction in NTBs	7.6%–1.89% /2.11%†	8.40%	—	—
World Bank (2020)	Gradual removal of 97% of tariffs on intra-AfCFTA trade	2.24%	51.85%	18.84%	19.58%
ECA (2023)	Gradual removal of 97% of tariffs + 50% of actionable NTMs on goods and services (within Africa only)	GDP: 0.95% (USD 108b)	IAT: 34.2% (USD 195b)	Exports: 5.8% (USD 71.9b)	Imports: 5.5% (USD 171.6b)

Removal of tariffs and NTBs on intra–AfCFTA trade and implementation of TFA

AfDB (2019)	Removal of all tariffs on intra-AfCFTA trade; removal of NTBs; implementation of TFA	3.50% (USD 100.0[†])	132.7% (USD 92.0[†])	51.10% (USD 295.6[†])	46.20% (USD 292.8[†])
World Bank (2020)	Gradual removal of 97% of tariffs on intra-AfCFTA trade; 50% reduction in NTBs with Africa and rest of world	4.20% (USD 413.0[†])	92.07% (USD 556.0[†])	28.64% (USD 560.0[†])	40.61% (USD 714.0[†])

b. Common external tariff: NTBs, non-tariff barriers; NTMs, non-tariff trade measures; TFA, trade facilitation agreement.

[†] Values expressed in terms of welfare gain.

Source: Kassa et al. (2022); authors' elaboration.

They can be classified in three broad categories: (1) non-tariff trade measures (NTMs); (2) infrastructure gaps; and (3) other trade-related transactions costs. Technical, and sanitary/phytosanitary barriers are the two most prevalent NTMs in Africa. Large infrastructure gaps and significant trade-related transaction costs also serve as barriers to trade in Africa. The methodologies for measuring NTBs vary, but are often conveyed in terms of 'tariff equivalents'. The estimated values can in some cases be very large (e.g. in excess of 300% of the value of the exported merchandise).[40]

Given such high levels of NTBs, it can be easily understood that a simulation that reduces them across the board (by say 20%) is likely to produce a much larger impact on welfare and trade than tariff liberalisation. And effectively, this is what Table 11.2 tells us, with GDP gains ranging from 1.25% of GDP up to as much as 7.6%.

Box 11.1. Employment challenges for the AfCFTA

The perceptive reader may have noticed a striking omission in our discussion of empirical studies into the AfCFTA—employment. Employment is barely dealt with in the simulation work. This is particularly strange given the fact that job creation is one of the major challenges for the African continent. According to the ILO,[41] an estimated 86% of people are employed in the informal sector.

Creating more job opportunities is clearly one of the pressing political, economic and social problems for Africa. Opinion polls carried out across the continent repeatedly show that the principal concern among young people is the creation of employment.[42] You would thus expect studies on the AfCFTA would focus on its potential to create employment.

Yet there are good reasons why the AfCFTA simulations reviewed in this chapter do not do so. Modelling the labour market in an African context is problematic because of the lack of reliable employment and unemployment data, the high levels of informality and the difficulty in modelling wage determination. Some studies[43] show variations in wages (e.g. skilled vs unskilled; male vs female), but it is questionable whether this is really meaningful in light of the lack of underlying modelling efforts of the labour market. One study by ECA/TMEA (2020) did make some tentative calculations of the employment impacts, by applying existing estimates of growth/employment elasticities. Depending on the range of GDP impacts, it was estimated that anywhere between 2–8 million jobs could be created in East Africa. However, such estimates are very tentative.

Finally, the other trick up the sleeve of the modellers is to incorporate changes in the model closure to reflect additional financing through trade facilitation measures. This makes the most pronounced difference of all, in terms of the boost to GDP and trade volumes. This is essentially due to the way both NTB reduction and trade facilitation measures are modelled, as in some cases,[44] they do not discriminate between intra- and extra-African trade. As such, they significantly reduce the cost of imports from the rest of the world as well as from the African continent and hence increase the perceived 'welfare gains'. Yet as we have stressed in earlier chapters, the AfCFTA's mandate focused on reducing the frictions to intra-African trade and investment.

To sum up, it is clear that CGE modelling is highly sensitive to the type of model closure, underlying assumptions, data availability, whether or not it incorporates services trade, any reductions in NTBs, trade facilitation measures, and whether the overall framework is static or 'dynamic'. This makes a straightforward comparison between the results of different studies fraught with difficulties.

Forecasting impacts is difficult

Nonetheless, it is worth stressing that discrepancies from different modelling methodologies are to be expected. For instance, CGE studies on the impact of the EU SMP and NAFTA displayed large variations. The Cecchini Report (1988) estimated total one-off benefits of the European single market from removing barriers to trade, technical barriers, economies of scale and competition ranging from 5.8% to 6.4% of GDP,[45] while early studies by Gasiorek et al.,[46] Haaland and

Norman[47] and Baldwin[48] estimated that the EU SMP would improve welfare by only 1.2%, 0.5%, and 0.3%, respectively. Landau examined the impact of the European Common Market on the economic growth of its member countries using an econometric approach, finding no statistically significant difference between the growth of member and non-member economies.[49]

At odds with these early studies, and more in line with the initial Cecchini Report, a recent extensive (and presumably much more reliable *ex-ante*) econometric study by Mayer et al. studied the impact of the establishment of the European single market over the period from 1950 and 2012 and found that it increased trade between EU members by 109% on average for goods and 58% for tradeable services.[50] The study's authors found that the trade impact was more than three times larger than the effect of simple tariff removal. The associated welfare gains were estimated to reach 4.4%, with many poorer peripheral countries gaining proportionately more than core countries. These figures were still below those proffered by the Cecchini Report, but much closer. With hindsight, then, and from a longer-term perspective, we can say that the impact of deeper European integration may have been significantly larger than had been previously anticipated by some of the published research.

By contrast, empirical studies on NAFTA generally reported much more modest trade and welfare effects. It is important to realise that NAFTA was quite a different proposition to either the AfCFTA or the SMP, as it focused exclusively on trade liberalisation and, beyond forcing Canada and Mexico to accept certain provisions liberalising investment, did not have elements of a 'deep integration' agenda. As a consequence, it is no surprise that studies estimated much smaller welfare and trade impacts. An early CGE study on NAFTA by Brown estimated welfare effects that varied from 0.1–0.7% for the USA and Canada. Mexico, the poorest country in the bloc, was actually estimated to be the biggest beneficiary, with a 1.6% improvement in welfare.[51] This certainly tallies with the subsequent trade impact of NAFTA, which led to a dramatic increase in the country's exports to the US and Canada, particularly from the Maquilla industries.[52] Yet Bachrach and Mizrahi estimated welfare effects of just 0.32% for Mexico and 0.02% for the United States.[53] The anticipated welfare gains from these studies were thus clearly small.[54] As Krugman pointed out at the time, any benefits from NAFTA were likely to be marginal, particularly in terms of job creation. Few studies indicate that NAFTA added much more than 0.1% to US real incomes.[55]

Limited tax implications

There is, however, one area in which the empirical studies of AfCFTA concur, and that is on the limited negative impacts on government revenue of the tariff liberalisation. Taxes on international trade have historically provided an unusually large portion of government revenues in Africa, dating back to the colonial period.[56]

One summary of existing CGE studies found that the AfCFTA would generate tax revenue losses in the range of 0.14–0.22% of GDP for the continent as whole.[57] In terms of total government revenues, estimates for East Africa by ECA/TMEA foresaw average revenue losses for the region amounting to less than 1% of total government revenues (Table 11.3).[58] As such, it may well be considered by policymakers a price worth paying.

Indeed, on this topic, it is not actually necessary to go to the length of performing such simulations: a few stylised facts are sufficient to establish that tariff revenue losses are likely to be limited and could well be compensated for over the mid- to long-term by higher VAT receipts and other taxes due to the greater intensity of economic activity following AfCFTA implementation. Moreover, although it is true that Africa has historically had a high dependence on tariff revenues, that dependence on tariff revenues as a source of government revenue has been declining over time, as governments have sought new sources of revenue, such as VAT. This was particularly the case during the period of SAPs, when the IMF and other IFIs pressured African countries to instigate trade-friendly policies and reduce taxes on imports. It is a trend which has continued over the last two decades (Figure 11.1).

In addition, the negotiations allow for 3% of product lines to be excluded from the AfCFTA tariff liberalisation. Countries are being encouraged to avoid limiting the extent of the trade liberalisation under AfCFTA rules. However, if they choose their excluded products judiciously, they can limit the extent of revenue losses.

Table 11.3: Estimated tariff revenue losses

		Tariff revenue loss (millions USD)	As % of total tariff revenue	As % of total government revenue
Ethiopia		61	6.1%	0.7%
Kenya		67	3.2%	0.6%
Madagascar		2	0.7%	0.1%
Rwanda		6	4.0%	0.3%
Tanzania		91	6.2%	1.3%
Uganda		23	8.4%	0.6%

Created with Datawrapper

Source: ECA/TMEA (2020).

Finally, because of the relatively low share of formal sector imports that currently are sourced from the continent, the share of revenues at stake with the tariff liberalisation is modest. Intra-Africa trade tariff revenue equated to just 0.1% of African GDP in 2015. By contrast, approximately 1.5% of African GDP comes from tariffs on imports from the rest of the world.[59] As noted by a recent AU publication,[60] the potential loss of USD 4.1 billion in tariff revenues for national governments is expected to be offset by increased employment and better use of domestic resources, among other benefits.

Figure 11.1: The decline of customs and import duties as a share of total tax revenue (2000–16)

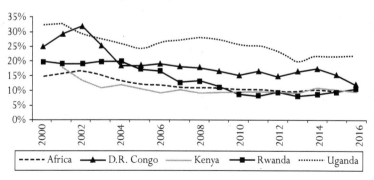

Source: OECDStat (2019).

Conclusions

To sum up, this review of empirical studies shows that the results crucially depend on the choice of model, the assumptions made and the quality of the data. The outcomes of CGEs, in particular, depend on the initial calibration and base-year data used for modelling.[61] Recognition of these limitations could admittedly result in scepticism towards the whole exercise. In fact, however, for a host of reasons, the modelling techniques discussed here may actually systematically underestimate the potential gains from deep regional integration, for various reasons:

1. **Inability to foresee the emergence of new activities or trade**—Both partial and general equilibrium models struggle to predict the emergence of new sectors or trade in products where there was none previously. This is because product categories for which there are initially no bilateral trade flows cannot be projected to become non-zero after the introduction of zero tariffs.[62]

2. **Neglect of the benefits from the services trade**—Services trade liberalisation is more difficult to model because of deficiencies in both bilateral service trade and tariff equivalents, yet the services sectors are often a major source of gains from deeper regional integration. This is beginning to change, however, as the coverage of bilateral service trade databases improve. ECA (2023) reports a 39.2% increase in service exports by 2045 compared with the baseline, with financial, business and communication services expanding by more than 50%, followed by tourism and transport (around 50%).

3. **Failure to model benefits derived from scale economies**—Most CGE global models assume constant returns to scale. Yet by expanding the size of the market, scale economies are one of the principal sources of gains from regional integration. Although technically feasible, introducing increasing returns to scale into this kind of modelling approach can make the model less tractable and is usually avoided.

4. **The long-term impact on productivity and incomes**—Competition is the spur of faster productivity growth and technological acquisition. Yet the positive impact of the AfCFTA through

inducing greater competition and the reduction of 'x-inefficien-cies'[63] is not captured through these models.

5. **Lack of sufficient data**—Input–output tables form the empiri-cal backbone of CGE models, but only 26 of 54 African countries currently have input–output tables in the GTAP 10 database. Although organisations like ECA have been making significant efforts to add additional countries to the database, the lack of country-specific data limits the degree of disaggregation possible. In addition, informal cross-border trade, which represents a sig-nificant portion of intra-African trade, is not captured in the simu-lations (see Chapter 8).

Arguably, then, the most important economic gains of forming a continental market derive from the dynamic gains associated with increased competition, higher inflows of FDI, economies of scale, greater transfer of knowledge and technology, increased productiv-ity, and economic diversification.[64] Current modelling techniques can only capture these gains in a proximate fashion.

Finally, it is worth stressing that the terms of trade and income impacts will also be divergent across countries. One early CGE simula-tion,[65] for instance, shows that the largest AfCFTA gains would go to countries with larger manufacturing bases and developed transporta-tion infrastructure, while a few more agriculturally based economies could actually suffer modest declines. ECA's most recent simulations do not support this contention.[66] However, it is still critical that AfCFTA countries adopt strategies so that the weaker economies are not left behind. We return to these points in the concluding chapter.

12

THE FREE MOVEMENT PROTOCOL

AN ATTAINABLE GOAL?

No African is a foreigner in Africa! No African is a migrant in Africa! Africa is where we all belong, notwithstanding the foolishness of our boundaries. No amount of national-chauvinism will erase this.

Achille Mbembe[1]

Introduction

The emotive nature worldwide of migratory movements tends to spur lots of misconceptions. Frequently migrants—including refugees and displaced persons—are treated as scapegoats in national politics, manifested in xenophobia, racism and discrimination. These attitudes in turn are often premised on false concerns over national public order, counter-terrorism, public health and employment.[2] This kind of misconception has dogged the Protocol to the Treaty Establishing the African Economic Community Relating to Free Movement of Persons, Right of Residence and Right of Establishment, which we shall refer to as the Free Movement Protocol (FMP), adversely affecting its signature, ratification and implementation.

Such scaremongering misses the important contribution that migrants make to economies of host states, as well as their home states. Migrants bring skills and build the capital base, contribute to technological progress, pay taxes, take up jobs locals would find unattractive, establish businesses that provide employment and products, and contribute to social and cultural diversity.[3]

Migration is commonly recognised as a handmaiden of cross-border trade and investment. A greater mobility of labour across the continent will help address skill shortages, contribute to a faster rate of economic growth and reduce unemployment, particularly for younger people—who we argue will be the principal beneficiaries of the implementation of the protocol. Without free movement, the continental agreement will be firing on three cylinders, not four.

In this chapter, we argue the case for full implementation of the FMP. As the African Union leadership agreed in its 50-year blueprint, Agenda 2063, the continent should aspire to attain 'seamless borders'.[4] It is a goal that may take time to accomplish, but it is a worthy aspiration that will bring many benefits for Africa. It is also one that, according to opinion polls, attracts a significant degree of popular support, with one recent poll across 18 African countries finding that 55% of respondents favour free movement of people across borders for work.[5]

The chapter sets out the case for free movement of persons, discusses the legal basis for the protocol and describes the progress to date. It also discusses the misconceptions and challenges that impede further progress. We argue that the practical obstacles to the implementation of the FMP—for instance, security concerns and border controls—can be resolved. But we also stress that the political obstacles can also easily be overcome, provided there are certain safeguards, and that the implementation of the protocol is gradual. We start with an overview of the context and a brief discussion of the drivers of intra-African migration.

The historical and global context

As the cradle of humanity, Africa has an almost timeless history of migratory movements. Possibly one of the least known and most remarkable events in terms of the history of migratory movements was the dispersal of Bantu-speaking peoples from their cradleland in the Benue valley of eastern Nigeria and in the adjacent grasslands of western Cameroon[6] around 5,000 years ago. By around 2,000 years ago, the suffusion of Bantu languages and associated ways of life was total, from the Sahel in the north to the south-west Cape, spanning 6,000 miles of equatorial forests, deserts, mountains and savannah. Bantu-speaking peoples changed the human landscape of sub-Saharan Africa from a region thinly populated by groups of hunter-gatherers to one that was dominated by farmers living in villages. It was, as noted by anthropologist John Reader, 'an event unmatched in human history'.[7]

Without artificial boundaries to constrain them, population movements on the continent were commonplace in the pre-colonial period. Many African societies have had great nomadic traditions— for instance, the Tuareg, Fulani, Peuls, and Maures of West Africa, the Afar and Maasai of East Africa, the San people of Southern Africa, or the Meshwesh of North Africa. We discussed briefly in Chapter 2 the creation of borders by the Europeans in the late nineteenth and early twentieth century, which limited some of these movements. But the borders were not effectively imposed, and indeed the colonialists often encouraged cross-border movements for their own economic benefits (for instance, the movement of workers from Zimbabwe to work in the mines of South Africa).

However, before we jump to the conclusion that human migrations on the African continent are somehow atypical in their intensity, it is worth considering the history of Europe. In the nineteenth century the pace of outward migration from Europe was tremendous. Overall, two out of every five surviving babies left Europe permanently in the nineteenth century, with about 60% (around 33 million) of them going to the United States.[8] Africa (or indeed any other continent) has never seen an exodus on an equivalent scale. Even today, the propensity of Africans to live outside their country of origin is much lower than in Europe: only 3.0% of the African population are living outside their home country in 2020 compared with 8.5% of the European population.[9]

Yet the impression is often given in the Western media that Africa is one of the principal sources of global migration. It is not. There were around 280 million international migrants in the world in 2020,[10] but just 14% of them were of African origin.[11] According to IOM data, on the list of the 20 leading source countries of migrants in the world, only one—Egypt—is an African country, and it ranks at the bottom of the list.[12] Table 12.1 summarises what we know about migratory movements *a grosso modo*, on the African continent since 1960. At the time of independence, it is estimated that cross-border movements amounted to over 6 million people, at a time when the total continental population was just 227 million. At that time, the African continent was also a net recipient of migrants from the rest of the world. Since then, migration both within and to outside the continent has grown significantly, with a notable acceleration in the last two decades.

Table 12.1: Migration within and outside Africa (1960–2020)

	From Africa to the rest of the world	Within Africa	Total
Millions of people			
1960	1.8	6.2	8
1980	5.4	8.0	13.4
2000	8.7	10.5	19.2
2020	19.7	20.9	40.6
% shares			
1960	22%	78%	100%
1980	40%	60%	100%
2000	45%	55%	100%
2020	49%	51%	100%

Sources: Authors' calculations, using data from Flahaux and De Haas (2016); UNDESA (2022).

However, what is perhaps not appreciated sufficiently is the extent to which intra-African migration has persistently outweighed migration to the rest of the world. Ever since independence, the intra-African share has stayed consistently over 50% of total migratory flows. But even this underestimates the importance of the phenomenon for the average African country because the continental totals are dragged down by North Africa, whose migration, for historic and geographical reasons, is strongly oriented towards Europe. In 2020, only 13% of its migrants headed towards the African continent, compared with 69% in East Africa, 70% in Central Africa and 75% within West Africa (Figure 12.1). Another striking characteristic of African migratory trends is the extent to which the majority of migrants stay within their region of provenance: 61%, 82% and 91% of intra-African migratory movements from East, Southern and West Africa stay, respectively, within their own sub-region.

Other studies confirm this pattern of a heavy predominance of intra-African flows. Kihato (2020)[13] reported that out of the top 20 destinations for African migrants in 2017, only four were in Europe (the UK, France, Italy and Portugal), and the rest were all in Africa. For instance, about two thirds of its international migrants from the ECOWAS region live elsewhere within West Africa, and only a small percentage of its migrants from the sub-region actually move to the West.[14] Out of the 10 million international migrants moving to or from ECOWAS countries in 2020, more than 6 million moved within ECOWAS.[15] A survey by the IOM of 88,000 people on popular migration routes in West Africa found that 90% planned to stay in Africa.[16] For sub-Saharan Africa as a whole—a denomination that we try to avoid in this book but which in this case is appropriate—around 80% of migrants choose to stay in the region.[17]

Figure 12.1: Shares of intra-African (as a % of total) and intra-regional (as a % of African) migratory flows (2020)

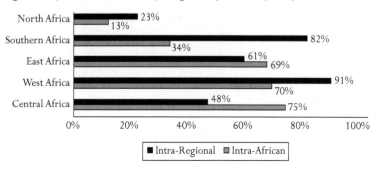

Source: Calculated from UNDESA data (2022).

And where are the intra-African migrants going? In terms of the total number of immigrants, South Africa remains the most significant destination country in Africa, with around 2.9 million international migrants residing in the country. Among the other important host countries are Nigeria and Côte d'Ivoire in West Africa, and Kenya and Uganda in East Africa. Other countries with high immigrant populations as a proportion of their total populations tend to be smaller but wealthier (in per capita terms) countries, including Gabon (19%), Equatorial Guinea (16%) and Seychelles (13%).[18]

Given this, there is a very real sense in which Africa is already sustaining high levels of cross-border migration. The FMP is required to formalise these flows and harness them in a way that helps accelerate the continent's economic development.

The drivers of intra-African migration

Research has established that there are a number of drivers of intra-African migration.[19] One is obviously the search for economic opportunities. Many people in Africa move from rural to urban areas or from one country to another in search of better-paying jobs or business opportunities. This movement is often driven by a lack of employment opportunities in their home countries or regions—a point which we develop further in the next section. Political instability is another factor that drives intra-African migration. In some countries, political unrest, conflict and persecution force people to flee their homes and seek refuge in other countries within the continent. However, this motivation should not be overplayed—fewer than 1% in one survey said conflict was their main reason for moving.[20] Additionally, cultural and social factors also contribute to intra-African migration; for example, some people may move to join family members or to seek better social support networks in other regions.

It is said that African youth seek to emigrate to escape poverty, disease, insecurity and corruption. Many are certainly preoccupied with these questions. But that broad brush stroke too is a simplification. According to the 2022 Africa Youth Survey, covering 4,500 people aged between 18 and 24 years,[21] the leading reasons for a wish to emigrate were economic (44%), educational (41%), seeking new experiences (25%), and fleeing from corruption (18%), politics

(12%) and insecurity (9%). That was the sensational part. However, the survey also found that a high percentage of youth believed their countries were making good progress and preferred to stay. On average, 64% of African youth maintain that their countries have a moral obligation to welcome refugees, and in Ethiopia, Kenya and Rwanda, that number was even higher.

Finally, we should not ignore the growing impact of climate change, which is increasingly forcing large-scale displacements of populations (particularly in the Sahel and the Horn of Africa, but also in parts of Southern Africa). In the Horn of Africa, for instance, severe drought in 2021–22 led to a large number of displaced peoples, both internally and across borders. The World Bank believes that by 2050 over 50 million people in sub-Saharan Africa might be displaced because of climate change alone.[22]

The trends towards greater intra-African migration described in the previous section are likely to accelerate for a number of reasons. Studies confirm that the majority of African migrants are young and relatively well-educated. But moving costs money: migrants need enough to cover at least a bus fare and accommodation while looking for a job. Many Africans cannot yet afford to do so, but one day they will. Global research suggests that as poor countries grow richer, more of their people tend to emigrate, until average incomes reach a threshhold of around USD 10,000 a year.[23] Income per head on the African continent is currently around USD 1,900,[24] so there is a lot of room for growth. In line with this research, Ethiopian economist Abebe Shimeles provides some empirical evidence that the wealthier African countries support higher net migration rates than their poorer counterparts. As the population expands and per capita incomes rise, Africans are thus likely to become more mobile.[25] There is already evidence that the pace of intra-African migration has been accelerating: it increased by 44% in the decade since 2010, compared with 26% growth in African migration towards Europe.[26]

The legal framework of the FMP

The FMP Protocol explains its rationale in the following terms:

> … the free movement of persons, capital, goods and services will promote integration, Pan-Africanism, enhance science, technology,

education, research and foster tourism, facilitate inter-African trade and investment, increase remittances within Africa, promote mobility of labour, create employment, improve the standards of living of the people of Africa and facilitate the mobilization and utilization of the human and material resources of Africa in order to achieve self-reliance and development ....[27]

The protocol defines free movement as the right of nationals of a member state to enter, move within and exit another member state, always in accordance with the national laws and procedures of the host member state. The right of entry is defined for a period of stay of up to 90 days, and abolition of the visa requirements will be undertaken after December 2023. Any person entering another member state should use a designated point of entry, and possess a recognised and valid travel document, but should not be prohibited from entry.[28] Also, member states are to enter arrangements for facilitating the movement of border communities, to recognise the right of workers to seek and accept employment, and to give visas to students and researchers.[29] Movement of persons also includes the right of residence and the right of establishment. Establishment means to set up a business, trade, profession, vocation or be self-employed.[30] The protocol envisages additional arrangements for 'vulnerable groups', set out as refugees, victims of smuggling and human trafficking, asylum seekers and pastoralists.[31]

In an important sense, the FMP will simply facilitate trends which have already been ongoing. One of Pan-Africanism's focal points has always been the right of Africans to cross national borders without undue restrictions. In principle, the free movement of persons, rights of residence and establishment by Africans across the borders of African Union member states was established in Article 4(2)(i) of the Abuja Treaty, which officially came into force in 1994 (see Chapter 3). The Abuja Treaty provides for creation of the African Common Market by 2023, during the fifth of the six stages, with the four freedoms: the free movement of goods, services, persons and capital, as well as the right of residence and establishment.[32] The free movement of people is to be further consolidated during the sixth stage—that is, in the period from 2023 to 2028.[33]

In addition, a Migration Policy Framework for Africa was endorsed by African Union members in 2006 in the Gambian capital of Bangui; this framework also included the right to gainful employment across African borders. Finally, after over 18 months of consultations, Africa's Agenda 2063 was concluded in 2013 and adopted in 2015, which included 'The African Passport and the free movement of people' as one of its 11 flagship projects. The African Passport was launched at an African Union meeting held in Kigali in 2016 and was meant to facilitate the free movement of people on the continent, although the take-up has been slow.[34] In 2017, the Peace and Security Council of the African Union acknowledged that the benefits of free movement of Africans across African borders outweigh both real and imagined economic and security challenges that such a reform might pose.

To sum up, there is therefore a strong political case—a matter of political credibility in fact—for the implementation of the FMP, in terms of compliance with existing obligations. It is also something reflected in the commitments of the RECs. In particular, the prioritisation of free movement of persons in ECOWAS has stood out over the years as part of its vision, with incremental programmes that include frameworks, the ECOWAS passport and the biometric card (Box 12.1). The EAC has, especially since the introduction of its common market in 2010, also registered significant progress in freeing the movement of persons, including the adoption of the East African Passport and the use of travel cards. Implementation, though, falters here and there.[35]

Box 12.1: The example of the ECOWAS Free Movement Protocol

ECOWAS adopted a protocol on the 'Free Movement of People and the Right of Residence and Establishment' in 1979. ECOWAS was only four years old at the time, having been established through the Treaty of Lagos in 1975. The 15 founding member countries crossed what was, until then, a rigid anglophone-francophone divide in West Africa. ECOWAS set out a long-term goal of 'freedom of movement and residence within the community'. In the 1979 protocol, ECOWAS members committed themselves to ultimately achieve a 'common market', including the right of citizens to enter, reside, work and establish businesses in the territory of member states. The protocol provides for a three-phased process of implementation intended to take 15 years. Phase one was the right of entry, which meant visa-free entry for a period of at least 90 days, after which the person would need to apply for an extension of stay. However, a member state could refuse admission to 'inadmissible immigrants under its laws'. Though the protocol came into force in 1980, in 1983 Nigeria expelled illegal 'unskilled workers' when recession hit following an oil boom, and later revoked two articles of the 1979 protocol.

Nevertheless, phase two of the protocol—the right to residence—was adopted. This included the right to carry out income-earning employment, and the right to equal treatment relative to nationals of the host member state. In 1990, phase three—the right to establishment—was adopted by the ECOWAS states through a supplementary protocol. This gave ECOWAS citizens the right to set up and manage enterprises under the same conditions as nationals of the host member state. The protocols would appear to offer a 'solid basis for establishing free movement and are widely recognised as a best practice for international cooperation on labour migration'. However, only phase one has been comprehensively implemented. This is an important achievement—entry visas have been abolished, effectively, for ECOWAS citizens; a regional travel document has been issued in at least seven ECOWAS countries; and ECOWAS passports, modelled on EU passports, have been issued in some ECOWAS countries too.

Reasons for the failure to progress significantly beyond phase one include 'the absence of adequate mechanisms to control the infiltration of criminals, perverse corruption of border officials, [and] diverse and incompatible national laws and policies on migration and labour'. Little further progress has been made despite a further attempt to agree on a common regional position on migration in 2008.

Sources: Hirsch 2021, p. 9; AUC 2022, p. 105.

It is important to note that the FMP includes a number of important 'safety measures' which protect the rights of member states to regulate matters related to migratory movements. The protocol specifically adds three principles: non-discrimination, transparency and 'respect for laws and policies for protection of national security, public order, public health, environment and any other factors that would be detrimental to the host state'.[36] Together, these principles provide assurance that there are adequate safeguards against possible adverse consequences of free movement, which should provide solace, especially to immigration departments.

Finally the name of the FMP might as well have been the 'Protocol on Movement of African Nationals', as it is limited to citizens of the member states, rather than simply residents. This is a distinct approach from, say, the AfCFTA Protocol on Trade in Services, which is not restricted by nationality. The approach is also different from the COMESA-EAC-SADC Tripartite Agreement on Movement of Businesspersons, which seeks to facilitate movement for all businesspeople resident in the member states.

Progress to date

Out of the 55 African Union member states, 33 have signed but only four (Rwanda, Niger, São Tomé and Príncipe, and Mali) have ratified the FMP Protocol since January 2018 when it was opened for signature and ratification. By contrast, the agreement establishing the AfCFTA was opened for signature and ratification on 21 March 2018 and had 54 signatures and 46 ratifications as of June 2023.[37] The FMP requires 15 ratifications before it can go into force.

The AUC and its partners have undertaken a series of activities since 2018 to create awareness and ownership of the FMP with a view to increasing ratifications and implementing it. Both the Specialised Technical Committee on Migration, Refugees and Internally Displaced Persons and the Pan-African Parliament have held sessions to consider the protocol. A media and communications event was organised jointly with the ECOWAS Commission for the West African region. Youth, researchers and civil society have been engaged. Preparation of strategies and policies has been ongoing, as well as advocacy with member states.

The African Union has adopted a number of complementary initiatives. For example, the Joint Labour Migration Programme, together with the African Qualifications Framework and Labour Market Information Systems, will promote skills portability and the mutual recognition of qualifications, and assist in addressing labour and skills shortages in deficit areas through flows from surplus areas. It will also contribute to acceptance of diversity and strengthen the African identity through social integration.[38]

Table 12.2 shows the status on the roadmap for the FMP. A number of key activities have already been missed which require that the roadmap be revised. Some of the activities are foundational in nature and form the premise for the protocol, such as the required 15 ratifications before the protocol can enter into force. Other activities, while not foundational, have been regarded as pre-conditions for operationalisation of the protocol, such as creation of a continental database of vehicles with links to national systems. Such an activity need not be a pre-condition; it could be coincidental. Other activities with short timeframes—such as the adoption, by 2019, of laws on acquisition of property by persons having the right of residence or establishment—relate to rights that will only be available after 2023. Such short timeframes could be considered inappropriate, especially if they begin to be regarded as pre-conditions for the signature, ratification or implementation of the protocol.

Moreover, the roadmap introduced certain details that are not in the substantive provisions of the protocol, which has contributed to a backlog of prerequisite conditions for signature or ratification of the protocol—quite unnecessarily, we might add, since they are not substantive requirements in the actual provisions of the protocol. For instance, drawing on Article 5 on the right of entry and Article 26 on harmonisation of national regimes with REC regimes (and REC regimes with the FMP), the roadmap lists a number of activities to be undertaken under the headings of strengthening national civil registration systems, movement control systems and border governance mechanisms through extensive IT infrastructure, all of which were to be carried out continuously after 2018. These activities in the roadmap now constitute backlogs.

It is worth insisitng that the FMP will not result in loss of sovereignty. This is because the FMP contains enabling provisions for national measures to ensure public order and public health, as well as maintenance of peace and security. What is more, the rights the protocol provides are to be granted and exercised in accordance with national regimes of the host state. This is a fundamental condition that gives assurance to national authorities, including immigration and security agencies, that the FMP maintains the existing flexibility and space for managing the public policy objectives of maintaining law and order, peace and security, good public health and morals, and the political economy of xenophobia.

Table 12.2: Performance on the roadmap for the FMP (July 2023)

Activity / obligation	Timeframe	Success
Signature and ratification (15 ratifications required for entry into force)	Jan–Dec 2018	Missed—only four ratifications; 33/55 signatures
Vehicles—specimens, systems and procedures, continental database, national links to the database	2019	Missed
Deportation procedures	2018	Missed
Property laws on right of residence and establishment	2019	Missed
Establishment of REC focal points	2018	Missed
Remedies in national laws	2018	Missed
Criteria for admission under right of entry	2018	Missed
Regionally recognised travel documents	2019	Missed—only implemented in EAC and ECOWAS

E-visa	Dec 2018	Missed—only implemented by some member states
Right of entry—90-day stay and abolition of visa requirement	Dec 2023	Running but likely to be missed
Right of residence	To be determined by the Executive Council after 2023	Running
Right of establishment	To be determined by the Executive Council	Running
Publish conditions on denial of entry	2018; continuous	Running
Publish official entry and exit points	2018; continuous	Running
Harmonisation of laws and procedures	Continuous	Running
Upgrade passports to e-passports	Continuous	Running
Issue the African Passport	Continuous	Running
Arrangements for border communities	2022–23	Running
Procedures for vulnerable/specific groups	2023	Running
Portability of social security benefits	2023	Running

Source: Compiled from the Roadmap attached to the Protocol.

Finally, it is important to stress that the FMP takes a phased approach. Three progressive stages are provided for—namely, the right of entry and abolition of visa requirements during the first phase, right of residence during the second phase, and right of establishment during the third phase.[39] The first phase—on right of entry and visa abolition—for instance, is to be implemented after December 2023, beginning on a date to be set by the Executive Council of the African Union. The dates for the other two phases will be determined by the Executive Council after review of implementation of the prior phase. The protocol also provides for cooperation and information sharing among member states,[40] and for the movement of students, researchers and workers, the portability of benefits, arrangements for travel of border communities and vulnerable groups, and roles for RECs as well as the member states and the African Union Commission. The protocol is therefore considered quite comprehensive and progressive.[41]

Creating a continental labour market

As noted in the introductory chapter, the timeframe for the implementation of the AfCFTA is ambitious, especially in view of the scale and scope of the agreement, but it will still take until 2034 before the removal of tariffs has been fully achieved. If past precedent of similar agreements worldwide is anything to go by, it will foreseeably take longer still to fully implement some other crucial parts of the agreement (e.g. services trade liberalisation or the competition protocol, etc). Yet many of the continent's developmental challenges require urgent solutions, and Africa does not have the luxury of time.

Youth unemployment is one of the most pressing challenges in this regard. The example of Kenya is illustrative. Kenya's employment challenges appear manageable on the surface: approximately 800,000 young Kenyans enter the labour market every year, a number that will continue to rise until the middle of the century because of the country's demographic expansion.[42] Yet prior to the global pandemic, the Kenyan economy was creating between 825,000 and 850,000 jobs annually.[43] At first sight, it looks as if the ever-growing ranks of new job-seekers are being absorbed by the labour market, and that is something that also appears to be reflected in the official unemployment figures. According to the ILO's strict definition of unemployment, Kenya's headline unemployment rate is still in single figures. In the first quarter of 2021, after an unprecedented global pandemic, only 1.2 million Kenyans were officially classified as unemployed, representing just 6.6% of the active labour force.[44]

However, such statistics are misleading. More than 90% of the new jobs generated are in the informal sector (known as the '*jua kali*' in Swahili).[45] And the livelihood of most of those informal workers is characterised by subsistence and precarity. Sadly, among the *jua kali* workers are an increasing number of well-educated men and women who aspire to be doctors, nurses, engineers, accountants and lawyers. They do not want to be selling phone time on street corners, waiting on passers-by in a roadside café or pulling *mkokoteni* (handcarts) simply to make ends meet.[46] The difficulty in finding work is most severe among the young. Over three quarters of the unemployed in 2021 were under 35 years old, and underemployment among the youth is the norm. Even the best-educated struggle: among Kenyans with tertiary education, more than a quarter were 'economically inactive'.

The Kenyan example is apposite, precisely because it is far from atypical. Using the UN's population database, it is possible to estimate the annual expansion of Africa's working-age population.[47] On this basis, across the continent, there is a need to find gainful employment for an additional 10–12 million youth every single year.[48] For Africa's most populous countries, the challenges are proportionally largest, with Nigeria adding around four million people a year to the working-age population. Implicit in these figures is the need for governments to do one of two things: either find higher education/training opportunities for school leavers or integrate them in the labour market. In this, clearly the majority of governments are failing. ILO statistics show that a staggering number of African youth are economically 'inactive' (Figure 12.2).

There is an extreme irony in these statistics. Surveys persistently show that companies in many sectors are suffering severe skills shortages. Despite high unemployment rates across Africa, 79% of firms surveyed say they expect losses on revenues due to skills shortages.[49] These shortages seem to impact on services sectors as much as manufacturing (Figures 10.3 and 10.4). According to a report by McKinsey & Company, only 10% of young people in sub-Saharan Africa have the skills needed to work in modern jobs. This is due to a lack of access to quality education and training programmes, as well as a lack of opportunities for work experience and on-the-job training.[50] What seems to be lacking most are skills related to production. A survey of country experts from 45 countries for the African Economic Outlook (2013) found that over 50% of respondents cited lack of specialised skills as a major obstacle keeping African firms from becoming competitive.

There are only two possible explanations for these phenomena: a lack of the requisite skills, or 'mismatched skills'. On the first point, it is important to recognise that there has been impressive progress in terms of improving educational outcomes—certainly compared with

Figure 12.2: Estimates of youth inactivity among 15–29-year-olds (latest year)

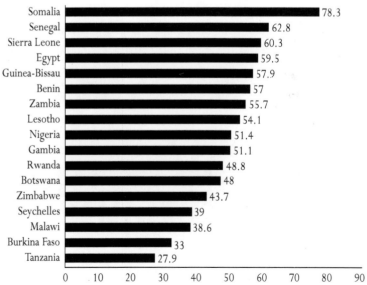

Data are given in percentages.
Source: ILO YouthStat (2022).

the colonial period when there was an almost criminal neglect in providing sufficient educational opportunities. Education systems have improved markedly, with secondary school enrolment increasing from 5% in 1971 to 43% in 2018.[51]

Nonetheless, there is also no denying that educational systems across the continent continue to suffer major deficiencies, including inadequate funding, poor infrastructure, and a lack of qualified teachers, reflected in excessively low levels of literacy and numeracy among many young people in Africa.[52] In a classic study on the link between literacy and industrialisation, Bowman and Anderson (1963) argued that historical data showed that countries could not grow sustainably unless a country achieved 40% adult literacy, and could not industrialise unless literacy levels reached 70–80%.[53]

There is a lot of contemporary evidence which lends credence to this hypothesis. According to a study by Newman et al. among firms owned by indigenous entrepreneurs, those with university-educated owners tend to have higher growth rates.[54] In Mozambique, firms with better-educated managers were found to be more likely to survive and expand in terms of employment. There is also evidence to suggest that enterprises managed by university graduates in Africa have a higher propensity to export. Cross-country research also indicates that there is a strong link between export sophistication and the percentage of the labour force with post-primary schooling.

Figure 12.3: Percentage of firms identifying inadequately educated workforce as major constraint

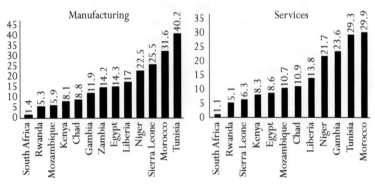

Source: World Bank Enterprise Surveys (latest years available).

Figure 12.4: Average skill mismatch among employed youth per country (2012–15)

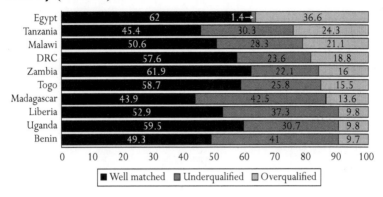

Source: Morsy and Mukasa (2019).

But this cannot explain why so many well-qualified graduates also struggle to find gainful employment opportunities. Returning to the example of Kenya, for instance, more than 50,000 students graduate from Kenyan universities each year, yet graduate unemployment is rife among young people with tertiary education.[55] A better explanation is what is known amongst economists as the 'skills mismatch'— that is, the extent to which firms end up employing workers that are either overqualified or underqualified for the tasks they are doing. One recent study for the African Development Bank[56] has tried to quantify the scale of the skills mismatch. Although the study was restricted to just ten countries on the continent, the results were nonetheless revealing (see Figure 12.4). In conformity with the aforementioned research, underqualified workers were definitely a major problem, particularly in lower-income economies like Benin, Liberia and Madagascar. But there were also very significant numbers of workers who were deemed by their employers to be 'overqualified' for the work that they were doing. In the face of so many companies complaining of skills shortages, this finding is clearly paradoxical and indicative of high levels of skills mismatches.

This observation lies at the core of arguments regarding the need to start establishing a continental labour market through the implementation of the FMP. Creating a regional labour market will help reduce skills mismatch by providing a larger pool of job opportunities for workers with specific skills. This can help reduce the number of workers who are unemployed or underemployed due to a lack of available jobs that match their skills. Additionally, creating a regional labour market can help employers find workers with the specific skills they need, which can help reduce the number of job vacancies that go unfilled due to a lack of qualified candidates.[57] For the millions of under- and unemployed young people on the continent, this is arguably the greatest gift that the AfCFTA can give them.

Other economic benefits of the FMP

To be sure, there are many other economic arguments in favour of FMP implementation. For one thing, free movement is a great catalyst of trade, and the positive relationship between higher levels of migration and trade has proven to be a powerful one.[58] A quantitative review of 48 econometric studies between 1994 and 2010 showed a 10% increase in the number of migrants causes trade to grow by 1.5% on average.[59] These arguments are particularly pertinent to services trade because having a physical presence in another country is the principal way in which many services are delivered (Chapter 10). Ottaviano et al. find that a 1% increase in immigrants from a particular country enables its firms to export 6–10% more services to that country.[60] The conclusion from this research is obvious: the trade impacts of the AfCFTA might be muted unless it is also accompanied by greater intra-regional migration.

A second powerful reason is that studies have repeatedly stressed that economic convergence is accelerated appreciably by the free movement of labour. During the recent history of globalisation, while trade and capital have been increasingly liberalised, the free movement of persons has been the perpetual laggard. Yet there are strong economic reasons why the movement of persons and labour should keep pace with the liberalisation of movement of goods and capital or investment. In a review of the existing literature, Clemens stressed that the gains from eliminating migration barriers dwarf the gains from eliminating the remaining barriers to trade and capital flows as the latter would provide estimated gains that amount to less than a few percent of global GDP, while eliminating the barriers to labour mobility could lead to gains in the range of 50–150% of world GDP.[61]

According to Kennan, if open borders were implemented globally, an average Angolan's income would increase by USD 10,000 a year, while a Nigerian's would increase by USD 22,000.[62] The gains from implementing a similar policy of open borders at the continental rather than the global level would obviously be smaller, but still highly appreciable. Wages in South Africa are five times higher than in Zimbabwe or Mozambique, which is one reason why 700,000 Zimbabweans and 350,000 Mozambicans live there. Some 1.4 million migrants from Burkina Faso are in Côte d'Ivoire, where income per head (USD 5,500) is twice as high.[63] So the personal gains are potentially very large.

More generally, there are also reasons to believe that the FMP would help accelerate the process of economic convergence between African countries. One route through which this could occur is remittances. In 2021, Africa received an estimated USD 19 billion worth of remittances from its citizens resident in other African countries.[64] There is evidence that remittances sent within Africa tend to reduce poverty more, because intra-African migrants have poorer families than migrants who cross oceans, and also because they tend to be flows sent from wealthier African countries towards poorer ones.[65]

The other route through which faster economic convergence could occur is the positive impact of skilled migrants on the economic development of their destination countries. When skilled individuals move to a new country, they bring with them valuable knowledge, skills and expertise, which can contribute to the development of their new home. In the case of intra-African migration, this 'brain gain' phenomenon can lead to a number of benefits.[66] Firstly, as noted above, there is evidence that it helps to address skills shortages in destination countries, particularly in sectors such as healthcare, engineering and information technology, leading to increased productivity, higher economic growth and improved living standards for local communities. Secondly, the brain gain phenomenon can promote knowledge and technology transfer, as migrants bring with them new ideas, practices and ways of doing things. This can lead to innovation and the development of new industries, which can create jobs and increase competitiveness within the continental economy. One recent econometric paper by Gnimassoun studied the impact of immigration on labour productivity for 187 countries over the period 1990–2019; it found that a 10% increase in the intra-African immigration rate led to an increase in labour productivity of 0.42%, more than twice as high as the estimated global average.[67] Furthermore, the service sector was the one that benefits the most from this positive effect.

Perhaps the most appealing economic benefit of all in the AfCFTA/FMP package is increasing the attractiveness of the continent to the African diaspora and encouraging greater return migration, while further dissuading the extra-African migration of skilled workers. There is an interesting parallel here with the literature on Chinese 'sea turtles' (*haigui* in Chinese)—slang for people who are born in mainland China, spend a few years abroad studying or working, and return home as highly skilled talent.[68] Since China initiated its economic reforms and opened the door to the world in 1978, over 1,905,400 students and scholars have studied abroad at various levels of education, and 632,200 of these have become 'sea turtles' (as of 2010). As the volume of return migrants rises over time, many of them have become pioneers in the sciences, the IT industry, the financial sector, and many other high-technology and innovative fields.[69]

While the exodus of skilled Africans has some potential benefits like receiving remittances, transfer of knowledge and skills, and investment, there is growing evidence that those gains for Africa have been overblown in the literature.[70] For instance, although the global flows of remittances to the African continent are large, with the continent having received an estimated USD 95.6 billion in 2021,[71] the benefits of large-scale remittances tend to be highly concentrated, with just three countries (Egypt, Nigeria and Morocco) accounting for around two thirds of the total. While there is evidence that remittances can help reduce poverty,[72] there is much less compelling evidence that it can impact positively on long-term economic performance.[73]

On balance, the phenomenon of the brain drain has a profound effect on the African continent's economic growth and development, exhausting the continent of its most valuable resource—human capital.

Africa has experienced a dramatic increase in its stock of skilled emigrants to OECD countries over the past three decades, a loss it can ill afford. Indeed, 3.6 million skilled Africans lived and worked in OECD countries in 2015 compared with 0.7 million in 1990.[74]

The impact has been perhaps most apparent in the medical profession.[75] For instance, in 2016 there were reportedly about 8,000 Nigerian doctors working in the United States, yet only about 35,000 doctors were attending to Nigeria's 173 million citizens.[76] Across the continent, exoduses such as these will inevitably lead to strained healthcare systems. In 1973, for instance, there were 7.8 doctors per 100,000 people in Liberia; by 2008, this had dropped to 1.4 doctors, leaving the country ill-equipped to deal with the Ebola pandemic of 2014–16.[77]

Annually, it is estimated that Africa loses around USD 2 billion through brain drain in the health sector alone, but this phenomenon is not limited to the medical field. South Africa, for instance, loses nearly as many engineers through migration as it trains annually.[78] In 2016, former South Africa president Thabo Mbeki labelled Africa's brain drain as 'frightening', claiming that the continent had lost 20,000 academics and 10% of its highly skilled information technology and finance professionals. Mbeki claimed more African scientists and engineers live and work in the US and the UK than on the African continent.[79]

By promoting the rapid implementation of the FMP and creating a continental labour market, there is an opportunity to turn things around. As we saw in the previous section, the lack of skilled professionals is considered a major constraint on growth. On average, it costs each African country between USD 21,000 and USD 59,000 to train a medical doctor. According to one study,[80] nine countries—Ethiopia, Kenya, Malawi, Nigeria, South Africa, Tanzania, Uganda, Zambia, and Zimbabwe—have lost more than USD 2 billion since 2010 from training doctors who subsequently migrated. And this sword is double-edged, given that destination countries do not pay for the cost of training the African doctors they recruit. For instance, one in ten doctors working in the UK comes from Africa, allowing the UK to save on average USD 2.7 billion on training costs. It is estimated that Africa has lost USD 4.6 billion in home-training doctors who are then recruited by just four destination countries (the UK, the US,

Australia and Canada). A major way to reverse these trends is for the FMP and the AfCFTA to jointly make it more attractive for African nationals to stay on the continent. Research suggests, for instance, that those returning to Mozambique are 25% more likely to own a business than those who have not been abroad, even controlling for the possibility that more talented people may travel abroad.[81]

Security concerns—the Achilles heel of the protocol?

During the negotiation of the FMP, a number of challenges were repeatedly highlighted: national security threats, including violent extremism and terrorism, cross-border crime, human trafficking, the proliferation of small arms and drug smuggling, shrinking financial resources, and health epidemics such as Ebola and Covid-19.[82] There also appeared to be an underlying fear among some leaders that its implementation could trigger political instability. In South Africa, many politicians have been quick to blame migrants for problems at home. In 2019, mobs of armed men looted and torched shops owned by migrants, with at least 18 foreigners killed, according to Human Rights Watch.[83] More recently, in Tunisia, there have been some highly incendiary declarations against migrants, which led the African Union to release a statement a day after, urging the country to avoid 'racialised hate speech'. Such was the depth of feeling that a previously planned African Union meeting in Tunis for mid-March 2023 was cancelled.[84]

Yet not all the concerns are groundless. Borders can get shut down for various reasons. In 2015 alone, it was assessed that there were over 100 border disputes in Africa, with 58 potential secessionist territories in 29 countries.[85] In August 2019, Nigeria closed its borders with Benin, Cameroon, Chad and Niger, citing transhipment concerns. A claim was made that Benin was not adhering to the ECOWAS rules of origin, allowing foreign products preferential treatment. The Rwandan government closed the border with Uganda in February 2019, after a dispute between the two countries.[86]

Sometimes the disputes are long-standing ones. For instance, despite otherwise fairly cordial bilateral relations, Kenya and Tanzania have experienced repeated tensions over the movement of border communities and their cattle. For communities and ethnic groups that straddle borders, the existing frontiers simply do not make sense, and represent an inconvenience to family and communal relations, and to traditions of cross-border trade that go back to pre-colonial times (see Chapter 3). This reality underpins a lot of the cross-border conflict that exists on the continent.

Ultimately, however, the economic ramifications come to the forefront. Several of Africa's richer countries seem to be concerned that once the protocol comes into force, they will experience a sudden influx of low-skilled economic migrants from poorer countries. The complaint that immigrants take jobs from locals or drag down wages is especially loud in South Africa, where wages are high compared with the rest of the region and unemployment is rife.

The SADC's official stance highlights the challenges that the FMP faces. South Africa has outlined a series of preconditions that must be met before implementing the protocol, including achieving peace and security, economic convergence between countries, effective civil registration systems, reliable movement control systems, machine-readable passports that comply with international standards, and bilateral return agreements. Such tough pre-conditions are clearly unrealistic and would render the FMP protocol a non-starter.[87]

The way forward for the FMP

Professor Alan Hirsch makes the valid point that the FMP has many safeguards to deal with some of the above concerns. For instance, the protocol has sufficient built-in flexibility to ensure the protection of public order, security and health. Certain parts of the FMP intentionally exhibit what might be called 'constructive ambiguity'. There is a right of entry, residence or establishment under the protocol, but as noted earlier these rights are also subject to national policies, laws, regulations and procedures.

Indeed, the African Union is already putting in place legal instruments on extradition and mutual assistance, as well as a framework for issuing an African passport. They are also collaborating with Interpol to develop an interface for controlling movement (a 'red notice system' at frontiers) that is compatible with individual member states' prohibition/undesirable person and UN warning lists. A compatible ICT system is required at ports of entry to facilitate information exchange. Furthermore, a continental-wide institution called AfriPol[88] was established in 2015 with a mandate to strengthen cooperation between the police agencies of member states, and this has a vital role to play here.

In the course of the negotiations on the FMP, it is notable that the African Union's Department of Political Affairs, rather than the Department of Trade and Industry, handled the FMP negotiations. This clearly coloured perspectives on the agreement. Instead of being framed principally as a security issue, there is a need to shift the narrative and frame it largely as an economic one.[89] And in this sense, there is a need to better familiarise people with the positive consequences of migration, particularly at a time when there is so much misinformation. That implies conveying better the findings of research.

In most measurable ways, migration benefits both locals and the local economy. A World Bank study on South Africa concludes that, far from representing a drag on wages or employment, greater immigration is conducive to both increased employment and wages for nationals too.[90] In Côte d'Ivoire, migrants contribute a disproportionately large share of GDP—around 19%—despite constituting only 10% of the population. Migrants tend to be more productive than nationals because they are more likely to be of working age. In Rwanda, migrants pay on average three times more tax than locals.[91] And they often bring complementary skills. Some are hired to fill niches, while others move to places where their skills are in demand. It is of particular note that Rwanda has a high share of skilled workers in its inward migration profile and has not flinched when it has needed to import talents which are scarce at home (for instance, through efforts to import primary and secondary school teachers from Zimbabwe).[92] According to an UNCTAD study, intra-African migration also has a positive role to play in structural change on the continent—a 1% increase in the number of migrants to a country is associated with a 0.2–0.4% increase in manufacturing output. This is possibly because migrants bring skills and ideas, and the better educated they are, the stronger the impact.[93]

Some of the benefits from FMP implementation are more tangible still. African nationals, for example, will benefit from the abolition of visa requirements. According to one evaluation carried out in 2016, East Africa and Central Africa were the most restrictive;[94] North Africa had even displayed a marked increase in visa restrictiveness since the 1970s, partly reflecting the political process of 'externalisation' of European border controls. Richer countries on the continent also tended to be more restrictive. Among the 20 most visa-open African countries, 18 belong to low- or lower-middle-income countries.[95] Yet over recent years, there has been notable progress—by 2021, 54% of Africans either did not need a visa to travel or could obtain visas on arrival; three African countries now offer visa-free travel to the citizens of all other African countries; 22 countries offer visa-free travel to the nationals of at least five other African countries.[96]

Small countries will not suddenly face an avalanche of migrants seeking to permanently settle and to change the face of the country. Seychelles and Rwanda have relaxed visa requirements for holders of African passports, yet both countries have gained from this policy. Benin, the Gambia and Seychelles (again) offer visa-free entry to African passport holders.[97] For Rwanda, within a year of adopting the policy, tourism increased by 24% and trade with neighbouring countries by 50%. Tourism to the Seychelles has been growing by 7% annually since the relaxation of visa requirements, while in Mauritius it stagnated. Once Mauritius relaxed their rules, however, its performance also improved.[98]

While 51% of African countries require African passport holders to have a visa before arrival, 25% do not require visas and 24% granted visas on arrival in 2021.[99] The performance on visa openness has improved since 2016, with 24 countries now offering e-visas, up from nine in 2016.[100]

Finally, it is important that progress in implementation of the protocol builds on existing advances made under the aegis of the RECs. We have already discussed the example of ECOWAS. Some countries, such as Côte d'Ivoire, are trying to include migrants in their planning by applying a free-movement protocol, and migrants are now entitled to the same access to healthcare and education at the same cost as nationals. Indeed, surveys find they are more likely to go to health centres than locals (though, struggling to pay costs, they are less likely to use local schools).[101] Since the introduction of its common market in 2010, the EAC too has registered significant progress in freeing the movement of persons, including the adoption of the East African Passport and use of travel cards (Box 12.2).[102]

Box 12.2: The EAC Common Market Protocol

The EAC Common Market Protocol came into force in 2010 and includes the commitment to 'the free movement of people, the free movement of labour, the right of establishment and the right of residence', but requires the partner states to implement these commitments. These commitments protect the rights of EAC citizens in partner states, but are limited on grounds of public policy, public security, or public health. Some economic benefits materialised rapidly. Since 2014, for instance, Rwanda, Kenya and Uganda have allowed movement across their borders with just an identity card. Within two years, this reportedly had helped increase cross-border trade by 50%.

The Common Market Protocol provides for free movement of labour in the region, under equal treatment with nationals of the partner East African state, but a cross-border worker is required to obtain a 30-day work permit and to present a travel document and a contract of employment of more than 90 days. These systems are not standardised; Kenya, for example, imposes charges of USD 93 (10,000 Kenyan shillings) for processing and USD 1,856 (200,000 Kenyan shillings) per year for issuance. The free movement of labour provision also has a commitment to the mutual recognition of various types of qualification and includes a commitment to harmonise labour policies and law. The right of residence entails a standardised system of application for a permit, and can also be limited on public policy, public health and public security grounds, subject to mutual notification. It does not apply to all citizens of the EAC, but only to those who have been granted work permits, whether as employees or as self-employed people.

The system of free movement is by no means perfect in East Africa. The subjection of residence rights to work permits makes it

---

inferior to EU law, for example. Yet, it does represent a significant advance towards the free movement of Africans within a region, especially when compared with other African economic regions.

Sources: Hirsch (2021, pp. 8–10); *The Economist* (2021).

Conclusions

This chapter has argued that the AfCFTA will be firing on three cylinders, not four, if there is a failure to implement the FMP. To be sure, tensions will continue to exist around intra-continental migration. But it is striking that while the ten least-accepting countries in Gallup's 2019 Migration Acceptance Index are in Europe, four of the ten most-accepting countries at world level are in Africa (in order: Sierra Leone, Burkina Faso, Chad, Rwanda). No African country features among the ten least-accepting countries.[103] If framed in the right way by policymakers and politicians, there is every chance that the FMP will become one of the most popular elements in the AfCFTA package.

While recognising that intra-African migration is not without its challenges, it is likely to grow in the future as people search for better opportunities and stability. To ensure that migration is managed effectively and equitably, it is crucial for countries to work together to develop policies and strategies that promote safe, legal and orderly migration. The best way to do that is through adopting and implementing the common framework of the FMP.

PART III

13

HELP NOT HINDER

THE ROLE OF EXTERNAL PARTNERS IN THE CONSTRUCTION OF A CONTINENTAL MARKET

Introduction

This book began with the premise that there are social, cultural and political factors that unify the African continent more naturally as a bloc than may be the case, for instance, in Asia or Latin America, or indeed Europe or North America. Yet African governments are not operating in a similar context to the time when many Asian economies achieved their acceleration towards convergence with high-income economies. It is clear that policy space for African countries has shrunk over the last four decades in various spheres, due not only to more intrusive donor policies, but also a gradual process by private and public interests of 'hemming in' the viable options open to developing countries, through the actions of bodies like the WTO, the IMF, preferential market access agreements like AGOA, and the informal power of global value chains. Very few African regimes can set their development goals independently from foreign interests. In short, donor countries and international organisations have a strong handle on African domestic economic policies.[1]

Against this backdrop, although it is a welcome development that external partners have generally expressed their support for the AfCFTA, their actions have not always been compatible with the expressed goal. In particular, just after the signing of the AfCFTA in 2018, there was a flurry of offers for signing bilateral free trade agreements with African member states, but this kind of action risks undermining the coherence of the AfCFTA agreement. This chapter stresses the importance of trading and development partners adopting the principle of 'doing no harm' and the need to avoid destabilising the agreement, by focusing their support in a way that helps maximise continental unity and does not expressly aim at 'dividing and ruling'.

Mixed messages from international experts

In previous chapters, we discussed the scepticism and even hostility that projects of regional integration have traditionally provoked on the African continent. Yang and Gupta epitomise this kind of sentiment:

> Regionalism may distract Africa from its focus on the core objective of its trade policy—creating a liberal trade regime ... RTAs aimed at helping local industries through import substitution in Africa are unlikely to expand the continent's overall trade—even intraregional trade—given the low complementarity of natural endowments, the region's small markets, and administrative capacity constraints.[2]

'Progressive' economists also often have a blind spot when it comes to regional integration. In an otherwise informative collection of essays on Africa's development strategies, a book edited by Noman, Botchwey, Stein and Stiglitz does not contain a single reference to regional integration.[3] Cramer et al. are openly damning, arguing that:

> One reason to query high expectations for intra-African trade is the 'dismally poor implementation record' of regional integration agreements .... Despite decades of negotiations and agreements within subregions and RECs in Africa, intra-African trade remains a tiny proportion of the continent's overall trade.[4]

Reflecting such views, in the past the IFIs and many other development partners have tended to give at best limited support to regional cooperation schemes. A clear statement of the World Bank position was given by Foroutan, who maintained that regional trade integration should be 'pursued as a complement rather than as a substitute for global trade liberalisation'.[5] Of course, regional cooperation 'pursued as a complement' is no regional integration policy at all, since it makes cross-border trade merely derivative from general trade liberalisation.[6] Another example of the ambiguous attitude to continental integration is the refusal to treat the continent as a single entity (Box 13.1).

Box 13.1: Why do the IFIs refuse to classify Africa as a single continent?

For historic and their own operational reasons, the IMF and World Bank have divided up the continent. North Africa is integrated into the Middle East and North African countries (the MENA region), and the countries located south of the Sahara are put in sub-Saharan Africa (SSA). Djibouti, Mauritania, Sudan, Somalia and South Sudan are also placed in the MENA region. This might not matter so much—it could simply be an internal operational matter for the World Bank and IMF—but in many of their databases these organisations do not even provide the option for a disaggregation of the continent. The result is that World Bank and IMF research persistently refer to the SSA or MENA regions, but—with some notable exceptions—only rarely to the African continent.

The message this conveys is clearly contrary to African unity. Yet the solution would be straightforward and very easy to implement: to provide the disaggregation for the African continent in their databases and start referring more frequently in their reports to Africa rather than SSA. This would send a strong signal that these institutions are serious about supporting the continental project. The US has woken up to the implications of this way of treating the continent and in a positive step forward, the 'US Strategy Toward Sub-Saharan Africa' announced by the Biden administration in August 2022 called for the US to 'address the artificial bureaucratic division between North Africa and sub-Saharan Africa'.[7]

In recent years, there has been a significant shift in opinion. Institutions like the World Bank have abandoned their sceptical stance, and now openly support regional integration on the continent. This is reflected in reports on the AfCFTA like that launched by the World Bank in 2020.[8] In another World Bank publication sympathetic to continental integration, the authors hit the proverbial nail on the head when they state that:

> The pessimistic view that regional integration can only play a limited role in Africa … is still common. Our studies challenge this conventional wisdom. It is becoming increasingly apparent that there is enormous scope for increased cross border trade and investment in Africa. Moreover, with rising incomes in Africa there are growing opportunities for cross border trade in basic manufactures, such as metal and plastic products, and processed food that are costly to import from outside the region. The potential for regional production chains has yet to be exploited and cross border trade in services offers similarly untapped opportunities.[9]

The reasons behind this shift in opinion are complex but are partially at least instrumentalist in nature. Some professionals working in the World Bank and other institutions see the AfCFTA as a useful tool to continue with the pursuit of the liberalisation agenda—'liberalisation by stealth', as it were. This is hinted at in the aforementioned World Bank report: 'Implementing the AfCFTA would help usher in the kinds of deep reforms necessary to enhance long-term growth in African countries'.[10] This also might explain the generous amount of funding that trade-facilitation organisations like TradeMark Africa—reputedly, the largest trade facilitation organisation in the world—get from donors. This is not to denigrate the very valuable work that these organisations do in trade facilitation, but it does inevitably generate a suspicion that the agenda is to focus principally on liberalising imports—a continuation of the policies of the 1980s and 1990s to achieve trade liberalisation through the back door, rather than promote the development of productive capacities in export-oriented industries.

Indeed, arguably, part of the donor community is in denial with regard to the extent that the AfCFTA is still a 'preferential agreement'; binding and reciprocal, yes, but still meant to favour only

African trading partners or African-based investors to better access the larger African market.[11] There is a risk here for the success of the AfCFTA. As Mkandawire noted with regard to the fate of earlier Pan-African schemes, 'One major premise of regional integration is preferential treatment of members of a particular integration scheme. Liberalisations sought opening to [the] entire world. This [is what] put paid to the Lagos Plan of Action'.[12]

Support for the AfCFTA is therefore in a rather strange position of actually cutting across the normal ideological lines within the economics profession. As noted by Odijie:

> There are grounds to think that both mainstream economists and development scholars … are likely to support the promotion of continental free trade in Africa. Mainstream economists generally support trade liberalization based on the argument that it leads to the most efficient allocation of resources …. In contrast, neo-Listians like Ha-Joon Chang and Erik Reinert would probably support the AfCFTA for reasons relating to market size. For example, due to their relatively small populations, countries like Ghana and Rwanda cannot provide the market basis for the promotion of large-scale manufacturing. Friedrich List and his followers were aware of this problem; List proposed unifying small countries to create an internal market big enough for industrialization.[13]

An equally odd coalition of opponents to the AfCFTA has emerged alongside this—from heterodox economists who believe that the AfCFTA is simply a manifestation of neoliberalism, to orthodox economists that have a trenchant belief that liberalisation and the free market is still the only way forward and, disregarding the overwhelming body of evidence shared in Parts I and II of this book, are still attached to their belief that regional integration is a 'second-best' or even 'third-best' policy option. Strange bedfellows indeed.[14] The battle lines are thus blurred. Regardless of these controversies, in this chapter we stress that there are specific ways that the donor community and multilaterals could better help in the construction of the continental market.

Aid conditionality and reduced policy space

Aid has been disproportionally directed towards Africa since the beginning of the 'aid era' in the post-war period. On the face of it, the global totals involved seemed impressive. Already by the 1980s the African share of aid per person was higher than anywhere else in the developing world. OECD countries had, by 1990, probably ploughed USD 50–60 billion into Africa, a sum that had risen to about USD 1.3 trillion by 2012.[15]

Because of the scope and scale of its influence, Mkandawire called the donor community the 'aid juggernaut'. From the 1990s he argued that aid in Africa was no longer focused on providing funds to fill resource gaps, but instead focused on ways of doing things, the implementation of objectives, standards-setting and conditionalities. The contemporary discourse on the importance of maximising 'ownership' of policies has been very difficult to square with the still pervasive nature of conditionality in many of the poorest developing countries.[16] The ultimate consequence of conditionality has often been perverse, as spelled out by Whitfield and Fraser:[17]

> If African governments are to be accountable to their citizens, then they must determine their development strategy and priorities, the set of policies to achieve those priorities, the instruments to implement those policies, and the timing and sequencing of implementation. If recipient governments do not have sufficient room to do this due to donor demands, or if they cede responsibility for policy choices and their outcomes to donors, then aid creates additional obstacles for citizens in holding their governments accountable.

There is an additional dimension to all this. Donor support often comes with a large foreign presence in African institutions, with foreigners often assuming key decision-making activities and responsibilities. This would be difficult enough if they were recommending a coherent set of practices or norms. However, reflecting the diversity of foreign actors and the parcelisation of African institutions among different donors, the striking feature is the array of institutional idiosyncrasies that recipient countries must live with.[18] The result of all this is that African governments often get cajoled in contrary directions, resulting in policy incoherence. Take, for instance, the FMP. Because of a heavy dependence on donor financing, migration policy in Africa often echoes European rather than continental priorities, with a lot of funding dedicated to persuading African governments to halt migrant flows north:

[This] legitimises a whole lot of really nasty things that can be done to migrants [within Africa]. It also works against any kind of sensible discussion about what countries could be doing .... European-funded anti-migration campaigns tell Africans harrowing stories of death and disaster.[19]

As a consequence of this kind of pervasive influence, some authors have questioned whether African countries are able to pursue the same kind of effective industrialisation policies that the Asian economies pursued in their push towards development.[20] There are a few purposeful governments on the continent that have managed to carve out more leeway than the average, such as Ethiopia, Morocco and Rwanda.[21] But they tend to be the exceptions rather than the rule, and this often happens in the context of less aid-dependent economies (though Ethiopia and Rwanda are obvious exceptions to this rule of thumb). Consciously or not, the donor community simply is not in the business of building up industrial capacity in what could become competing economies, which explains the extremely low share of donor money that goes to productive activities outside of small-scale agriculture, SMEs, and micro-financing.[22] 'Thinking small' is thus subtly imposed on African governments (see Chapters 9 and 14)—but economic history tells us most resoundingly that this is not the route to long-term sustainable development.

The (unpalatable) alternatives to preferential market access

In Chapter 6, we explained at some length why preferential market access agreements have broadly failed to deliver on their promise. Strict rules of origin, the arbitrary application of phytosanitary standards, heavy-handed conditionality, preferential tariff erosion and the impermanence of the agreements have in essence undermined their usefulness. Yet the fact that AGOA, EPAs and other preferential schemes have not produced the desired results does not necessarily imply that the next option is to move towards reciprocal market access. That is very strange logic indeed. Not only is it unclear where the economic benefits are going to come from, it is also doubtful it would help African firms address their supply-side constraints and limitations. While it is true that firms could source capital goods and intermediate products more easily under a bilateral free trade deal from their higher-income and higher-productivity trading partner, such trading arrangements could also induce trade diversion away from lower-cost suppliers not benefiting from the free trade deal, thereby undermining long-term competitiveness.

More fundamentally, North–South negotiations are particularly challenging for developing countries, and they often end up trading away their policy space in areas like intellectual property and investment in exchange for improved access to the developed partners' markets.[23] Regional bilateral trade agreements typically extend external constraints beyond those found in the WTO. These agreements are in effect a means for the United States and the EU to export their own regulatory approaches to developing nations. They often encompass measures which the US and the EU have tried but failed to get adopted in the WTO. In addition, in its free trade agreements with developing countries, the United States aggressively pushes for the lifting of restrictions designed to regulate capital flows.[24] And it impacts on other areas too. As part of the original NAFTA negotiations, for instance, Mexico accepted virtually all the US demands on intellectual property protection, clearly to the benefit of US firms.[25]

Not only are there the power imbalances to take into account, but North–South agreements have tended to create 'hub-and-spoke' trade relationships, with large high-income economies being the 'hub' and small developing ones being the 'spokes.' Because their economies are small, African countries have always been the spokes in their trade relations with industrial countries, especially those in Western Europe.[26] These agreements benefit the hub disproportionately because of differing rules of origin, product exclusions, and trade and investment diversion. There is even evidence that hub countries enjoy higher R&D and productivity levels, whereas the opposite is true for spoke countries: regional trade liberalisation may decrease productivity of periphery economies if the level of competition with the hub countries is too ferocious.[27]

For its part, the United States has often struggled to reach FTAs with developing regions. For instance, negotiations for the Free Trade Area of the Americas were proposed in 1994 but never concluded.[28] The US subsequently turned towards bilateral agreements with individual Latin American countries (Chile, Panama, Colombia and Peru), as well as in other regions. The evidence is mixed on the effectiveness of these agreements, however—US exports to signatory countries have boomed in some cases, but imports from Latin American countries to the United States have experienced a far weaker response, with the result that the Latin American countries ended up sustaining larger trade deficits with the US.[29]

Similarly, the prospects for African countries to make significant inroads with their agricultural exports into the US market are quite poor. The US farming lobby is extremely vocal, and still receives major subsidies to the tune of USD 20 billion annually in direct transfers (and much more indirectly). This makes it very difficult for African farmers to compete on an even-footing, as has been noted in Chapter 9. Yet that does not stop US officials explicitly flagging Africa as a growth market for its own agricultural exports:

> Africa remains a continent of great, yet mostly untapped, potential for U.S. agricultural exports .... [In 2022] only one African country (Egypt) was in the United States' top 15 agricultural export markets, and only four additional countries (Nigeria, Morocco, Algeria, and South Africa) were in the United States' top 50 agricultural export markets—but we expect this to change significantly in the future.[30]

Similar challenges bedevil economic relations with the European Union and their proposed EPAs. Over two decades ago, even before it became official policy, African analysts were aware of the potential problems with the EPAs.[31] Most African exports were already entering the EU market free of tariffs under preferential market access schemes (Chapter 6); as such, the scheme basically provided improved market access for EU exporters to African markets, but the converse was not true. Thus, the only significant additional market access gains derived from the scheme by African countries would be through laxer rules of origin or less arbitrary phytosanitary controls and the like.

Moreover, given their fragile industrial sectors, the impact of the EPAs in terms of increased competitive pressures and lost fiscal revenues would inevitably be quite large. Furthermore, granting free access only to EU exporters would discriminate against Africa's other trading partners and cause trade diversion. Finally, as noted earlier, the 'hub-and-spoke' approach to regionalism generally favoured by the EU will bias investment towards the hub (i.e. the EU) rather than towards the spokes (i.e. African countries). Multiple studies have supported these concerns.[32]

The fact that the negotiations have taken over two decades speaks volumes and reflects the lack of enthusiasm by African countries to sign up to the deals. By mid-2022, only the EU interim EPAs with Ghana and Côte d'Ivoire had entered into force and were being provisionally applied.[33] The EPA with six SADC states had been ratified, but for East Africa the EPA encountered intra-EAC opposition/friction due to concerns that they may be detrimental to intra-African trade, leading Kenya to negotiate bilaterally with the EU.[34] This makes a total of nine out of 48 African countries that have EPAs with the EU—after 20 years of exertion.

As an example of how such agreements can cause problems for the AfCFTA, the unilateral agreement between the EU and South Africa has already caused strain within SADC, contributing to an indefinite suspension in working towards a customs union. Particularly problematic was the fact that South Africa negotiated the agreement without involving the other four members of SACU.[35]

Perhaps most controversial of all is the way in which the EPAs are seemingly being used to pursue 'Singapore issues'; that is, issues related to investment, competition policy, transparency in government procurement and trade facilitation (see Chapter 7). In the face of firm opposition from developing countries they were considered too divisive during the Doha Round of WTO negotiations and were subsequently dropped. The fact that they have reappeared in the EPA negotiations suggests the EU is now pursuing a similar agenda bilaterally. Similar arguments could apply to the USA. As Jawara and Kwa argued:

> Since Cancun, many have bemoaned the possible demise of multilateralism, represented by the WTO; its replacement with bilateral negotiations has been held over the developing countries as a dire threat. This is a false choice. For the USA and EC, bilateral agreements and the WTO are not alternatives but two parts of the same strategy. What cannot be attained in one arena is pursued in the other, and 'progress' in one strengthens the other.[36]

China's role—neither saint nor sinner

A special mention is warranted for bilateral relations between the African continent and China. Although China had economic relations with the African continent dating back centuries, beyond a few specific interventions in East Africa (notably the construction of the Tanzam railways between Zambia and Tanzania), the Asian giant's economic engagement on the continent had been relatively modest until the early 2000s. But thereafter there was a remarkable increase in Chinese investment and trade on the continent, driven in part by the need to secure sources of raw materials and fuel to feed its demand for inputs into its prodigious manufacturing sector.[37] What implications does this have for the AfCFTA?

It is quite clear that China is not in Africa for philanthropic reasons. Western analysts have often been extraordinarily critical in their appreciations of Chinese influence on the continent, claiming that China is only interested in exploiting the continent's natural resources—given the long history of Western extractive industries in Africa, this claim strikes many Africans as rather like the kettle calling the pot black. Some European analysts have even suggested that China's engagement on the continent has changed the political landscape and that Africa has experienced a major reverse in political reform and the consolidation of democracy on the continent due to China's support of authoritarian regimes.[38] While Chinese engagement on the continent is clearly not for philanthropic reasons, the evidence provides relatively little support for such contentions.[39] One recent study finds that Chinese FDI is not even primarily attracted to Africa for its oil and gas reserves (although they do note that Chinese FDI is correlated with high levels of mineral deposits—aluminium, bauxite, copper, gold and diamonds).[40] Indeed, the authors note that larger markets are a significant determinant of Chinese FDI in Africa, something reflected in considerable amounts of Chinese investment into the continent's manufacturing sector.[41]

What China's increased engagement on the continent has done is change the framework within which development cooperation is provided. Whereas some Western analysts and governments see the entry of China as undermining their efforts to 'discipline' certain 'errant' governments, others see it as a promising, more workmanlike, relationship between African governments and donors.[42] Indeed, this would explain why African countries have been so accommodating to the overtures of the Chinese on the continent— there are no political conditionalities attached, and consequently African countries know (or at least think they know) where they stand. China, above all, is challenging the received wisdom on ownership and conditionality, principally by giving aid under the same modality that the DAC members and the World Bank did in the 1960s and 1970s—namely, project-based aid, tied in with agreements on trade and aid, and with minimal conditionality and no political dimension.[43]

The benefits from the African perspective are tangible. If, for instance, we accept the earlier arguments that a revitalisation of industrial policy is a necessary prerequisite for African countries to successfully take advantage of the opportunities stemming from the AfCFTA, then the additional policy space that China's presence has afforded them is to be welcomed. The other area where there is a clear positive impact on the prospects of the AfCFTA is the massive Chinese support for infrastructure projects (roads, railways, bridges and energy), physical structures and government facilities. This is all integral to the functioning of the continental agreement.

As with all relationships, however, Sino-African relations have their own set of problems. Unease at working conditions in Chinese-owned mines and factories has spilled over into protests on several occasions, from Zambia to Nigeria. We mentioned in Chapter 6 the challenge represented by the surge of Chinese imports into the continent, often of finished goods of sometimes debatable quality. Although frequently exaggerated, high levels of indebtedness are also a challenge in countries with heavy exposure to Chinese loans.[44] Nonetheless, on balance, Africa-China relations are characterised by a degree of 'possibilism':

> When you come from a rich country, poor countries look the same .... You can see people writing about a city like Nairobi and they see no changes because it still looks poor compared to London and Paris .... That is why so much of the Western aid establishment simply can't see Africa industrialising. Asians can see easily because they are not far off from where we are, and that's why they can imagine Africa

industrialising. The Japanese and the Chinese have always thought Africa can industrialise ... because their own experience is quite recent in their memories.[45]

More diversified investment as an alternative to free trade agreements

Before we leave the story of the Chinese influence on the continent, there is one further aspect of Sino-African economic relations that is worth stressing. Although in the popular imagination Chinese firms are focused on exploiting Africa's energy and mineral wealth, in reality Chinese firms operate across many sectors of the African economy. Nearly a third are involved in manufacturing, a quarter in services, and around a fifth in trade, construction and real estate. In infrastructure, Chinese firms' dominance is pronounced, claiming nearly 50% of Africa's internationally contracted construction market. In manufacturing, McKinsey has estimated that 12% of Africa's industrial production—valued at some USD 500 billion a year in total—is already handled by Chinese firms. Moreover, unlike in China (where many factories are oriented to international markets), many Chinese factories in Africa are largely serving its fast-growing markets. According to a McKinsey survey, 93% of the revenues of Chinese-owned manufacturers came from regional sales.[46] In line with our observations in Chapter 9 about the high returns in many sectors of the African economy, the firms are also profitable; nearly one third of those surveyed reported 2015 profit margins of more than 20%, and more than half reported that they had taken four years or less to recoup their initial investment. For example, the owner of a Chinese manufacturing firm in Kenya was reported as saying, 'I expect to make back my investment in less than a year because the prevailing market price is so high for my product'.[47] Chinese firms also seem agile and quick to adapt to new opportunities.[48]

At a time of AfCFTA implementation, such investment activity is very much welcome, and will hopefully act as a spur to greater investment by Western countries and other important investors from emerging economies (e.g. India, Brazil, etc.) to establish production facilities on the continent. European and North American firms certainly have a major presence, but it is not as pronounced as it could be. For instance, of the UK's investment stock on the continent, around half of the total is accounted for by the mining sector, and another quarter is in banking and finance. What's more, just one country—South Africa—takes the lion's share of that capital. The profile of EU and US investment is similar (Figure 13.1).

Clearly, from an African perspective, a more diversified investment portfolio would be advantageous. As explained in Chapters 9 and 10, there is a need for much more investment on the continent in the productive sectors—in high-valued services and segments of agriculture, yes, but particularly in manufacturing. While the preference should be for investments from other African countries, as stressed in Chapter 10, there is clearly also a major role for investment from outside the continent. The hope is that Chinese economic activity on the continent will spur investors from elsewhere to also take action and consider investing more in the African market. To some extent, that is already happening. France has recently been announcing a series of investments in East Africa—a region where in the past its companies have tended to be conspicuous by their

Figure 13.1: Sectoral distribution of direct investments from EU and the United States (2020)

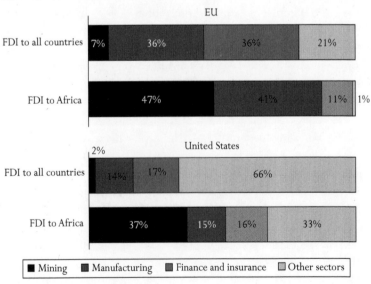

Sources: US Department of Commerce (2023); MacLeod and Luke (2023).

absence.[49] And US firms like Ford have already announced large investments to strengthen their regional presence.

Help with focusing on the right (not the wrong) things

For developing country governments with serious resource con-straints, focusing on the right things is fundamental. And that can be informed, at least in part, by research. But there are often serious disconnects between the research community and the policy one. For instance, as noted in Chapter 9, policy discussions in recent years have tended to focus on encouraging the growth of 'small enterprises' or SMEs. This, Mkandawire noted (as usual, way ahead of the curve of most analysts), is part of a Manichean discourse in which 'small is beautiful' and big is ugly.[50] By contrast, successful development strate-gies in Asia and Latin America have tended to focus on the develop-ment of DBGs.[51] Where there is a role for SMEs in these development strategies, it hinges on their relationships with larger enterprises.

Private sector development strategies in most African countries receive a lot of support from the IFIs and donors like the United States, and they consequently have an almost ideological predisposi-tion towards supporting the development of small firms. Most of these strategies tend to focus their attention on encouraging more businesses to operate or be registered in a country or on improving the general business environment.[52] As such, weaknesses in private sector development are portrayed as a supply-side problem, including deficiencies in both government policy and within the private sector itself. But this, as Behuria rightly notes, fails to acknowledge the demand side of the economy—a considerable oversight, since many of the largest African DBGs have grown through responding to domestic and regional demand.[53]

Can a special emphasis on SMEs and labour-intensive technologies be justified within the context of the AfCFTA? The African economic landscape's dominant feature—an informal sector comprising micro-enterprises, household production, and unofficial activities—absorbs the growing urban labour force and acts as a social safety net. But, as reported in Chapter 9, the evidence suggests it cannot provide the missing productive dynamism. Studies show that very few micro-enterprises grow out of informality, just as the bulk of successful established firms do not start out as small, informal enterprises.[54] Although it is often ignored in popular discourse, it is well recognised in the literature that SMEs tend to exhibit below-average productivity and offer comparatively low levels of salary and less secure employment than large enterprises. It is mainly large enterprises that can exploit economies of scale, invest resources in R&D, and develop new, more efficient technologies. Even when it is accepted that SMEs exhibit relatively low productivity, it is commonly argued that they contribute more to employment creation. Yet even here the evidence is ambiguous. For instance, of an estimated 128,000 manufacturing jobs created in Ethiopia between 1996 and 2016, all were created in establishments employing ten workers or more, and most were concentrated in larger establishments.[55]

An excessive focus on the SME sector ignores the realities of how the global economy ticks. Although there are important structural differences between all the market economies, in general terms large firms are the anchor around which the rest of the economy is built (the baobabs, in the words of Ache Leke; see Chapter 10). In a world where huge standalone firms are a thing of the past, and supply chains have become the norm, there is a real need to develop a strong ecosystem of SMEs dependent on the activities and operations of larger companies. It is precisely the absence of a sufficient number of large companies that handicaps the development of a structurally resilient economy in many African countries.

Arguably, the discourse on structural transformation[56]—one that is heard across the continent and crucial for understanding the dynamics of development—has been shifted excessively towards the activities of small firms. This could exact a heavy price on the implementation of the AfCFTA if energies are almost exclusively diverted towards supporting the development of the SME sector. One outcome could be that industrial policies skewed towards small firms might succeed in increasing their productivity, yet exert a negative influence on aggregative productivity levels at the same time, simply by preserving a size composition of enterprises that is suboptimal from an economic growth perspective.[57]

An alternative, more evidence-based strategy proposed by Duflo and Banerjee[58] would involve using governmental resources to help create more large businesses by providing loan guarantees to medium-sized ventures. This kind of strategy may set off a virtuous circle: stable and higher wages of larger firms would give workers the financial security and the necessary optimism both to invest in their children and save more. With higher savings, and access to easier credit that a steady job brings, the most talented among them would also eventually be able to start businesses large enough to hire other people.

Finally, another example of the way that the contemporary donor discourse shapes African policies in ways which are not always helpful is migration policy (Chapter 12). For instance, EU migration initiatives on the African continent have been criticised for concentrating on migration management in 'the northern route' towards Europe and for focusing on North Africa, West Africa and the Horn of Africa regions, while neglecting the impact of migration on other parts of the continent.[59]

For domestic politcal reasons, the EU seems intent on spending a lot of money to 'deter' migrants. One example is the European Union Emergency Trust. The European Commission's (2016) stated aim is to 'invest in long-term economic and social development, improving people's life and tackling the drivers of migration'. With over 4 billion euros already committed, this is a major undertaking.[60] Yet there is little evidence that these policies are effective. Indeed, one study even finds that development assistance made conditional on reducing migratory outflows towards Europe backfires and creates even more migratory pressures.[61]

Even from the perspective of self-interest, it would seem better if more of these funds were spent helping increase the attractiveness of intra-African migration, through assisting with the implementation of the free movement protocol. According to Afrobarometer, the first preference of African migrants is to stay on the African continent, with 36% of respondents preferring to go to another African country, compared with 27% who aspire to go to Europe. Why not leverage that sentiment, support the implementation of the FMP, and increase the attractiveness of Africa as a destination for migration? The benefits for the continent, as spelled out in Chapter 12, would be manifold. Moreover, this is one area where the EU has a rich history of successfully adopting a progressive internal migration policy, especially since its full endorsement of free movement since 1993.[62] This experience could be shared with Africa and help inform the implementation of the FMP. Funding more regional initiatives on the continent would be a powerful way to go.

Conclusions

It is important to recognise from the outset that there are limitations to how much the international community can achieve. To paraphrase John Maynard Keynes, development is essentially home-spun—and there is now a wide consensus on this point among the development community, both inside and outside Africa.[63] However, the financial and intellectual impact of the donor community on the African continent since independence has been pervasive. That is why it is important that in future their policy advice be better attuned to the priorities of the AfCFTA.

Fortunately, there is a lot of empirical evidence to draw upon when deciding priorities for providing financial and technical support—it just requires that the technicians keep abreast of the literature and correctly interpret it. Yet at the moment, policy support seems to follow fashion more than being evidence-based.

No single study should form the basis of policy action, but as an example of the kind of insights which can be gleaned from existing research, one recent econometric analysis found that, all else being equal, lower tariffs, better infrastructure and easier access to credit all favoured larger trade flows. The study also stressed that the gap to be breached on the African continent was a large one, with the quality of infrastructure about 50% lower in the region than elsewhere in the world, with credit to GDP ratios about 25% lower, and tariffs on average four times higher than elsewhere.[64]

Why not use such evidence to guide policy? For instance, donors could work with institutions like the African Development Bank or Afreximbank to increase the resources available for investments in infrastructure, and by supporting the African Union's Action Plan for Boosting Intra-African Trade and the Associated Programme for Infrastructure Development in Africa (PIDA). Out of 409 projects launched by the PIDA in 2012, only 155 (38%) are under construction or already operational; 15% are currently in the pre-feasibility or feasibility study phases, while 10% are still in the stage of project definition.[65]

We know the payoffs could be large from completing these programmes. For instance, Coulibaly and Fontagné estimated the elasticity of trade performance to infrastructure endowments of seven West African Economic and Monetary Union (WAEMU) countries and found that trade flows within them would be 3.2 times higher if 100% of interstate roads were paved.[66] Buys, Deichmann and Wheeler, meanwhile, established that the coordinated upgrading and maintenance of road networks could expand intra-African trade by 18% annually over a 15-year period. These are massive impacts. Aligning donor programmes better with the continent's own priorities would thus be a great step forward.[67]

14

CONCLUSIONS

TOWARDS A UNIVERSAL AFRICA

Introduction

This book has tried to convey the sense of urgency that surrounds the AfCFTA. Over the last few years, Africa's development challenges have come into sharp focus with the onset of the Covid-19 pandemic, the war in Ukraine, global inflationary pressures, a rise in the intensity of extreme climatic events, increasing food insecurity, and the risk of an impending debt crisis in some countries, all lending credence to the idea that Africa needs to press the reset button and approach its developmental aspirations in a new way. We (and fortunately many others) believe the way in which to do this is the AfCFTA.

Part I of this book is based essentially on the premise that the alternatives have been tried and found wanting. But a true attempt at Pan-African integration has not. Part II explained the economic rationale behind the AfCFTA. They may be guilty of exaggeration, but Woolfrey et al. paint a futuristic nightmare of what could go wrong over the coming decades if the AfCFTA fails to catalyse the kind of changes necessary, including urban riots, a sharp rise of displaced populations, a collapse in intra-African transport networks and general economic malaise.[1]

Fortunately, the goals of the AfCFTA are broadly supported by public opinion. An initial polling in 2018 of more than 2,000 respondents from 42 African countries found that an overwhelming 77% expressed strong confidence that the AfCFTA is an important step toward economic growth and prosperity for Africa. When asked about the most significant outcome of the AfCFTA, most respondents cited employment creation, economic development and integration, and increased market access. This reflects the clear promise the AfCFTA offers for advancing Africa's socio-economic development and the attainment of the African Union's Agenda 2063, as well as highlighting the importance of continuously engaging stakeholders.[2]

Nonetheless, there is a need for realism too. The founder of the European Economic Community (and French prime minister) Robert Schuman said in 1950, 'Europe will not be made all at once, or according to a single plan. It will be built through concrete achievements which first create a de facto solidarity'.[3] In other words, if you build the mechanisms of economic cooperation first, this will prepare the ground for broader political cooperation and institutions. This is the pragmatic approach that Africa too has chosen. Implementing the continental free trade area will be a long process that will be achieved by a thousand small steps.[4] Notwithstanding Mo Ibrahim's recent (and wise) exaltations for the continent to reduce its dependence on external support for achieving its integrational goals,[5] leveraging foreign investment and the donor community will also remain important elements in the success of the continental project for the foreseeable future. Far from wishing to disengage economically, the AfCFTA is a project to facilitate the continent's incorporation into the global economy on a stronger footing. This final chapter makes some observations about what we consider to be some of the critical aspects for the effective implementation of the agreement.

The need for regional champions

A finding common to many studies is that a regional agreement is more likely to succeed if at least one government takes the lead in implementing it.[6] There are two main reasons for this. Firstly, enacting regional integration agreements requires an extensive amount of intergovernmental coordination. As a result, it is subject to the problems associated with collective action.[7] Implementation is more likely to succeed if at least one government takes the lead in solving these coordination problems. Secondly, although there are net gains, regional integration can cause losses for some sectors of certain economies. If the voices representing those sectors are loud enough, it is understandable that some governments may be reluctant to implement agreements.

The EU is a particularly salient example of the importance of one country taking the lead in a regional agreement. That country was Germany, which took a lead role in pressing for deeper regional integration and, as the largest single net contributor to the EU budget, being prepared to finance the lion's share of costs. Because it has the largest economy in the EU and its private sector is broadly supportive of deeper integration, it has been able to fulfil this lead role effectively.[8] Moreover, Germany clearly saw taking on this role in its own best interest too, not just for trade, but for its sense of purpose. As the former German Chancellor Angela Merkel once conceded in an interview, 'I see the European Union as our life insurance. Germany is far too small to exert geo-political influence on its own'.[9] If that is true for Germany within the EU, how much truer for individual African economies?

Sadly for the continent, as noted in Chapter 4, Africa has lacked a regional hegemon with the same proclivities. Being such a large continent, it surely has the economic space for several sub-regional hegemons. In Southern Africa, for instance, South Africa might have been a natural candidate to assume this role. But it did not do so, initially because of the way the legacy of apartheid had made the country a pariah state with its regional neighbours. After South Africa's democratic transition and global diplomatic normalisation in the 1990s, it is true that the country's private sector aggressively pursued economic opportunities throughout the region,[10] and today South African firms trade and invest in a range of sectors across the continent, including in mining, construction and manufacturing, agriculture and food processing, financial services, consumer retailing, transport, tourism and hospitality, and telecommunications. In addition to this, some strong regional value chains have been established across economies that neighbour South Africa.[11] The expansion of apparel exports from Lesotho, Eswatini and Madagascar into the South African market is a good example of this phenomenon.[12] But so too are firms like the telecom giant MTN Group, which has operations across the continent—and is potentially a great integrator of economic activity across borders.[13] Above all, as we saw in Chapter 9, South Africa is already the continent's largest regional trader, and enjoys a positive trade balance with the rest of the continent.

Yet although South Africa is in a strong economic position to take a lead role in the roll-out of the AfCFTA, on some scores, it seems reluctant to do so. This is also reflected in South Africa's sometimes ambiguous attitudes towards its own regional economic community—the SADC. The reluctance is possibly attributable to several factors:

- The country tends to view global integration as a more promising development strategy than regional integration. As a result, its export-oriented growth strategy focuses on international markets, especially toward the EU, with which it has an FTA.[14]
- While South African firms have a strong regional presence, the government does not always advocate for the interests of its domestic private sector abroad.[15] This is partly an inheritance of the era of apartheid—the government appears to have concerns over a potential backlash to its economic interests due to perceived South African hegemony.[16]
- The country also continues to struggle with high rates of domestic unemployment and the Congress of South African Trade Unions is very vocal in challenging policies that may negatively impact its members. Economic liberalisation has already adversely impacted South Africa's labour-intensive manufacturing sectors. As a result, many are understandably cautious about further economic liberalisation, whether this is within SADC or under the aegis of the AfCFTA.[17]

As a consequence of this hesitancy, some authors allege that South Africa actually risks losing its reputation as the 'gateway to Africa'.[18] However, there are two regional integration efforts that are clearly a priority for the government.[19] The first is the highly successful Maputo Development Corridor project, which has been responsible for the massive growth in bilateral trade and FDI between South Africa and Mozambique since the turn of the millennium. Notwithstanding the controversies that exploded around the company in 2023, due to persistent power outages, there have been efforts to place the South African company Eskom at the centre of Southern Africa's electricity generation and distribution networks. While Eskom imports from Lesotho and Mozambique, and exports to Botswana, Lesotho, Namibia, and Eswatini, the government of South Africa reportedly has much greater ambitions in the region.[20] Looked at in the cold light of day, projects like these should persuade South Africa to take a more proactive stance with regards to the creation of the continental market. A very positive sign that South Africa does take its role seriously is the fact that a young and dynamic South African national, Wamkele Mene, took over in February 2020 as the first Secretary-General of the AfCFTA Secretariat in Accra.

Beyond South Africa, economic research makes it clear that regional hubs are evolving in other parts of the continent. Allard et al. use a measure of 'centrality', which reveals the emergence of trade sub-regions, with hubs such as Côte d'Ivoire, Nigeria, and, to a lesser extent, Senegal in West Africa, and Kenya in East Africa.[21] In economic terms, some Kenyan firms have taken a leading role in certain sectors across the region, including a few companies that have become household names, such as Safaricom (telecommunications) and the Serena group (hospitality), not to mention the success that the Kenyan banking sector has had in its Pan-African operations.[22]

Kenya has been arguably rather more neglectful of its regional role in recent years, however, as revealed by a slowing down of its trade with the EAC and declining intra-regional investment made by Kenyan firms from 2015–20.[23] From this point of view, Kenya also needs, like South Africa, to step up to the mark and assume its regional economic leadership. It is clear from policy documents and public pronouncements from its officials that Kenya is starting to rethink its strategy towards the continent and give it a higher priority. It is also reinvigorating its unquestionable leadership role within the EAC, and a Kenyan national—Ambassador Peter Mathuki—is currently heading that institution as Secretary-General.

And then there is the North African question. Of all the sub-regions on the continent, the one that is most separated from the rest is clearly North Africa. This is partly a function of economic geography—with the Mediterranean binding Europe and North Africa together, and the Sahara separating it from the rest of the continent—and partly a function of North Africa's historical cultural and political ties with Europe and the Middle East.

Yet in developmental terms, North Africa has an enormous amount to bring to the continental agreement, both in terms of its human capital (with the best-qualified workers on the continent) and its expansive trading links with the rest of the world. Of all the North African countries, Egypt has the largest economy, but is not 'pulling its weight' in terms of continental integration, with a very low share of its total trade with the continent (see Chapter 8). Yet like South Africa and Kenya, Egypt has a strong manufacturing base and many competitive firms.

It is clearly in the long-term interest of the Egyptian economy to leverage the continental market to the advantage of its large manufacturing sector, and also to procure more in the way of intermediate goods and agricultural products from the continental market. Morocco could perhaps show the way; in recent years, it has been expanding its economic interests in the rest of the continent, both through trade and, crucially, investment. The country has even applied to become part of ECOWAS. Part of the driver here is political,[24] but ultimately, it may not matter what the motivation is from the point of view of achieving deeper continental integration—the end objective is to achieve a more integrated African economy.

Finally, we have intentionally not elaborated on the more positive role on AfCFTA implementation that could be played in West Africa by Nigeria. Its internal political economy and attitudes towards continental and regional projects are complicated and would warrant more space than is available.[25] But it is clearly a major actor with the potential to exercise a monumental influence on the implementation of the AfCFTA. Adedeji summed up the situation succinctly in a speech he delivered back in 1985:

> What happens to the Nigerian economy is not the affair or concern of Nigerians alone; it is of concern to the wider continent as most African countries look up to it as the beacon. Will Nigeria rise up to the challenge?[26]

CONCLUSIONS

To sum up, leading economic hubs such as Egypt, Kenya, Nigeria and South Africa can exert positive spill-over effects into regional markets.[27] Many of their larger firms have already expanded into the region, and not only draw in their domestic suppliers, but also use suppliers from elsewhere in the region. Above all, as stressed in Chapter 9, the continent's net exporters to the African market could shift their positions and actively promote greater imports. This is particularly the case for South Africa, which is not only by far the largest exporter to the continental market, but also enjoys the largest positive trade balance (worth nearly USD 10 billion in 2022).[28] In this vein, one proposal recently put forward by Macleod et al. is that regional 'leaders' should set an example and start immediately allowing duty-free imports from other African countries. They cite the example of Kenya taking leadership in the East African Community, when it immediately allowed duty-free imports into its market from its neighbours when the customs union was formed in 2005, while letting its exports be progressively liberalised over a longer time period.[29] Indeed, this is a message that needs to be conveyed to all member states. Promoting new exports is relatively hard—it takes time to develop new products and services and identify market opportunities. But removing the barriers to greater intra-African imports is something that can almost be achieved with the stroke of a customs officer's pen.

Greater economic policy coordination

Increased trade will not in itself drive industrialisation or development; it must be accompanied by appropriate policies.[30] There is now a wide consensus on the need for modern industrial policies for the African continent, often framed as 'smart industrial policies'.[31] Yet the AfCFTA currently has no programme specifically governing industrial policy. As a result, a mechanism must be found to promote industrialisation and deal with the lack of coordination that is likely to occur at a continental level.

Recent developments in the global economy are probably giving African countries greater leeway to experiment with different forms of industrial policy. For instance, under the Inflation Reduction Act implemented in late 2022, the US government committed nearly USD 370 billion of subsidies for clean energy projects. Arguing that such subsidies create an uneven playing field and were unfair to European companies, the EU retaliated with its own investment plan to support the development of green industries, worth USD 800 billion.[32] China too has been investing enormous sums to support its green economy, much to the chagrin of the European Commission.[33] The likelihood of African countries being rebuked or falling foul of WTO rules for attempting their own (much more modest) industrial policies is diminished when such practices become generalised.

The challenge for the continent is, of course, that it simply does not have the same level of resources to throw into its industrial policies as do China, the EU or the United States. So if it is going to do so effectively, it will need to do it in a coordinated manner. While industrial policies can 'tilt' the playing field toward sectors or technologies with positive spill-overs or externalities,[34] there can be some risks associated with countries selecting similar sectors to promote. For instance, in West Africa, in line with its industrial policy, Nigeria selected cement for protection. But this prompted Ghana, Côte d'Ivoire, Togo, Sierra Leone, Benin and Burkina Faso to institute similar policies promoting cement production.[35]

How then to tackle the issue of coordinating industrial policies? In theory, implementing regional industrial policies through RECs could enhance scale economies and complementarities, leading to increased production, processing, higher-value exports, and industrialisation through the development of regional value chains.[36] However, this regional approach has not been very effective through bodies such as the EAC, ECOWAS, SADC or COMESA, mainly because their plans lack funding and member states are hesitant to align their national policies with regional ones.

Arguably, the only effective way to meet these challenges will be through concrete partnerships built on the realities of particular sectors—the formation of sectorial coalitions in areas like agro-processing, automobile manufacturing, pharmaceuticals, textiles and clothing, etc.—all sectors with specific needs and with a vested interest in making sure the AfCFTA works for them. Giving substance to such ideas, a 2022 ICT report undertook research to identify promising value chains, based on extensive data analysis and interviews with 10,000 firms as well as business support organisations, industry experts and other stakeholders. From an analysis of 415 possibilities, the study identified no less than 94 promising value chains, though the AfCFTA Private Sector Strategy identifies four priority sectors to start with: agro-processing, automotives, pharmaceuticals, and transport and logistics.[37]

One way to address the development needs of these value chains is through the establishment of industrial partnership agreements (IPAs). These agreements allow groups to collaboratively build the complex environment necessary for modern industrialisation within sectoral production and trade systems, rather than on an individual economy basis. The African Auto Pact is a concrete example of how an IPA could function.[38] These groups could also serve as effective advocates for the full implementation of the AfCFTA.

Fortunately, there are positive signs of progress in the quality and ambition of industrial policy in Africa. Morocco's car industry is a prime example of a next-generation industrial policy. Its automotive industry increased its export revenue from USD 400 million in 2004 to USD 5 billion by 2015, creating 67,000 jobs.[39] This success is due to good infrastructure, consistent policy, and a focus on exports to foreign markets where efficiency and quality control are crucial. The state provides oversight while promoting rigorous private-sector competition.[40]

The achievements of the Ethiopian Industrial Parks programme also merits a mention. In 2000, the government set a goal to achieve lower middle-income status through robust industrial growth. Despite very low initial per capita incomes, a complex political backdrop, regional instability, and some major domestic challenges related to agricultural performance and climate change,[41] the programme's results have been impressive. By mid-2019, Ethiopia's industrial parks had created about 70,000 jobs. For example, the Hawassa Industrial Park is a 300-hectare eco-friendly park focused on textile and garment production.[42] It involves a USD 250 million investment and employed more than 15,000 people.[43]

What unifies these two examples is the fact that the industrial policies are focused principally on serving developed country markets.

And therein lies their fundamental weakness. For instance, the Ethiopian strategy hit severe problems when civil conflict erupted in the country in 2020–22, leading to the suspension of the country from the provisions of AGOA in January 2021. Immediately, there were reports of job losses at Hawassa Industrial Park, and a great concern about how to reorient exports towards alternative markets—particularly on the African continent. Adedeji alerted us to the weakness of this kind of strategy, and his words still ring true:

> When entrepreneurs in the Western World talk about producing for the market, they invariably have in mind the domestic markets. When they venture into foreign markets, their main aim is to sell with a view to procuring those goods and services which they do not have at home. Such goods and services do not constitute the bulk of their activities so that when the external markets are no more viable, they can fall back on the domestic markets. *In our case, the situation is the reverse.* We do not even have a fall-back position since the goods and services which we produce at present are complementary to those of international markets. This trickle-down approach to development and economic growth will not serve our purpose. Up to now, we have usually caught more of the cold of the sneezing of the rest of the world. More of it will lead to chronic pneumonia.[44]

Instilling greater competition

In Chapter 9, we noted the high average prices paid for food products on the African continent. This also applies to many other types of consumption, intermediate and capital goods. More often than not, African consumers, firms and governments are, not to put too fine a point on it, being 'ripped off'. This is not to point a finger in any particular direction—many parties are involved—and predatory pricing practices are found across sectors. In 2009, for instance, the Competition Commission of South Africa uncovered cartel arrangements which affected the SACU market as a whole, resulting in prices being an estimated 7.5–19.9% higher than they should have been. In neighbouring Zambia, the country's Competition and Consumer Protection Commission initiated an investigation against Lafarge Zambia in 2014 for abuse of dominance in the cement market. They made an adverse finding in 2017 and, following the entry of Dangote

CONCLUSIONS

Cement in 2015, they found that Lafarge Zambia and Dangote had colluded to fix prices.[45]

Although often an imperfect policy tool, the enforcement of competition rules and regulations could help address some of these structural problems in African markets, by inducing more competition and better contestability of markets.[46] It could also help in allaying fears that the AfCFTA will unfairly favour large firms. By curbing anti-competitive practices, a strong competition legal framework should make markets work better for both businesses and consumers.

In recent decades, 44 African countries have adopted competition laws and established competition agencies.[47] However, progress in improving market conditions has been slow. About nine countries lack competition authorities or institutions to enforce their laws, rendering them ineffective.[48] Effective antitrust frameworks require a sound legal setup, independent regulatory bodies, adequate financial resources, and qualified staff. However, antitrust frameworks in the region present a mixed picture. About one third of countries with competition laws have agencies under the purview of another government body, potentially undermining their independence. Financial resources and technical staff availability also vary. On average, agencies in the region investigate just a few cases each year. The exceptions are the Kenyan and South African authorities, which investigate about 500 cases a year and are among the best performers on the continent according to the World Economic Forum's Effectiveness of Anti-Monopoly Policy Index.[49] There is also the issue of overlapping regional competition regimes, such as those shared by COMESA and EAC member states or the case of WAEMU. These regional authorities have already started to prove their mettle. For instance, the COMESA Competition Authority, established in 2013, was the first regional competition authority in Africa and the second in the world.[50] It has demonstrated its utility by opening investigations into firms suspected of collusive behaviour and price-rigging in various sectors.[51] In its first ten years, it handled over 360 merger cases and investigated 40 cases of restrictive business practices.

The AfCFTA's Competition Protocol was finally approved by the AU's Assembly in January 2023. After a lot of deliberations, pragmatism ruled the day, and the Protocol adopted a multi-tiered-hybrid approach to leverage the best practices of the existing national and regional competition authorities. The Protocol established an over-arching AfCFTA Competition Authority, which will function as an autonomous body with powers to administer and enforce provisions of the Protocol. The Protocol strives to create an integrated conti-nental competition regime, prohibiting cartels and abuse of dominant position, and regulating mergers and acquisitions. One area that was considered but not included in the provisions of the protocol is con-sumer protection. This is regrettable, as ultimately regional blocs are formed not only for the benefit of the private sector but also for its citizens. As discussed in Chapters 9 and 10, purposefully prioritising measures that will benefit African citizens is the best way to build popular support behind the AfCFTA.

Brexit as a warning

In the latter half of 2022, the United Kingdom's economic and politi-cal woes dominated discussions within mainstream and social media. In just four months, the country had in quick succession no less than four finance ministers, three home secretaries and three prime minis-ters. Although apparently unrelated, this whole sorry episode does have a lot of lessons for Africa and the AfCFTA.[52] When the Brexit referendum took place in 2016, many people in Europe were fearful other EU countries would follow the UK's example. Certainly, opin-ion polls in quite a few EU member states were becoming increasingly unfavourable to the EU. What people did not count on—particularly the supporters of Brexit—was the tremendously difficult job of extri-cating yourself from a long-standing agreement like the EU.

If you ask political leaders in the rest of Europe about leaving the EU today (including self-professed Europhobes like Marine Le Pen), no one seems to be asking for the door.[53] The UK's recent predica-ments highlight the enormous costs—even for quite large econo-mies—of either abandoning or not implementing an established regional bloc. If you stay on the sidelines, your economy will get trampled. UK trade has declined significantly, with exports falling by 25% in 2021 when compared to 2019, and both investment and growth are well below their trend rate prior to leaving the EU.[54] By the second quarter of 2022, Brexit had hit GDP by as much as 6% relative to a counterfactual scenario where the UK had not voted to leave the EU.[55] In addition, the depreciation of the exchange rate had a deleterious effect on real incomes and contributed to stoking inflationary pressures.[56]

Underlying the recent economic and political problems of the UK are the reduced options regarding the way to turn things around. Beyond rolling over existing trade deals from which the UK benefited as part of the EU and a highly controversial bilateral deal with Australia,[57] new trade deals with other countries have not materialised—most pointedly including the United States.

The other main lesson regards sovereignty and regional integration. In a recent Twitter space discussion on the AfCFTA, the question was asked whether African authorities were not concerned about a 'loss of sovereignty'. That fear is what underpinned Brexit too— because of media disinformation, people became obsessed that the EU meant a loss of power of the UK government to decide what was best for its own citizens.

But most of that perceived loss of sovereignty was trivial. During his career as a journalist in the 1990s, former UK Prime Minister Boris Johnson reported a story about how Brussels would not allow 'curved bananas' to be sold. It was largely made-up, but it did have a notable impact on public opinion in the UK that the EU was intruding on people's daily lives in a way that was unnecessary and unwarranted.[58]

This story conveys a very important truth. Agreement on a common set of standards, rules and regulations which facilitate business and trade between signatories is a dimension to regional integration which is very boring to the layperson. It almost does not matter so much what those standards are; the important thing is all member states of the regional bloc agree to abide by them. So the loss of sovereignty is normally quite banal, compared to the large benefits from belonging to and negotiating as a regional bloc. In this sense, a little national sovereignty is sacrificed in exchange for much larger gains in collective sovereignty. Basically, Africa either sets its own standards, rules and regulations for its own benefit, or they get set by larger more powerful trading partners like the EU or the US.[59]

This is the crux of the dilemma now for the UK. The more extreme 'Brexiteers' forced a hard Brexit on the UK, and the result is that the UK's 'regulatory freedom' has come at the cost of partially freezing the country out of the largest market in the world. It is no small irony that the only part of the UK economy that remains in the European Single Market—Northern Ireland—is currently posting the highest rates of economic growth.[60] This is essentially due to the fact that businesses in Northern Ireland can still do business both with the Republic of Ireland and the rest of the EU unhindered by the paper-work and border controls which are impacting negatively on the UK. All this should drive home to African policymakers the impor-tance of not staying on the sidelines and implementing the AfCFTA agreement as expeditiously as possible. The costs of not doing so could be much higher than they expect.

Learning the right lessons from the European Union

There is also a case to be made that a lot can be learnt from Europe's own missteps. The impression is often given that progress towards a united Europe was smooth, well-planned and executed. One notable example of this in East Africa is when, in 2010, the European Central Bank conducted a study for the EAC that was meant to serve as a guide to how the region could adopt a single currency—one of the explicit goals of the EAC.[61] The document was a lofty one, running to more than 800 pages, and presumed to show the EAC the path to single currency based on the experience of the EU with the euro.[62] Ironically, the document was published in 2010, just months before the Greek crisis exploded in Europe—a crisis which nearly brought the house down around Europe's single currency.

In a recent paper,[63] Mold argued that by examining Europe's record in regional integration, both with regards to what went well and what went wrong, valuable insights can be learnt that can help advance the AfCFTA agenda. For instance, quantitative studies into EU integration tend to concur that the benefits of the European SMP sprung essen-tially from increased competition, innovation, productivity and invest-ment, rather than from static gains from trade. Mold concludes that African policymakers should not overly obsess on the minutiae of trade liberalisation alone, but rather focus on the bigger picture of creating a continental market. This means going beyond tariff reduction and

CONCLUSIONS

addressing non-tariff barriers, regulatory harmonisation, trade facilitation, infrastructure development and services liberalisation. It also
includes recognising the need to promote greater cross-border investment between member states (Chapter 10).

Another core lesson from Europe is related to the distribution of
benefits from regional integration. Like on the African continent,
fears of the centralising impact of regional integration were commonplace on the European periphery in the 1970s and 1980s (for
instance, in Portugal, Ireland, Spain and Greece).[64] It was hypothesised, most notably by Krugman and Venables, that larger, higher-
income and centrally located countries might gain from deeper
integration more than poorer members.[65] In the end, those fears
proved to be misplaced, and in fact there is considerable empirical
evidence that the peripheral countries of the EU benefited proportionally more than the higher-income economies.[66] The simulation
results reported in Chapter 11 tend to predict a similar outcome for
the African economy.

One key lesson from the European experience is the centrality of
the private sector in pushing the integration agenda forward. Europe
suffered from lack of government interest in integration for many
decades prior to the rapid and unexpected progress it started making
in the 1980s. And this was despite the enormous political support for
a united Europe.[67] It was principally when Europe's powerful business sector became active in pushing for achieving a single market that
the agenda lurched forward: in January 1985, the CEO of Philips,
Wisse Dekker, unveiled the 'Europe 1990' plan before 500 commission and industry officials in Brussels. The so-called 'Dekker Plan' laid
out steps in four key areas: the elimination of border formalities, the
opening up of public procurement markets, the harmonisation of
technical standards, and fiscal harmonisation to create a European
market within five years. Just a few days later, the new president of
the European Commission, Jacques Delors, announced the Commission's intention to create a single market by 1992. As Delors himself
noted, the SMP came about 'thanks to many people and actors in
what became a process ... the 1992 process. And I must admit the
business actors mattered; they made a lot of it happen'.[68]

For the African continent, some key business sector organisations
have similarly expressed their enthusiasm for the AfCFTA (e.g.

Afrochampions, East African Business Council). Many prominent businesspeople have also made public pronouncements about the potential of a unified continental market under the AfCFTA.[69] But awareness about the AfCFTA is still relatively limited among the broader business community,[70] and they are far from being in the driving seat regarding moving the agenda forward. This is something that needs to change. As Mkandawire stressed, 'the failure to bring on board these interests is tantamount to a performance of Hamlet without the prince'.[71]

To sum up, regional integration requires public support and participation. It should involve consultations with stakeholders, communication of benefits and costs, compensation of losers, and protection of vulnerable groups. Brexit is a warning of what can go wrong if such public support is lacking.

The future for Africa will not resemble the past

As stressed in Part I of this book, African development strategies built on export-led growth to high-income markets have been fraught with problems. Of course, there is nothing new about 'export pessimism'—it can be traced back to the arguments of Singer and Prebisch (Chapter 4), and also debates around the 'fallacy of composition' of the 1980s, which warned that it would not be possible for other developing countries to follow the path of the 'Asian Tigers' (Hong Kong, Singapore, Taiwan and South Korea) because of the saturation of Western markets and the limited capacity to absorb more manufactured goods.[72] Those arguments proved excessively pessimistic.

Notwithstanding those previous debates, in Part I we documented the structural impediments to any significant growth of manufactured exports from Africa to high-income countries. The current global environment—a slowing China, anaemic growth in Europe, volatile commodity prices, and the risks of global financial instability as the advanced economies normalise their monetary policy—may make matters more challenging over the course of the decade.

This adverse environment, however, provides a unique opportunity to refocus policies on economic diversification and on fostering structural transformation. Necessity is the mother of invention. That was the case for South America in the 1930s and 1940s, when its traditional export markets in Europe and the United States were closed off by protectionism in the aftermath of the 1929 Great Depression, and then the Second World War, thereby accelerating the pace of economic industrialisation and diversification.[73] For Africa too, the current turmoil and uncertainty in the global economy may end up actually helping the continent to move forward decisively with the continental project. Africa is clearly going to have to trace its own path to economic development.[74]

At the beginning of this book, we alluded to fundamental shifts in the dominant 'techno-economic paradigm'[75] driving the global economy.[76] Despite the persistence of scale economies as a key source of competitive advantage (Chapter 9), the Fordist model of mass production is gradually being eclipsed by ICTs, which are the new motor of the emerging techno-economic paradigm. This is not just about digitalisation, but also about its integration into manufacturing processes, facilitated through improvements in sensors, advanced materials, robotics, artificial intelligence and big-data analytics. This is enabling the customisation of goods through additive manufacturing (3D printing) and new business models, such as production on-demand.[77] Collectively, these trends are termed the 'Fourth Industrial Revolution'.[78]

Some analysts are concerned that this new wave of labour-saving technologies will make it even harder for lower-income countries to participate in global manufacturing.[79] However, this concern may be overblown, as Africa can turn adversity into an advantage and benefit from the Fourth Industrial Revolution. ICTs are decentralising production, making manufacturing easier, cheaper and more sustainable. As manufacturing relocates closer to consumer markets, a window of opportunity opens for the African continent.

At the same time, Africa's demographic boom, while presenting considerable challenges,[80] is driving a rapid acceleration in the pace of urbanisation. This is stimulating the intensification and diversification of rural-urban exchange networks, and fuelling a process of domestic market integration.[81] This is creating new opportunities for economies of scale in tradeable commodities and services that enjoy a degree of natural protection against foreign imports, such as perishables, culture-specific products, and products with high per-unit transportation costs. All of this creates conditions that are favourable for the expansion of local and regional firms to cater to these demands.[82]

Pointedly, the new economic paradigm is all about connectivity; that is, how well a country is connected with other countries. As Parag Khanna writes:

> The transition beyond export-led growth toward higher value-added services and consumption begins with infrastructure investment .... Borders tell us who is divided from whom by political geography. Infrastructure tells us who is connected to whom via functional geography. As the lines that connect us supersede the borders that divide us, functional geography is becoming more important than political geography ... the paramount factor in determining the importance of a State is not its location or population but its connectedness—physically, economically, digitally—to flows of resources, capital, data, talent and other valuable assets.[83]

All these profound changes mitigate in favour of the success of the AfCFTA and its policies to eliminate those economic boundaries, but it means that policy must be duly aligned to these new realities. It is why the service-sector provisions of the AfCFTA are so important, and why there is a need to approach the economy differently under the AfCFTA. It is also why the incessant calls for African economies to try harder to integrate into global value chains may no longer be as pertinent, as the regional option is an increasingly viable one.

Added into this heady mix of profound technological changes is the imperative of catalysing a 'green industrial revolution' on the continent. Africa is home to many critical minerals which are increasingly required in emerging digital and green technologies, such as cobalt (which is needed for batteries) and caesium and rubidium (used in mobile cellular global positioning systems). An estimated 42 of the 63 elements used by low-carbon technologies and the so-called Fourth Industrial Revolution are found in Africa.[84] By embracing the technologies of the Fourth Industrial Revolution, and leveraging the continent's prodigious renewable energy sources, the continent should be able to leapfrog towards a more energy-efficient future.[85] Africa is rich in sources of renewable energy—whether that is geothermal, wind-power, or hydro-electric. For instance, more than 90% of Ethiopia's energy is already produced from renewable (principally hydroelectric) sources.[86] Stronger regional energy markets could prove extremely useful in terms of reducing emissions, for instance through the completion of the Zambia-Tanzania-Kenya interconnector for the Eastern Africa and Southern Africa Power Pools.

As far as we are aware, there is only one study which looks at how the implementation of the AfCFTA will impact directly on the environment.[87] While the study conceded that greater intra-regional trade and the concomitant boost to economic growth would lead to a modest increase in greenhouse gas emissions, it could also be associated with an improvement in air quality. This is no small thing—during the last two decades of fast economic growth, a number of African countries have seen air quality plummet in their largest cities. Nairobi, for instance, now has some of the most polluted air on the continent.[88] Although much improved by a recently opened expressway, its road network suffers serious congestion during peak hours, due to the abundance of vehicles on the road. Nearly 80% of those vehicles are imported, second-hand vehicles from Europe and Asia, which are old and do not meet emissions standards.

To sum up, by priming regional trade and encouraging firms and businesses to cater more to local tastes and demands, rather than focusing excessively on low-value-added or niche products destined for often elusive and fickle consumer markets in high-income countries, the AfCFTA could truly live up to its moniker of 'transformative'.

The centrality of the RECs in the construction of the continental economy

The AfCFTA is not a *tabula rasa*: the RECs have arguably laid a bedrock on which the continental project can be built. As was stressed in Part I, regional schemes on the African continent are often unfairly denigrated in a lot of mainstream literature. While it is true that some African RECs have been blighted by a weak commitment to implementation and have been seriously underfunded, Africa is hardly unique in this regard.[89] In Chapter 11, we established that early studies purporting to show no impact of African RECs on intra-regional trade were methodologically flawed, with more robust studies showing an average increment in trade between signatories of between 28–32%, with even larger impacts in manufacturing trade. RECs have made notable achievements in other areas too, sometimes in a very innovative manner:[90]

- Important strides have been taken by ECOWAS towards implementing its protocol governing free movement (see Chapter 12).
- By eliminating mobile roaming charges between signatories (Kenya, Uganda and Rwanda), the EAC's One-Area Network agreement of 2014 led to an increase in inbound roaming calls between Kenya and Rwanda of over 950% in the first few months.[91]
- Within SADC, the Chinyanja Triangle Soybean Trade initiative links a total of 22,179 smallholder farmers to regional markets and supplies over 7,070 million metric tonnes of soybeans.[92]
- Through its Protocol on Education and Training, which came into force in July 2000, tuition fees at universities within SADC are fixed at the same levels for all citizens from member states.[93]

Perhaps most interesting has been the contribution of the RECs to institution-building. We mentioned earlier the important work of the COMESA Competition Authority. COMESA has also created various trade facilitation instruments and financial institutions such as the Trade and Development Bank, Africa Trade Insurance Agency, the COMESA Clearing House and its regional payment and settlement system. Underpinning the contribution of the RECs to continental integration are the judicial innovations, a prime example being the East African Court of Justice (Box 14.1).

Box 14.1: The East African Court of Justice

The East African Court of Justice (EACJ) was established in November 2001 under Article 9 of the Treaty for the Establishment of the East African Community, and has exclusive jurisdiction over the interpretation of the treaty.[94] Any one who has ever listened to the passionate legal defence of the EAC by the former Chief Justice of the EACJ Issac Lenaola will have little doubt about the importance of the institution in defending the progress made, much in the same way that the European Court of Justice does in the EU. The EACJ can award damages, giving its rulings 'teeth', and review domestic legislation to determine whether there has been a breach of the treaty.[95] Individual citizens can take their governments to court directly and seek redress through the regional court, without first having to exhaust all possible domestic channels of justice. A recent example of how the EACJ has endeavoured to protect the integrity of the EAC market is its judgment delivered on 2 December 2022, in the case between Christopher Ayieko vs Attorney General of the Republic of Kenya (reference No. 5/2019). That judgment found that in negotiating a bilateral trade agreement with the United States, Kenya had acted in contravention of the East African Community Treaty and the Customs Union Protocol. There is every likelihood that jurisprudence from regional courts like the EACJ will be used under the AfCFTA dispute settlement system, even if just as inputs into the panel and appellate body processes.

RECs have already contributed a great deal to AfCFTA negotiations by aggregating their tariff offers. This aggregation was the case for members of ECOWAS, ECCAS and the EAC, which submitted collective tariff offers. RECs also fill capacity gaps for their less-resourced countries that may not be able to participate fully in the AfCFTA trade negotiations. Critically, in an effort to achieve harmonisation, the Rules of Origin negotiations have been heavily influenced by the preferential trade areas created by some RECs.[96]

In principle, the central role of the RECs in implementing the AfCFTA is accepted. In the preamble to the AfCFTA Treaty (and again in Article 5 of the AfCFTA Framework Agreement), the eight officially recognised RECs are designated as 'building blocks', meaning that their best practices and achievements are to be followed and incorporated into AfCFTA implementation. Yet, as per Article 12 of the AfCFTA Treaty, the RECs currently have only had an advisory role in the AfCFTA negotiations. A step in the right direction is that the AfCFTA Secretariat held its first coordination meeting among the heads of RECs to discuss the implementation of the AfCFTA in September 2021,[97] and two subsequent meetings had been held by July 2023. However, things will need to go further to truly leverage the groundwork already laid down by the RECs.

A need for a concerted campaign against NTBs

One of the central political economic obstacles to economic integration on the continent is that a great deal of money is currently made, both officially and unofficially, at Africa's borders. Vested interests will inevitably feel threatened by the dismantling of the barriers to intra-African trade. Some countries' domestic lobbies initially delayed signing the AfCFTA. In Nigeria, for instance, the Manufacturers Association of Nigeria urged the federal government not to sign the agreement.[98] Nigeria is alleged to have one of the most restrictive trade regimes on the continent, consisting of numerous import bans and prohibitively high tariff peaks.[99]

But it is obviously wrong to single out Nigeria—many countries across the continent indulge in unfair trade practices with the intention of both revenue raising and stemming the flow of imports. If they continue doing this to their African trading partners, there is no doubt that it will undermine the effective implementation of the AfCFTA. In Chapter 11, it was noted that benefits from the agreement will be relatively limited if restricted to tariff liberalisation alone, and so the positive trade impact is heavily dependent on measures to also reduce NTBs. Yet studies have persistently shown that tariff liberalisation positively correlates with an increase in NTBs, as countries scramble around for new ways to protect their domestic market. For instance, COMESA observed that tariff liberalisation among its members also saw an increase in NTBs that stifled trade.[100]

There is an institutional response to this within the AfCFTA framework. Annex 5 to the Protocol on Trade in Goods includes detailed plans to deal with the NTBs by establishing a reporting, monitoring and elimination mechanism whereby the private sector can file complaints. Once again, the regional experience is instructive—in

CONCLUSIONS

COMESA, the establishment of reporting mechanisms proved effective in reducing and/or eliminating NTBs.[101] One important action will be the aforementioned creation of sectoral coalitions (IPAs) that have the resources to lobby at the highest levels for the removal of the NTBs in their particular sectors.

Other practices antithetical to intra-African trade are simply self-defeating and arguably could easily be terminated. For instance, contrary to standard practice in many countries, customs officials on the continent often charge tariffs on the Cost, Insurance and Freight (CIF) value of imported goods rather than on the Free-on-Board (FOB) value—which is in effect placing a tariff on a business cost. In land-locked Rwanda, for instance, the CIF cost of imports is more than 20% higher than the FOB cost. Unfortunately, the AfCFTA does not have a Customs Valuation Agreement, which could have addressed this issue. A further constraint is that to engage in import/export of goods, African customs authorities usually insist on exporting to a legally registered trading company or clearing authority in the destination country. For firms that have no affiliate in the counterpart country, this clearly leads to the additional cost of hiring the services of a trading company. Removing practices like these will help contribute to making business across the continent easier and less expensive.[102]

A good precedent is that in October 2022, eight African countries (Cameroon, Egypt, Ghana, Kenya, Mauritius, Rwanda, Tanzania and Tunisia) took part in a pilot AfCFTA implementation scheme. This provided a powerful 'demonstration effect' of how to put all the policy work into practice.[103] Admittedly for the exporters involved, the experience was a mixed one—a number of them had difficulties in getting the necessary documentation approved, and there were also some severe logistical problems.[104] But that was the whole point of the initiative—to highlight areas for action and focus attention on the barriers.

Managing opposition to continental integration

This final topic is a thorny one. As with all regional arrangements, the political economy of implementing the AfCFTA is complicated. To make sure that implementation is effective, we must ask ourselves who has a stake in making sure that the agreement is fully implemented and who are likely to be its opponents. In a speech made at the University of Ife-Ife in 1984, Adedeji recognised that the Pan-African project had many potential foes:

> Because of the various political orientations of African countries and group interests, there may be various coalitions between African and foreign governments, between African and foreign professional groups including business interests, and other coalitions too numerous to mention, that may prevent or slow down the implementation of the [Lagos Action] Plan and the Act. I believe such coalitions are possible and constitute potential sources of diversion.[105]

Breaking down the different interest groups is a good place to start. Parts of the business community can be expected to be highly supportive of the AfCFTA[106]—but other factions may not be. Distinguishing between the two is important. Acknowledging the changed circumstances on the continent, Nigerian businessman Tony Elumelu coined the term 'Africapitalism' to denote an economic philosophy that has gathered pace among African businesspeople, and which aims to combine profit motives with the political and economic ideas of African unity.[107]

Yet it is important to recognise that there has been historic antagonism towards domestic capitalists that the AfCFTA must help address. Post-independence governments were perceived to be reluctant to support domestic businessmen because they feared such individuals would develop alternative sources of power, thereby threatening political stability.[108] And because of the domestic orientation of economic policy and strong economic links with former colonial powers, few African businesspeople had an interest in regional markets. Yet as Thandika Mkandawire stressed, things have changed over time and there are now plenty of African businesspeople who are interested in regional markets:

> Such interests can be important to a regional project .... How do you reconcile their interests with those of the continent or the regional schemes that we are talking about? ... We are talking here as bureaucrats and academics, and the actual big actors are not involved. And we don't fully understand what their interest is.[109]

In a recent publication, Echandi et al. do a good job of breaking down what those interests may be. African private sector representatives

CONCLUSIONS

have recognised that attitudes toward the AfCFTA within Africa itself vary among three categories of businesspeople.[110]

First among these is a group consisting mostly of African multinationals which are highly enthusiastic about the prospects of establishing a continent-wide market. Many of these companies participate in the aforementioned AfroChampions Initiative, a project that seeks to raise awareness of the AfCFTA and mobilise USD 1 trillion in investment funds by 2030 to support African economic integration.

A second group comprises African enterprises that, for many reasons, perceive the AfCFTA as a threat to their existing interests and do not necessarily want to see it succeed. Most of the enterprises within this category are oriented towards serving domestic markets, and many of them are associated with strong interest groups that benefit from protectionist trade policies that they fear will be eroded by continental free trade. This sentiment tends to prevail in those African countries where the domestic political economy has traditionally been less favourable to regional trade integration.[111] But it is also widespread in other countries.

Finally, a third segment of the African private sector is currently indifferent toward the AfCFTA. Many reasons can explain such sceptical attitudes, but the need for further information may be one factor. Perceptions that the AfCFTA may just be another grand political gesture calling for African integration, but failing to lead to concrete implementation, is another source of scepticism.[112] Many of the firms in this category are smaller businesses focused on domestic markets who think that their potential to become directly involved in cross-border trade, although theoretically possible, is still a long way from their current capacity.

To these three categories we can add a fourth. Many of the traders and trading companies that facilitate the import of goods are important additional constituents of the sceptical, nay, hostile group against the AfCFTA. Importers are often extremely powerful. Their existing trade links are with supermarket chains in Europe, companies in Dubai, and manufacturers in Asia. They are unlikely to wish to break up their existing business model, which serves them so well. Changing their modus operandi and making them more amenable to sourcing more from the African continent may prove challenging.

Managing these different interest groups will be fundamental to making the AfCFTA work. The AfCFTA's potential for supporting industrialisation and economic diversification will depend heavily on whether it can alter the interests and incentives of business and political elites, either by creating new opportunities for commercial benefit or by facilitating the formation of new coalitions of actors with more to gain from the AfCFTA.[113]

For countries concerned over the economic impact of opening their borders to intra-African competition, it is reassuring that a compensatory mechanism has been put in place. In March 2023, Rwanda signed a host agreement with the Secretariat of the AfCFTA and the Afreximbank for a USD 10 billion adjustment fund. The AfCFTA Adjustment Fund will provide grants and technical assistance to address tariff revenue losses that could result from the implementation of the AfCFTA agreement, as well as finance for the development of trade-enabling infrastructure. But to be really impactful, it would be important to make such adjustment support conditional on countries following the agreed tariff schedules and admitting the bulk of their intra-African imports under AfCFTA rules.[114]

Amongst the general public, we hinted earlier at the varying attitudes towards introducing more liberal trading regimes. According to Afrobarometer survey evidence, support for freer trade is highest in Uganda (70%), Burkina Faso (63%) and Mali (61%). But similarly, strong majorities support protectionism for domestic producers in Tunisia (70%), Lesotho (63%) and Botswana (62%). Emblematic of mixed feelings on the continent, Kenyans appear evenly split (49% each) on the question of free trade versus protectionism.[115] These represent, however, far larger constituencies in favour of a more liberal trading environment than currently prevail in the United States or many European countries.[116]

It is thus essential to convey to the general public that the ultimate beneficiaries of the AfCFTA are themselves. Many of the discussions on the AfCFTA revolve around the opportunities for exporters under the AfCFTA, but this is to misconceive what regional integration is really about. In the final instance, very few people in any country are engaged directly in exporting. Nonetheless, we are all beneficiaries of greater economic efficiency, faster job creation and lower prices for goods and services, to name but a few of the benefits that spring from deeper economic integration. And, as we stressed in Chapter 12, young people will be the principal beneficiaries from the implementation of the FMP. Mobilising their enthusiasm and abilities to 'hustle' for change will be key for making sure the AfCFTA stays on track.[117]

Thus, a better understanding of what the agreement entails is essential if the AfCFTA is to gain broad traction. Under the leadership of the AfCFTA Secretariat and the African Union Commission, the United Nations ECA, the African Export-Import Bank and other organisations have held numerous events and activities geared toward private sector stakeholders, reiterating the importance of their engagement. But that engagement needs to be broadened and deepened. When asked in a recent survey of African youth about their level of familiarity with the AfCFTA, just over 22% say they are very or somewhat familiar with the agreement. Nearly half of African youth had never even heard of AfCFTA before, while another 17% only knew of it by name.[118] In another recent survey of 800 private sector players, 62% said that they did not know where and how to access useful information regarding the AfCFTA.[119] That is clearly not good enough and requires more concerted efforts to improve awareness of the AfCFTA.

Africa in the world

By embracing the AfCFTA, Africa is not turning its back on the world. Far from it. The continent is simply seeking to be more effectively represented and heard, and being able to make constructive inputs into global outcomes that adequately reflect its own priorities.[120] The vision of the African Union is to achieve an integrated, prosperous and peaceful Africa, driven by its own citizens and representing a dynamic force in the global arena. This vision is articulated in Agenda 2063—an admittedly aspirational document, but one rooted in the historic and contemporary realities of the continent. However, to achieve these goals, it is of paramount importance that Africa is internally strong as a pre-condition for international diplomatic agency—thus making the AfCFTA an idea whose time has come. Symbolic of the desired changes are moves to give the African Union a permanent seat at the G20, just as the EU already has.

One of the biggest gains from the AfCFTA will be obliging member states to adopt common positions in their negotiations with the rest of the world. Speaking with one voice is not an easy goal to achieve, and it is certainly not going to happen immediately. However, member states at least need to avoid outright conflict and the taking up of contradictory positions. For instance, the AfCFTA will operate within WTO regulations, similar to how the EU operates. Each African WTO member will represent itself during WTO negotiations, but the AfCFTA will utilise the Geneva-based group of ambassadors that speaks for the entirety of the agreement on the basis of common African positions at all WTO meetings until Africa develops a supranational mechanism with exclusive competence in trade negotiations and trade-related matters. Like the EU, the AfCFTA may in due course become a member of the WTO in its own right.[121] The Kenyan activist and Nobel Prize-winner Wangari Maathai spoke passionately and bluntly on this point:

> By raising their voices in unison at a regional and continent-wide level, Africa can both demand and achieve more in the negotiating rooms and halls of power. It is not too much to say that unless African leaders embrace their common goals and work together to make their individual nations and the whole continent stronger, Africa will remain a victim of globalization and unfair global trade rules, not a beneficiary.[122]

At the same time, there have been complaints that the political dimensions of regional integration are being neglected. This book admittedly tries to steer clear of political analysis as it is beyond the areas of professional competence of the authors. However, it is true that the Abuja Treaty is mainly focused on trade and economic integration. Gumede[123] makes a strong case for what he terms 'pan-African developmental regional integration', which he describes as 'a political agenda grounded in African nationalism, not an economistic affair aimed at increasing market access and associated factors'.[124] He has a point. It is a topic that would be worthy of a future African Arguments book.

As noted in Chapter 2, arguments about whether political integration should precede or follow economic integration are long-standing ones—and a topic on which we have not really dedicated much space.

CONCLUSIONS

Yet right from the beginning, African decolonisation champions focused not so much on the material wealth of the continent but on its political unification as a prerequisite for economic transformation. This outlook is engraved on the plinth of Ghana's first president, Kwame Nkrumah, outside Parliament House in Accra: 'Seek ye first the political kingdom and all other things shall be added unto you'.[125]

It is a common debate everywhere in the world where bold plans of economic and social transformation have been embraced: should politics precede economic changes on the ground? We would argue that the balance of evidence is in the opposite direction—economic reform is required first before political reform.[126] Julius Nyerere's intuition on these matters was right (Chapter 3). And that is why progress on AfCFTA implementation is so crucial.

This book makes the case for moving towards a borderless Africa. This view is not utopian—we have laid out the main developmental and economic arguments in favour of the agreement. We believe most of these arguments are incontrovertible. But clearly this is a project that is going to be decades in the making.

In fact, we share concerns with other authors[127] that the AfCFTA is currently being oversold, and the hyperbole is excessive. There is an inherent danger in letting the rhetoric get carried away with itself and 'overselling' the AfCFTA. The AfCFTA is becoming all things to all people—a mechanism to achieve greater intra-regional trade, yes, but also a way of reducing inequalities, eliminating conflicts, delivering more environmental sustainability, empowering women, etc.

It is critical to remind people that the AfCFTA is, in its essence, a mechanism to increase the intensity of intra-African economic activity—cross-border investment and trade. It is an admittedly ambitious agreement, aiming for deep rather than shallow integration. It will have beneficial impacts in many spheres (for instance, by freeing up the movement of people across borders). But the AfCFTA is not able to address all Africa's development challenges. Nor does it exonerate member states from the responsibility of having well-developed national policies to tackle some of these other developmental challenges.

One final observation. The entry into force of the agreement will lead to a pooling and sharing of a certain degree of economic sovereignty for African member states; sometimes provocatively and unnecessarily called 'ceding of sovereignty'. This sharing is the inevitable consequence of any regional agreement, and is especially true when it involves a 'deep integration' project like the AfCFTA. In the move towards greater harmonisation of economic policy in areas like competition, investment regimes, intellectual property and rules of origin (which constitute the nuts and bolts of any cross-border regulation), African governments will lose a certain amount of autonomy in their domestic affairs, and share it in the context of the oversight of intergovernmental bodies such as the Council of Ministers, or the supranational continent-wide bodies established along the lines of regional bodies such as the COMESA Competition Commission or the EAC Parliament, or even the African Peace and Security Architecture. But they will win enormously in terms of economic efficiency and policy space vis-à-vis third-party countries outside Africa. It is a price worth paying for greater collective sovereignty and agency on the African continent.

NOTES

1. MAKING THE CASE FOR THE AFCFTA

1. Akinkugbe (2021, pp. 296–7) summarises a number of the criticisms of the AfCFTA from different African authors.
2. However, we will also insist that those arguments are not always the ones which are most frequently mustered in favour of the AfCFTA.
3. In economics, a 'binding constraint' refers to a lacking factor or condition that can only be a constraint to growth where the supply of it is low and demand for it is strong. For example, a country may have a shortage of skilled labour or inadequate roads, which can be considered as binding constraints to its economic growth. Binding constraints can also relate to economic or market-related factors, policy or regulatory gaps, or institutional and capacity constraints. Typically, countries face a multitude of such constraints, and addressing all of them at once is neither possible nor practical. Priorities will have to be set. See Rodrik 2008.
4. In line with the Treaty of Abuja (1991), it will in fact evolve into an African Common Market. See Chapters 2 and 3 for a discussion.
5. The single market seeks to guarantee the free movement of goods, capital, services and people, known collectively as the 'four freedoms'.
6. See Seong et al. 2022, p. 19.
7. Perez 2002.
8. The process began in the 1990s, when an impressive number of mergers and acquisitions occurred across various industries (aerospace and defence, automobiles, trucks, power equipment, oil and petrochemicals, pharmaceuticals, and banking), resulting in the emergence of global firms. To boost their competitiveness in increasingly oligopolistic markets, these new global giants selected suppliers from their networks, raised entry barriers, and consolidated their market shares in capital- and knowledge-intensive sectors. All this made it more difficult for developing countries to compete in many sectors by taking advantage of low labour costs. See Nolan 2001; UNCTAD 2020b, p. 128.

9. This is discussed more fully in Chapters 4 and 14.
10. See Rodrik 2011.
11. The official title was 'The AfCFTA Agreement and its Protocols on Trade in Goods, Trade in Services and on Rules and Procedures on the Settlement of Disputes'.
12. These included the Annexes on Customs Co-operation and Mutual Administrative Assistance, Trade Facilitation, Non-Tariff Barriers, Technical Barriers to Trade, Sanitary and Phytosanitary Measures, Transit, and Trade Remedies.
13. Luke 2023.
14. Erasmus 2019.
15. The Agreement stipulates that the percentage for sensitive products should not exceed 7% of the total tariff lines and the exclusion list should not exceed 3% of total tariff lines, Moreover, the exclusion list should not amount to more than 10% of the total value of imports (AU 2019).
16. Under international trade law, there are basically two legal approaches to liberalisation: positive or negative lists. The positive list approach is more conservative and specifies which sectors are to be liberalised—if a sector is not mentioned, it is not liberalised. However, the level of the ambition of the AfCFTA is again large, and the intention is to liberalise all 12 service sectors according to the standard WTO classification (WTO 1991).
17. Least developed countries (or LDCs) are low-income countries that are confronting severe structural impediments to sustainable development. They are highly vulnerable to economic and environmental shocks and have low levels of human assets. There are currently 46 countries on the list of LDCs which is reviewed every three years by the Committee for Development (CDP) (UNCTAD 2023).
18. For example, see Pilling 2020; Nwuke 2022.
19. Schiff and Winters 2003, p. 72.
20. ASEAN had initially been agreed in 1967, but it was not until the Fourth Summit in January 1992 that the ASEAN leaders confounded critics and moved forward decisively towards the creation of the ASEAN Free Trade Area (AFTA). See Naya and Plummer 1997.
21. Mkandawire 2014, p. 7.
22. It might be argued that at the time the level of comprehension about what the AfCFTA was about was minimal, but then that is often the way of public opinion polls. Few British people, for instance, probably understood what the referendum on leaving the EU actually entailed. Arguably, although they are open to manipulation in the way the questions are framed, polls like this simply pick up on the general sentiment—and, in the African case, that sentiment is very pro-African economic integration.
23. PAFTRAC 2022.
24. Ichikowitz Family Foundation 2022.
25. The details of the survey reveal some interesting distinctions. On average across 18 countries, Africans are almost evenly divided in their views on free trade: 47% support policies that protect domestic industries, whereas 49% prefer open bor-

ders. Resistance to open borders was particularly strong in Tunisia (70%), Lesotho (63%), Botswana (62%) and Gabon (60%). Botswana is the only country where a clear majority (68%) prefer limiting cross-border movement in the region (Sanny and Patel 2021, p. 2).

26. Sanny and Patel 2021, p. 1.

27. The respondents were also asked whether they would be likely to support their member of Congress in the next elections if they had voted in favour of the agreement. Just 9% responded yes. This resulted in US negotiators reflecting the misgivings of Congress and the general public in the text of the draft agreement. Although NAFTA aimed at reducing border obstacles, hundreds of pages of the agreement were devoted to listing the exceptions that the US negotiators demanded and obtained (Vernon 1998, p. 161).

28. For example, see Luke and Macleod 2019; AfDB 2019; AUC, ECA, AfDB 2019; AUC, ECA, AfDB 2010; AUC 2022; FAO 2021; Fofack and Mold 2021; ECA/TMEA 2020.

29. Mkandawire 2014; Brenton and Hoffman 2016.

30. The organisation's main purpose was to isolate South Africa regionally, push for the end of apartheid, and press for Namibia's independence. It grew out of an earlier initiative of the Front-Line States (Angola, Botswana, Mozambique, Tanzania and Zambia) to secure these objectives as well as assist in Zimbabwe's efforts at independence.

31. See, inter alia, UNDP 2020.

32. Chang 2002.

2. THE HISTORICAL ANTECEDENTS

1. Davidson 2001, p. 72. See Bairoch (1995) on the vitality of the trans-Saharan trade; Reader (1998) on the salt trade; Parker (2020) on Egypt's trade with both sub-Saharan Africa and as the main supplier of grain in the Roman Empire, etc. Iliffe (1995) has some wonderful examples of the vibrancy of trade and manufacturing activities across the continent in pre-colonial times.

2. Iliffe 1995, p. 172.

3. Inikori 2007; Austin 2014, p. 4.

4. Chirikure 2021.

5. Davidson 2001, p. 72.

6. Frankema and van Waijenburg 2018, p. 563.

7. Herbst 2000, Chapter 2.

8. Young 1994; Michalopoulos and Papaioannou 2011.

9. Faloyin 2022.

10. Ibid., p. 30.

11. This division is reflected today in the five stars on the Somali national flag.

12. Gashaw 2017.

13. Alesina et al. 2011.

14. Adebajo 2021.
15. The names of the participants were illustrious, with W. E. B. Du Bois leading the movement; and three future presidents among the attendees—Kwame Nkrumah, Jomo Kenyatta, and Hastings Banda.
16. Michalopoulos and Papaioannou 2011.
17. This kind of debate is often traced back to disputes between Stalinists and Maoists over whether to give primacy to technological economic development or to 'put politics in charge' (Spitz 1996). But there are also shades of these tensions in many areas related to regional integration—thus, for instance, within the European Union, there was a dispute in the early 1990s between France and Germany over how to successfully achieve monetary union, with France preferring the 'political' approach of rapid implementation of the euro, without waiting for the groundwork of achieving a fiscal union first.
18. Adebajo 2021, p. 50.
19. It did not help matters that sometimes Senghor waxed lyrically about the contribution of France to the African continent: 'Colonialism has had its dark moments and its moments of light. If it destroyed some of the values of our civilization, Europe sometimes brought its substitutes, almost always fertile ones, complementary ones' (cited by Adebajo 2021, p. 50).
20. Like Nkrumah, Anta Diop also stressed the enormous economic potential of Africa's economy if it were treated as a single entity. In his book *Black Africa: The Economic and Cultural Basis for a Federated State*, he speaks at length about the continent's abundant natural resources and the potential for developing an elaborate industrial infrastructure. He also argued that 'Africa must win a hold in a large part of its own domestic market, one of the greatest in the world. A whole book should be devoted to the study of this market with a view to organizing the economies of the African states.' See Anta Diop 1987; Martin 2020.
21. The French government mounted a campaign of subterfuge to destabilise the newly independent government of Guinea. See 'Opération "Persil"', *Le Monde diplomatique*, 1 April 2018. It was not an isolated example—many campaigns (including direct involvement in assassination plots) to destabilise the new governments were carried out by the European colonial powers.
22. Nyerere 1963.
23. Adebajo 2021, p. 49.
24. Michalopoulos and Papaioannou 2011, p. 7.
25. Cited by Faloyin 2022, p. 60.
26. Mangeni and Juma 2018.
28. Adebajo 2021, p. 27.
29. According to Adedeji (1970, p. 9), the UDAO was not effective because of political rivalries, the widely differing levels of economic development of the countries, and the practical difficulties of coordinating investment policies and redistributing the gains from the union through inter-country payments.
30. Adedeji 1970, p. 11.

31. Mshomba 2017. For lengthy discussion of the reasons for the earlier collapse, see Hazlewood 1979; Mugomba 1978; Potholm 1979.
32. World Bank 1981.
33. Weeks 1996, p. 117.
34. See Mangeni and Juma 2018, Chapter 3.
35. AUC 2022, p. 32. The Community Levy Protocol of 1996 legislates for the imposition of a levy on imported goods originating from third countries.
36. Mold and Mukwaya 2017.
37. Luke and MacLeod 2023.

3. THE INTELLECTUAL UNDERPINNINGS OF THE AFCFTA

1. This is not meant to disregard the tremendous role that women played in the Pan-African movement from the very beginning. As eloquently noted by Professor Adekeye Adebajo:

    [A] serious pitfall of the 'father of Pan-Africanism' trope is that it ignores major contributions by black women …. From the time of the first Pan-African Conference, women such as Ida Gibbs Hunt, Anna Julia Cooper, Anna H. Jones, Addie Waites Hunton, Helen Curtis, Jessie Fauset and Coralie Franklin Cook were actively involved in the movement. These women were Congress organisers, fundraisers and thinkers who in their own right provided critical intellectual contributions desperately needed by the movement …. These were the 'mothers of Pan-Africanism', without whom Blyden, Du Bois, and others could not have been its fathers. (Adebajo 2021, p. 3)

2. There were some notable exceptions. Cheikh Anta Diop wrote a fascinating description of how to achieve economic integration in his book *Black Africa: Economic and Cultural Basis for a Federal State* (1987). Likewise, Kwame Nkrumah wrote a lengthy discussion on the economic dimensions of continental integration in his classic books *Africa Must Unite* (1963) and *Neo-Colonialism—The Last Stage of Imperialism* (1965).
3. Lest the reader doubt the 'drama', one is well advised to read the stories associated with some of the dramatic confrontations with the Bretton Woods institutions in the 1980s during the period of structural adjustment.
4. Paez 2016, p. 183. These three phases of integration are not to be confused with the two phases for the formation of regional economic communities.
5. Adebajo also makes some interesting parallels between the Latin American economist Raúl Prebisch and Adedeji. Prebisch was the executive secretary of CEPAL, the first of the UN's regional commissions, which was founded in 1948, a full decade before ECA: 'Both Prebisch and Adedeji … had a keen political understanding of what regional governments would support and championed the idea of "home-grown" development and self-reliance theories built on the specific experiences of Latin America and Africa, as well as on regional ownership of development ideas. Prebisch and Adedeji consistently sought private sector participation in their

regional initiatives. Both acted as public intellectuals who often wrote their own speeches and sought to appeal directly above the heads of government to audiences in universities, think-tanks, the private sector, and other fora, employing impressive communication skills to explain complicated economic ideas. Both turned the ECLA and the ECA into intellectual think-tanks acting as secular monks in monasteries in which disciples were encouraged to dream up heretical plans to transform the global economic system in ways that addressed the acute disadvantages of their respective continents. If both prophets ultimately failed to achieve their goals, it was a heroic failure born not of lack of ambition or application, but of power' (Adebajo 2014, p. 33).

6. Sawyer et al. 2015, p. 9.
7. Amoako 2020, p. 162.
8. Adedeji and Colley Senghor 1989, bibliographical note.
9. Adebajo 2014, p. 82; Adedeji and Colley Senghor 1989.
10. Adedeji 1970, pp. 213–31.
11. Sawyer et al. 2015, p. 9.
12. The first was ECLAC (or CEPAL, in Spanish) which was formed in 1948 in Santiago, with the distinguished Argentinian economist Raúl Prebisch at the helm.
13. UNECA 2018.
14. As an example of the kind of Pan-African solidarity that the colonial powers were keen on suppressing, when Guinea Conakry chose independence in 1958, under the leadership of Ahmed Sékou Touré, it was Ghana that initially offered economic support, despite its own challenges. *The Washington Post* observed how 'brutal' the French were in tearing down all that they thought were their contributions to Guinea: 'In reaction, and as a warning to other French-speaking territories, the French pulled out of Guinea over a two-month period, taking everything they could with them. They unscrewed lightbulbs, removed plans for sewage pipelines in Conakry, the capital, and even burned medicines rather than leave them for the Guineans' (Dash 1984).
15. Jolly 2015.
16. Adebajo 2014, p. 22.
17. Ibid., pp. 258–9.
18. Amoako 2020, p. 102.
19. Adedeji 2004.
20. The currency of Nigeria is the naira, and each naira is divided into a hundred kobo.
21. Adedeji and Senghor 1989, p. 342.
22. K. Y. Amoako had worked on the Berg Report—an association that was to haunt him later in his career—but in his autobiography he also provides some insights and criticism into how the report was drawn up, without any real consultative process or attempt to reflect African perspectives. In the end, it was to prove a millstone around the neck of the Bretton Woods institutions too, and they gradually had to disassociate themselves from many of the report's recommendations. That they did so was in part a testimony to the success of Adedeji's ECA, which moved the frame-

work of the debate with the 'Alternative Framework for Structural Adjustment Programmes for Socio-Economic Recovery and Transformation' paper (Adedeji 1990). Strangely, for a number of years, copies of this influential document were nearly impossible to find in the ECA archives.

23. Amoako 2020, p. 101.
24. World Bank 1994; World Bank 2000.
25. Jolly 2015, p. 22. In challenging these perspectives, Adedeji was at his best and his most loyal to Africa—although he was to be largely unsuccessful (Jolly 2015, p. 20).
26. The Lagos Plan of Action also had African critics. During a Council for the Development of Economic and Social Research in Africa (CODESRIA) conference with the ECA in 1982, several authors castigated the plan for being quiet or ambiguous on certain issues, including: communal versus private ownership of land; the need to define how to prioritise agricultural and industrial exports; and the role of foreign investment in development. African scholars further criticised the Plan as having been naïve about state agricultural policies in Africa, for ignoring the class dimensions of governing regimes on the continent, and for assuming that African leaders were interested in promoting the welfare of their own citizens (Adebajo 2014, p. 30). See also Barrett-Brown 1997.
27. Adedeji and Senghor 1989, p. 498.
28. It is also arguable that greater African dynamism would have also benefited industrial countries through more trade and investment opportunities, through rising African incomes and arguably through more political stability in African countries (Jolly 2015, p. 24).
29. Mkandawire 2014, p. 19.
30. Amoako 2020.
31. See, for instance, Anta Diop 1987.
32. Adedeji 1993, p. 214.
33. Currently, there are eight RECs recognised by the African Union: the East African Community (EAC), the Economic Community of Central African States (ECCAS), the Community of Sahel-Saharan States (CEN-SAD), the Common Market for Eastern and Southern Africa (COMESA), the Economic Community of West African States (ECOWAS), the Intergovernmental Authority on Development (IGAD), the Southern African Development Community (SADC), and the Arab Maghreb Union (UMA).
34. AUC, ECA, AfDB 2012, p. 11.
35. The AU aims to have the African Common Market (Internal Market) in place by 2023, five years before the establishment of the African Economic Community (AUC, ECA, AfDB 2019). See also Mangeni and Juma 2018.
36. Biswaro 2012, p. 348.
37. Asante 1991.
38. Zeleza 2020.
39. Gumede 2019.

40. Nonetheless, he was under no illusions about the nature of Chinese engagement on the continent:

    I always assume that these countries have their interests and that Africa must be able to assert its own interests too … China is not in Africa for philanthropic reasons. In fact, our main headache is that China has a plan for Africa, but Africa has no plan for China (Mkandawire 2019).

41. Mkandawire 2014, p. 18; Amoako 2020.

42. Mkandawire and Soludo 1999.

43. Mkandawire 2001; 2019.

44. For sub-Saharan Africa, there was a minus 15% decline in per capita GNP, compared with a positive growth of 36% achieved from 1960 to 1980 (Weisbrot et al. 2000, cited by Jolly 2015, p. 22).

45. Mkandawire 2019.

46. Sender 1999.

47. Mkandawire 2014, p. 3. As noted in Chapter 11, it is a view that is broadly supported by the econometric evidence.

48. In fact, the original use of the term 'spaghetti bowl' phenomenon was by Bhagwati 1995 to describe what he perceived as the US's obsession with recurring to FTAs. But it soon became applied most frequently to describe the complexity of regional arrangements on the African continent.

49. See, inter alia, AUC 2020; De Melo 2015.

50. Mkandawire 2014, p. 4.

51. Krugman 1995.

52. Rodrik 2012.

53. Mkandawire 2019, p. 538.

54. Mkandawire 2014, p. 5.

55. Ibid., p. 10.

56. He also lamented the fact that 'much of the NGO world today has no interest in the Pan-African project, they are much more interested in the North-South international arrangements …. But we have to bring back the projects of Pan-Africanism' (Mkandawire 2014, p. 25).

57. Bach 2016, p. 13.

58. Palma and Marcel 1989.

59. Ibid., p. 14.

60. Fukuyama 1992; Darian-Smith 2019.

61. Mkandawire 2014, p. 13.

62. Ibid., p. 10.

63. African Union 2022.

64. TRALAC 2022.

65. Pharatlhatlhe and Vanheukelom 2019.

66. Mkandawire 2014, p. 27.

67. Ibid.

68. Hirsch et al. 2021.
69. Mkandawire 2014, p. 29.
70. Ibid.
71. Ibid., p. 15.
72. Nyerere 1963, p. 3.
73. Ibid., p. 249.
74. Adedeji and Senghor 1989.

4. THE HEART OF THE MATTER: A LACK OF ECONOMIC DIVERSIFICATION

1. World Bank 2000, p. 21.
2. See, inter alia, Gibbon and Ponte 2005; Helleiner 2002; Rodrik 1999; Sachs and Warner 1997.
3. Sachs and Warner 1997.
4. Collier and Gunning 1999.
5. Rodrik 1999, p. 113.
6. Helleiner 2002.
7. Fosu 2011.
8. See Bouët 2008; Coe and Hoffmaister 1999; Foroutan and Pritchett 1993.
9. The reasons for the dynamism in global trade are complex during this period, but are as much tied up with technological changes (particularly the boom in containerisation and reduction in transport costs) as they are in policy changes towards a more liberal trade policy. See the discussion in Rose (2007).
10. Mkandawire 2019.
11. See, inter alia, Fosu 1990; 1996; Collier and Gunning 1999.
12. Grimwade 2000, Table 1.6.
13. Desai 2004; Barrett-Brown 1997, Chapter 9.
14. Iliffe 1995, p. 261.
15. Amsden 2007; Whitfield et al. 2015.
16. For a summary of that literature, see Morris et al. 2012.
17. Prebisch 1950; Singer 1950.
18. Both Prebisch (1950) and Singer (1950) reported that the terms of trade for the UK in the years 1870–1938 showed a 40% improvement, thereby implying, by assumption, a corresponding decline in the terms of trade of commodity-exporting developing countries.
19. Cited by Coulson 2012, p. 4.
20. As another example, between 1960 and 1970, while imports of cotton textiles doubled in the United States, imports of synthetics grew ten times (Schwartz 1994, p. 290).
21. There are a few discrepant studies. For instance, Brahmbhatt, Canuto and Vostroknutova (2010) argue that there is no evidence of any deterministic trend.
22. As noted by Moore et al., the international market prices of products such as cocoa, coffee, copper, cotton, diamonds, gold, groundnuts, palm oil, sisal and tobacco

311

had soared in the mid-1950s during the Korean War, offering false hope about future market potential to the soon-to-be independent countries on the African continent (Moore et al. 2018, p. 25).

23. See Morris et al. 2012, Chapter 2 for an overview. Cashin et al. 2002 showed a downward trend in the terms of trade of around 1% per year over the period between 1862 and 1999. Using 1900–80 data (and excluding petroleum prices), Sapsford (1985) estimated a decrease of 1.3% per year in terms of trade for primary commodities, interrupted briefly by the 1951–53 commodity price boom.

24. Maizels 2003, cited by Amsden 2007, p. 83.

25. Stein 2000, p. 3.

26. Bulmer-Thomas (2003) coins the phrase 'commodity lottery' to draw attention to the arbitrary nature of shifts in commodity prices. Some, such as meat, have a relatively high-income elasticity of demand, so that a 5% increase in real-world income brings an increase in demand in terms of quantity of more than 5%. Others, such as coffee, have seen income elasticities that decline over time, as the commodity in question has moved from being a luxury good to being an article of basic consumption. Some commodities (e.g. gold) have no close substitute, whereas others (e.g. cotton) face competition from synthetic products so that the price elasticity in terms of demand is high. For some commodities (e.g. cobalt), there are few alternative sources of supply; in others (e.g. sugar), international competition is fierce.

27. Iliffe 1995, p. 261.

28. Oxfam International 2002.

29. Wuyts 2005.

30. Santos-Paulino (2007) points to a relationship between aid inflows and a more rapid acceleration of imports. This occurs both because of the extent to which increased aid inflows facilitate the purchase of imports, and also because the bulk of 'trade facilitation' measures funded by the donor community were directed at liberalising imports. Little donor funding was directed to investing in domestic productive capacities to enable an improved export performance.

31. Buffie (2001) described the scale of the change thus: 'The most disturbing evidence comes from post 1980 liberalization episodes in sub-Saharan Africa'.

32. Summarised from Buffie 2001, pp. 190–2.

33. UNCTAD 1999.

34. Boratav 2001.

35. Ul Haque 2004.

36. Amsden (2007) suggests that there would be a logic in exporters of minerals forming a cartel like OPEC but concedes that any such initiative would likely be undermined by the hegemonic power.

37. Cavalcanti et al. 2012.

38. See Collier and Gunning 1999, p. 6.

39. Morris et al. 2012, p. 31.

40. See Amsden 2007; Haggard and Affairs 1990.

41. Kholi 2004.

42. In particular, the Cold War played out differently in Asia compared with Africa. In Asia, US policy was focused on building up the economies of 'allied' countries (Japan, South Korea, Taiwan, etc.) as a buttress against communism. As a consequence, these countries were given much more leeway, in terms of policy space and access to the US market to develop their own industries and export sectors than was the case in Latin America and Africa. For an engaging discussion on this theme, see Amsden 2007.
43. Roessler et al. 2022.
44. Enns and Bersaglio 2019.
45. Rodrik et al. 2004; Luke and Macleod 2019.
46. Adebajo 2021, p. 63.
47. Macleod and Luke 2023b; p. 3.
48. Figures from UNCTADStat 2023.
49. Havinden and Meredith 1993.
50. See Leubuscher 1940.
51. Austin 2014, p. 8.
52. Amsden 2007.
53. Fieldhouse 1999.
54. For some tentative answers to that question, see Amsden 2007; Kholi 2004; Thompson and Thompson 2001.
55. Lancaster 2006.
56. See Blomqvist 1996.
57. Schwartz 2018.
58. Mold and Chekwoti 2022.
59. Brautigam 2009, p. 194.
60. Interestingly, for reasons related to political uncertainty at home, Chinese investors from Hong Kong and Taiwan were among the first to make investments in the African garment sector. Brautigam (2009, pp. 204–5) reports that Taiwan industrialists set up 300 factories in Lesotho and Hong Kong nationals were responsible for more than 90% of the early capital invested in Mauritian export processing zones.
61. See, inter alia, Mitchell 2008; Headey and Fan 2008; Von Braun 2008; Farooki and Kaplinsky 2013; Cuddington and Jerrett 2008.
62. At the turn of the century, it was thought that Africa possessed roughly 10% of the world's remaining crude oil reserves and 8% of natural gas reserves. Since then, however, almost 30% of all new discoveries of oil and gas worldwide have been located in Africa. This recent wave of discoveries has revealed new basins in Mauritania (2001), Uganda (2006), Kenya (2007), Mozambique, Tanzania and Sierra Leone (2010), and Liberia and Kenya (2012). As a result, proven reserves of oil on the continent have increased by approximately 150%, from 53 billion barrels in 1980 to over 130 billion barrels at the end of 2013 (Signé 2021).
63. See the excellent explanation on this in Ghazvinian 2007, Chapter 1.
64. Freeman 2006.

65. Selwyn 2018.
66. Kaplinsky and Morris 2009.
67. Lederman and Maloney 2007.
68. Morris et al. 2012, p. 33.
69. Piketty 2014, Chapters 7–8.
70. Mold and Prizzon 2014.
71. Blas and Farchy 2022, p. 248.
72. Deaton 1999, p. 10.
73. Bulte et al. 2005; Isham et al. 2005.
74. Deaton 1999, p. 12.
75. Carmignani and Avom 2010.
76. Nkurunziza et al. 2017.
77. Bahar and Santos 2018.
78. Csordás 2017.
79. Fosu 1990.
80. Fosu 1996.
81. Fosu 2000, p. 12. Usman and Landry (2021) provide a very useful recent overview of the evidence. Another useful reference is IMF (2014), an econometric study that confirms Durlauf et al.'s (2008) earlier results wherein aggregate trade measures are not robust growth determinants, but once export diversification is introduced, the results show that it is a crucial determinant of economic growth for low-income countries. The effect is not only statistically significant but also economically important: a one standard deviation increase in export diversification is shown to increase the average annual growth rate by 0.8 percentage points for low-income countries.
82. For example, Zambia and Nigeria (see UNCTAD 2021a).
83. Collier 2008.
84. Cramer et al. 2020, p. 59.
85. Cited in Meagher 2019, p. 529.
86. Bawumia and Halland 2018.
87. UNCTAD's (2021a, p. xii) analysis uses empirical data over the period from 1995 to 2018 and covers 206 countries and territories. During the sample period, 95% of commodity-dependent countries remained within this group. The authors concluded that the likelihood that a strongly commodity-dependent country loses its dependency on commodities over the 24-year period was very small.

5. THE FLIP SIDE OF COMMODITY DEPENDENCE: THE MANUFACTURING DEFICIT

1. Bell 1974.
2. As noted by Rodrik (2018, p. 228), once shoes can be produced cheaply with 3D printing technologies, the winners will be countries like Germany, not Ethiopia.
3. Baccini et al. 2021, p. 1.
4. Helleiner et al. 1976.

5. Kuznets 1966.
6. Lal 1985.
7. See, inter alia, Agarwal et al. 2022; Ndung'u, Abebe and Ngui 2022. For a summary of the debate, see UNECA 2016.
8. Rowden 2015.
9. See also Rodrik 2015; Gelb et al. 2020.
10. Macleod and Luke 2023, p. 5.
11. Moussa 2016, p. 4.
12. Cramer et al. 2020, p. 102.
13. Figures are for sub-Saharan Africa.
14. Amsden 2007, p. 81.
15. For instance, Britain faced a financial crisis in 1976. The Labour government was forced to apply to the IMF for a loan of nearly USD 4 billion. IMF negotiators insisted on deep cuts in public expenditure, greatly affecting economic and social policy. See British National Archives 2023.
16. IMF 2022.
17. Mold 2009; Dreher 2009; Easterly 2007.
18. Thirlwall 2012.
19. Note that the same methodology has been applied to (and found pertinent) in high-income countries like the UK and Spain, which have at times experienced a lacklustre performance in terms of their merchandise trade balance. See Alonso and Garcimartín 1998.
20. The authors contrasted the 'benchmark economy' by identifying a group of currently middle-income countries that have crossed the USD 1,045 low-income threshold, specifically China (2000), India (2007), Indonesia (2004), Korea (1968), Malaysia (1968), the Philippines (1976) and Thailand (1987). The economic structure of the benchmark is simply the average of the shares of value added and employment in four broad sectors (agriculture, manufacturing, other industry, and services) for these seven countries in the relevant year (Newman et al. 2016).
21. Amsden (2001; 2007) claims that there may be another payoff from a greater prioritisation of manufacturing, as the development of manufacturing sectors is less associated with corruption than with the 'point rents' of minerals and fuels.
22. Naudé 2018, p. 3.
23. McMillan and Headey 2014; Naudé 2018, p. 3.
24. Allard et al. 2016, p. 31.
25. For example, Bigsten et al. 2004; Van Biesebroeck 2005.
26. Jones et al. 2019; Abreha et al. 2021, p. 73.
27. Amsden 2001. On data for 1950 and 1994 for a group of 29 developing countries, when she regressed per capita manufacturing output in 1950 against per capita manufacturing output in 1994; she found that the adjusted R-squared was 0.75.
28. Conceiçao et al. 2014; Abreha et al. 2020.
29. Rodrik (2018) has some insights as to how the policy parameters for developing countries have changed recently, and the space for industrial development has

diminished. He notes how for six decades in the post-war period, 'governments in rich countries for the most part looked the other way while Japan, South Korea, Taiwan, and China protected their home markets, appropriated "intellectual property", subsidized their producers, and managed their currencies. We have now reached the end of this happy coexistence' (Rodrik 2018, Chapter 5).

30. For example, Newfarmer et al. 2018; Dadush 2015.

31. It would be nonetheless wrong to overstate this shift. In 1970, for the African continent as a whole, value added in services was already estimated to account for 47% of continental GDP; in 2020 it was just 6% higher, standing at 53%. Manufacturing over the same period contracted, but from 16% to 12% (calculated from UNCTADStat 2023). It should also be borne in mind that because of much higher average productivity growth in manufacturing than in services, this decline in the share reflects in part a sharper fall in manufacturing prices compared with services. The shifts are there, but not on a dramatic scale.

32. Dihel and Goswami 2016.

33. Gervais and Jensen 2019; Loungani and Mishra 2014.

34. Young 2014. Pointedly, it should be noted that Young's study referred specifically to developed countries and was looking at average productivity growth. As noted by UNCTAD (2020a, p. 44), many service activities are, by their very nature, inherently impervious to productivity increases, and there is a qualitative aspect that needs to be taken into account. A lot of the increases in retail service productivity in countries such as the United States and the United Kingdom have been brought about by lowering the quality of the retail service itself—fewer shop assistants, longer drives to the supermarket, lengthier waits for deliveries, etc. The 2008 global financial crisis also revealed that much of the recent productivity growth in finance had been achieved through the debasement of the products—that is, the creation of overly complex, riskier and even fraudulent products.

35. Baccini et al. 2021, p. 3; Chang 2022; UNCTAD 2020.

36. Chang 2022, p. 165.

37. Kaplinsky 2014.

38. Behuria and Goodfellow 2019.

39. Baccini et al. 2021, p. 1.

40. The authors further note that, if merged and separated countries are excluded, the manufacturing value-added share in developing countries has not changed since 1970, even at current prices (Haraguchi et al, 2017, p. 9). It should be noted, however, that the difference in the result is caused by the breakup of the USSR alone.

41. See CBS News 2015.

42. Handy 2004.

43. The one important caveat to make here is that when we consider the trade-in-value added, rather than the gross trade values, services trade takes on a much more substantial role in total trade. World Bank (2019) calculations suggest that while services' trade share of gross exports was just 21% in 2009, it was more than double that (43%) as a share of trade in value-added. Those figures drive home the rela-

tive importance of the service sector in total value addition. More is said on this in Chapter 9.

44. See Szirmai (2013) for an update on Cornwell's hypothesis. Lall and Kraemer-Mbula (2005, Chapter 2) also provide some compelling arguments on this point.

45. Marconi et al. 2016.

46. Szirmai and Verspagen 2015.

47. Their findings for more recent periods suggest that a higher level of human capital (at least seven to eight years of education) is necessary for manufacturing to play a role as an engine of growth in developing countries. This might have some negative implications for the continent. For instance, Ethiopia has achieved some success in attracting FDI into its manufacturing sector, but despite improvements, its average educational levels are still low (Chen et al. 2015).

48. UNCTAD (2021, p. 39) finds that measures of human capital, technological development and investment have a statistically significant impact on labour productivity growth in the manufacturing sector. The same was true for high productivity services, but not for agriculture. The IMF (2018) also finds evidence of unconditional convergence of productivity levels in most sectors, but not in agriculture. Using a steady-state model (which allows parameter values to vary over time), Acevedo et al. 2009 analyse Latin American growth performance over the period 1950–2006, and while they confirm the role of manufacturing as the leading growth sector, they also find similar qualities in certain sub-sectors of services.

49. Su and Yao 2016. In addition, exploratory analysis by Baccini et al. (2021) of the relationship between services and economic development, using per capita nightlight luminosity as a proxy for growth, reveals no evidence that services in aggregate are associated with economic development. There is, however, substantial heterogeneity across different services industries. Disaggregating the tertiary sector by skill intensity reveals that higher-skilled services are strongly associated with development. Health services, public services and, to a lesser extent, business services are positively associated with economic development. Conversely, transport and private household services are negatively correlated with development indicators.

50. Chang 2022, p. 156.

51. McMillan and Headey 2014.

52. Naudé 2018, p. 5.

53. Hallward-Driemeier and Nayyar 2017. See also Rodrik 2012; McMillan et al. 2014; Rodrik 2015.

54. Newman et al. 2016.

55. Hallak and Sivadasan 2013.

56. In a recent study into the role of trade openness in the economic reallocation from the agricultural to the manufacturing sector in 34 sub-Saharan African countries between 1970 and 2016, Kaba et al. (2022) find that commodity exports have a negative impact on structural change, whereas manufacturing exports positively impact structural change. The authors conclude that commodity exporters have

failed to use the revenues from commodities exports sufficiently in infrastructure, thereby removing the constraints on the development and relocation of labour-intensive manufacturing activities.

57. Kruse et al. 2021.
58. Abreha et al. 2021, p. 29.
59. Kruse et al. 2021.
60. According to Abreha et al. (2021, pp. 6–7), the region experienced a 148% increase in manufacturing jobs, from a total of 8.6 million in 1990 to 21.3 million in 2018. Some authors talk of much larger magnitudes. Naudé, for instance, claims that

    Countries such as Ethiopia, Kenya, Nigeria, and Burkina Faso have experienced notable increases in manufacturing employment; for example, in Ethiopia, manufacturing employment levels grew from just about one million workers in 2004 to more than 5.6 million workers by 2015. Adding 4 million jobs to manufacturing in less than a decade is an indication of revival, not decline (Naudé 2018, p. 4).

61. Leke et al. 2018.
62. Abreha et al. 2021.
63. Signé 2021; Naudé 2018.
64. McMillan et al. 2014.
65. Harrison et al. 2014.
66. Austin 2016, p. 16; Robertson 2022.
67. Sender 1999.
68. African Union Statistical Yearbook 2020.
69. Austin 2016, p. 16.
70. Typifying this kind of view, Cheru cites Jackie Selebi, who at the time was Director-General of the South African Department of Foreign Affairs: 'It is meaningless to open markets when these economies do not produce anything to trade' (cited in Cheru 2002, p. 122).
71. Hirschman 1958. See also Streeten 1959.
72. Abreha et al. 2021, p. 156.
73. Odijie 2019.
74. Abreha et al. 2021, p. 156.

6. WEAKNESSES OF AFRICA'S CURRENT PATTERNS OF INTEGRATION INTO THE GLOBAL ECONOMY

1. To this trend we must also consider the impact of the exit of the United Kingdom from the bloc. For an analysis of the impact of Brexit on African economies, see Mold 2018.
2. This contention is broadly supported by ICP data, which found that the two largest economies in the world in 2017 were China and the United States, each of whom recorded a PPP-based GDP of just under USD 20 trillion (ICP 2020). This implies that, under current growth rates, the size of the US economy would have been surpassed by the Chinese economy within a few years after 2017.

3. Coulibaly et al. 2022.
4. See Luke and Macleod 2023.
5. Cilliers 2020, p. 200.
6. Using 1995 trade data on 126 exporting countries to 59 importing countries in 5,000 product categories, Hummels and Klenow (2005) find that the extensive margin accounts for 62% of the growth of exports of larger economies.
7. IMF 2023.
8. Rodrik 2018, p. 132. According to Kaplinsky, two main factors explain the decline in the rates of productivity growth and investment rates in high-income economies: the first is the atrophy of the mass production paradigm and the second the inappropriate neo-liberal policy response to the underlying slowdown, which exacerbated systemic inequality, the precarity of livelihoods and the fragility of economic systems (Kaplinsky 2021, Chapters 2 and 5). Indicative of the scale of the decline is the fact that the United States is now no longer a leading exporter of high-tech goods; high-tech exports represented just 20% of the total value of its manufactured exports in 2019, ranking it as 28th globally, according to World Bank WDI data. Leading the pack in terms of the share of high-tech manufactured exports are Asian economies such as Hong Kong (China), Malaysia and Singapore, all with shares higher than 50% (Chang 2022, p. 84).
9. See ILO 2014, Chapter 2; Weisbrot 2015, Chapter 3.
10. See World Bank 2023.
11. Coulibaly et al. 2022.
12. For example, see UNECA 2019.
13. Standard Bank 2020, p. 7.
14. Grimwade 2000, p. 256.
15. Mold 2005.
16. This stance is supported by the fact that productivity differences between the industrialised and African countries are so large as to be almost without historical precedent. To give an approximate idea of the scale of the productivity gap, if we take GDP per capita at purchasing power parities to reflect the differences in productivity levels, then the differential between the richest European countries and the poorest African countries is likely to be in the order of 40:1. At market exchange rates, the scale of the difference is much larger.
17. Even within the African continent—a continent that is usually regarded as highly protectionist—average tariff levels are only around 6.5% (UNCTAD 2019), meaning that there is a limit to how much can be gained under the AfCFTA through the elimination of tariffs alone.
18. Cernat et al. 2002.
19. Schwartz 2018, p. 284.
20. See, for instance, Newman et al. 2016; Cramer et al. 2020, p. 105.
21. Mold 2005a. There is a lot of evidence that domestic pressures for protection mount during bad times and safety regulations are often used as an excuse to protect the domestic producers. For instance, researchers found that during the 2008 financial

crisis in the United States, the Food and Drug Administration suddenly became more likely to refuse shipments of imported foods coming from developing countries on food-safety grounds. For exporters from developing countries, the cost associated with shipments being refused quadrupled during the period (Banerjee and Duflo 2019, p. 66).

22. Yeshiwas and Workie 2018; Lim et al. 2013.

23. See Oya (2011) Jarzebski et al. (2019).

24. Cook and Jones 2015.

25. These rules of origin emulated the 'triple transformation' principle already prevalent in other US preferential trade agreements such as NAFTA and the Caribbean Basin Initiative. These rules of origin had a prejudicial impact on the long-term development of the Mexican clothing industry, with restrictive rules of origin stipulating that clothing must be cut and made from fibre originating in North America in order to qualify for duty-free access. This allowed the United States to charge higher prices on textiles for apparel producers in Mexico, undermining the long-term competitiveness of the Mexican clothing industry (UNCTAD 2019, p. 76). Mexico's greatly increased share of US clothing imports in the 1990s thus proved to be ephemeral. By contrast, China's share of US clothing imports rebounded, and, by 2011, Chinese clothing imports into the USA were more than eight times greater than Mexico's (Dicken 2015, pp. 471–3).

26. Although the country-level quotas have been removed, a regional AGOA quota remains for apparel. The quota was initially set at 1.5% of US imports but was increased to 3.5% over eight years. These caps were doubled under a set of amendments called AGOA II (Abreha et al. 2021, p. 149).

27. Mullings and Mahabir 2018, p. 247.

28. A few early studies established a positive impact of AGOA on SSA exports. Collier and Venables (2007) and Tadesse and Fayissa (2008) found that AGOA promoted exports of apparel to the US. Frazer and Van Biesebroeck (2010) concluded that AGOA had a large and robust impact on US imports for apparel and manufactured products and a smaller but significant impact on agricultural products. Notice, however, that these positive appraisals were undertaken relatively early in AGOA's lifetime, and thus did not capture the slide in African exports to the US after the financial crisis of 2008–09, as commodity prices declined.

29. Condon and Stern 2011.

30. Mueller 2008, cited by Mullings and Mahabir 2018.

31. Seyoum 2007.

32. Nilsson and Davies 2013.

33. UNECA 2015; Eicher and Kuenzel 2016.

34. Coulibaly et al. 2022.

35. Cook and Jones 2015.

36. In principle, to comply with GATT/WTO rules, and because they are exceptions to the 'most favoured nation' principle, all preferential market access schemes are supposed to require a special dispensation through the World Trade Organization. It is of note that the US has never asked for such a waiver.

37. Wolff 2020.
38. It is clear that, in some cases, the national body politic was to blame for the situation created. Collier (2008), for instance, explains the circumstances surrounding the suspension of Madagascar and the mismanagement not only of the economy but the domestic political situation, resulting in the contraction of employment in the export processing zone from 300,000 to just 40,000 people.
39. Hochberg 2020.
40. Davies and Nilsson 2019.
41. Gasiorek and López González 2011.
42. It is interesting to note that the authors did their econometric work on a sample of exports from developing countries to the EU and the US for the period 2007–10 (Davies and Nilsson 2019, p. 619). Given the context of a global financial crisis that initially struck the US economy much harder than that of the EU, this possibly impacts on the results in a way favourable to the EBA case.
43. Persson and Wilhelmsson 2015.
44. See, for instance, Persson and Wilhelmsson 2007; Thelle et al. 2015; Cirera et al. 2015, among others.
45. EUC 2015.
46. Davies and Nilsson 2019, p. 619.
47. See Chapter 11 for an explanation.
48. Cipollina et al. 2016.
49. Gradeva and Martínez-Zarzoso 2015.
50. Manchin and Francois 2006.
51. Mullings and Mahabir 2018, p. 246.
52. UNECA 2015.
53. Manchin and Francois 2006.
54. Chinese membership of the WTO was a policy that both Europe and the US supported, expecting it to handicap the Chinese economy with the rules and regulations incumbent on WTO members. In the end, Chinese officials had the last laugh, and the expansion of their exports to high-income markets on MFN terms was phenomenal.
55. Gelb et al. (2017) look at African labour costs and conclude that only Ethiopia might have a chance in competing on costs with China.
56. See World Development Report (World Bank 2020b). It should be stressed that all the major trading partners with Africa are guilty of this malpractice. In fact, the data provided by the World Development Report shows that China places the highest tariffs on semi-processed and final goods (although the multiple of raw material tariffs is smaller than in the case of the EU).
57. See Brenton and Hoppe 2006; Naumann 2010, cited by Mullings and Mahabir 2018.
58. In a study by Kareem (2014), 52 African countries are considered in an empirical analysis covering the period 1995 to 2012 which looks at fish, cocoa, vegetables and coffee.
59. Collier points to a further problem with European market access under EBA guide-

lines for the Ugandan fish industry: if the boat used to catch the fish has a single crew member from Kenya, the production cannot be exported to the EU under the EBA's strict rules of origin that do not allow non-LDCs to benefit (and Kenya is a non-LDC) (Collier 2008, p. 164).

60. Green bean exports to the EU are often presented as an African success story. Led by Kenya, African countries captured a significant share of a rapidly expanding but demanding export market. Their success was attributed to the leading role played by private companies in establishing the industry, the Kenyan government's supportive role, secure land tenure, and the inclusion of smallholders in the supply chain. However, by 2013, the World Bank was reporting challenges associated with increasingly stringent food safety and other standards by the EU (Headey 2013).

61. Kaplinsky and Morris 2019, p. 8.

62. Luke and Macleod 2023, p. 6.

63. One fear that is often raised, for example, is aflatoxins. Yet research shows that the risks are minimal from this source. See Mold 2006.

64. See Nelsen 2022.

65. UNCTAD 2021b.

66. A similar story of thwarted hopes of rising exports to the EU market relates to biofuels. When the EU first embarked on its policy to foster biofuels in its transport sector in the mid-2000s, most developing countries expected to benefit, and there was a prediction that there would be a rise in African biofuel exports to the EU. However, this rise has not materialised. The EU biofuel policy was structured in ways that act as an NTB under the EU Renewable Energy Directive, which has limited Africa's access to the EU biofuel market (Abreha et al. 2021, p. 148).

67. See Brautigam 2009; Mullings and Mahabir 2018.

68. Minson 2008, cited by Mullings and Mahabir 2018.

69. Minson 2008. Brautigam notes that Minson's figures were based on early data and might have underestimated possible increases in the value of exports due to the preferential scheme. She contrasts Minson's figures with the 2006–08 figures provided by China's Minister of Commerce Chen Deming who claimed that the programme had transferred USD 680 million in tariff exemptions to 31 countries (Brautigam 2009, p. 96).

70. Co and Dimova 2014.

71. Mullings and Mahabir 2018.

72. Busse et al. (2019) conducted an econometric analysis using panel data for 43 African countries over the period 1991–2010.

73. Baliamoune-Lutz 2011.

74. Mold and Chekwoti 2022.

75. Ibid.

76. OECD 2021.

77 Mullings and Mahabir 2018.

78. Abreha et al. 2021, p. 149.

79. Collier 2008.

80. Newman et al. 2016.
81. Although the authors don't recognise it, this proposal had already been made earlier by Collier (2008). It was unrealistic then, however, and remains unrealistic.
82. See also Coulibaly et al. (2022).

7. AFRICA'S TRIALS AND TRIBULATIONS WITH GLOBAL TRADE GOVERNANCE

1. Oyejide 2000.
2. Gereffi 1994.
3. Gibbon and Ponte 2005.
4. In fact, the GATT's remit fell considerably short of the blueprint laid out by John
Maynard Keynes for an international trade organisation (Skidelsky 2000). The draft
charter of Keynes' organisation was ambitious, extending beyond world trade dis-
ciplines to include rules on employment, commodity agreements, restrictive business practices, international investment and services. Its foundation met with significant opposition, however, particularly from the United States. Pointedly, the
bottom line in the negotiations for the British delegation was the defence of 'imperial preference'.
5. See WTO 1995, Article XXVI (5). This must be taken in context. They did not all
exercise such a choice because the choice was of the colonising country as was provided in Article XXVI(5)(a) of the GATT: 'Each government accepting the
Agreement does so in respect of its metropolitan territory and of the other territories for which it has international responsibility'.
6. Gathii 2006, p. 1370.
7. There is some debate in the literature on the impact of the different rounds on
average tariffs. Baldwin claimed that 'Multilateral liberalisation since WWII has
been wildly successful at cutting developed nations. industrial tariffs' (1997, p. 1).
The average tariff in 1947 is often reported as around 40%, but a paper by Brown
(2016) which reviewed extensive historic documentation on tariff schedules found
that among the key GATT participants—the US, Western Europe and Japan—
the average tariff was only about 22% (World Bank 1987). Moreover, this figure
refers to the unweighted tariff average; the import-weighted tariff average would
have been much lower than this (Brown and Irwin 2016). This subsequently must
colour our impressions about the success of GATT and subsequently the WTO in
reducing tariffs.
8. Calculated from Our World in Data (Oxford Martin School 2023).
9. Grimwade 2000, p. 330.
10. See Mold and Chekwoti 2022.
11. Chang 2007. The WTO has a specific 'safeguard' mechanism that enables countries to raise import tariffs temporarily when imports cause 'serious injury' to
domestic firms. But the procedural hurdles are higher for safeguards, and countries
that use them must compensate exporters who are adversely affected. The numbers speak for themselves. Since the WTO was established in 1995, in excess of

3,000 anti-dumping duties have been put in place (with India, the United States, and the EU being the heaviest users). The corresponding number for safeguard measures is a mere 155 (with developing countries being the heaviest users). Clearly, anti-dumping is the trade remedy of choice (Rodrik 2018; p. 214).

12. Baldwin 1997, p. 1.

13. Grimwade 2003, p. 13. See also Chapter 6.

14. Schwartz 2018, p. 284. In 1955, the US had successfully lobbied for the exclusion of its agricultural sector from GATT. Neither the European Union nor Japan were especially interested in agricultural liberalisation, although from 1986 onwards, a group of 14 agricultural-exporting countries formed a group called the Cairns group which lobbied for greater liberalisation in agriculture.

15. However, far from impeding market forces, this creative protection often ended up magnifying market pressures on local producers by accelerating industrial dispersal and thus helping to give rise to the new manufactured goods exporters (Schwartz 2018, p. 282).

16. Amsden 2007, p. 49.

17. Schwartz 2018, p. 283.

18. Both agriculture and services were major US exports, and represented two areas where the United States had a trade surplus (USD 72.1 billion in 1998) and Japan and Germany large deficits (USD 48.7 billion and USD 88 billion, respectively) (WTO 1999).

19. See Gathii 2006.

20. Stiglitz and Charlton 2005.

21. Cilliers 2020. The WTO established an Aid for Trade initiative in 2006, and as of mid-2017, over USD 300 billion had been disbursed for various programmes to help developing countries trade. Behind all such initiatives and funding is the belief that trade is a route out of poverty for these countries. Yet in practice, facilitating trade has been a lot harder than might have been anticipated (see Banerjee and Duflo 2019, p. 67).

22. See Hochberg 2020.

23. Collier 2008.

24. Gathii 2006, p. 1379.

25. See Urban et al. 2016.

26. This figure is based on the averages presented in Schnepf (2021, Table 2) for the years 2015–17. In an effort to avoid falling foul of WTO rulings on trade-distorting subsidies, a lot of the agricultural support has been shifted towards ones which are tolerated to some extent under 'Green Box' outlays. Over 80% of the total figure of agricultural support cited here are considered 'Green Box' outlays, and hence are nominally allowed under WTO rules. However, critics still insist that a subsidy of any kind will eventually end up distorting trade outcomes, particularly in comparison with developing regions like Africa where, beyond subsidised fertilisers, most farmers receive no support whatsoever from their governments. Banga (2016) provides evidence that Green Box subsidies are also trade-distorting.

27. Cilliers 2020.
28. Brooks 2015.
29. Cilliers 2020.
30. Jawara and Kwa 2004.
31. Oyejide 2000. It is not perhaps coincidental that during the Doha Round of WTO negotiations in Cancun in September 2003, such was the rift in positions on the controversial 'Singapore issues' that it was Kenya that was the first country to abandon the negotiations (Stiglitz and Charlton 2005).
32. Gathii 2006, p. 1363.
33. Van der Ven and Luke 2023, p. 131.
34. Jawara and Kwa 2004.
35. Tandon 2015.
36. Wolff 2020.
37. Brooks 2015. Illustrative of the competitive pressures, according to one study cited by Brooks, nearly 80% of all clothing purchased in Uganda is now second-hand clothing.
38. Mkandawire 2001; Gallagher and Kumar 2007.
39. Fosu 2012, p. 8. For instance, the WTO bans the use of 'local contents requirement' (that is, a government requiring that MNCs buy more than a certain proportion of their inputs locally, rather than importing them). This rule disproportionately benefits rich countries because most MNCs are from rich countries. These examples show that, even if all countries abide by the same rules, the more powerful countries are likely to benefit more from the system because they have already ensured that the content of the rules favours themselves. See Chang 2022, p. 73; Gathii 2012.
40. Amsden 2000.
41. See the discussion in Cramer et al. 2020, pp. 199–223.
42. Chortareas and Pelagidis 2004.
43. UNDP 1997, p. 82, cited by Stiglitz and Charlton 2005, p. 47.
44. Francois 2000.
45. Fosu and Mold 2007.
46. Ibid.
47. One interesting dimension to the results reported by Fosu and Mold is that the region that had the most to gain from the elimination of tariffs was the 'Rest of North Africa' region, a composite aggregation of the Egyptian, Algerian and Libyan economies. The explanation resides in the degree and structure of the distortions of the domestic economies; the largest gains from multilateral liberalisation are likely to occur in those sectors and economies where initial tariffs are highest.
48. Sachs 2005, p. 281.
49. Gereffi 1994.
50. Hopkins and Wallerstein 1986. For an explanation of the evolution of the concept, see Gibbon and Ponte 2005.
51. As reported by Morris and Kaplinsky 2014. According to the World Bank's WDR

2020, that was around the time that GVCs peaked, and since 2015, GVCs experienced a degree of retrenchment—a retrenchment which is likely to have accelerated since the onset of the Covid-19 pandemic.

52. Gibbon and Ponte 2005; Kaplinsky and Morris 2016.
53. Oya 2010.
54. Allard et al. 2016, p. 28.
55. Ibid.; Abreha et al. 2021.
56. Selwyn 2018, p. 18.
57. Nolan 2003, p. 18.
58. For an explanation of why this has occurred, see World Bank 2020, pp. 82–3.
59. Choi et al. 2021.
60. South African firms with a medium (11–25%) and large (more than 25%) share of exports charge markups that are 1.8% and 2.3% lower than those of non-exporters, respectively (World Bank 2020, p. 85).
61. World Bank 2020, p. 88.
62. Fagerberg et al. 2018; Kummritz 2015. The former paper's analysis is based on data from 125 countries over the period 1997–2013, and finds that countries that increase GVC participation do not grow faster than other countries when other relevant factors are controlled for. Small countries, and countries with low capabilities, appear to be particularly disadvantaged.
63. Greenville et al. 2017; Selwyn 2018.
64. UNCTAD 2021; Montalbano and Nenci 2020.
65. Allard et al. 2016. The cited figures pertain to sub-Saharan Africa.
66. UNCTAD 2019.
67. ACET 2014.
68. UNCTAD 2019.
69. Kaplinsky and Morris 2019, p. 9.
70. Examples include the Comprehensive and Progressive Agreement for Trans-Pacific Partnership (CPTPP), which came into effect in December 2018, and the Regional Comprehensive Partnership (RCEP) among Asia-Pacific countries, which is the largest trade agreement globally by value.
71. Mkandawire 2019, p. 539.
72. Oyejide et al. 1997; Oyejide et al. 1999.
73. It is worth noting that that view did not go unchallenged. According to Wang and Winters (1997), greater African unity during the negotiations may not have improved the outcome for Africa since, acting as a group, African countries probably had little more clout than when they act individually.
74. Selwyn 2018, p. 3.

8. THE ECONOMIC SIGNIFICANCE OF INTRA-AFRICAN TRADE: GETTING THE NARRATIVE RIGHT

1. An earlier draft of this chapter appeared as a Brookings Institution Working Paper (Mold 2022).

2. See, inter alia, Yang and Gupta 2005; Ngepah and Udeagha 2018; Cramer et al. 2020.

3. To add insult to injury, the adjectives employed to describe intra-African trade are often visceral, including descriptions such as 'dismal', 'chronically low', 'tiny', 'anaemic' and 'insignificant'.

4. Cramer et al. 2020, p. 65.

5. Rosling et al. (2018) draw attention to a series of ten cognitive biases—'gaps'—that impinge on our perceptions of data and data trends, including errors related to a lack of proper appreciation of magnitudes, assumptions that things are worse than the data reveals, and the tendency to extrapolate in a linear manner from existing trends.

6. On the problems of trade data, see Ortiz-Ospina and Beltekian 2018; OECD-WTO 2012. Double counting is a particularly serious problem and may result in an overvaluing of trade by around 25%. The treatment of re-exports is also a challenge (Koopman et al. 2012). On the challenges specifically of intra-African trade statistics, see Yeats 1990; Jerven 2014.

7. See Chapter 2.

8. Austin 2014; Frankema and Booth 2019.

9. Adedeji 1970; Akyeampong 2017.

10. On interpreting these historical data trends, it is important to stress the extent to which shifts in the share of intra-African trade depends on the denominator—total extra-African exports. The denominator is volatile because commodities account for the majority of the continent's exports. For instance, in 2015 alone, total African exports declined by more than 30%. As a result, the share of intra-African trade can change dramatically, not because of any change in the underlying amount of intra-African trade, but simply because the denominator has fallen or risen sharply.

11. Expressed in purchasing power parities (rather than at market exchange rates).

12. A word of caution here is that changes in membership can occur over the period of study. If we hold as constant the number of members of the EU to the EU-15 (which was the number of constituent member between 1995 and 2004), for instance, we would see that they experienced the second-largest decline of any of the regional blocks listed in Table 8.3.

13. This includes the IGAD, SADC and the Central American Common Market (CACM).

14. One recent example is an article in *African Business*, where Nwuke (2022) cites UNCTAD to claim intra-African trade 'to have averaged, excluding informal cross-border trade, 2% between 2015 and 2017'. Even based on official statistics, the figure is clearly erroneous, by a factor of eight or nine.

15. In absolute terms, it should be stressed that South Africa is by far the most important trader on the African continent. But it is also better integrated into global markets than the African average and hence the intra-African share is only around the average for the continent as a whole. From the perspective of attaining higher lev-

els of intra-African trade, this is a pity because, given its primary role as a hub for intra-regional trade in Southern Africa, in principle it could push up the continental intra-African share.

16. AU 2021.
17. Morris et al. 2012. See Annex Table.
18. For example, after nearly three decades of existence, the share of MERCOSUR's trade that is intra-regional is still lower than the African average. This is largely because the bloc is dominated by one of the world's largest commodity exporters—Brazil—and the principal demand for its commodities comes from outside the region.
19. According to the author's calculations, based again on the UNCTADStat 2023 dataset.
20. According to UNCTADStat data (2022), in 2020, 19 African countries were net commodity importers. A further 12 countries are only marginally net commodity exporters (i.e. less than USD 400 million a year).
21. Golub 2015.
22. For example, see Montalbano and Nenci 2020; Afreximbank, 2020.
23. Koroma et al. 2017.
24. Harding 2019.
25. Bridges 2018.
26. Golub 2015. The following review is drawn in part from Afreximbank 2020.
27. Little, Tiki and Debsu 2015.
28. Ibid.
29. Ayadi et al. 2013.
30. Afrika and Ajumbo 2012.
31. Njiwa et al. 2012.
32. Economic Commission for Africa and Afreximbank 2020.
33. Timmis 2017.
34. Ndumbe 2013, Titeca 2009, Chikanda and Tawodzera 2017.
35. See the Annex for the classifications of different African economies.
36. It also belies the contention that 'even if ICBT is included, the total level of intra-African trade is not likely to be more than 20% of the total trade' (African Union Commission 2012).
37. There is certainly a degree of inconsistency between those that stress simultaneously that formal sector trade is very low, while exaggerating the developmental potential of ICBT. It is a kind of argument that resonates with the stance taken by De Soto (1989) about the alleged vibrancy of the informal sector, which is contrasted against the stagnancy of the formal sector, an argument that was soundly rebutted by, inter alia, Bromley 1990.

9. THE PROMISE OF THE AFCFTA: THE ECONOMIC CASE FOR ESTABLISHING A CONTINENTAL MARKET

1. See, for instance, World Bank 2000, p. 7, which observes that 'the region's total

income is not much more than Belgium's and is divided among 48 countries with median GDP of just over USD 2 billion—about the output of a town of 60,000 in a rich country.'

2. France, the former colonial power, ranks last in the top ten economies of the world, and the United Kingdom, the other principal former colonial power, does not even make it onto the list. Cognisant of the shift of the global economy towards the emerging economies, all four BRIC economies (Brazil, China, India and Russia) make it into the top ten.
3. Standard Bank 2020, p. 7.
4. McKinsey Global Insitute (2023), 'Reimagining Economic Growth in Africa—Turning Diversity into Opportunity', June.
5. Leke et al. 2018, p. xii.
6. Lopes 2018, p. 71.
7. Kharas 2017.
8. Roxborough 2009.
9. Deloitte 2017, p. 1.
10. Signé 2020, p. 12.
11. Ibid., p. 22.
12. Frankema and van Waijenburg 2018.
13. See Lamarque and Nugent 2022.
14. Collier and Gunning 1999.
15. Dollar and Collier 1999.
16. See Mold 2004.
17. Kremer 1993.
18. World Bank 2016; Allard et al. 2016, p. 34; Roberts et al. 2023.
19. Yusuf and Nabeshima 2012.
20. Kaplinsky 2021. See also Kaplinsky and Morris 2019.
21. We discuss some of the implications of this for Africa's development model in Chapter 14.
22. Schwartz 2018.
23. It would be wrong to overestimate this even in the garment industry, however. For instance, Bangladesh's success in terms of promoting apparel exports is often ascribed to small firms, yet in reality exports are dominated by a group of medium-sized to relatively large firms. There are currently over 4,400 firms producing garment items for export purposes in Bangladesh, but the average size of a Bangladeshi firm is 797 employees per firm, much higher even than some competitor countries like Vietnam (426 employees per firm) and China (269 employees per firm) (Swazan and Das 2022). In comparison, few of the major players in Africa could currently be considered as major global players.
24. Agarwal et al. 2022, p. 15.
25. Schwartz 2018, pp. 289–90.
26. The fact that certain processes are 'scale-specific' also implies that firms cannot decide to increase and reach efficient operational scale without 'making jumps'. In

other words, investments are 'lumpy' and require significant increases in investments, financial commitments and risks, something small firms are ill-equipped to do, especially in countries where both the supply of raw materials and the final demand is very unstable (UNCTAD 2020, p. 32).

27. Kaplinsky and Morris 2019.

28. Chandler Jr 1990.

29. See UNCTAD 2020. The study notes that capacity utilisation rates in South Africa are high relative to other regional averages, something the author attributes to the fact that the South African firms are larger companies (UNCTAD 2020, p. 73).

30. Kaplinsky and Morris 2019.

31. For examples, see Leke et al. 2018; Signé 2020.

32. Fortune 2022.

33. See, for instance, Cockcroft and Riddell 1991; Stewart, Lall and Wangwe 1992.

34. Leke et al. 2018, pp. 21–2.

35. Page and Söderbom 2015. There is, however, discrepancy with studies such as Ayyagari et al. (2007), who, in a study of the relationship between the relative size of the SME sector and the business environment in 76 countries, find that small firms (5–19 employees) have higher employment growth than medium and large firms across all country income groups, which is explainable by the fact that this latter study provides no data on job destruction. Moreover, their data are subject to survivorship bias since they only include continuing firms.

36. See Van Biesebroeck 2005; Iacovone et al. 2014; Kerr et al. 2014; Aga et al. 2015.

37. In contrast, in Asian comparator countries, the share of employment in small manufacturing firms is flat or falling.

38. Diao et al. 2021; McMillan and Zeufack 2021.

39. Masson and Pattillo 2005.

40. Hummels and Klenow 2005.

41. Amurgo-Pacheco and Pierola 2008.

42. Brenton and Newfarmer 2007, cited in Fosu 2018, p. 19.

43. Haddad and Shepherd 2011.

44. World Bank 2020. The World Development Report notes that MFN tariffs on South–South trade are higher than those on North–South trade. What the authors don't stress, however, is that preferential tariffs on South–South trade (i.e. trade undertaken within the framework of some regional or bilateral agreements) are actually lower on South–South trade than South–North trade. And Southern countries face higher tariffs on their exports to the North than the North faces with regard to their exports to the South. Clearly, if tariff data like this are brought to bear on international negotiations through the WTO, it is clear that there is no 'level-playing field', and developing countries are actually better off focusing on export growth in the 'global South'.

45. This graphic excludes South African and all the North African economies, simply because they have a different dynamic in their external trading relations—North Africa is more reliant on the European market, and South Africa is the most globalised economy on the continent.

46. Abreha et al. 2021, p. 118.
47. Hirschman (1958).
48. By way of example, Chang (2022, pp. 42–3) notes that Japan—perhaps the epitome today of a high-tech economy—would still be producing silk and other textile products if the country had never engaged in import substitution policies in the 1950s and 1960s in sectors like steel and automobiles. In the 1950s, Japan simply could not compete in the international market in these industries, but by the 1980s, it was a world leader in many.
49. Buffie 2001, pp. 96–7.
50. For example, Yang and Gupta 2005.
51. Austin 2016, p. 15. The most likely exception would have been the Southern African settler states, South Africa and Rhodesia, where much of the rural male population had long been pressured into migrant labour. Even there, though manufacturing continued to expand in the 1950s and 1960s, it was behind protectionist tariffs.
52. Noman et al. 2012.
53. As Coulson (2012, p. 24) notes with regards to the Tanzanian situation: 'At independence, there were hardly any Tanzanian African engineers, accountants or architects, and very few doctors or agriculturalists. There was no quick way of changing the inherited economies' structure'.
54. Whitfield et al. 2015; Amsden 2001.
55. Mkandawire 2014, p. 13.
56. A remarkable example of the volte-face is a candid and insightful paper by IMF economists Cherif and Hasanov (2019).
57. Rwanda is one example of a country that in recent years has pragmatically shifted its strategy to embrace a domestic market recapturing strategy (Republic of Rwanda 2015). In that strategy document, seven high-priority sectors were identified: cement, textiles and garments, soaps and detergents, packaging materials, fertilisers, edible oils and maize.
58. Signé 2020, p. 42.
59. Leke et al. 2018, p. 54.
60. Cilliers 2020, p. 151.
61. Harrison et al. 2014.
62. Notably, the 'conditional' African advantage applies only to manufacturing firms—in the service sector, the African 'advantage' ceases to exist.
63. Harrison et al. 2014, p. 2.
64. Cilliers 2020, p. 151.
65. Behuria 2017.
66. Over the past 20 years, supermarket chains, in particular South African chains, have expanded into the SADC region and, less successfully, into other regions in Africa. Four large retailers—Shoprite, Pick n Pay, Spar and Woolworths—collectively have a market share of 72%, based on turnover figures for 2015. Some of the factors attributed to the 'supermarketisation' of food retail in countries in the SADC

are increased urbanisation and the newly developing middle class (UNCTAD 2021a, p. 86).

67. Andreoni et al. 2021, p. 61.

68. TMEA 2022.

69. Preliminary data shared with the authors.

70. Weeks 1996, p. 117.

71. Between 2005 and 2018, the country increased the share of its high-technology exports in total merchandise exports from 6% to 35%, while the share of exports of primary resources fell from 52% to 22% of total merchandise exports (UNCTAD 2021a).

72. Lewis 1958, p. 43. See also Weiss 2017. It is demonstrably the case that agricultural revolutions—in the sense of a pronounced increase in agricultural productivity—have tended to precede any shift towards higher value-added activities in manufacturing and services.

73. For the historic cases in Europe, see Bairoch 1995. For the case of China in the 1980s and 1990s, see Yasheng. 2005; Nolan 2001.

74. See, for instance, Oya 2010.

75. Woolfrey (2021, p. 74) claims that 'the continent was dependent on imports for almost 30% of its food demand in the early 2020s'. An UNCTAD official also argues that Africa imports about 85% of its food from outside the continent (UNCTAD 2021a, p. 116).

76. The share is lowest in North African countries and South Africa. But it is as high as two thirds of all employment in the poorer countries of Eastern Africa, for example (ILO 2019).

77. Fox and Jayne 2020. Of course, this conclusion is heavily dependent on the timeframe for the analysis. The FAO (2021, p. 19) comes to a different conclusion by looking at the data for the period 1996–2016: 'While exports have been growing at a compound annual growth rate of 4% over the last two decades (1996–2016), this has been outpaced by the annual growth in imports, which was 6% over the same period. Africa is thus a growing net importer of agricultural products'.

78. See Fox and Jayne 2020; Oya 2010.

79. Monbiot 2022.

80. Ibid., pp. 32–3. At the level of individual firms, the level of control is perhaps even more shocking. Just four companies—Cargill, Archer Daniels Midland, Bunge and Louis Dreyfus—control, in one estimate, 90% of the global grain trade. They are consolidating vertically as well as horizontally, buying into seed, fertiliser, processing, packing, distribution and retail businesses. Another four companies—ChemChina, Corteva, Bayer and BASF—control 66% of the world's agricultural chemicals market, while a similar cluster—ChemChina, Corteva, Bayer and Lima Grain—owns 53% of the global seed market (ibid., p. 37).

81. Morsy et al. 2021.

82. Tunisia is a net exporter, however, due to the export of products like olives to the European market. Similarly, Morocco also has a smaller imbalance because of horticultural exports to the European market.

83. Overall, Northern Africa is a significant and growing net importer. Central and Western Africa are also net importers (although traded volumes are much smaller and more volatile in Central Africa). Southern Africa has been close to parity between imports and exports, and East Africa, which had largely been a net exporter, has in recent years become a net importer (FAO 2021, p. 19).
84. Weeks 1996, p. 167. The process of urbanisation is driving greater food demand, coupled with the rapid shift in diets from cereal-based food to non-grain products such as fruits and vegetables; roots and tubers; meat, fish and dairy; and edible oils (World Bank 2021).
85. Cherif et al. 2020.
86. FAO 2021, p. 12; Morsy et al. 2021.
87. World Bank 2021, p. 48.
88. Diao et al. 2007.
89. Weeks 1996; World Bank 2013, p. 47.
90. World Bank 2013, p. 19.
91. Morsy et al. 2021.
92. FAO 2021. For comparison's sake, the effectively applied tariff weighted average (customs duty) for sub-Saharan Africa for all merchandise was 5.67% in 2017 while the MFN weighted average tariff was 7.85%.
93. Brenton and Hoffman 2016, p. 4.
94. Fox and Jayne 2020. Juma (2011, p. 11) noted that investment in R&D in the agricultural sector was one of the best investments that one could make to increase productivity, with an estimated average rate of return of 33% over the period 1970–2004.
95. In his 2011 book, Juma cites many examples of regional R&D projects in agriculture, such as WABNet project in West Africa looking into sorghum genetic resources (Juma 2011).
96. World Bank 2021, p. 48.
97. World Bank 2013, p. 47.
98. Leke et al. 2018, p. 74.
99. Signé 2020, p. 61.

10. THE IMPORTANCE OF CATALYSING CROSS-BORDER INVESTMENT

1. Blomström and Kokko 2003.
2. In particular, there is econometric evidence that FDI from other developing countries (the 'South') positively affects the ability of African countries to diversify their export baskets and to raise export quality, especially within manufacturing—significantly more so compared with FDI from high-income economies (the 'North') (Amighini and Sanfilippo 2014).
3. Matthee et al. 2017.
4. Gathani and Stoelinga 2013, p. 74. The authors also estimate that 80% of output in Rwanda's 47 largest manufacturing and agribusiness is controlled by large groups, 70% of which is owned by foreign capital.

5. Edwards 2020.
6. Since 2005, World Bank Enterprise Surveys have surveyed over 37,000 firms on the African continent (and 180,000 globally). This makes it one of the most comprehensive sources for data on African business activity.
7. Small firms are defined here as having between five and 19 employees.
8. Bateman and Chang 2012; Banerjee and Jackson 2017. These results are confirmed in research undertaken elsewhere. Using a sample of more than 30 developing countries, Freund and Pierola (2015) show that, on average, the top five firms account for one third of the value of all exports. These findings imply that attracting a 'superstar' exporter can transform a country's industrial specialisation. Sometimes countries attract such a firm through foreign investment. One often cited example is Intel's investment in Costa Rica in 1997 which gave the country a comparative advantage in semiconductors. Although Intel eventually withdrew (in 2014), by that stage the country had built up an ecosystem of firms around the electronics sector, helping it to sustain the sectoral diversification. As another example, the world's first semi-conductor companies, like Fairchild and Motorola, set up their assembly operations in the mid-1960s in South Korea—now one of the superpowers of the semi-conductor industry but then a poor country in which the assembly of transistor radios, mostly with imported parts, counted among the most advanced industries (Chang 2022, p. 82). In other cases, the investment is indigenous (for example, Ahmet Zorlu and his Vestel Group significantly expanded Türkiye's television exports) (Freund 2016).
9. Bernard et al. 2007.
10. Freund 2016.
11. ITC and UNCTAD 2021.
12. Leke et al. 2018.
13. Shaxson 2019; UNCTAD 2013.
14. Seong et al. 2022, p. 31.
15. This typology of the strategic motivations behind FDI is forever associated with John Dunning (1980), who laid out the main tenets of what he named the 'eclectic paradigm' of FDI. Dunning and Narula (2000) lay out a more nuanced framework which relates to developing countries.
16. Thomsen and Woolcock 1993, Phelps 1997.
17. Blomström and Kokko 1997; Im 2016; Jang 2011, as reported by Echandi et al. 2022.
18. Blomström and Kokko 1997. Blomström and Kokko actually refer to intra-regional FDI inflows, but the argument is equally valid for FDI from outside the region by firms with an existing presence in the markets in question.
19. Anderson et al. 2015. The simulations suggest that Nigeria, Tanzania, Zimbabwe and Morocco would all experience declines in exports in excess of 40%.
20. Mijiyawa 2016.
21. Cuevas et al. 2005; MacDermott 2007.
22. Baltagi et al. 2008.

23. Thangavelu and Narjoko 2014; Li et al. 2016.
24. Kox and Rojas-Romagosa 2020.
25. The literature review in this paragraph is drawn from Echandi et al. 2022.
26. Shingal and Mendez-Parra 2020; Echandi et al. 2022.
27. Inward FDI is expected to increase in their study most in relatively poor countries in Africa, including Somalia (31%), Gabon (30%), Mauritania (28%), Mali (28%) and Burkina Faso (25%). Outward FDI, on the other hand, is predicted to rise most in large regional players, including Nigeria (26%), Morocco (17%), Egypt (15%), and South Africa (14%). Significantly, none of the African countries is found to attract lower levels of FDI.
28. Echandi et al. 2022.
29. According to their analysis, some of Africa's least integrated economies stand to gain the most in relative terms, including Angola, Cameroon, DRC, Republic of Congo, Equatorial Guinea, Gabon and Nigeria. In terms of the value of investment, Angola, Mauritius, Mozambique, Nigeria and South Africa attract the most additional inward investment directed to the continent.
30. FDI flows to Africa did actually reach a record USD 83 billion in 2021, raising the continent's total, but that figure was inflated by a single intrafirm financial transaction (worth USD 42 billion) in South Africa in the second half of 2021 (a share exchange between Naspers and Prosus) (UNCTAD 2022b).
31. We do need to exert quite a lot of care in interpreting these figures, however. FDI stock and flows figures are often highly unreliable, particularly in a developing country setting (although even high-income countries often lack the necessary surveys of the investment undertaken by their firms). According to the UNCTADStat database, for instance, Kenya in 2018 had just USD 84 million of outward FDI stock, yet Kenya's own national source (from the Central Bank of Kenya and KenInvest 2020) has an outward FDI stock of 151.5 billion Kenyan shillings (or approximately USD 1.5 billion) for the same year. Meanwhile, Echandi et al. (2022) cite an FDI outward stock for Kenya in 2017 of USD 2.6 billion. There are clearly some worrying incompatibilities in the statistics like these. The fact that Kenyan firms and banks have quite an active presence in Eastern Africa suggests that the UNCTADStat figure seriously underestimates Kenya's investment abroad.
32. As a prime example of Pan-African operations, Heineken has more than 40 breweries in 16 countries and exports its products to virtually every other. It started brewing locally as early as the 1930s (van Beemen 2019).
33. Echandi et al. 2022.
34. Ownership advantages refer to competitive advantages of the enterprises seeking to engage in FDI (or increase their existing FDI), which are specific to the ownership of the investing enterprises (i.e. their ownership-specific advantages).
35. As calculated from UNCTAD 2022b.
36. IMF (2021b).
37. Gomez-Mera and Varela 2017.
38. Amighini and Sanfilippo 2014.

39. Gomez-Mera and Varela 2017.
40. Blonigen and Piger 2014.
41. Gold et al. 2017.
42. ECA/TMEA 2020.
43. Leke et al. 2018.
44. Iacovone et al. (2014) found that African manufacturing firms, at any age, tend to be about 20–24% smaller than firms in other regions of the world. African firms that start small remain small, rather than converging towards the 'missing middle' (Gelb et al. 2017).
45. Elumelu 2011.
46. Evenett and Fritz 2021.
47. Gonzalez-Garcia and Yang 2020, p. 26.
48. van Beemen 2019, p. xi.
49. According to the UK Office for National Statistics (2022), profitability for UK firms averaged 9.7% and 10.1% for 2020 and 2021 respectively, very similar to the rates we are reporting here for African firms.
50. Cited by Echandi et al. 2022, p. 106.
51. UNCTAD 2021c; Kaplinsky and Morris 2019.
52. Southwood 2022, p. 23. Ultimately, it has been the customers that have benefited the most from this expansion of Pan-African investment in telecommunications. For example, when MTN launched in Uganda, it forced the only other mobile operator, Celtel, to cut its rates from 49–66 US cents a minute to 16–33 US cents a minute. Once the market opened up to two mobile operators, the number of subscribers exploded, from around 30,000 in 1998 to 150,000 by the end of 2000. Competition had lowered prices and driven demand. In Nigeria, the price of mobile phone starter packs fell from 20,000 naira (USD 145) in 2001 to 1 naira (less than one US cent) in 2004 for basic pre-paid minutes.
53. UNCTAD 2017.
54. Kedem 2019.
55. Ibid.
56. Leke et al. 2018.
57. OCP 2022.
58. Abreha et al. 2021, p. 111.
59. Leke et al. 2018, pp. 92–3.
60. For instance, in his classic text *How Europe Underdeveloped Africa*, Walter Rodney talks at length about the Anglo-Dutch firm Unilever 'as a major beneficiary of African exploitation' (1972, p. 198).
61. See for instance Oqubay's (2015) fascinating account of how Ethiopia changed its policy stance from around 2003 and set about attracting greater FDI into selected sectors.
62. Vernon 1998.
63. Narula and Dunning 2010.
64. Asiedu 2004.

65. See the review by Narula and Driffield 2011.
66. See Aitken and Harrison 1999; Blalock and Gertler 2008; Javorcik and Spatareanu 2008.
67. Alfaro et al. 2002; Abreha et al. 2021, p. 74.
68. Agostin and Machado 2007.
69. For a discussion of the related issues, see Dunning and Lundan 2010, p. 471.
70. For instance, using cross-country data, Borensztein et al. (1998) examine data on OECD multinational investments in 69 developing countries, and find that FDI had no discernible effect on per capita income growth below a threshold level of human capital development.
71. For instance, in Taiwan and Korea, managerial and technical assistance from Japanese companies played an important role. For instance, with help from companies such as Kawasaki Shipbuilding Corporation and Nippon Steel from Japan, world-class industries were created within the space of a decade in Korea (Kozul-Wright and Rowthorn 1998, p. 82). Amsden (2001) provides a magistral overview of how different countries solved the problem of technological acquisition without depending on FDI.
72. The AfroChampions Initiative has spearheaded several flagship projects aimed towards proffering Africa's economic integration. These include AfCFTA sensitisation meetings, training, capacity-building and research (AfroChampions 2022).
73. Mold 2003.
74. Vernon 1971, p. 252.
75. Clearly, in the US case, this is linked to the high share of extractive industries in total FDI to the continent.
76. Signé 2020, p. 30.
77. WEF 2021.
78. Pilling 2021. The Moroccan car industry now directly employs some 220,000 people, most of whom work for roughly 250 suppliers.
79. Oqubay 2015, p. 88.
80. Adedeji 1982.
81. Behuria (2019) provides a list of examples of DBGs in East Africa (Kenya, Rwanda and Tanzania). See also Kelsall 2013.
82. Behuria 2019, p. 9.

11. WHAT THE STUDIES SAY ON THE AFCFTA'S IMPACT—AND HOW TO INTERPRET THEM

1. We review some of these in Chapter 10.
2. For a review of a wide selection of those studies, see Mold 2021.
3. Banerjee and Duflo 2019.
4. Rodrik 2017; Banerjee and Duflo 2019.
5. See the discussions on this matter in Banerjee and Duflo 2019; Rodrik 2018.
6. Meade 1955.

7. Panagariya 2000, p. 41.
8. AUC, ECA, AfDB 2017.
9. Laird and Yeats 1986; WITS 2011; WTO 2012.
10. De Maio et al. 1999.
11. Stiglitz and Charlton 2005.
12. See, inter alia, Panagariya and Duttagupta 1999.
13. Panagariya 2000, p. 40.
14. Some modellers try to get around this by introducing tiny non-zero flows to ensure trade can pick up where there was none before.
15. IMF 2019a, p. 57. That said, some GCE models, like GTAP, MIRAGE and Linkage (in their dynamic versions), are getting more sophisticated in their grasp of these elements. See Ianchovichina and Walmsley 2012.
16. Abrego et al. 2019, p. 59.
17. Piermartini and Teh 2005.
18. Among those, we can cite Foroutan and Pritchett 1993; Oyejide et al. 1997; Longo and Sekkat 2004; Kirkpatrick and Watanabe 2005; Geda and Kebret 2007; Kasekende and Ng'eno 1999; Lyakurwa 1998; Robson 1998.
19. The two main econometric concerns raised by Afesorgbor (2016) relate to: (1) the lack of a multilateral resistance term in the regressions, which reflects an economy's position relative to other trading partners beyond the bilateral relations under study, and (2) the treatment of zero trade flows. Intra-African trade data are characterised by a considerable number of zeros, arising either from missing data or the absence of any trade in many product lines (since the average African country trades in only a small number of products), with Longo and Sekkat (2004) putting the percentage of zero flows in African bilateral trade at around 25% and Afesorgbor (2016) claiming that, over longer time periods, the proportion of zero flows can be as high as 55%. None of the earlier methods to deal with these problems led to econometrically consistent and robust findings.
20. In an important methodological contribution to econometrically estimating gravity models, Santos Silva and Tenreyro (2006) proposed the PPML estimator as a better alternative to the techniques used in earlier studies. PPML estimators have been confirmed by other studies as both consistent in the presence of heteroscedasticity and well-behaved when the proportion of zero flows is large (e.g. Head and Mayer 2014; Shepherd 2021).
21. MacPhee and Sattayanuwat 2014.
22. To close observers of the African economy, the poor results for ECCAS are not surprising, as it is a region dominated by oil exporters and countries with little incentive to engage in more intense intra-regional trade. See Byiers et al. 2018.
23. Deme and Ndrianasy 2017.
24. Afesorgbor 2016.
25. IMF 2019a.
26. Gravity models have also been used to assess the level in which countries/RECs are under-trading. For instance, a study by AUC, ECA, AfDB (2010) indicated that

on average East and Southern African countries were found to be trading at about 75% (40%, using the trade-weighted average) of their potential. A similar study undertaken on the EAC for the EAC Secretariat found that intra-regional trading was at only 55% of potential (ECA 2019).

27. It is quite possible with PE models to do the calculations by hand or simply on a spreadsheet, as Milner and Kubota (2005) did.

28. Milner and Kubota 2005; Karingi et al. 2006.

29. Mashura 2020.

30. ECA/TMEA 2020. Data on trade flows and tariffs used in the model were extracted from the COMTRADE and UNCTAD TRAINS database, with the underlying data referring to a 2014 baseline. The elasticities incorporated in the simulation were for import demand, and infinite export supply elasticities were assumed (under the reasonable assumption that the small regional economies are 'price-takers' in the global market). The standard Armington substitution elasticity between products of different countries was also utilised in the model to avoid unrealistically large responses to price changes.

31. WITS is a piece of online software developed by the World Bank, in collaboration with the various other international organisations, including UNCTAD, the International Trade Center, United Nations Statistical Division and the WTO.

32. This may appear to be an extreme simulation—100% liberalisation will not occur under the AfCFTA—but is arguably the best option in the absence of prior knowledge about which products will be excluded under the sensitive item list.

33. Fosu and Mold 2008.

34. FAO 2021, p. 30.

35. Abrego et al. 2019, p. 22.

36. For more on this point, see Jerven 2014.

37. Jensen and Sandrey 2013.

38. Strachan 2012.

39. Fosu and Mold 2007.

40. See, for instance, Abrego et al. 2019, p. 9.

41. ILO 2018.

42. According to the Youth Survey (2022), 28% of young people respond that the leading priority for the continent should be creating new, well-paying jobs. Youth in Kenya (41%) and Mozambique (41%) are most likely to prioritise this goal. In Ethiopia, Gabon and Sudan, youth have a slightly different perspective—Ethiopian youth want the continent to prioritise modernising the education system (22%) and achieving peace and stability (22%); Sudanese youth also want to prioritise modernising the education system (22%); and Gabonese youth think the continent's priority should be granting more personal freedoms to citizens (20%).

43. For example, see World Bank 2020.

44. For example, see World Bank 2022.

45. Cecchini 1988.

46. Gasiorek et al. 1991.

47. Haaland and Norman 1992.

48. Baldwin et al. 1989.
49. Landau 1997.
50. Mayer et al. 2018.
51. Brown 1992.
52. Caliendo and Parro (2014) estimate that tariff reductions under NAFTA increased Mexico's intra-bloc trade by 118%, compared with 41% for the United States and 11% for Canada.
53. Bachrach and Mizrahi 1992. With the benefit of hindsight, Caliendo and Parro (2014) reach similar results of tiny welfare gains under NAFTA. What is equally interesting from their results is that fully half of the miniscule 0.08% gain for the United States is not an efficiency gain but a benefit due to terms-of-trade improvement. In other words, they estimate that the world prices of what the United States imports fell relative to what it exports. These are not efficiency gains but income transfers from other countries (principally from Mexico and Canada). These gains came at the expense of other countries (Rodrik 2018, p. 262).
54. These CGE studies were extensively cited in the early 1990s to support the case for NAFTA, but the results were very wide of the mark in terms of underestimating the rate of export growth between Mexico and the United States (Bergoeing and Kehoe 2003).
55. For an explanation on why the gains were so small, see Krugman and Hanson 1993, Rodrik 2018.
56. Moore et al. 2018; AUDA-NEPAD 2020.
57. Abrego et al. 2019, p. 4. Abrego et al.'s own study put the revenue losses as even smaller. Estimated revenue losses for the continent from the elimination of import tariffs in the baseline model amount to 0.03% of GDP.
58. ECA/TMEA 2020.
59. AUDA-NEPAD 2020.
60. AUC 2022, p. 117.
61. IMF 2019, p. 57.
62. IMF 2019.
63. Leibenstein (1966) introduced the concept of 'x-inefficiencies' to capture the under-utilisation of resources under conditions of imperfect competition.
64. Baldwin et al. 1989. Kassa et al. 2022, p. 249.
65. Jensen and Sandrey 2013.
66. ECA (2023).

12. THE FREE MOVEMENT PROTOCOL: AN ATTAINABLE GOAL?

1. 'Achille Mbembe writes about Xenophobic South Africa', Africa is a Country, 16 April 2015. Available at: https://africasacountry.com/2015/04/achille-mbembe-writes-about-xenophobic-south-africa/. CC BY 4.0.
2. Erisen et al. 2019.
3. OECD 2014.

4. AUC 2013, aspiration no. 2.
5. See Sanny and Patel 2021. On average, two thirds (66%) of respondents say it is currently 'difficult' or 'very difficult' to cross borders to work or trade, while only one in five (21%) describe it as easy.
6. We know that these are the cradlelands because of their 'linguistic proximity', where the word roots survive most extensively in the least modified form.
7. Reader 1998, Chapter 19.
8. Brinley 1973, cited by Schwartz 2018. Argentina alone absorbed 5.4 million immigrants and Canada 4.5 million. Notably, 370,000 went to South Africa (Schwartz 2018, p. 177).
9. Mo Ibrahim Foundation 2022.
10. These figures also need to be put in their proper global context. Despite popular opinions to the contrary, migrants as a share of the global population have increased only marginally over the last three decades: from 2.9% of the global population in 1990 to 3.6% in 2020 (IOM 2022).
11. The major source countries of migration in the whole world are not where most people would think. With 17.9 million international migrants in 2020, India has been a large source of international migrants for more than a century, followed by Mexico and Russia (Hirsch 2021).
12. IOM 2022, p. 25.
13. Kihato 2020.
14. Lücke 2015.
15. IOM 2022.
16. *The Economist* 2021.
17. Shimeles 2018; Brookings Institution 2018. The intra-African migration figures for the continent as a whole are distorted by the strong tendency of North Africans to emigrate towards Europe, with Egypt and Morocco being especially important source countries.
18. IOM 2022.
19. Flahaux and De Haas 2016.
20. Allie et al. 2021.
21. Ichikowitz Family Foundation 2022.
22. Nonetheless, the effects may be more ambiguous than we might at first believe. For instance, a study in Burkina Faso (reported by *The Economist* 2021) found that, because droughts make people poorer, they can actually reduce cross-border migration.
23. Clemens 2020.
24. UNCTADStat 2023.
25. Shimeles 2018.
26. Mo Ibrahim Foundation 2022.
27. As cited in Hirsch 2021.
28. AUC 2018b, articles 1, 6 and 7.
29. AUC 2018b, articles 12–14.

30. AUC 2018b, articles 16–17.
31. AUC 2018b, article 24.
32. OAU 1991, article 6(2)(e)(iii) and article 43(2).
33. OAU 1991, article 6(2)(f)(i).
34. AUC 2013, paragraph 72(l).
35. AUC 2022.
36. AUC 2018b, article 3.
37. AUC 2022.
38. Ibid.
39. AUC 2018b, article 5.
40. AUC 2018b, article 25.
41. Amadi and Lenaghan 2020.
42. Kenya Vision 2030, 2018.
43. Kamer 2022.
44. KNBS 2021. Even if the underemployed are added to the figures, that figure rises to just 2.5 million, or 12.3% of the population.
45. This Swahili expression translates to 'hot sun' in English, described thus because the workers toil under the 'hot sun' (Ramadhan and Otieno 2020).
46. Paice 2021, pp. 360–2.
47. This should be distinguished from the 'active workforce'. For multiple reasons, people may decide not to join the workforce at all, and either voluntarily or involuntarily withdraw (e.g. because of taking up higher education, physical incapacity, looking after a child, or because of a decision to stay at home and look after an elderly family member). As noted by Fox (2021), the labour force participation rate on the continent is low and declining, standing at around 45%.
48. AfDB 2016.
49. PWC 2019. Almost one third of businesses (30%) expressed their feeling that the losses were large. An urgent need for skilled personnel was also reflected in the demand for different types of employees. Sales experts (46%) are most in demand across Africa, with engineers and technicians among those also in demand. Digital experts were more in demand (27%) than upper management.
50. McKinsey 2020.
51. World Bank figures, cited by Komminoth 2023.
52. World Bank 2018.
53. Cited by Robertson 2022.
54. Newman et al. 2016, p. 163.
55. Ramadhan and Otieno 2020.
56. Morsy and Mukasa 2019.
57. Hane-Weijman 2021.
58. Cottier and Anirudh 2019.
59. Genc et al. 2012.
60. Ottaviano et al. 2018.
61. Clemens 2011.

62. Kennan 2012.
63. *The Economist* 2021; Flahaux and De Haas 2016.
64. This must be set against a continental total of USD 96 billion of remittances in the same year (Ford 2023).
65. *The Economist* 2021.
66. Beine et al. 2008; Docquier et al. 2015.
67. Gnimassoun 2019.
68. The authors are grateful to Raphie Kaplinsky for highlighting this parallel.
69. Sun 2013.
70. Schiff (2005) suggests that positive impacts of skilled emigration are greatly exaggerated. In particular, the author shows that both the size of the human capital gain, as well as the impact on the return to education, are smaller than those implied by the brain-gain literature. See also Gonzalez-Garcia et al. 2016.
71. AfDB 2022a.
72. Shimeles 2018.
73. Gonzalez-Garcia et al. 2016; Barajas et al. 2009.
74. Cha'ngom 2020.
75. Gonzalez-Garcia et al. 2016.
76. Ighobor 2016.
77. LSE 2016.
78. Mangeni and Juma 2018.
79. LSE 2016.
80. Reported by Kweitsu 2018.
81. Research by Catia Batista, Nova School of Business and Economics, Lisbon, cited by *The Economist* 2021.
82. AUC 2022.
83. *The Economist* 2021.
84. Abbassi 2023.
85. Oduntan 2015.
86. AFP 2019.
87. Hirsch 2021.
88. AU 2015.
89. Mangeni 2022.
90. World Bank 2018.
91. *The Economist* 2021.
92. Buningwire 2022.
93. Ibid.
94. Flahaux and De Haas 2016.
95. Signé 2017.
96. AfDB 2022b; Madden 2020. These more liberal visa policies have entailed shouldering a fiscal cost. In 2022, South Sudan, for instance, aligned itself with EAC rules by removing visa requirements for all EAC nationals travelling to the country. Because of the quite large numbers of Kenyans and Ugandans travelling to South Sudan daily

(usually on business-related trips), it was estimated that this would cost the treasury upwards of USD 300,000 a day—a significant amount for a small and very poor East African country. So it is commendable that such actions are being taken (personal communication from Ministry of East African Affairs, Juba).

97. AfDB 2021.
98. AfDB 2013; Signé 2020; AUC 2022.
99. AfDB 2021.
100. Ibid.
101. *The Economist* 2021.
102. AUC 2022.
103. Mo Ibrahim Foundation 2022.

13. HELP NOT HINDER: THE ROLE OF EXTERNAL PARTNERS IN THE CONSTRUCTION OF A CONTINENTAL MARKET

1. Frankema and van Waijenburg 2018, p. 548.
2. Yang and Gupta 2005, p. 4.
3. Noman et al. 2012.
4. Cramer et al. 2020.
5. Foroutan 1992.
6. Weeks 1996, p. 100.
7. Reported by Luke and MacLeod 2023, p. 13.
8. World Bank 2020.
9. Brenton and Hoffman 2016, p. 9.
10. World Bank 2020. See Chapter 11 for a discussion of this report, and some of its shortcomings.
11. The encouragement of greater FDI by external partners is also of course part of the core objectives, and by giving access to the continental market, the incentives to such FDI is greatly increased. Designated in the literature 'tariff-jumping FDI' because it reflects attempts by investors to avoid tariffs by investing directly in the target market, research suggests it was a common motivation of Japanese and American investors into the European Common Market. See Chapter 10.
12. Mkandawire 2014, p. 18.
13. Odijie 2018, p. 185.
14. We develop these points further in Chapter 14.
15. Young 2020, p. 37. Although this sounds a lot, it should not be forgotten that developed countries spend twice as much annually on subsidising domestic agriculture as they do on foreign aid. The OECD estimates that poor countries lose three times as much to tax evasion as they receive in foreign aid (Rutger 2017, p. 203).
16. Mold 2009; Easterly 2014; Dreher, Sturm and Vreeland 2015.
17. Whitfield and Fraser 2010, p. 13.
18. Mkandawire 2012, p. 94.
19. Landau, cited by *The Economist* 2021.

20. Rodrik 2011, p. 200; Frankema and van Waijenburg 2018, p. 548.
21. For instance, despite the unease among parts of the donor community, Rwanda has managed to maintain its economic support to its fledgling national airline, RwandAir. The financial record of regional airlines is not good—Kenya Airways, for instance, regularly loses hundreds of millions of US dollars a year (with only Ethiopian Airlines bucking that negative trend). However, Rwanda sees its national airline as an intrinsic part of its economic strategy and will not willingly reduce its support to the airline until it is economically viable in its own right. Ethiopia is another country that has managed to impose its will in terms of the development of its system of industrial parks (Oqubay 2015). The breakdown of relations with the donor community over the conflict in Tigray which broke out in 2021 is ironically likely to increase autonomous policy-making. For a review of the issues, see Whitfield 2009; Whitfield et al. 2015.
22. Mold 2009.
23. Herreros 2019.
24. Rodrik 2011, p. 200.
25. Bhagwati 1992, p. 553.
26. Yang and Gupta 2005, p. 5.
27. Teteryatnikova 2008.
28. Herreros 2019.
29. DeRosa and Gilbert 2003; Varas 2017.
30. Congress 2023.
31. Oyejide 2000.
32. Stender et al. 2021; Langan and Price 2021; Luke and Suominen 2019.
33. Stender et al. 2021.
34. Cilliers 2020, pp. 198–9.
35. According to Brenton and Hoffman (2016), this leads to a number of negative consequences. Firstly, because the agreement lowered South Africa's common external tariff, other members of SACU had concerns that they would lose revenue from imports under the revenue-sharing agreement. Secondly, the South Africa-EU FTA contributed to the fragmentation of other SADC members into three different blocs to negotiate EPAs with the EU. Finally, because the various trade agreements among SADC member states with the EU are different from each other, they substantially complicate the development of a SADC customs union.
36. Jawara and Kwa 2004, p. xxii. See also Narlikar 2004.
37. Brautigam 2009; Farooki and Kaplinsky 2013. Notably, the panorama has changed somewhat in recent years, with a slowdown in economic growth in China accompanied by a relative decline in the growth of its demand for mineral imports.
38. See the discussion on this in Alden 2007; Brautigam 2009.
39. Benabdallah et al. 2016; Dorrie 2015.
40. There is nothing particularly surprising in this latter finding. We have noted in Chapter 11 the high share of Western investments in the mining sector.
41. Utesch-Xiong and Kambhampati 2021.

42. Oya (2006, p. 26) is explicit about the benefits of Chinese aid compared with OECD aid, and argues that there are four potential advantages: 1) the aid is more targeted to important infrastructure projects with long maturity and long-term potential (no hurry for disbursements); 2) it is less bureaucratic and with lower transaction costs; 3) it is more efficient, with lower costs and faster input; and 4) it allows more policy space (lower conditionality) and increases the bargaining power of African countries vis-à-vis other donors.

43. Mold 2009.

44. For example, Djibouti, Kenya and Zambia.

45. Mkandawire 2019, p. 528.

46. Although not directly comparable, it is worth remembering that only 17% of US firms' sales in Africa are directed towards the continental market. See Figure 10.6.

47. Leke et al. 2018, p. 53.

48. Yuan Sun (2017, p. 10) notes that Chinese firms are often accused of not employing enough African staff. Studies do not tend to support this narrative. A meta-analysis of previous studies revealed no sample in which the proportion of local workers dips below 78%, and in some companies with thousands of employees, the figure exceeds 99%. A large-scale Chinese-language survey in Kenya found that 90% of the employees in Chinese manufacturing and construction companies were local hires and, moreover, that as Chinese enterprises operated in Kenya over time, their percentage of local hires increased (Yuan Sun 2017, p. 5).

49. *African Business* 2019.

50. Mkandawire 1999.

51. Amsden 2001; Chang 2007; Freund 2016. Fukuyama (1995) noted how General Park in South Korea was 'obsessed' with the development of DMGs—large corporations capable of competing with the Japanese *keiretsu*.

52. An example being the World Bank's *Doing Business Index*, which was abandoned in 2020 in the face of criticisms about its objectivity and transparency.

53. Behuria 2019, p. 9.

54. Rodrik 2018, p. 229.

55. Abreha et al. 2021, p. 44.

56. McMillan and Headey 2014; Newman et al. 2016.

57. Pages-Serra 2010, p. 213, cited by Altenburg and Lütkenhorst 2015, p. 19.

58. Banerjee and Duflo 2011, p. 228.

59. Hirsch 2021, p. 7.

60. Clist and Restelli 2020, p. 1281.

61. Research has consistently found that aid inflows correlate positively with emigration from Africa, inferring that the more aid countries receive, the more migration there is (Mugh 2011; Clist and Restelli 2020). The reasons are related to the fact that there is no linear relationship between the level of development and migration: higher levels of development may in fact facilitate outward migration, as the act of migration is far from costless, and the poorest of the poor simply do not migrate.

62. To pile irony on irony, free movement within the European Union did not lead to

massively larger numbers of people migrating between member states. In 1973, there were 3.9 million EU workers living in other EU member states. By the year 2000, that number had declined to 2.9 million. As noted by Molle (2017, p. 109), the figures seem to suggest that migration diminishes as free trade grows.

63. See Dercon 2022.
64. Allard et al. 2016.
65. AUDA-NEPAD 2020. Lisinge and van Dijk 2021, p. 3.
66. Coulibaly and Fontagné 2006.
67. Chuku, Simpasa and Ekpo (2022) used panel data analysis to show that the infrastructure sector with the strongest multiplier effect on economic activity is the information and communication technology sector, followed by the transport sector, the electricity sector and the water sector.

14. CONCLUSIONS: TOWARDS A UNIVERSAL AFRICA

1. Woolfrey et al. 2021, pp. 76–84.
2. Biteye and Songwe 2019.
3. Rodrik 2017, p. 79.
4. PAFTRAC 2022, p. 1.
5. Mo Ibrahim 2023.
6. Brenton and Hoffman 2016, p. 5.
7. Olson 1971.
8. Brenton and Hoffman 2016.
9. Cited by Kampfner 2020, p. 175.
10. Alden and Soko 2005; Krapohl, Meissner and Muntschick 2013.
11. Abreha et al. 2021, p. 11.
12. Kaplinsky and Morris 2019, p. 10.
13. For instance, MTN already allows seamless mobile money payments across several countries in Africa.
14. By contrast, there is no EU/SADC free trade area since the EU refused to grant South Africa the same types of preferential market access as it has to low-income economies in the region (Brenton and Hoffman 2016, p. 5).
15. Alden and Soko 2005.
16. In this context, it is useful to recall that SADC grew out of an older regional integration effort, the Southern African Development Coordination Conference (SADCC), whose main purpose was to reduce Southern Africa's economic ties to South Africa (Brenton and Hoffman 2016, p. 5).
17. Brenton and Hoffman 2016. As noted in Chapter 12, xenophobia has also become a concern in South Africa, particularly towards migrant groups from Zimbabwe and other neighbouring countries.
18. E.g. Oppong-Amoako 2018.
19. They have not yet come to fruition due, in part, to shortages within South Africa and challenges with the development of the Inga Dam in the DRC. See Brenton and Hoffman 2016.

20. Brenton and Hoffman 2016, p. 5. Those projects have become derailed by growing controversy around Eskom. See Bowman 2020.
21. Allard et al. 2016, p. 37; AUC 2022, p. 118.
22. Brenton and Hoffman 2016, p. 7. To incentivise economic and trading ties, former President Uhuru also gifted land to both Uganda and Rwanda to set up dry ports in Naivasha. See IGIHE 2022.
23. UNECA 2020.
24. The issue of Western Sahara colours a lot of Moroccan decisions with regards to foreign policy on the continent, and it clearly wishes to influence other African countries to support it in its claims to ownership of Western Sahara. For a discussion on this, see Abderrahim and Aggad 2018; Khan and Saleh 2021.
25. There is an in-depth and compelling discussion on contemporary internal politics of Nigeria towards the AfCFTA contained in Byiers and Woolfrey (2022).
26. Adedeji and Colley Senghor 1989, p. 138.
27. Omoshoro-Jones and Bonga-Bonga 2021.
28. Figures from IMF DOTS 2023.
29. Macleod, Luke and Guepie 2023.
30. Cannard 2019.
31. E.g. Oqubay 2015; UNECA 2015; Lopes 2018.
32. Chu, Brower and Williams 2023.
33. See Fleming et al. 2023.
34. Cimoli, Dosi and Stiglitz 2009, p. 34.
35. Odijie 2019, p. 19.
36. Odijie 2019; Abreha et al. 2021, p. 16. For instance, see the EAC Industrialisation Policy (2012–2032).
37. Based on further analysis of trade patterns, supply, demand, market access and sustainable development indicators, the diagnostic eventually settled on four pilot strategic sectors: cars, pharmaceuticals, cotton clothing and baby food.
38. AAAM & AfCFTA 2021.
39. Leke, Chironga and Desvaux 2018, p. 54.
40. Pilling 2020.
41. Prunier and Ficquet 2015.
42. Paice 2021, p. 356.
43. Oqubay 2015. Arkebe Oqubay was the architect and key implementer of the industrial park strategy, embodying the ambition and drive to attract FDI. He pulled off a deal with clothing giant PVH for the Hawassa Industrial Park, and many others.
44. Adedeji 1980; italics added.
45. Roberts et al. (2023) point out that the cement industry has been characterised around the world by cartels which have divided markets and fixed prices. For instance, cement cartels have been uncovered across Europe, including Germany, Norway, Austria and Poland, with markups in the German cartel ranging from 20.7–26.5%.
46. Baumol (1982) first introduced the idea that the competitiveness of a sector does

not depend exclusively on the number of firms present, but rather how strong the possibilities are that new entrants can enter into the market. The theoretical perspective has a particular relevance to regulation in sectors like telecommunications, which have elements of natural monopolies.

47. Ojakol 2021, p. 5.
48. Ibid., p. 2.
49. Cherif et al. 2020, p. 21.
50. SADC 2023.
51. COMESA 2023.
52. Mold 2022.
53. TLDR News EU 2023.
54. O'Carroll 2022.
55. *The Economist* (2023), citing a study by John Springford of the Centre for European Reform.
56. Portes 2021.
57. Alim 2023.
58. Fanta 2020.
59. Mold 2022.
60. *Financial Times* 2021.
61. Ruzuhuzwa 2012.
62. ECB 2009.
63. Mold 2021.
64. See, for instance, the collected essays contained in the book by Dudley Seers (1979).
65. Krugman and Venables 1990.
66. See, for instance, Mayer et al. 2018.
67. Bhagwati 1992, p. 145.
68. Cowles 2012, p. 114.
69. See, inter alia, Masiyiwa, cited by Reporter 2018; Dangote, cited by Onwuamaeze 2021.
70. Vanguard 2020.
71. Mkandawire 2014, p. 14.
72. Harris 1998.
73. See Bulmer-Thomas 2003; Hirschman 1958.
74. Allard et al. 2016, p. 40.
75. Carlota Perez (2002) defines technological revolution as a powerful and highly visible cluster of new and dynamic technologies, products and industries capable of bringing about an upheaval in the whole fabric of the economy and propelling a long-term upsurge of development.
76. Kaplinsky 2021; Naudé 2019.
77. Naudé 2019, p. 6; Abreha et al. 2021, p. 33.
78. Kaplinsky 2021.
79. See, inter alia, Nayyar and Vargas Da Cruz 2018.
80. Paice 2021; Robertson 2022.

81. This transformation was a crucial element in the historic long-term development processes of all industrialised economies, including Britain and Japan, and especially in the case of China. See Qingqing et al. 2011; Huang 2008.

82. Frankema and van Waijenburg 2018, p. 565.

83. Khanna 2016.

84. United Nations University—Institute for Natural Resources in Africa 2019, cited by Luke 2023, p. 4.

85. An interesting but somewhat neglected report was produced in 2017 on this topic by the World Bank/China Development Bank. Chapter 5 focuses on the opportunities for technological leapfrogging in the energy sector.

86. World Bank 2022.

87. Bengoa et al. 2021.

88. BBC News Africa 2019.

89. Mattli 1999; Mold 2021. For instance, the European Free Trade Area—established in 1960 as an alternative to the emerging European Economic Community—is broadly considered as a poorly designed and unsuccessful attempt at integration. Latin America too has had its share of failed RECs, such as LAFTA and the CACM. ASEAN languished for many years, suffered poor leadership and interest in integration, and traded little among member states before developing into a more cohesive organisation (Brenton and Hoffman 2016).

90. AUC 2022, p. 31.

91. Wandera 2023.

92. Dessalegn 2023.

93. SADC 2023.

94. EACJ 2023.

96. EACJ 2014; EACJ 2017.

97. Tayo 2023.

98. Luke and MacLeod 2023.

99. Odijie 2019, p. 192; Coulibaly, Kassa and Zeufack 2022, p. 24.

99. In addition to outright bans, a number of products face tariffs at or 'exceeding the ECOWAS maximum of 35 percent' (Afreximbank 2020, pp. 30–1).

100. AUDA-NEPAD 2020, p. 19.

101. Abreha et al. 2021, p. 156.

102. For a collection of insightful essays on the challenges of Africa's transport infrastructure, see Lamarque and Nugent 2022; Lisinge and van Dijk 2021.

103. These arguments carry over to migratory policy and the FMP too (Chapter 12). Upper middle-income countries on the continent are clearly more reluctant to liberalise. Perhaps paradoxically, the countries which are more inclined to liberalise their immigration systems tend to be the poorer African countries. Yet larger countries, in particular, can influence regional outcomes towards free movement of labour, even though some smaller countries (e.g. Rwanda and Benin) could be pacesetters in the right environment (Hirsch 2021, p. 14).

104. See Tayo 2023.

105. Adedeji and Senghor 1989, p. 348. However, Adedeji was also clear that in the long run the factors propelling the continent towards greater integration would prevail:

    > In view of the pull and push factors that are ever present in the African situation, such diversion is not likely to last long. The push factors are mainly the increasingly hostile external environment. The pull factors are the growing aspirations of the youth and other groups in African countries.

106. The AfroChampions Initiative, for instance, calls for governments to '[e]ncourage the private sector to take advantage of AfCFTA to make investments in the following "core business opportunity areas" that create jobs and wealth and raise living standards of Africans: Feeding the People, Clothing the people, Housing the People, Moving the People & Goods, Value-Addition, Tourism & Creative Industries, Digital Economy, Skills & Healthcare and Financial services' (AfroChampions 2019).
107. Behuria 2019.
108. Mkandawire and Soludo 1998.
109. Mkandawire 2019, p. 13.
110. Remarks of Michael Kottoh, Head of Strategy and Research AfroChampions, at the webinar 'Implementing the AfCFTA: The Need for Deepening Private Sector Engagement and Commitment', 2021, cited by Echandi, Maliszewska and Steenbergen 2022.
111. Woolfrey, Apiko and Pharatlhatlhe 2019.
112. Remarks of H. E. Mr Alan Kyerematen, Minister of Trade and Industry of Ghana at the webinar 'Implementing the AfCFTA: The Need for Deepening Private Sector Engagement and Commitment' (AfDB 2021).
113. Woolfrey and Byiers 2019.
114. Karuhanga 2023.
115. Sanny and Patel 2021, p. 4.
116. See the World Bank Development Report (2020, Chapter 9), which explains the increasing hostility to open trade regimes.
117. A useful guide to how to mobilise for change is provided by Green for Growth Fund (ECDPM 2016).
118. Ichikowitz Family Foundation 2022.
119. PAFTRAC 2022.
120. Mangeni and Atta-Mensah 2022, pp. 1–10.
121. AUDA-NEPAD 2020, p. 14.
122. Maathai 2009, p. 106.
123. Gumede 2019.
124. Cited by Leshoele 2020, p. 2.
125. Mangeni and Juma 2018.
126. In the dying days of the Soviet Union, Mikhail Gorbachev embraced the idea of *glasnost* preceding *perestroika*. He felt that without political reform, there could be

no reform of the economy. Nolan (1990) contrasts this attitude with that of the Chinese leadership under Den Xiao Ping, where there was economic reform without any political reform at all, and ends concluding that the Chinese position was right. The subsequent economic performance of the two countries would clearly support Nolan's position.

127. E.g. Parker 2022; Nwuke 2022.

REFERENCES

AAAM & AfCFTA (2021), *The African Association of Automotive Manufacturers and the African Continental Free Trade Area: An AAAM Position Paper on Rules of Origin in the Auto Sector Within the AfCFTA.*

Abbassi, N. (2023), 'Tunisia: President's offensive statements targeted black migrants—with widespread fallout', *The Conversation*, 16 March. Available at: https://theconversation.com/tunisia-presidents-offensive-statements-targeted-black-migrants-with-widespread-fallout-201593

Abderrahim, T. and Aggad, F. (2018), 'Starting afresh: The Maghreb's relations with sub-Saharan Africa', *ECDPM*, 30 April. Available at: https://ecdpm.org/work/starting-afresh-the-maghrebs-relations-with-sub-saharan-africa

Abrego, L. et al. (2019), 'The African Continental Free Trade Agreement: Welfare Gains Estimates from a General Equilibrium Model', International Monetary Fund Working Paper No. 2019/124. Available at: https://EconPapers.repec.org/RePEc:imf:imfwpa:2019/124.

Abreha, K. et al. (2020), 'Africa in Manufacturing Global Value Chains: Cross-Country Patterns in the Dynamics of Linkages', Policy Research Paper No. 8. Available at: https://doi.org/10.1596/1813-9450-9439

Abreha, K.G. et al. (2021), 'Industrialization in Sub-Saharan Africa: Seizing Opportunities in Global Value Chains', Africa Development Forum. Available at: https://doi.org/10.1596/978-1-4648-1673-4

ACET (2014), 'African Transformation Report 2014', African Center for Economic Transformation. Available at: https://acetforafrica.org/publication_type/african-transformation-report-2014/

Acevedo, A., Mold, A. and Perez Caldentey, E. (2009), 'The Analysis of "Leading Sectors": A Long Term View of 18 Latin American Economies', University Library of Munich, Germany. Available at: https://EconPapers.repec.org/RePEc:pra:mprapa:15017

Adebajo, A. (2014), 'Two Prophets of Regional Integration: Prebisch and Adedeji', in

REFERENCES

B. Currie-Alder et al. (eds), *International Development: Ideas, Experience, and Prospects*, Oxford: Oxford University Press, pp. 323–38.

———— (2021), *The Pan-African Pantheon: Prophets, Poets, and Philosophers*, Manchester: Manchester University Press.

Adedeji, A. (1970), 'Prospects of Regional Economic Co-operation in West Africa', *Journal of Modern African Studies*, 8(2), pp. 213–31.

———— (1980), 'Africa in a Divided and Inequitable World Economy: The Permanent Underdog?' Lecture delivered in Commemoration of the 10th Anniversary Celebration of the International Development Research Centre of Canada, Ottawa, 3 December. Available at: https://api.pageplace.de/preview/DT0400.978113 5181024_A23800165/preview-9781135181024_A23800165.pdf

———— (1982), 'Africa in the World Economy', *Socialist People's Libyan Arab Jamahiriya*, Tripoli, April.

———— (1990), *African Alternative Framework to Structural Adjustment Programmes for Socio-economic Recovery and Transformation (AAF-SAP)*, Addis Ababa: United Nations Economic Commission for Africa. Available at: https://hdl.handle.net/10855/5670

———— (1993), *Africa within the World: Beyond Dispossession and Dependence*, London: Zed Books in association with African Centre for Development and Strategic Studies.

———— (2004), 'The ECA: Forging a Future for Africa', in Y. Berthelot (ed.), *Unity and Diversity in Development Ideas—Perspectives from the UN Regional Commissions*, Bloomington and Indianapolis: Indiana University Press.

Adedeji, A. and Colley Senghor, J. (1989), 'Towards an African Monetary Fund', in *Towards a Dynamic African Economy, Selected Speeches and Lectures 1975–1986*, Abingdon: Routledge.

AfDB (2013), 'Visa restrictions and economic consequences in Africa', African Development Bank Group, 10 June. Available at: https://blogs.afdb.org/fr/afdb-championing-inclusive-growth-across-africa/post/visa-restrictions-and-economic-consequences-in-africa-11987

———— (2016), 'Jobs for Youth in Africa: Catalyzing Youth Opportunity across Africa', March. Available at: https://www.afdb.org/fileadmin/uploads/afdb/Images/high_5s/Job_youth_Africa_Job_youth_Africa.pdf

———— (2019), 'African Economic Outlook', Abidjan: African Development Bank. Available at: https://www.afdb.org/en/news-keywords/african-economic-outlook-2019

———— (2021a), *Africa Visa Openness Report 2021*. Available at: https://www.visaopen-ness.org/fileadmin/uploads/afdb/Documents/VOI%E2%80%93 2021_fin_R20_14dec21_01.pdf

———— (2021b), 'Implementing the AfCFTA: The Need for Deepening Private Sector Engagement and Commitment', Joint webinar on the implementation of the AfCFTA within the WTO Aid-for-Trade Stocktaking Event 2021, March. Available at: https://www.afdb.org/en/news-and-events/events/implementing-afcfta-need-deepening-private-sector-engagement-and-commitment-42144

REFERENCES

———— (2022a), 'Diaspora's remittances, investment and expertise vital for Africa's future growth, say participants at African Development Bank Forum', African Development Bank Group, 2 December. Available at: https://www.afdb.org/en/news-and-events/press-releases/diasporas-remittances-investment-and-expertise-vital-africas-future-growth-say-participants-african-development-bank-forum-57024

———— (2022b), *Africa Visa Openness Report 2022*. Available at: https://www.afdb.org/en/documents/africa-visa-openness-report-2022

Afesorgbor, S. K. (2016), 'Revisiting the Effect of Regional Integration on African Trade: Evidence from Meta-analysis and Gravity Model', *Journal of International Trade & Economic Development*, 26(2), pp. 133–53.

AFP (2019), 'Feud between Rwanda, Uganda strongmen takes toll', *The Guardian* [Nigeria], 15 May. Available at: https://guardian.ng/news/world/feud-between-rwanda-uganda-strongmen-takes-toll/

Afreximbank (2020), *African Trade Report 2020*. Available at: https://www.afreximbank.com/reports/african-trade-report-2020/

Africa Renewal (2022), 'Horn of Africa: Extreme drought deepens hunger in a region facing conflict', 20 November. Available at: https://www.un.org/africarenewal/magazine/november-2022/horn-africa-extreme-drought-deepens-hunger-region-facing-conflict

African Business (2019), 'En Marche: Why French companies are exploring East Africa', 7 January. Available at: https://african.business/2019/01/trade-investment/en-marche-why-french-companies-are-exploring-east-africa/

———— (2023), 'Africa's Top 250 Companies', Special Report, May, pp. 38–54.

African Union Commission (AUC) (2012), *Synthesis Paper on Boosting Intra-African Trade and Fast Tracking the Continental Free Trade Area*, Addis Ababa: AUC.

Afrika, J. G. and Ajumbo, G. (2012), 'Informal Cross-Border Trade in Africa: Implications and Policy Recommendations', *Africa Economic Brief*, 3, pp. 1–15.

AfroChampions (2019), *The Trillion Dollar Investment Framework for Africa: In Support of AfCFTA Implementation*. Available at: https://www.afrochampions.org/assets/doc/Contenus%20Trillion%20Dollar%20Framework/THETRI~1.PDF

———— (2022), *AfroChampions*. Available at: https://www.afrochampions.org/drivingafricafoward.php

Aga, G., Francis, D. C. and Meza, J. R. (2015), 'SMEs, Age, and Jobs: A Review of the Literature, Metrics, and Evidence', World Bank Policy Research Working Paper. Available at: https://doi.org/10.1596/1813–9450–7493

Agarwal, P. et al. (2022), 'The African Continental Free Trade Area and the Automotive Value Chain', Overseas Development Institute Briefing Report.

Agostin, M. and Machado, R. (2007), 'Openness and the International Allocation of Foreign Direct Investment', *Journal of Development Studies*, 43, pp. 1234–47.

AGRA (2020), *Annual Report 2020: Nurturing Change Across African Agriculture*. Available at: https://agra.org/annual-report-2020/

Aitken, B. J. and Harrison, A. E. (1999), 'Do Domestic Firms Benefit from Direct Foreign Investment? Evidence from Venezuela', *American Economic Review*, 89(3), pp. 605–18.

REFERENCES

Akinkugbe, O. D. (2021), 'A Critical Appraisal of the African Continental Free Trade Area Agreement', in K. Kugler and F. Sucker (eds), *International Economic Law from a (South) African Perspective*, Cape Town: Juta, pp. 283–306.

Akyeampong, E. (2017), *History of African Trade*, Cairo: African Export-Import Bank. Available at: https://elibrary.acbfpact.org/acbf/collect/acbf/index/assoc/HASH0100/039e055d/606b9c4a/9550.dir/History-of-African-Trade.pdf

Alden, C. (2007), *China in Africa*, London: Zed Books.

Alden, C. and Soko, M. (2005), 'South Africa's Economic Relations with Africa: Hegemony and Its Discontents', *Journal of Modern African Studies*, 43(3), pp. 367–92.

Alesina, A., Matuszeski, J. and Easterly, W. (2011), 'Artificial States', *Journal of the European Economic Association*, 9(2), pp. 246–77.

Alfaro, L. et al. (2002), 'FDI and Economic Growth: The Role of Local Financial Markets', *Journal of International Economics*, 64(1), pp. 89–112.

Alim, A. N. (2023), 'UK government threatened with legal action over Australia trade deal', *Financial Times*, 31 March. Available at: https://www.ft.com/content/b3d55007-f5fe-4095-99f3-686376be7e42

Allard, C. et al. (2016), 'Trade Integration and Global Value Chains in Sub-Saharan Africa', International Monetary Fund Department Paper 2016:004. Available at: https://doi.org/10.5089/9781498349901.087

Allie, F. et al. (2021), 'Using IOM Flow Monitoring Data to Describe Migration in West and Central Africa', Immigration Policy Report, September. Available at: https://immigrationlab.org/content/uploads/2021/09/IPL-Report_African-Migration.pdf

Alonso, J. A. and Garcimartín, C. (1998), 'A New Approach to Balance-of-Payments Constraint: Some Empirical Evidence', *Journal of Post Keynesian Economics*, 21(2), pp. 259–82.

Altenburg, T. and Lütkenhorst, W. (2015), *Industrial Policy in Developing Countries: Failing Markets, Weak States*, Cheltenham: Edward Elgar Publishing.

Amadi, V. T. and Lenaghan, P. (2020), 'Advancing Regional Integration through the Free Movement of Persons in the Southern African Development Community (SADC)', *Spec Juris*, 34(1). Available at: http://www.saflii.org/za/journals/SPECJU/2020/5.pdf

Amighini, A. and Sanfilippo, M. (2014), 'Impact of South–South FDI and Trade on the Export Upgrading of African Economies', *World Development*, 64(C), pp. 1–17.

Amoako, K. Y. (2020), *Know the Beginning Well: An Inside Journey Through Five Decades of African Development*, Trenton, NJ: Africa World Press.

Amsden, A. (2000), 'Industrialization under New WTO Law', paper prepared for the High-level Round Table on Trade and Development: Directions for the Twenty-first Century, Bangkok, Thailand, 12 February.

———— (2001), *The Rise of 'The Rest': Challenges to the West from Late-Industrializing Economies*, New York: Oxford University Press.

———— (2007), *Escape from Empire—The Developing World's Journey Through Heaven and Hell*, Cambridge, MA: MIT Press.

REFERENCES

Amurgo-Pacheco, A. and Pierola, M. D. (2008), 'Patterns of Export Diversification in Developing Countries: Intensive and Extensive Margins', Policy Research Working Papers [Preprint]. Available at: https://doi.org/10.1596/1813–9450–4473

Anderson, J. E., Larch, M. and Yotov, Y. V. (2015), 'Growth and Trade with Frictions: A Structural Estimation Framework', National Bureau of Economic Research Working Paper 21377. Available at: https://www.nber.org/papers/w21377

Andreoni, M., Mondliwa, P. and Robert, S. (2021), *Structural Transformation in South Africa*, Oxford: Oxford University Press.

Anta Diop, C. (1987), *Black Africa—The Economic and Cultural Basis for a Federated State*, Chicago, IL: Lawrence Hill Books.

Anyanzwa, J. (2019), 'Disputes push countries into bilateral deals to ensure seamless flow of trade', *The East African*, 29 December. Available at: https://www.theeast-african.co.ke/tea/business/disputes-push-countries-into-bilateral-deals-to-ensure-seamless-flow-of-trade-1433784

Asante, S. K. B. (1991), *African Development: Adebayo Adedeji's Alternative Strategies*, Lochcarron: Hans Zell Publishing.

Asiedu, E. (2004), 'Policy Reform and Foreign Direct Investment in Africa: Absolute Progress but Relative Decline', *Development Policy Review*, 22(1), pp. 41–48.

AU (2015), *African Union Mechanism for Police Cooperation (AFRIPOL)*, Addis Ababa: African Union. Available at: https://afripol.africa-union.org/

———— (2019), *Draft Decisions, Declarations, Resolution and Motion*, Addis Ababa: African Union. Available at: https://informante.web.na/wp-content/uploads/2019/02/Assembly-AU-Draft-Dec-1-34-XXXII-_E.pdf

———— (2022), *Sustainable Financing*, Addis Ababa: African Union. Available at: https://au.int/en/aureforms/financing

AUC (2013), *Agenda 2063*, AUC Archives, Addis Ababa: African Union. Available at: https://au.int/en/agenda2063

———— (2018), *Protocol to the Treaty Establishing the African Economic Community Relating to Free Movement of Persons, Right of Residence and Right of Establishment*, AUC Archives, Addis Ababa: African Union. Available at: https://au.int/en/treaties/protocol-treaty-establishing-african-economic-community-relating-free-movement-persons

———— (2022), *African Integration Report, 2021—Putting Free Movement of Persons at the Centre of Continental Integration*, Addis Ababa: African Union. Available at: https://au.int/en/newsevents/20220314/2021-african-integration-report-put-ting-free-movement-persons-centre-continental

AUC, ECA, AfDB (2010), *Assessing Regional Integration in Africa IV*, Addis Ababa: Economic Commission for Africa. Available at: https://archive.uneca.org/sites/default/files/PublicationFiles/aria4full.pdf

———— (2012), *Assessing Regional Integration in Africa V: Towards an African Continental Free Trade Area*, Addis Ababa: Economic Commission for Africa. Available at: https://archive.uneca.org/sites/default/files/PublicationFiles/aria5_print_uneca_fin_20_july_1.pdf

REFERENCES

———— (2019), *Assessing Regional Integration in Africa ARIA IX: Next Steps for the African Continental Free Trade Area*, Addis Ababa: Economic Commission for Africa. Available at: https://repository.uneca.org/bitstream/handle/10855/42218/b11963189. pdf?sequence=1&isAllowed=y

AUDA-NEPAD (2020), 'Conditions for Success in the Implementation of the African Continental Free Trade Agreement', Denver, CO and Johannesburg: Frederick S. Pardee Center for International Futures and the African Union Development Agency. Available at: https://www.nepad.org/publication/conditions-success-implementation-of-african-continental-free-trade-agreement

Austin, G. (2014), 'The Economics of Colonialism in Africa', in C. Monga and J. Y. Lin (eds), *The Oxford Handbook of Africa and Economics: Volume 1: Context and Concepts*, Oxford: Oxford University Press.

———— (2016), 'Is Africa Too Late for "Late Development"? Gerschenkron South of the Sahara', in M. Andersson and T. Axelsson (eds), *Diverse Development Paths and Structural Transformation in the Escape from Poverty*, Oxford: Oxford University Press, pp. 206–35.

Ayadi, L. et al. (2013), 'Estimating Informal Trade across Tunisia's Land Borders', Policy Research Working Papers. Available at: https://doi.org/10.1596/1813–9450–6731

Ayyagari, M., Beck, T. and Demirguc-Kunt, A. (2007), 'Small and Medium Enterprises Across the Globe', *Small Business Economics*, 29(4), pp. 415–34.

Baccini, L. et al. (2021), 'Services and Economic Development in Africa', *The World Bank Research Observer*. Available at: https://doi.org/10.1093/wbro/lkac006

Bach, D. C. (2016), 'The diversity of African regionalism', *GREAT Insights*, 5(4). Available at: https://ecdpm.org/great-insights/regional-integration-dynamics-africa/diversity-african-regionalism/

Bachrach, C. and Mizrahi, L. (1992), 'The Economic Impact of a Free Trade Agreement Between the United States and Mexico: A CGE Analysis', unpublished manuscript.

Bahar, D. and Santos, M. A. (2018), 'One MoreResource Curse: Dutch Disease and Export Concentration', *Journal of Development Economics*, 132, pp. 102–14.

Bairoch, P. (1995), 'Economics and World History: Myths and Paradoxes', *American Historical Review*, 100(3).

———— (1997), 'The Causes of Regionalism', CEPR Press Discussion Paper No. 1599. Available at: https://cepr.org/publications/dp1599

Baldwin, R., Chiappori, P. A. and Venables, A. (1989), 'The Growth Effects of 1992', *Economic Policy*, 4(9), pp. 247–81.

Baliamoune-Lutz, M. (2011), 'Growth by Destination (Where You Export Matters): Trade with China and Growth in African Countries', *African Development Review*, 23(2), pp. 202–18.

Baltagi, B. H., Egger, P. and Pfaffermayr, M. (2008), 'Estimating Regional Trade Agreement Effects on FDI in an Interdependent World', *Journal of Econometrics*, 145(1–2), pp. 194–208.

REFERENCES

Banerjee, A. and Duflo, E. (2011), *Poor Economics: A Radical Rethinking of the Way to Fight Global Poverty*, New York: PublicAffairs.

———— (2019), *Good Economics for Hard Times*, New York, New Delhi and London: PublicAffairs, Juggernaut Books and Allen Lane.

Banerjee, S. B. and Jackson, L. (2017), 'Microfinance and the Business of Poverty Reduction: Critical Perspectives from Rural Bangladesh', *Human Relations*, 70(1), pp. 63–91.

Banga, R. (2016), 'Impact of Green Box Subsidies on Agricultural Productivity, Production and International Trade', International Trade Working Paper 2413–3175. Available at: https://doi.org/10.14217/5jm0zbqzszbs-en

Banga, K. and Balchin, N. (2022), 'Linking Southern Africa to South Africa's Exports: New Opportunities for Regional Value Chains', *The World Economy*, 46, pp. 346–62.

Barajas, A. et al. (2009), 'Do Workers Remittances Promote Economic Growth?' IMF Working Paper 09/153.

Barrett-Brown, M. (1997), *Africa's Choices after Thirty Years of the World Bank*, London: Taylor & Francis.

Bashir, S. et al. (2018), *Facing Forward: Schooling for Learning in Africa*, Washington, DC: World Bank. Available at: http://hdl.handle.net/10986/29377

Bateman, M. and Chang, H.-J. (2012), 'Microfinance and the Illusion of Development: From Hubris to Nemesis in Thirty Years', *World Economic Review* No. 1. Available at: https://ssrn.com/abstract=2385482

Baumol, W. (1982), 'Contestable Markets: An Uprising in the Theory of Industry Structure', *American Economic Review*, 72(1), pp. 1–15.

Bawumia, M. and Halland, H. (2018), 'Oil Discovery and Macroeconomic Management', in T. Addison and A. Roe (eds), *Extractive Industries: The Management of Resources as a Driver of Sustainable Development*, Oxford: Oxford University Press.

BBC News Africa (2019), 'Air pollution in Nairobi leaves Kenyan children struggling to breathe', 4 December. Available at: https://www.bbc.com/news/av/world-africa-50665548

van Beemen, O. (2019), *Heineken in Africa: A Multinational Unleashed*, London: Hurst.

Behuria, P. (2017), 'The cautious return of import substitution in Africa', International Growth Centre blog. Available at: https://www.theigc.org/blog/cautious-return-import-substitution-africa/

———— (2019), 'African Development and the Marginalisation of Domestic Capitalists', ESID Working Paper No. 115. Manchester: Effective States and Inclusive Development Research Centre, University of Manchester. Available at: https://doi.org/10.2139/ssrn.3381558

Behuria, P. and Goodfellow, T. (2019), 'Leapfrogging Manufacturing? Rwanda's Attempt to Build a Services-Led "Developmental State"', *European Journal of Development Research*, 31(3), pp. 581–603.

Beine, M., Docquier, F. and Rapoport, H. (2008), 'Brain Drain and Human Capital Formation in Developing Countries: Winners and Losers', *Economic Journal*, 118(528), pp. 631–52.

REFERENCES

Bell, D. (1974), 'The Coming of Post-Industrial Society: A Venture in Social Forecasting', *Science and Public Policy*, 1(7), pp. 158–9.

Benabdallah, L., Robertson, W. and Wangjune, Y. (2016), 'China loans Africa much less than you think (and four other lessons from a new database)', *African Arguments*, 6 June. Available at: https://africanarguments.org/2016/06/china-loans-africa-much-less-than-you-think-and-four-other-lessons-from-a-new-database/

Bengoa, M. et al. (2021), 'Environmental Effects of the African Continental Free Trade Agreement: A Computable General Equilibrium Model Approach', *Journal of African Trade*, 8(2), pp. 36–48.

Benjamin, N., Golub, S. and Mbaye, A. A. (2015), 'Informality, Trade Policies and Smuggling in West Africa', *Journal of Borderlands Studies*, 30(3), pp. 381–94.

Bensassi, S. et al. (2017), 'Algeria–Mali trade: The normality of informality', *Middle East Development Journal*, 9(2), pp. 161–83.

Bergoeing, R. and Kehoe, T. J. (2003), 'Trade Theory and Trade Facts', Federal Reserve Bank of Minneapolis Research Department Staff Report 284. Available at: https://users.nber.org/~confer/2003/efgf03/kehoe.pdf

Berhanu, W. (2016), 'Informal Cross border Livestock Trade Restrictions in Eastern Africa: Is there a Case for Free Flows in Ethiopia-Kenyan Borderlands?' *Ethiopian Journal of Economics*, 25, pp. 95–119.

Bernard, A. et al. (2007), 'Firms in International Trade', National Bureau of Economic Research Working Paper 13054. Available at: https://doi.org/10.3386/w13054

Bhagwati, J. (1992), 'Regionalism versus Multilateralism', *World Economy*, 15(5), pp. 535–56.

van Biesebroeck, J. (2005), 'Exporting Raises Productivity in Sub-Saharan African Manufacturing Firms', *Journal of International Economics*, 67(2), pp. 373–91.

Bigsten, A. et al. (2004), 'Do African Manufacturing Firms Learn from Exporting?' *Journal of Development Studies*, 40, pp. 115–41.

Biswaro, J. M. (2012), *The Quest for Regional Integration in the Twenty first Century—Rhetoric versus Reality—A Comparative Study*, Dar es Salaam: Mkuki Na Nyota.

Biteye, M. and Songwe, V. (2019), 'Africa's Voices on the AfCFTA: A Call for Inclusive Trade', The Rockefeller Foundation, 19 March. Available at: https://www.rockefellerfoundation.org/blog/africas-voices-afcfta-call-inclusive-trade/

Blalock, G. and Gertler, P. J. (2008), 'Welfare Gains from Foreign Direct Investment through Technology Yransfer to Local Suppliers', *Journal of International Economics*, 74(2), pp. 402–21.

Blas, J. and Farchy, J. (2022), 'The World for Sale: Money, Power and the Traders Who Barter the Earth's Resources', *Financial Markets and Portfolio Management*, 37, pp. 115–8.

Bleaney, M. and Greenaway, S. D. (1993), 'Long-run Trends in the Relative Price of Primary Commodities and in the Terms of Trade of Developing Countries', *Oxford Economic Papers*, 45(3), pp. 349–63.

Blomqvist, H. C. (1996), 'The "Flying Geese" Model of Regional Development: A Constructive Interpretation', *Journal of the Asia Pacific Economy*, 1, pp. 215–31.

REFERENCES

Blomström, M. and Kokko, A. (1997), 'Regional Integration and Foreign Direct Investment', Policy Research Working Paper 6019. Available at: https://www.nber.org/papers/w6019

——— (2003), 'The Economics of Foreign Direct Investment Incentives', National Bureau of Economic Research Working Paper 9849. Available at: https://doi.org/10.3386/w9489

Blonigen, B. A. and Piger, J. (2014), 'Determinants of Foreign Direct Investment', *Canadian Journal of Economics*, 47(3), pp. 697–1046.

Boratav, K. (2001), 'Movements of Relative Agricultural Prices in Sub-Saharan Africa', *Cambridge Journal of Economics*, 25(3), pp. 395–416.

Borensztein, E., De Gregorio, J. and Lee, J.-W. (1998), 'How Does Foreign Direct Investment Affect Economic Growth?' *Journal of International Economics*, 45(1), pp. 115–35.

Borrell, J. (2023), *United Nations: Address by the High Representative/Vice-President Josep Borrell to the UN Security Council on EU-UN cooperation*, 22 February. Available at: https://www.eeas.europa.eu/eeas/united-nations-address-high-representativevice-president-josep-borrell-un-security-council-eu_en

Bouët, A. (2008), *The Expected Benefits of Trade Liberalization for World Income and Development: Opening the "Black Box" of Global Trade Modeling*, Food Policy Review 8, International Food Policy Research Institute (IFPRI). Available at: https://doi.org/10.2499/0896295109fprev8

Brahmbhatt, M., Canuto, O. and Vostroknutova, E. (2010), 'Natural Resources and Development Strategy after the Crisis', in O. Canuto and M. Giugale (eds), *The Day After Tomorrow: A Handbook on the Future of Economic Policy in the Developing World*, Washington, DC: World Bank Publications, pp. 101–18.

Brautigam, D. (2009), *The Dragon's Gift: The Real Story of China in Africa*, New York: Oxford University Press.

Brenton, P. and Hoffman, B. (2016), *Political Economy of Regional Integration in Sub-Saharan Africa*, Washington, DC: World Bank. Available at: https://openknowledge.worldbank.org/handle/10986/24767

Brenton, P. and Hoppe, M. (2006), 'The African Growth and Opportunity Act, Exports, and Development in Sub-Saharan Africa', World Bank, Policy Research Working Paper Series. Available at: https://elibrary.worldbank.org/doi/abs/10.1596/1813-9450-3996

Brenton, P. and Newfarmer, R. (2007), 'Watching More Than the Discovery Channel: Export Cycles and Diversification in Development', Policy Research Working Paper. Available at: https://doi.org/10.1596/1813-9450-4302

Bridges Africa (2018), 'Supporting Small-scale Cross-border Traders across Africa', *Bridges Africa*, 7(4).

Brinley, T. (1973), *Migration and Economic Growth: A Study of Great Britain and the Atlantic Economy*, Cambridge: Cambridge University Press.

British National Archives (2023), 'IMF Crisis'. Available at: https://www.nationalarchives.gov.uk/cabinetpapers/themes/imf-crisis.htm

REFERENCES

Bromley, R. (1990), 'A New Path to Development? The Significance and Impact of Hernando De Soto's Ideas on Underdevelopment, Production, and Reproduction', *Economic Geography*, 66(4), p. 328.

Brookings Institution (2018), 'Foresight Africa: Top Priorities for the Continent in 2018', Brookings Institution Press, 11 January. Available at: https://www.brookings.edu/multi-chapter-report/foresight-africa-top-priorities-for-the-continent-in-2018/

Brooks, A. (2015), *Clothing Poverty*, London: Zed Books.

Brown, C. and Irwin, D. (2016), 'The GATT's Starting Point Tariff Levels circa 1947', World Bank Policy Research Working Paper No. 7649. Available at: https://openknowledge.worldbank.org/bitstream/handle/10986/24223/The0GATT0s0sta0ff0levels0circa01947.pdf?sequence=5&isAllowed=y

Buffie, E. (2001), *Trade Policy in Developing Countries*, Cambridge: Cambridge University Press.

Bulmer-Thomas, V. (2003), *The Economic History of Latin America since Independence*, Cambridge: Cambridge University Press.

Bulte, E., Damania, R. and Deacon, R. (2005), 'Resource Intensity, Institutions, and Development', *World Development*, 33(7), pp. 1029–44.

Buningwire, W. (2022), 'Over 160 Zimbabwean teachers expected to arrive in Rwanda', KT Press, 19 October. Available at: https://www.ktpress.rw/2022/10/84029-over-160-zimbabwean-teachers-expected-to-arrive-in-rwanda/

Busse, M., Erdogan, C. and Mühlen, H. (2019), 'Structural Transformation and Its Relevance for Economic Growth in Sub–Saharan Africa', *Review of Development Economics*, 23, pp. 33–53.

Buys, P., Deichmann, U. and Wheeler, D. (2006), 'Road Network Upgrading and OverLand Trade Expansion in Sub-Saharan Africa'. Policy Research Working Paper; No. 4097. World Bank, Washington, DC.

Byiers, B., de Melo, J. and Brown, E. (2018), 'Working with the grain of African integration', *ECDPM*, 28 September. Available at: https://ecdpm.org/publications/working-with-the-grain-of-african-integration/

Byiers, B. and Woolfrey, S. (2022), 'Nigeria and the AfCFTA as a Two-level Game', *World Economy*, 46, pp. 312–27.

Caliendo, L. and Parro, F. (2014), 'Estimates of the Trade and Welfare Effects of NAFTA', *Review of Economic Studies*, 82(1), pp. 1–44.

Campos, F. M. L. et al. (2019), *Profiting from Parity: Unlocking the Potential of Women's Businesses in Africa*, Washington, DC: World Bank Group. Available at: http://documents.worldbank.org/curated/en/501971553025918098/Main-Report

Cannard, J. (2019), 'The African Continental Free Trade Agreement: Loss of Sovereignty, Lack of Transparency', *Committee for the Abolition of Illegitimate Debt*, 19 August. Available at: https://www.cadtm.org/The-African-Continental-Free-Trade-Agreement-Loss-of-Sovereignty-Lack-of

Carmignani, F. and Avom, D. (2010), 'The Social Development Effects of Primary Commodity Export Dependence', *Ecological Economics*, 70(2), pp. 317–30.

REFERENCES

Carrère, C. (2004), 'Impact of African Regional Agreements on Foreign Trade: Evaluation Using a Panel Gravity Model', *Journal of African Economies*, 13(2), pp. 199–239.

Cashin, P. and McDermott, C. (2002), 'The Long-Run Behavior of Commodity Prices: Small Trends and Big Variability', IMF Working Papers 2001: 068. Available at: https://doi.org/10.5089/9781451848991.001

Cavalcanti, T., Mohaddes, K. and Raissi, M. (2012), 'Commodity Price Volatility and the Sources of Growth', SSRN Preprint. Available at: https://doi.org/10.2139/ssrn.1846429

CBS News (2015), 'A look at China's "Button Town"', 8 October. Available at: https://www.cbsnews.com/news/welcome-to-button-town-china/

Cecchini, P. (1988) *The European Challenge, 1992: The Benefits of a Single Market*, Aldershot: Gower.

Central Bank of Kenya and KenInvest (2020), *Foreign Investment Survey 2020*. Available at: https://www.centralbank.go.ke/wp-content/uploads/2021/08/Foreign-Investment-Survey-2020-Report.pdf

Cernat, L., Laird, S. and Turrini, A. (2002), 'How Important Are Market Access Issues for Developing Countries in the Doha Agenda?' Centre for Research in Economic Development and International Trade, University of Nottingham, 2/13(CREDIT Research Paper). Available at: https://www.nottingham.ac.uk/credit/documents/papers/02-13.pdf

Chandler Jr, A.D. (1990), *Scale and Scope: The Dynamics of Industrial Capitalism*, Cambridge, MA and London: Harvard University Press.

Chang, H.-J. (2002), *Kicking Away the Ladder: Development Strategy in Historical Perspective*, London: Anthem Press.

———— (2007), *Bad Samaritans: The Myth of Free Trade and the Secret History of Capitalism*, London: Bloomsbury Publishing.

———— (2022), *Edible Economics: A Hungry Economist Explains the World*, London: Allen Lane.

Cha'ngom, N. (2020), 'African Countries and the Brain Drain: Winners or Losers? Beyond Remittances', African Economic Research Consortium, 26 May. Available at: https://aercafrica.org/wp-content/uploads/2020/06/D8-NARCISSE_CHANGOM-WIP.pdf

Chen, G., Geiger, M. and Fu, M. (2015), *Manufacturing FDI in Sub-Saharan Africa: Trends, Determinants, and Impact*, Washington, DC: World Bank. Available at: https://www.worldbank.org/content/dam/Worldbank/Event/Africa/Investing%20in%20Africa%20Forum/2015/investing-in-africa-forum-manufacturing-fdi-in-sub-saharan-africa-trends-determinants-and-impact.pdf

Cherif, R. et al. (2020), 'Competition, Competitiveness and Growth in Sub-Saharan Africa', IMF Working Papers 2020:030. Available at: https://doi.org/10.5089/9781513526379.001

Cherif, R. and F. Hasanov (2019), 'The Return of the Policy that Shall Not Be Named: Principles of Industrial Policy', IMF Working Paper 2019/074, IMF, Washington.

REFERENCES

Cheru, F. (2002), *African Renaissance: Roadmaps to the Challenge of Globalization*, London: Zed Books.

Chikanda, A. and Tawodzera, G. (2017), *Informal Entrepreneurship and Cross-Border Trade between Zimbabwe and South Africa*. Southern African Migration Programme. Available at: https://doi.org/10.2307/j.ctvh8qz72

Chirikure, S. (2021), '"Unearthing the Truth" Christmas Specials', *The Economist*, 18 December. Available at: https://www.economist.com/interactive/christmas-specials/2021/12/18/great-zimbabwe-archaeology

Choi, J., Fukase, E. and Zeufack, A. G. (2021), 'Global Value Chain Participation, Competition, and Markups: Evidence from Ethiopian Manufacturing Firms', *Journal of Economic Integration*, 36(3), pp. 491–517.

Chortareas, G. E. and Pelagidis, T. (2004). 'Trade Flows: A Facet of Regionalism or Globalisation?', *Cambridge Journal of Economics*, 28(2), pp. 253–271. http://www.jstor.org/stable/236021263-271.jstor.org/stable/23602126

Chu, A., Brower, D. and Williams, A. (2023), 'US states recruit European clean tech groups with green subsidies', *Financial Review*, 24 January. Available at: https://www.afr.com/world/europe/us-states-recruit-european-clean-tech-groups-with-green-subsidies-20230124-p5cf5l

Chuku, C., Simpasa, A. and Ekpo, A. (2022), 'Catalysing Regional Integration in Africa: The Role of Infrastructure', *World Economy*, 46, pp. 472–95.

Cilliers, J. (2020), *Africa First!: Igniting a Growth Revolution*, Johannesburg: Jonathan Ball Publishers.

Cimoli, M., Dosi, G. and Stiglitz, J. E. (eds) (2009), *Industrial Policy and Development: The Political Economy of Capabilities Accumulation*, Oxford: Oxford University Press.

Cipollina, M., Debucquet, D. L. and Salvatici, L. (2016), 'The Tide that Does not Raise All Boats: An Assessment of EU Preferential Trade Policies', *Review of World Economics*, 153(1), pp. 199–231.

Cirera, X., Foliano, F. and Gasiorek, M. (2015), 'The Impact of Preferences on Developing Countries' Exports to the European Union: Bilateral Gravity Modelling at the Product Level', *Empirical Economics*, 50(1), pp. 59–102.

Clemens, M. A. (2011), 'Economics and Emigration: Trillion-Dollar Bills on the Sidewalk?' *Journal of Economic Perspectives*, 25(3), pp. 83–106.

——— (2020), 'The Emigration Life Cycle: How Development Shapes Emigration from Poor Countries', Institute of Labour Economics DP No. 13614. Available at: https://docs.iza.org/dp13614.pdf

Clist, P. and Restelli, G. (2020), 'Development Aid and International Migration to Italy: Does Aid Reduce Irregular Flows?' *World Economy*, 44, pp. 1281–311.

Co, C. Y. and Dimova, R. (2014), 'Preferential Market Access into the Chinese Market: How Good is it for Africa?' Brooks World Poverty Institute Working Paper No. 196. Available at: https://doi.org/10.2139/ssrn.2437456

Cockcroft, L. and Riddell, R. C. (1991), 'Foreign Direct Investment in Sub-Saharan Africa', World Bank Working Paper 619, March. Available at: https://documents1.worldbank.org/curated/en/795891468768335280/pdf/multi-page.pdf

REFERENCES

Coe, D. and Hoffmaister, A. W. (1999), 'North-South Trade: Is Africa Unusual?', *Journal of African Economics*, 8(2), pp. 228–56.

Collier, P. (2008), *The Bottom Billion: Why the Poorest Countries Are Failing and What Can Be Done About It*, Oxford: Oxford University Press.

Collier, P. and Gunning, J. W. (1999), 'Why Has Africa Grown Slowly?' *Journal of Economic Perspectives*, 13(3), pp. 3–22.

Collier, P. and Venables, A. J. (2007), 'Rethinking Trade Preferences: How Africa Can Diversify its Exports', *World Economy*, 30(8), pp. 1326–45.

COMESA (2023), 'Home page', *The Common Market for Eastern and Southern Africa*. Available at: https://www.comesa.int/

Conceiçao, P. et al. (2014), 'Are global value chains good News for Africa's industrialisation?' *GREAT Insights*, 3(5). Available at: https://ecdpm.org/great-insights/value-chains-industrialisation/global-value-chains-good-news-africas-industrialisation/

Condon, N. and Stern, M. (2011), *The Effectiveness of African Growth and Opportunity Act (AGOA) in Increasing Trade from Least Developed Countries: A Systematic Review*, London: EPPI-Centre, Social Science Research Unit, Institute of Education, University of London. Available at: https://eppi.ioe.ac.uk/cms/Portals/0/PDF%20reviews%20and%20summaries/AGOA%202011Condon%20report.pdf?ver=2011-05-20-150456-597

Cook, N. and Jones, J. (2015), 'The African Growth and Opportunity Act (AGOA) and Export Diversification', *Journal of International Trade & Economic Development*, 24(7), pp. 947–67.

Cooper, C. A. and Massell, B. F. (1965), 'Toward a General Theory of Customs Unions for Developing Countries', *Journal of Political Economy*, 73(5), pp. 461–76.

Cottier, T. and Anirudh, S. (2019), *Migration, International Trade and Foreign Direct Investment in the Twenty-first Century*, Geneva: International Organization for Migration.

Coulibaly, S. and Fontagné, L. (2006), 'South–South Trade: Geography Matters', *Journal of African Economies*, 15(2), pp. 313–41.

Coulibaly, S., Kassa, W. and Zeufack, A. G. (eds) (2022), *Africa in the New Trade Environment: Market Access in Troubled Times*, Washington, DC: World Bank. Available at: https://elibrary.worldbank.org/doi/abs/10.1596/978-1-4648-1756-4

Coulson, A. (2012), *Tanzania—A Political Economy*, 2nd edition, Oxford: Oxford University Press.

Cowles, M. G. (2012), 'The Single European Act', in E. Jones, A. Menon and S. Weatherill (eds), *The Oxford Handbook of the European Union*, Oxford: Oxford University Press, pp. 107–20.

Cramer, C., Sender, J. and Oqubay, A. (2020), *African Economic Development: Evidence, Theory, Policy*, Oxford: Oxford University Press.

Csordás, S. (2017), 'Commodity Exports and Labour Productivity in the Long Run', *Applied Economics Letters*, 25(6), pp. 362–5.

Cuddington, J. T. and Jerrett, D. (2008), 'Super Cycles in Real Metals Prices?', *IMF Staff Papers*, 55(4), pp. 541–65.

REFERENCES

Cuevas, A., Messmacher, M. and Werner, A. (2005), 'Foreign Direct Investment in Mexico since the Approval of NAFTA', *World Bank Economic Review*, 19(3), pp. 473–88.

Dadush, U. (2015), 'Is Manufacturing Still a Key to Growth?' Policy Center for the New South Paper 1507. Available at: https://ideas.repec.org/p/ocp/rpaper/pp-15–07.html

Darian-Smith, E. (2019), 'Globalizing Education in Times of Hyper-Nationalism, Rising Authoritarianism, and Shrinking Worldviews', *New Global Studies*, 14. Available at: https://doi.org/10.1515/ngs-2019–0020

Dash, L. (1984), 'Guinea's longtime president, Ahmed Sekou Toure, dies', *Washington Post*, 28 March. Available at: https://www.washingtonpost.com/archive/local/1984/03/28/guineas-longtime-president-ahmed-sekou-toure-dies/18f31685-878c-4759-8028-3bef7fbc568b/

Davidson, B. (2001), *Africa in History*, Cambridge: Touchstone Books.

Davies, E. and Nilsson, L. (2019), 'A Comparative Analysis of the EU and US Trade Policies Towards LDCs', *Development Policy Review*, 38, pp. 613–29.

Davies, R. B. and Markusen, J. R. (2020), 'The Structure of Multinational Firms' International Activities', CESifo Working Paper No. 8150. Available at: https://doi.org/10.2139/ssrn.3552390

Deaton, A. (1999), 'Commodity Prices and Growth in Africa', *Journal of Economic Perspectives*, 13(3), pp. 23–40.

de Grauwe, P. (1996), 'Monetary Union and Convergence Economics', *Papers and Proceedings of the Tenth Annual Congress of the European Economic Association*, 40(3), pp. 1091–101.

de Grauwe, P. and Ji, Y. (2014), 'The Future of the Eurozone', *The Manchester School*, 82, pp. 15–34.

de Maio, L., Stewart, F. and van der Hoeven, R. (1999), 'Computable General Equilibrium Models, Adjustment and the Poor in Africa', *World Development*, 27(3), pp. 453–470.

Deloitte (2017), *Deloitte on Africa: The Rise and Rise of the African Middle Class*. Available at: https://cisp.cachefly.net/assets/articles/attachments/41119_the-rise-and-rise-of-the-african-middle-class.pdf

Deme, M. and Ndrianasy, E. R. (2017), 'Trade-creation and Trade-Diversion Effects of Regional Trade Arrangements: Low-income Countries', *Applied Economics*, 49(22), pp. 2188–202.

Dercon, S. C. (2022), *Gambling on Development: Why Some Countries Win and Others Lose*, London: Hurst.

DeRosa, A. and Gilbert, J. (2003), 'Technical Appendix: Quantitative Estimates of the Economic Impact of US Bilateral Free Trade Agreements', *Institute for International Economics*, pp. 383–418. Available at: https://piie.com/publications/chapters_preview/375/14iie3616.pdf

REFERENCES

Desai, M. (2004), *Marx's Revenge: The Resurgence of Capitalism and the Death of Statist Socialism*, London: Verso.

Dessalegn, H. (2023), 'Food Security in Africa: Current Efforts and Challenges', Brookings, Chapter 2. Available at: https://www.brookings.edu/essay/food-security-strengthening-africas-food-systems/

De Soto (1989), *The Other Path—The Economic Answer to Terrorism*, New York: Basic Books.

Diao, X. et al. (2021), 'Africa's Manufacturing Puzzle: Evidence from Tanzanian and Ethiopian Firms', National Bureau of Economic Research Working Paper 28344. Available at: https://doi.org/10.3386/w28344

Dicken, P. (2015), *Global Shift*, New York: Guilford Press.

Dihel, N. and Goswami, A. G. (2016), *The Unexplored Potential of Trade in Services in Africa: From Hair Stylists and Teachers to Accountants and Doctors*, Washington, DC: World Bank. Available at: https://doi.org/10.1596/24968

Docquier, F., Machado, J. and Sekkat, K. (2015), 'Efficiency Gains from Liberalizing Labor Mobility', *Scandinavian Journal of Economics*, 117(2), pp. 303–46.

Dollar, D. and Collier, P. (1999), 'Aid Allocation and Poverty Reduction', SSRN Preprint. Available at: https://papers.ssrn.com/sol3/papers.cfm?abstract_id=629108

Dorrie, P. (2015), 'AAP#5: China in Africa with Deborah Brautigam', *African Arguments*, 26 November. Available at: https://africanarguments.org/2015/11/aap5-china-in-africa-with-deborah-brautigam/

Dreher, A. (2009), 'IMF Conditionality: Theory and Evidence', *Public Choice*, 141(1), pp. 233–67.

Dreher, A., Sturm, J.-E. and Vreeland, J. R. (2015), 'Politics and IMF Conditionality', *Journal of Conflict Resolution*, 59(1), pp. 120–48.

Dunning, J. (1980), 'Toward an Eclectic Theory of International Production: Some Empirical Tests', *Journal of International Business Studies*, 11(1), pp. 9–31.

Dunning, J. and Lundan, S. M. (2010), 'Multinational Enterprises and the Global Economy', *Transnational Corporations*, 19(3), pp. 103–06.

Durlauf, S. N., Kourtellos, A. and Tan, C. M. (2008), 'Are Any Growth Theories Robust?', *Economic Journal*, 118(527), pp. 329–46.

EACJ (2014), *Kyarimpa vs A.G. of Uganda*, Appeal No. 6 of 2014, East African Court of Justice. Available at: https://africanlii.org/ea/judgment/east-african-court-justice/2014/109

———— (2017), *Hon. Margaret Zziwa vs Secretary General of the East African Community*, Reference No. 17 OF 2014, East African Court of Justice. Available at: https://www.eacj.org/?cases=hon-margaret-zziwa-versus-secretary-general-of-the-east-african-community

———— (2023), 'Home page', East African Court of Justice. Available at: https://www.eacj.org/

REFERENCES

Easterly, W. (2007), 'Was Development Assistance a Mistake?' *American Economic Review*, 97(2), pp. 328–32.

———— (2014), *The Tyranny of Experts: Economists, Dictators, and the Forgotten Rights of the Poor*, New York: Basic Books.

Easterly, W. and Reshef, A. (2010), 'African Export Successes: Surprises, Stylized Facts, and Explanations', National Bureau of Economic Research Working Paper 16597. Available at: http://dx.doi.org/10.3386/w16597

ECA (2019), *Macroeconomic and Social Developments in Eastern Africa 2019: Towards the Implementation of the AfCFTA*, Addis Ababa: United Nations Economic Commission for Africa. Available at: https://archive.uneca.org/sites/default/files/uploaded-documents/SRO-EA/22ICE/Eng/sub-regional_profile_2019_executive_summary_eng.pdf

———— (2023), *AfCFTA What You Need to Know Frequently Asked Questions & Answers*, Addis Ababa: United Nations Economic Commission for Africa. Available at: https://repository.uneca.org/bitstream/handle/10855/49411/b12025574.pdf?sequence=3&isAllowed=y

ECA/TMEA (2020), 'New report highlights significant gains from AfCFTA implementation in East Africa', Addis Ababa: United Nations Economic Commission for Africa. Available at: https://www.un.org/africarenewal/news/new-report-highlights-significant-gains-afcfta-implementation-east-africa

ECB (2009), *Discussion Paper with Regard to a Study on the Establishment of a Monetary Union among the Partner States of the East African Community inPreparation of Visits to the EAC Partner States from 7 to 25 September 2009 by the Project Teams of the East African Community and the European Central Bank*. East African Community Secretariat. Available at: http://repository.eac.int/bitstream/handle/11671/268/EAMU%20Discussion%20Paper.pdf?sequence=1&isAllowed=y

ECDPM (2016), 'Mobilising private capital for sustainable development', *Great Insights Magazine*, 6 October. Available at: https://ecdpm.org/work/2030-smart-engagement-with-business-volume-5-issue-5-october-november-2016/mobilising-private-capital-for-sustainable-development

Echandi, R., Maliszewska, M. and Steenbergen, V. (2022), *Making the Most of the African Continental Free Trade Area: Leveraging Trade and Foreign Direct Investment to Boost Growth and Reduce Poverty*. Washington, DC: World Bank Group. Available at: https://documents.worldbank.org/curated/en/099305006222230294/P1722320bf22cd02c09f2b0b3b320afc4a7

ECMR (2020), 'Intra-African Foreign Direct Investment (FDI) and Employment: A Case Study', Working Paper Series No. 335, Abidjan: African Development Bank.

The Economist (2021), 'Many more Africans are migrating within Africa than to Europe (African Odyssey)', *The Economist*, 30 October. Available at: https://www.economist.com/briefing/2021/10/30/many-more-africans-are-migrating-within-africa-than-to-europe

———— (2023), 'The impact of Brexit, in charts', *The Economist*, 3 January. Available

REFERENCES

at: https://www.economist.com/britain/2023/01/03/the-impact-of-brexit-in-charts

Edwards, L. (2020), 'African manufacturing firms and their participation in global trade', UNIDO. Available at: https://iap.unido.org/articles/african-manufacturing-firms-and-their-participation-global-trade

Eicher, T. S. and Kuenzel, D. J. (2016), 'The Elusive Effects of Trade on Growth: Export Diversity and Economic Take–off', *Canadian Journal of Economics*, 49(1), pp. 264–95.

Elumelu, T. (2011), 'Africapitalism: The Path to Economic Prosperity and Social Wealth', Lagos: The Tony Elumelu Foundation. Available at: https://nccd-crc.issuelab.org/resources/15291/15291.pdf

Enns, C. and Bersaglio, B. (2019), 'On the Coloniality of "New" Mega-Infrastructure Projects in East Africa', *Antipode*, 52, pp. 101–23.

Erasmus, G. (2019), 'When will trade under AfCFTA preferences become a reality?' *TRALAC*, March. Available at: https://www.tralac.org/documents/events/tralac/2741-tralac-brief-when-will-trade-under-afcfta-preferences-become-a-reality-march-2019/file.html

Erisen, C., Vasilopoulou, S. and Kentmen-Cin, C. (2019), 'Emotional Reactions to Immigration and Support for EU Cooperation on Immigration and Terrorism', *Journal of European Public Policy*, 27(6), pp. 795–813.

EU (2021), 'Investment Facilitation in Sub Saharan Africa—How to Make it a Reality', 12 February. Available at: https://trade.ec.europa.eu/doclib/docs/2021/june/tradoc_159669.pdf

EUC (2015), *The EU's Generalised Scheme of Preferences (GSP)*. Available at: https://trade.ec.europa.eu/doclib/docs/2015/august/tradoc_153732.pdf

European Commission et al. (2015), *Assessment of Economic Benefits Generated by the EU Trade Regimes towards Developing Countries*, Brussels: European Commission Publications.

Evenett, S. J. and Fritz, J. (2021), 'Foreign investment: How to make it work for developing countries', Industrial Analytics Platform, June. Available at: https://iap.unido.org/articles/foreign-investment-how-make-it-work-developing-countries

Fagerberg, J., Lundvall, B.-Å. and Srholec, M. (2018), 'Global Value Chains, National Innovation Systems and Economic Development', *European Journal of Development Research*, 30(3), pp. 533–56.

Faloyin, D. (2022), *Africa Is Not A Country: Breaking Stereotypes of Modern Africa*, London: Vintage.

Fanon, F. (1967), *Black Skin, White Masks*, New York: Grove Press.

Fanta, A. (2020), 'The real story why "bonkers Brussels" went bananas', *EU Observer*, 5 October. Available at: https://euobserver.com/news/149607

FAO and AUC (2021), 'Framework for Boosting Intra-African Trade in Agricultural Commodities and Services', Addis Ababa: FAO and AUC. Available at: https://doi.org/10.4060/cb3172en

REFERENCES

Farooki, M. and Kaplinsky, R. (2013), *The Impact of China on Global Commodity Prices*, London: Routledge.

Federal Ministry for Economic Cooperation and Development (2002), *What Are the Aims Served by Promoting Legal and Judicial Reform in Development Cooperation?* Bonn: Federal Ministry for Economic Cooperation and Development.

Federico, G. and Tena-Junguito, A. (2017), 'A Tale of Two Globalizations: Gains from Trade and Openness 1800–2010', *Review of World Economics*, 153(3), pp. 601–26.

Fieldhouse, D. K. (1999), *The West and the Third World: Trade, Colonialism, Dependence, and Development*, Oxford and Malden, MA: Blackwell.

Flahaux, M.-L. and De Haas, H. (2016), 'African Migration: Trends, Patterns, Drivers', *Comparative Migration Studies*, 4(1), p. 1.

Fleming, S. et al (2023), 'EU vows to counter China over "massive" subsidies to its industries', *Financial Times*, 10 February. Available at: https://www.ft.com/content/9bfe7e7e-83b7-47f2-8d59-e180215d534a

Fofack, H. and Mold, A. (2021), 'The AfCFTA and African Trade—An Introduction to the Special Issue', *Journal of African Trade*, 8(2), p. 1.

Ford, N. (2023), 'Can Africa's remittances be put to long-term work?' *African Business*, 13 February. Available at: https://african.business/2023/02/finance-services/can-africas-remittances-be-put-to-long-term-work

Foroutan, F. (1992), 'Regional Integration in Sub-Saharan Africa: Experience and Prospect', World Bank Policy Research Working Paper 0992. Available at: https://documents1.worldbank.org/curated/en/626511468768341775/pdf/multi0page.pdf

Foroutan, F. and Pritchett, L. (1993), 'Intra-Sub-Saharan African trade: Is it Too Little?' *Journal of African Economies*, 2(1), pp. 74–105.

Fortune (2022), 'Global 500—The World's Largest Corporations, Fortune', September. Available at: https://www.fortune.com/ranking/global500/

Fosu, A. K. (1990), 'Exports and Economic Growth: The African Case', *World Development*, 18(6), pp. 831–5.

———— (1996), 'Primary Exports and Economic Growth in Developing Countries', *The World Economy*, 19(4), pp. 465–75.

———— (2000), 'The International Dimension of African Economic Growth', Explaining African Economic Growth Performance Conference Series, CID Working Paper No. 34. Available at: https://www.hks.harvard.edu/sites/default/files/centers/cid/files/publications/faculty-working-papers/034.pdf

———— (2011), *Growth, Inequality, and Poverty Reduction in Developing Countries: Recent Global Evidence*. World Institute for Development Economic Research (UNU-WIDER) Working Paper No. wp-2011–001. Available at: https://EconPapers.repec.org/RePEc:unu:wpaper:wp-2011-001

———— (2012), 'Development Success: Historical Accounts from More Advanced Countries', WIDER Working Paper Series No. 2012/71. Available at: https://www.wider.unu.edu/sites/default/files/wp2012–071.pdf

REFERENCES

————— (2018), *Exports Diversification and Employment in Africa*. UNCTAD. Available at: https://unctad.org/webflyer/exports-diversification-and-employment-africa

Fosu, A. and Mold, A. (2007), 'Gains from Trade: Implications for Labour Market Adjustment and Poverty Reduction in Africa', *African Development Review*, 20.

Fouquin and Hugot (2016), cited by Esteban Ortiz-Ospina, Diana Beltekian and Max Roser (2018), 'Trade and Globalization'. Available at: https://ourworldindata.org/trade-and-globalization

Fox, L. (2021), 'It's easy to exaggerate the scope of the jobs problem in Africa. The real story is nuanced', Brookings Institution Press, 19 April. Available at: https://www.brookings.edu/blog/africa-in-focus/2021/04/19/its-easy-to-exaggerate-the-scope-of-the-jobs-problem-in-africa-the-real-story-is-nuanced/

Fox, L. and Jayne, T. S. (2020), 'Unpacking the misconceptions about Africa's food imports', Brookings Institution Press, 14 December. Available at: https://www.brookings.edu/blog/africa-in-focus/2020/12/14/unpacking-the-misconceptions-about-africas-food-imports/

Francois, J. (2000), *Assessing the Results of General Equilibrium Studies of Multilateral Trade Negotiations*, New York and Geneva: United Nations.

Frankema, E. and Booth, A. (eds) (2019), 'Fiscal Capacity and the Colonial State: Lessons from a Comparative Perspective', in *Fiscal Capacity and the Colonial State in Asia and Africa, c.1850–1960*, Cambridge: Cambridge University Press, pp. 1–35.

Frankema, E. and van Waijenburg, M. (2018), 'Africa rising? A historical perspective', *African Affairs*, 117(469), pp. 543–68.

Frazer, G. and van Biesebroeck, J. (2010), 'Trade Growth under the African Growth and Opportunity Act', *Review of Economics and Statistics*, 92(1), pp. 128–44.

Freeman, R. (2006), 'The Great Doubling: The Challenge of the New Global Labor Market', August. Available at: https://eml.berkeley.edu/~webfac/eichengreen/e183_sp07/great_doub.pdf

Freund, C. (2016), *Rich People Poor Countries: The Rise of Emerging-Market Tycoons and Their Mega Firms* [e-book], Peterson Institute for International Economics. Available at: https://cup.columbia.edu/book/rich-people-poor-countries/9780881327038

Freund, C. and Pierola, M. D. (2015), 'Export Superstars', *Review of Economics and Statistics*, 97(5), pp. 1023–32.

Fukuyama, F. (1992), *The End of History and the Last Man*, New York: The Free Press.

————— (1995), *Trust: The Social Virtues and the Creation of Prosperity*, Chicago, IL: American Library Association.

Gallagher, K. P. and Kumar, N. (2007), 'Relevance of "Policy Space" for Development: Implications for Multilateral Trade Negotiations', RIS Discussion Paper, New Delhi.

Games, D. (2013), *Business in Africa: Corporate Insights*, South Africa: Penguin Books.

Gashaw, T. (2017), 'Colonial Borders in Africa: Improper Design and its Impact on African Borderland Communities', *Africa Up Close*, 17 November. Available at: https://africaupclose.wilsoncenter.org/colonial-borders-in-africa-improper-design-and-its-impact-on-african-borderland-communities/

REFERENCES

Gasiorek, M. and López González, J. (2011), 'A Preliminary Investigation into the Effects of the Changes in the EU's GSP', *Trade Negotiations Insights*, 10(5). Available at: http://sro.sussex.ac.uk/id/eprint/27365

Gasiorek, M., Smith, A. and Venables, A. J. (1991), 'Completing the Internal Market in the EC: Factor Demands and Comparative Advantage', in L. Winters and A. Venables (eds), *European Integration: Trade and Industry*, Cambridge: Cambridge University Press, pp. 9–30.

Gathani, S. and Stoelinga, D. (2013), 'Learning by Exporting in Rwanda: A Deep-drive into Rwanda's Export Sector Focusing on Designations, Products, and Firms', International Growth Centre Working Paper. Available at: https://www.theigc. org/publications/learning-exporting-rwanda-deep-drive-rwandas-export-sector-focusing-designations

Gathii, J. (2006), 'The High Stakes of WTO Reform: Review of Behind the Scenes at the WTO: The Real World of Trade Negotiations/The Lessons of Cancun by Fatoumata Jawara and Aileen Kwa. Review by James Gathii', *Michigan Law Review*, 104(6), pp. 1361–86.

Geda, A. and Kebret, H. (2007), 'Regional Economic Integration in Africa: A Review of Problems and Prospects with a Case Study of COMESA', *Journal of African Economies*, 17(3), pp. 357–94.

Gelb, A. et al. (2017), 'Can Africa Be a Manufacturing Destination? Labor Costs in Comparative Perspective', Center for Global Development Working Paper No. 466. Available at: https://doi.org/10.2139/ssrn.3062914

———— (2020), 'Can Sub-Saharan Africa Be a Manufacturing Destination? Labor Costs, Price Levels, and the Role of Industrial Policy', *Journal of Industry, Competition and Trade*, 20(2), pp. 335–57.

Genc, M. et al. (2012), 'Migration and trade', Migration Data Portal, last updated October 2021. Available at: https://www.migrationdataportal.org/themes/migration-and-trade

Gereffi, G. (1994), 'The Organization of Buyer-driven Global Commodity Chains: How US Retailers Shape Overseas Production Networks', in *Global Value Chains and Development*, Cambridge: Cambridge University Press, pp. 43–71.

Gervais, A. and Jensen, J. (2019), 'The Tradability of Services: Geographic Concentration and Trade Costs', *Journal of International Economics*, 118(C), pp. 331–50.

Ghazvinian, J. (2007), 'Untapped: The Scramble for Africa's Oil', *Choice Reviews Online*, 45(04), pp. 2143–45.

Gibbon, P. and Ponte, S. (2005), *Trading Down: Africa, Value Chains, and the Global Economy*, Philadelphia, PA: Temple University Press.

Gnimassoun, B. (2020), 'Regional Integration: Do Intra-African Trade and Migration Improve Income in Africa?' *International Regional Science Review*, 43(6), pp. 587–631.

Gold, R. et al. (2017), 'South–South FDI: Is it Really Different?', *Review of World Economics*, 153(4), pp. 657–73.

REFERENCES

Golub, S. (2015), 'Informal Cross-border Trade and Smuggling in Africa', *Handbook on Trade and Development*, Cheltenham: Edward Elgar Publishing, pp. 179–209.

Gomez-Mera, L. and Varela, G. J. (2017), 'A BIT Far? Geography, International Economic Agreements, and Foreign Direct Investment: Evidence from Emerging Markets', World Bank Policy Research Working Paper No. 8185. Available at: https://doi.org/10.1596/1813-9450-8185

Gonzalez-Garcia, J. R., et al. (2016), 'Sub-Saharan African Migration: Patterns and Spillovers', *Spillover Notes*, 2016(009), p. A001.

Gonzalez-Garcia, J. and Yang, Y. (2020), 'International Trade and Corporate Market Power', IMF Working Paper 20(131). Available at: https://doi.org/10.5089/9781513550473.001

Gradeva, K. and Martínez-Zarzoso, I. (2015), 'Are Trade Preferences More Effective than Aid in Supporting Exports? Evidence from the "Everything But Arms" Preference Scheme', *World Economy*, 39(8), pp. 1146–71.

Greenville, J., Kawasaki, K. and Beaujeu, R. (2017), 'How Policies Shape Global Food and Agriculture Value Chains', OECD Food, Agriculture and Fisheries Papers, No. 100, Paris: OECD Publishing. Available at: https://doi.org/10.1787/aaf0763a-en

Griffith-Jones, S. and Gottschalk, R. (2016), *Achieving Financial Stability and Growth in Africa*, London: Routledge.

Grilli, E. R. and Yang, M. C. (1988), 'Primary Commodity Prices, Manufactured Goods Prices, and the Terms of Trade of Developing Countries: What the Long Run Shows', *World Bank Economic Review*, 2(1), pp. 1–47.

Grimwade, N. (2000), *International Trade: New Patterns of Trade, Production and Investment*, 2nd edition, London: Routledge.

Gumede, V. (2019), 'Revisiting Regional Integration in Africa—Towards a Pan-African Developmental Regional Integration', *Africa Insight*, 49(1), pp. 97–111.

Haaland, J. and Norman, V. (1992), 'Global Production Effects of European Integration', in *Trade Flows and Trade Policies*, Cambridge: Cambridge University Press, pp. 67–88.

Haddad, M. and Shepherd, B. (2011), 'Export-led growth: Still a viable strategy after the crisis?' Centre for Economic Policy Research, 12 April. Available at: https://cepr.org/voxeu/columns/export-led-growth-still-viable-strategy-after-crisis

Haggard, S. (1990), *Pathways from the Periphery: The Politics of Growth in the Newly Industrializing Countries*, Cornell, NY: Cornell University Press.

Hallak, J. C. and Sivadasan, J. (2013), 'Product and Process Productivity: Implications for Quality Choice and Conditional Exporter Premia', *Journal of International Economics*, 91(1), pp. 53–67.

Hallward-Driemeier, M. and Nayyar, G. (2017), *Trouble in the Making? The Future of Manufacturing-Led Development*, Washington, DC: World Bank. Available at: https://doi.org/10.1596/978-1-4648-1174-6

Hane-Weijman, E. (2021), 'Skill Matching and Mismatching: Labour Market Trajectories of Redundant Manufacturing Workers', *Geografiska Annaler: Series B, Human Geography*, 103(1), pp. 21–38.

REFERENCES

Haraguchi, N., Cheng, C. F. C. and Smeets, E. (2017), 'The Importance of Manufacturing in Economic Development: Has This Changed?', *World Development*, 93(C), pp. 293–315.

Harding, R. (2019), 'Africa: Trade briefing', *Global Trade Review*, 13 August. Available at: https://www.gtreview.com/supplements/gtr-africa-2019/africa-trade-briefing/

Harrison, A. E., Lin, J. Y. and Xu, L. C. (2014), 'Explaining Africa's (Dis)advantage', *World Development*, 63, pp. 59–77.

Havinden, M. and Meredith, D. (1993), *Colonialism and Development: Britain and its Tropical Colonies, 1850–1960*, London: Routledge.

Head, K. and Mayer, T. (2014), 'Gravity Equations: Workhorse, Toolkit, and Cookbook', *Handbook of International Economics*, 4, pp. 131–95.

Headey, D. D. (2013), 'The Impact of the Global Food Crisis on Self-assessed Food Security', *The World Bank Economic Review*, 27(1), pp. 1–27.

Headey, D. and Fan, S. (2008), 'Anatomy of a Crisis: The Causes and Consequences of Surging Dood Prices', *Agricultural Economics*, 39, pp. 375–91.

Helleiner, G. K., Chenery, H. B. and Syrquin, M. (1976), 'Patterns of Development, 1950–1970', *African Economic History*, 2, p. 56.

Helleiner, G. (2002), *Non-traditional Export Promotion in Africa: Experience and Issues*, Basingstoke and New York: Palgrave and UN University.

Herbst, J. (2000), *States and Power in Africa*, Princeton, NJ: Princeton University Press.

Herreros, S. (2019), 'The Failure of the Free Trade Area of the Americas: A Cautionary Tale for the African Continental Free Trade Area', in D. Luke and J. Macleod (eds), *Inclusive Trade in Africa: The African Continental Free Trade Area in Comparative Perspective*, London: Routledge, p. 228.

Hirsch, A. (2021a), 'A Strategic Consideration of the African Union Free Movement of Persons Protocol and Other Initiatives towards the Freer Movement of People in Africa', South African Institute of International Affairs. Available at: http://www.jstor.org/stable/resrep29589

———— (2021b), 'The African Union's Free Movement of Persons Protocol: Why Has it Faltered and How Can its Objectives Be Achieved?', *South African Journal of International Affairs*, 28(4), pp. 497–517.

Hirsch, C., Adkins, W. and Busquets Guardia, A. (2021), 'How to join the EU bubble—Brussels careers by the numbers', *Politico*, 4 February. Available at: https://www.politico.eu/article/what-to-study-to-join-the-eu-bubble-careers-eu-university-studies-europe-parliament/

Hirschman, A. O. (1958), *The Strategy of Economic Development*, New Haven, CT: Yale University Press.

Hochberg, F. P. (2020), *Trade Is Not a Four-Letter Word: How Six Everyday Products Make the Case for Trade*, New York: Avid Reader Press.

Hopkins, T. K. and Wallerstein, I. (1986), 'Commodity Chains in the World-economy Prior to 1800', *Review (Fernand Braudel Center)*, 10(1), pp. 157–70.

Huang, Y. (2008), *Capitalism with Chinese Characteristics—Entrepreneurship and the State*, Cambridge, MA: Massachusetts Institute of Technology.

REFERENCES

Hummels, D. and Klenow, P. J. (2005), 'The Variety and Quality of a Nation's Exports', *American Economic Review*, 95(3), pp. 704–23.

Iacovone, L., Ramachandran, V. and Schmidt, M. (2014), 'Stunted Growth: Why Don't African Firms Create More Jobs?', Center for Global Development Working Paper No. 353. Available at: https://doi.org/10.2139/ssrn.2390897

Ianchovichina, E. and Walmsley, T. L. (2012), *Dynamic Modeling and Applications for Global Economic Analysis*, Cambridge: Cambridge University Press.

Ichikowitz Family Foundation (2022), *Africa Youth Survey 2022*. Available at: https://ichikowitzfoundation.com/ays2022/ (accessed 26 June 2022).

ICP (2020), 'ICP 2017 results', in *Purchasing Power Parities and the Size of World Economies: Results from the 2017 International Comparison Program*, Washington, DC: World Bank, pp. 17–61. Available at: https://doi.org/10.1596/978–1–4648–1530–0_ch2

Ighobor, K. (2016), 'A green path to industrialization', *Africa Renewal*, November. Available at: https://www.un.org/africarenewal/magazine/august-2016/green-path-industrialization

IGIHE (2022), 'Rwanda gifted four hectares of land in Kenya', 6 August. Available at: https://en.igihe.com/news/article/rwanda-gifted-four-hectares-in-kenya

Iliffe, J. (1995), *Africans: The History of a Continent*, Cambridge: Cambridge University Press.

ILO (2014), *World of Work 2014: Developing with Jobs*, Geneva: International Labour Organization. Available at: https://www.ilo.org/global/research/global-reports/world-of-work/2014/WCMS_243961/lang—en/index.htm

——— (2018), 'More than 60 per cent of the world's employed population are in the informal economy', Geneva: International Labour Organization. Available at: https://www.ilo.org/global/about-the-ilo/newsroom/news/WCMS_627189/lang—en/index.htm

——— (2019), *Africa's Employment Landscape*, Geneva: International Labour Organization. Available at: https://ilostat.ilo.org/africas-changing-employment-landscape/

——— YouthStat (2022), *Statistics on Youth*, Geneva: International Labour Organization. Available at: https://ilostat.ilo.org/topics/youth/

Im, H. (2016), 'The Effects of Regional Trade Agreements on FDI by its Origin and Type: Evidence from U.S. Multinational Enterprises Activities', *Japan and the World Economy*, 39, pp. 1–11.

IMF (2014), 'Sustaining Long-Run Growth and Macroeconomic Stability in Low Income Countries—the Role of Structural Transformation and Diversification—Background Notes', International Monetary Fund Policy Paper 2014(39). Available at: https://doi.org/10.5089/9781498343664.007

——— (2018), 'Manufacturing Jobs: Implications for Productivity and Inequality', in *World Economic Outlook, April 2018: Cyclical Upswing, Structural Change*, Washington, DC: International Monetary Fund, Chapter 3. Available at: https://www.elibrary.imf.org/display/book/9781484338278/ch003.xml

REFERENCES

———— (2019a), 'Is the African Continental Free Trade Area a Game Changer for the Continent?' in *Regional Economic Outlook, April 2019, Sub-Saharan Africa: Recovery Amid Elevated Uncertainty*, Washington, DC: International Monetary Fund, Chapter 3. Available at: https://doi.org/10.5089/9781484396865.086

———— (2019b), *Statistical Appendix*, Washington, DC: International Monetary Fund. Available at: https://www.imf.org/-/media/Files/Publications/REO/AFR/2019/April/English/statapp.ashx

———— (2021a), *Direction of Trade Statistics. Exports, FOB to Partners Countries*, Washington, DC: International Monetary Fund. Available at: https://data.imf.org/regular.aspx?key=61013712

———— (2021b), *IMF Coordinated Direct Investment Survey*, Washington, DC: International Monetary Fund. Available at: https://data.imf.org/?sk=40313609-F037-48C1-84B1-E1F1CE54D6D5

———— (2022), *Extended Credit Facility (ECF)*, Washington, DC: International Monetary Fund. Available at: https://www.imf.org/external/np/fin/tad/extarr11.aspx?memberKey1=ZZZZ&date1key=2022-07-31

———— DOTS (2023), *Exports and Imports by Areas and Countries*, Washington, DC: International Monetary Fund. Available at: https://data.imf.org/regular.aspx?key=61013712

Inikori, J. (2007), 'Africa and the Globalization Process: Western Africa, 1450–1850', *Journal of Global History*, 2(1), pp. 63–86.

IOM (2022), *World Migration Report 2022*, New York: UN International Organization for Migration. Available at: https://worldmigrationreport.iom.int/wmr-2022-interactive/

IPCC (2004), *IPCC Workshop on Describing Scientific Uncertainties in Climate Change to Support Analysis of Risk and of Options*, Geneva: Intergovernmental Panel on Climate Change. Available at: https://www.ipcc.ch/event/ipcc-workshop-on-describing-scientific-uncertainties-in-climate-change-to-support-analysis-of-risk-and-of-options/

Isham, J. et al. (2005), 'The Varieties of Resource Experience: Natural Resource Export Structures and the Political Economy of Economic Growth', *World Bank Economic Review*, 19(2), pp. 141–74.

ITC and UNCTAD (2021), 'Sustainable and Inclusive: Regional Integration in Africa'. Available at: https://tradebriefs.intracen.org/2021/7/special-topic

Jang, Y. J. (2011), 'The Impact of Bilateral Free Trade Agreements on Bilateral Foreign Direct Investment among Developed Countries', *World Economy*, 34(9), pp. 1628–51.

Jarzebski, M. P. et al. (2019), 'Food Security Impacts of Industrial Crop Production in Sub-Saharan Africa: A Systematic Review of the Impact Mechanisms', *Food Security*, 12(1), pp. 105–35.

Javorcik, B. S. and Spatareanu, M. (2008), 'Liquidity Constraints and Linkages with Multinationals', LICOS Discussion Paper No. 225/2008. Available at: https://doi.org/10.2139/ssrn.1360685

REFERENCES

Jawara, F. and Kwa, A. (2004), *Behind the Scenes at the WTO: The Real World of International Trade Negotiations*, London: Zed Books.

Jensen, H. G. and Sandrey, R. (2013), 'A New Approach to a Regional Free Trade Agreement in East Africa: "willing participants"', TRALAC Working Paper No. S13WP09/2013. Available at: https://www.tralac.org/files/2013/07/S13WP092013-Jensen-Sandrey-A-new-approach-to-a-regional-Free-Trade-Agreement-in-east-Africa-20130626-fin.pdf

Jerven, M. (2014), 'On the Accuracy of Trade and GDP Statistics in Africa: Errors of Commission and Omission', *Journal of African Trade*, 1(1), pp. 45–52.

Jolly, R. (2015), 'Contemporary Perspectives on the Lagos Plan of Action and Structural Adjustment in the 1980s', in A. Sawyer, A. Jerome and E. Otobo, *African Development in the 21st Century: Reflection on Adebayo Adedeji's Theories and Contributions*, Trenton, NJ: Africa World Press.

Jones, P. et al. (2019), 'Sources of Manufacturing Productivity Growth in Africa', World Bank Policy Research Working Paper No. 8988. Available at: https://doi.org/10.1596/1813–9450–8988

Juma, C. (2011), 'Science Meets Farming in Africa', *Science*, 334(6061), p. 1323.

Juompan-Yakam, C. (2020), 'Nigeria's Chimamanda Ngozi Adichie talks colonialism, politics and pop culture', *The Africa Report*, 8 May. Available at: https://www.theafricareport.com/27060/nigerias-chimamanda-ngozi-adichie-talks-colonialism-politics-and-pop-culture/

Kaba, K., Lin, J. Y. and Renard, M. (2022), 'Structural Change and Trade Openness in Sub–Saharan African Countries', *World Economy*, 45(7), pp. 2101–34.

Kamer, L. (2022), 'Formal and informal new jobs created in Kenya from 2015 to 2019', *Statista*, April 2020. Available at: https://www.statista.com/statistics/1134125/formal-and-informal-new-jobs-created-in-kenya/

Kampfner, J. (2020), *Why the Germans Do it Better: Notes from a Grown-Up Country*, London: Atlantic Books.

Kaplinsky, R. (2014), 'Raphael Kaplinsky: Not whether, but how to participate in the global economy'. Available at: http://www.gc2014.org/2014/07/raphael-kaplinsky-not-whether-but-how-to-participate-in-the-global-economy/

———— (2021), *Sustainable Futures: An Agenda for Action*, Hoboken, NJ: John Wiley & Sons.

Kaplinsky, R. and Morris, M. (2009), 'Chinese FDI in Sub-Saharan Africa: Engaging with Large Dragons', *European Journal of Development Research*, 21(4), pp. 551–69.

———— (2016), 'Thinning and Thickening: Productive Sector Policies in the Era of Global Value Chains', *European Journal of Development Research*, 28, pp. 625–45.

———— (2019), 'Trade and Industrialisation in Africa: SMEs, Manufacturing and Cluster Dynamics', *Journal of African Trade*, 6(1), article 2.

Kareem, O. I. (2014), 'European Union's Sanitary and Phytosanitary Measures and Food Exports', *International Journal of Trade and Global Markets*, 9(4), p. 287.

Karingi, S. et al. (2006), 'Assessment of the Impact of the Economic Partnership

REFERENCES

Agreement between the COMESA Countries and the European Union', MPRA Paper 13294, University Library of Munich.

Karuhanga, J. (2023), '7 continental priorities region's business community presented to AfCFTA boss', *The New Times*, 13 March. Available at: https://www.newtimes. co.rw/article/5720/news/economy/7-continental-priorities-regions-business-community-presented-to-afcfta-boss

Kasekende, L. A. and Ng'eno, N. (1999), 'Regional Integration and Economic Liberalization in Eastern and Southern Africa', in P. Collier and A. Oyejide (eds), *Regional Integration and Trade Liberalization in SubSaharan Africa*, London: Palgrave Macmillan, pp. 148–96.

Kassa, W., Edjigu, H. T. and Zeufack, A. G. (2022), 'The Promise and Challenge of the African Continental Free Trade Area', in A. G. Zeufack and W. Kassa (eds), *Africa in the New Trade Environment: Market Access in Troubled Times*, Washington, DC: The World Bank, p. 2011.

Kedem, S. (2019), 'Morocco continues its push into Africa', *African Business*, 8 May. Available at: https://african.business/2019/05/economy/morocco-continues-its-push-into-africa/

Kelly, T. and Kemei, C. (2016), *One Network Area in East Africa*, Digital Dividends World Development Report 2016. Available at: https://pubdocs.worldbank.org/en/499731452529894303/WDR16-BN-One-Network-Area-in-East-Africa-Kelly-Kemei.pdf

Kelsall, T. (2013), *Business, Politics, and the State in Africa Challenging the Orthodoxies on Growth and Transformation*, London: Zed Books.

Kennan, J. (2012), 'Open Borders', National Bureau of Economic Research Working Paper 18307. Available at: https://www.nber.org/system/files/working_papers/w18307/w18307.pdf

Kenya Vision 2030 (2018), *Youth Employment Initiatives in Kenya*. Available at: https://vision2030.go.ke/wp-content/uploads/2018/05/WB_Youth-Employment-Initiatives-Report-13515.pdf

Kerr, A., Wittenberg, M. and Arrow, J. (2014), 'Job Creation and Destruction in South Africa', *South African Journal of Economics*, 82(1), pp. 1–18.

Khan, M. and Saleh, H. (2021), 'EU court strikes down trade deals with Morocco over Western Sahara', *Financial Times*, 29 September. Available at: https://www.ft.com/content/55568d85-c65d-484c-bd35-295daaf5f325

Khanna, P. (2016), *Connectography: Mapping the Future of Global Civilization*, New York: Random House.

Kharas, H. (2017), *The Unprecedented Expansion of the Global Middle Class: An Update*, Washington, DC: Brookings Institution. Available at: https://www.brookings.edu/wp-content/uploads/2017/02/global_20170228_global-middle-class.pdf

Kholi, A. (2004), *State-Directed Development: Political Power and Industrialization in the Global Periphery*, Cambridge: Cambridge University Press.

Kihato, C. W. (2020), 'Paolo Boccagni 2017: *Migration and the Search for Home: Mapping*

REFERENCES

Domestic Space in Migrants' Everyday Lives, New York: Palgrave Macmillan', *International Journal of Urban and Regional Research*, 44, pp. 389–90.

Kirkpatrick, C. and Watanabe, M. (2005), 'Regional Trade in Sub-Saharan Africa: An Analysis of East African Trade Cooperation, 1970–2001', *The Manchester School*, 73(2), pp. 141–64.

KNBS (2021), *Quarterly Labour Force Report January—March 2021*, Nairobi: Kenya National Bureau of Statistics. Available at: https://africacheck.org/sites/default/files/media/documents/2022–03/Kenya%20Quarterly%20Labour%20Force%20Survey-09_2021.pdf

Kohl, T. (2014), 'Do We Really Know that Trade Agreements Increase Trade?', *Review of World Economics*, 150(3), pp. 443–69.

Komminoth, L. (2023), 'Africa's demographic dilemma: Can half a billion jobs be created by 2050?', *African Business*, 1 March. Available at: https://african.business/2023/03/trade-investment/africas-demographic-dilemma-can-half-a-million-jobs-be-created-by-2050.

Koopman, R., Wang, Z. and Wei, S.-J. (2012), *Tracing Value-added and Double Counting in Gross Exports*, National Bureau of Economic Research Working Paper 18579. Available at: https://doi.org/10.3386/w18579

Koroma, S., Nimarkoh, J. and Ogalo, V. (2017), *Formalization of Informal Trade in Africa: Trends, Experiences and Socio-Economic Impact*, Accra: Food and Agriculture Organization of the United Nations.

Kox, H. and Rojas-Romagosa, H. (2020), 'How Trade and Investment Agreements Affect Bilateral Foreign Direct Investment: Results from a Structural Gravity Mode', KVL Discussion Paper No. 2020–02. Available at: https://doi.org/10.2139/ssrn.3667034

Kozul-Wright, R. and Rowthorn, R. (eds) (1998), *Transnational Corporations and the Global Economy*. London: Palgrave Macmillan.

Krapohl, S., Meissner, K. L. and Muntschick, J. (2013), 'Regional Powers as Leaders or Rambos? The Ambivalent Behaviour of Brazil and South Africa in Regional Economic Integration', *JCMS: Journal of Common Market Studies*, 52(4), pp. 879–95.

Kremer, M. (1993), 'Population Growth and Technological Change: One Million B.C. to 1990', *Quarterly Journal of Economics*, 108(3), pp. 681–716.

Kruse, H., et al. (2021), 'A Manufacturing Renaissance? Industrialization Trends in the Developing World', UNU-WIDER Working Paper 2021/28. Available at: https://doi.org/10.35188/UNU-WIDER/2021/966–2

Krugman, P. and Hanson, G. (1993), 'Mexico-U.S. Free Trade and the Location of Production', in P. M. Garber (ed.), *The Mexico-US Free Trade Agreement*, London and Cambridge, MA: MIT Press.

Kummritz, V. (2015), 'Global Value Chains: Benefiting the Domestic Economy?' IHEID Working Paper 02–2015. Available at: https://EconPapers.repec.org/RePEc:gii:giihei:heidwp02-2015

Kuznets, S. (1966), *Modern Economic Growth: Rate, Structure and Spread*, New Haven, CT and London: Yale University Press.

REFERENCES

Kweitsu, R. (2018), 'Brain drain: A bane to Africa's potential', Mo Ibrahim Foundation, 9 August. Available at: https://mo.ibrahim.foundation/news/2018/brain-drain-bane-africas-potential

Laird, S. and Yeats, A. J. (1986), 'The UNCTAD Trade Policy Simulation Model: A Note on the Methodology, Data and Uses', UNCTAD Discussion Paper No. 19. Available at: https://wits.worldbank.org/data/public/SMARTMethodology.pdf

Lakmeeharan, K (2020), 'Solving Africa's infrastructure paradox', McKinsey Global Institute, 6 March. Available at: https://www.mckinsey.com/capabilities/operations/our-insights/solving-africas-infrastructure-paradox

Lal, D. (1985), 'The Poverty of Development Economics', *Population and Development Review*, 11(3), p. 553.

Lall, S. and Kraemer-Mbula, E. (2005), *Industrial Competitiveness in Africa*, Rugby: Practical Action Publishing.

Lamarque, H. and Nugent, P. (2022), *Transport Corridors in Africa*, Rochester, NY: Boydell and Brewer.

Lancaster, C. (2006), *Foreign Aid*, Chicago, IL: University of Chicago Press.

Landau, A. and Whitman, R. (eds) (1997), *Rethinking the European Union: Institutions, Interests and Identities*, Basingstoke: Macmillan Press.

Langan, M. and Price, S. (2021), 'Migration, Development and EU Free Trade Deals: The Paradox of Economic Partnership Agreements as a Push Factor for Migration', *Global Affairs*, 7(4), pp. 505–21.

Le Bars, B. (2018), 'The Evolution of Investment Arbitration in Africa', *Global Arbitration Review*, 11 May. Available at: https://globalarbitrationreview.com/review/the-middle-eastern-and-african-arbitration-review/2018/article/the-evolution-of-investment-arbitration-in-africa

Lederman, D. and Maloney, W. F. (2007), 'Natural Resources Neither Curse nor Destiny', *Natural Resources Forum*, 31(3), pp. 245–6.

Leibenstein, H. (1966), 'Allocative Efficiency vs. X-Efficiency', *American Economic Review*, 56, pp. 392–415.

Leke, A., Chironga, M. and Desvaux, G. (2018), *Africa's Business Revolution: How to Succeed in the World's Next Big Growth Market*, Cambridge, MA: Harvard Business Review Press.

Leshoele, M. (2020), 'AfCFTA and Regional Integration in Africa: Is African Union Government a Dream Deferred or Denied?', *Journal of Contemporary African Studies*, pp. 1–15.

Leubuscher, C. (1940), '*Capital Investment in Africa. Its Course and Effects*. By S. Herbert Frankel. Issued by the Committee of the African Research Survey under the auspices of the Royal Institute of International Affairs. Oxford University Press. 1938. pp. viii + 487. 10s. 6d', *Africa*, 13(3), pp. 302–3.

Lewis, W. A. (1958), 'Unlimited Labour: Further Notes', *The Manchester School*, 26, pp. 1–32.

Li, Q., Scollay, R. and Maani, S. (2016), 'Effects on China and ASEAN of the ASEAN-China FTA: The FDI Perspective', *Journal of Asian Economics*, 44(C), pp. 1–19.

REFERENCES

Lim, F., Nabeegh, S. V. and Qing, H. (2013), 'The Progress and Issues in the Dutch, Chinese and Kenyan Floriculture Industries', *International Journal of Horticulture and Floriculture*, 2(1), pp. 33–9.

Liptak, K. (2022), 'Biden says he'll travel to Africa soon as he announces billions in new commitments', CNN, 15 December. Available at: https://edition.cnn.com/2022/12/15/politics/joe-biden-africa-commitment/index.html

Lisinge, R. and van Dijk, M. (2021), 'Regional Transport Infrastructure Programmes in Africa: What Factors Influence Their Performance?', *Canadian Journal of African Studies*, 56(1), pp. 99–121.

Little, P. D. (2005), 'Unofficial Trade When States Are Weak: The Case of Cross-Border Commerce in the Horn of Africa', UNU-WIDER Wider Working Paper No. RP2005–13. Available at: https://EconPapers.repec.org/RePEc:unu:wpaper:rp2005–13

Little, P., Tiki, W. and Debsu, D. (2015), 'Formal or Informal, Legal or Illegal: The Ambiguous Nature of Cross-border Livestock Trade in the Horn of Africa', *Journal of Borderlands Studies*, 30(3), pp. 405–21.

Longo, R. and Sekkat, K. (2004), 'Economic Obstacles to Expanding Intra-African Trade', *World Development*, 32(8), pp. 1309–21.

Lopes, C. (2018), *Africa in Transformation: Economic Development in the Age of Doubt*, Cham: Palgrave Macmillan.

Loungani, P. and Mishra, S. (2014), 'Not Your Father's Service Sector', *Finance & Development*, 51(2), p. ii.

LSE (2016), 'How severe is Africa's brain drain?', LSE Blog, 18 January. Available at: https://blogs.lse.ac.uk/africaatlse/2016/01/18/how-severe-is-africas-brain-drain/

Lücke, M. (2015), 'Remittances: Does Human Capital Follow Financial Capital?—The Development Potential of the West African Diaspora', in A. B. Akoutou et al. (eds), *Migration and Civil Society as Development Drivers—A Regional Perspective*, Bonn: Zei Centre for European Integration Studies, pp. 125–52.

Luke, D. (ed.) (2023), *How Africa Trades*, London: LSE Press.

Luke, D. and Macleod, J. (2019), *Inclusive Trade in Africa: the African Continental Free Trade Area in Comparative Perspective*, London: Routledge.

———— (2023), *A New Trade Deal for Africa, Please!*, Bonn: Friedrich Ebert Stiftung.

Luke, D. and Suominen, H. (2019), 'Towards Rethinking the Economic Partnership Agreements', in *Perspectives on the Soft Power of EU Trade Policy*, London: CEPR Press, pp. 143–50.

Lyakurwa, W.M. (2003), 'Primary Exports and Primary Processing for Export in Sub-Saharan Africa', in E. Aryeetey, J. Court, M. Nissanke and B. Weder (eds), Asia and Africa in the Global Economy, pp. 175–207, Tokyo, New York and Paris: United Nations University Press.

Maathai, W. (2009), *The Challenge for Africa*, New York: Pantheon Publishers.

MacDermott, R. (2007), 'Regional Trade Agreement and Foreign Direct Investment', *North American Journal of Economics and Finance*, 18(1), pp. 107–16.

REFERENCES

MacLeod, J. and Luke, D. (2013), 'Trade and Investment Flows and a Perspective for Analysing Trade Policy in Africa', in D. Luke (ed.), *How Africa Trades*, London: LSE Press, pp. 1–21.

Macleod, J. Luke, D. and Guepie, G. (2023), 'The AfCFTA and Regional Trade', in D. Luke (ed.), *How Africa Trades*, London: LSE Press, pp. 23–50.

MacPhee, C. and Sattayanuwat, W. (2014), 'Consequence of Regional Trade Agreements to Developing Countries', *Journal of Economic Integration*, 29, pp. 64–94.

Madden, P. (2020), 'Figure of the week: Africa's visa openness continues to improve', Brookings Institution Press, 16 December. Available at: https://www.brookings.edu/blog/africa-in-focus/2020/12/16/figure-of-the-week-africas-visa-openness-continues-to-improve/

Maizels, A. (2003), 'Economic Dependence on Commodities', in J. Toye (ed.), *Trade and Development*, Cheltenham: Edward Elgar Publishing, pp. 169–85.

Manchin, M. and Francois, J. (2006), 'Institutional Quality, Infrastructure and the Propensity to Export', Citeseer. Available at: https://citeseerx.ist.psu.edu/viewdoc/download?doi=10.1.1.557.5080&rep=rep1&type=pdf

Mangeni, F. (2022), 'The Why, the Bane and Ways Forward on Regional Integration in Africa', in F. Mangeni, J. Atta-Mensah and United Nations Economic Commission for Africa (eds), *Existential Priorities for the African Continental Free Trade Area*, Addis Ababa: UN Economic Commission for Africa. Available at: https://hdl.handle.net/10855/47860

Mangeni, F., Atta-Mensah, J. and United Nations Economic Commission for Africa (eds), *Existential Priorities for the African Continental Free Trade Area*, Addis Ababa: UN Economic Commission for Africa. Available at: https://hdl.handle.net/10855/47860

Mangeni, F. and Juma, C. (2019), *Emergent Africa: Evolution of Regional Economic Integration*, London: Headline Books.

Marconi, N., Reis, C. F. de Borja and Araújo, E. C. (2016), 'Manufacturing and Economic Development: The Actuality of Kaldor's First and Second Laws', *Structural Change and Economic Dynamics*, 37, pp. 75–89.

Martin, G. (2020), 'Pan-Africanism and African Unity', in R. Rabaka (ed.), *Routledge Handbook of Pan-Africanism*, Abingdon: Routledge, pp. 527–36.

Mashura, S. (2020), 'A Partial Equilibrium Analysis of the effects of the African Continental Free Trade Area on Intra-COMESA Trade, Tariff Revenue and Welfare'. Available at: https://www.comesa.int/wp-content/uploads/2020/10/Partial-equlibrium-Analysis-Mashura.pdf

Masson, P. R. and Pattillo, C. (2005), 'The Monetary Geography of Africa', *Journal of African Studies*, (69), pp. 189–91.

Matthee, M. et al. (2017), 'Understanding Manufactured Exporters at the Firm-level: New Insights from Using SARS Administrative Data', *South African Journal of Economics*, 86, pp. 96–119.

Mattli, W. (1999), *The Logic of Regional Integration*, Cambridge: Cambridge University Press.

REFERENCES

Mayer, T., Vicard, V. and Zignago, S. (2018), 'The Cost of Non-Europe, Revisited', Banque de France Working Paper No. 673. Available at: https://doi.org/10.2139/ssrn.3160818

May, L. and Mold, A. (2021), 'Charting a new course in US-Africa relations: The importance of learning from others' mistakes', Africa in Focus: Brookings Institution, 21 June. Available at: https://www.brookings.edu/blog/africa-in-focus/2021/06/21/charting-a-new-course-in-us-africa-relations-the-importance-of-learning-from-others-mistakes/

McMillan, M. and Headey, D. (2014), 'Introduction—Understanding Structural Transformation in Africa', World Development, 63, pp. 1–10.

McMillan, M., Rodrik, D. and Verduzco-Gallo, Í. (2014), 'Globalization, Structural Change, and Productivity Growth, with an Update on Africa', World Development, 63, pp. 11–32.

McMillan, M. and Zeufack, A. (2021), 'Labor Productivity Growth and Industrialization in Africa', National Bureau of Economic Research Working Paper 29570. Available at: https://doi.org/10.3386/w29570

Meade, J. E. (1955), The Theory of International Economic Policy, Volume II. Trade and Welfare, London: Oxford University Press for the Royal Institute of International Affairs.

Meattle, C. et al. (2022), 'Landscape of Climate Finance in Africa', Climate Policy Initiative, 21 September. Available at: https://www.climatepolicyinitiative.org/publication/landscape-of-climate-finance-in-africa/

Mevel, S. and Karingi, S. (2012), 'Deepening Regional Integration in Africa: A Computable General Equilibrium Assessment of the Establishment of a Continental Free Trade Area Followed by a Continental customs Union', Selected paper for presentation at the 7th African Economic Conference Kigali, Rwanda, 30 October–2 November.

Michalopoulos, S. and Papaioannou, E. (2011), 'The Long-Run Effects of the Scramble for Africa', NBER Working Paper No. 17620.

Mijiyawa, A. (2016), 'Does Foreign Direct Investment Promote Exports? Evidence from African Countries', World Economy, 40, pp. 1934–57.

Milner, H. V. and Kubota, K. (2005), 'Why the Move to Free Trade? Democracy and Trade Policy in the Developing Countries', International Organization, 59(1), pp. 107–43.

Mitchell, D. (2008), 'A Note on Rising Food Prices', Policy Research Working Papers. Available at: https://doi.org/10.1596/1813-9450-4682

Mkandawire, P. T. (2001), 'Thinking about Developmental States in Africa', Cambridge Journal of Economics, 25(3), pp. 289–314.

———— (2014), 'On the Politics of Regional Integration'. TRALAC Annual Conference, Cape Town, South Africa. Available at: http://www.nelsonmandelaschool.uct.ac.za/sites/default/files/image_tool/images/78/News/MKANDAWIRE_Regional_Integration_Transcript.pdf

REFERENCES

———— (2019), 'Reflections of an Engaged Economist: An Interview by Kate Meagher', *Development and Change*, 50(2), pp. 511–41.

———— and Soludo, C. C. (1999), *Our Continent, Our Future: African Perspectives on Structural Adjustment*, Dakar: CODESRIA.

Mkandawire, T. (1999), 'Developmental States and Small Enterprises', in K. King (ed.), *Enterprise in Africa*, Rugby: Practical Action Publishing, pp. 33–47.

————(2012), 'Institutional Monocropping and Monotasking in Africa', in A. Noman et al. (eds), *Good Growth and Governance in Africa: Rethinking Development Strategies, Initiative for Policy Dialogue*, Oxford: Oxford University Press, pp. 80–113.

Mo Ibrahim Foundation (2022), *Africa and Europe Facts and Figures on African Migrations*, London and Dakar: Mo Ibrahim Foundation. Available at: https://mo.ibrahim. foundation/sites/default/files/2022–02/aef_summit_african-migrations.pdf

Mold, A. (2003), 'The Impact of the Single Market Programme on the Locational Determinants of US Manufacturing Affiliates: An Econometric Analysis', *Journal of Common Market Studies*, 41(1), pp. 37–62.

———— (2004), 'FDI and Poverty Reduction: A Critical Reappraisal of the Arguments', *Région et Développement*, 20, pp. 91–122.

———— (2005a), 'Non-tariff barriers: their prevalence and relevance for African countries', *African Trade Policy Centre*, 25. Available at: https://repository.uneca.org/ handle/10855/25017

———— (2005b), 'Trade Preferences and Africa: The State of Play and the Issues at Stake', Africa Trade Policy Centre Work in Progress 12. Available at: https:// repository.uneca.org/bitstream/handle/10855/5577/bib.%2040943.pdf

———— (2006), 'Are Improving Terms of Trade Helping Reduce Poverty in Africa?', in *Are Improving Terms of Trade Helping Reduce Poverty in Africa?*, International Policy Centre for Inclusive Growth. Available at: https://ideas.repec.org/p/ipc/ opager/24.html

———— (2009), *Policy Ownership and Aid Conditionality in the Light of the Financial Crisis*, Paris: OECD Development Centre. Available at: https://openlibrary.org/books/ OL24048544M/Policy_ownership_and_aid_conditionality_in_the_light_of_the_ financial_crisis

———— (2018), 'The Consequences of Brexit for Africa: The Case of the East African Community', *Journal of African Trade*, 5(1–2), pp. 1–17.

———— (2021), 'Proving Hegel Wrong: Learning the Right Lessons from European Integration for the African Continental Free Trade Area', *Journal of African Trade*, 8(2), pp. 115–32.

———— (2022a), 'The Economic Significance of Intra-African Trade—Getting the Narrative Right', Brookings Global Working Paper No. 44. Available at: https:// www.brookings.edu/wp-content/uploads/2022/08/Economic-significance_of_ intra-African_trade.pdf

———— (2022b), 'It's cold out here: UK's predicament a handy lesson in implementing AfCFTA', *The East African Newspaper*, 4 November. Available at: https://www.

REFERENCES

theeastafrican.co.ke/tea/oped/comment/it-s-cold-out-here-uk-s-predicament-a-handy-lesson-in-implementing-afcfta-4008630

Mold, A. (2023) 'Why South-South trade is already greater than North-North trade—and what it means for Africa', Brookings Institution, 11 December. Available at: https://www.brookings.edu/articles/why-south-south-trade-is-already-greater-than-north-north-trade-and-what-it-means-for-africa/

Mold, A. and Chekwoti, C. (2022), 'The Textile and Clothing Sector in the Context of the African Continental Free Trade Area', in *Existential Priorities for the African Continental Free Trade Area*. Addis Ababa: Economic Commission for Africa. Available at: https://hdl.handle.net/10855/47860

Mold, A. and Mukwaya, R. (2017), 'Modelling the Economic Impact of the Tripartite Free Trade Area: Its Implications for the Economic Geography of Southern, Eastern and Northern Africa', *Journal of African Trade*, 3(1–2), p. 57.

Mold, A. and Mveyange, A. (2020), 'Trade in uncertain times: Prioritizing regional over global value chains to accelerate economic development in East Africa', Brookings Institution Press, 15 April. Available at: https://www.brookings.edu/blog/africa-in-focus/2020/04/15/trade-in-uncertain-times-prioritizing-regional-over-global-value-chains-to-accelerate-economic-development-in-east-africa/

Mold, A. and Prizzon, A. (2014), 'Commodity Prices and Export Performance in Sub-Saharan African Countries', in O. Morrissey, R. Lopez and K. Sharma (eds), *Handbook on Trade and Development*, Cheltenham: Edward Elgar Publishing, pp. 232–44.

Molle, W. (2017), *The Economics of European Integration*, London: Routledge.

Monbiot, G. (2022), *Regenesis: Feeding the World without Devouring the Planet*, Milton Keynes: Allen Lane.

Montalbano, P. and Nenci, S. (2020), *The Effects of Global Value Chain (GVC) Participation on the Economic Growth of the Agricultural and Food Sectors*, Rome: FAO. Available at: https://doi.org/10.4060/cb0714en

Moore, M., Prichard, W. and Fjeldstad, O.-H. (2018), *Taxing Africa*, London: Zed Books.

Morris, M., Kaplinsky, R. and Kaplan, D. (2012), '"One Thing Leads to Another"—Commodities, Linkages and Industrial Development', *Resources Policy*, 37(4), pp. 408–16.

Morris, M. and Kaplinsky, R. (2014), 'Developing Industrial Clusters and Supply Chains to Support Diversification and Sustainable Development of Exports in Africa', Report for the African Export-Import Bank. Available at: https://www.research-gate.net/profile/Mike-Morris-11/publication/275518116_Developing_Industrial_Clusters_and_Supply_Chains_to_Support_Diversification_and_Sustainable_Development_of_Exports_in_Africa_-_The_Composite_Report/links/553e04110cf2fbfe509b835d/Developing-Industrial-Clusters-and-Supply-Chains-to-Support-Diversification-and-Sustainable-Development-of-Exports-in-Africa-The-Composite-Report.pdf

Morsy, H. and Mukasa, A. (2019), *Youth Jobs, Skill and Educational Mismatches in Africa*,

REFERENCES

MPRA Paper No. 100394, University Library of Munich. Available at: https://ideas. repec.org/p/pra/mprapa/100394.html

Morsy, H., Salami, A. and Mukasa, A. N. (2021), 'Opportunities amid COVID-19: Advancing Intra-African Food Integration', *World Development*, 139: 105308.

Moussa, N. (2016), 'Trade and Current Account Balances in Sub-Saharan Africa: Stylized Facts and Implications for Poverty', Trade and Poverty Paper, Series 1. Available at: https://unctad.org/system/files/official-document/webaldc2016d2_en.pdf

Muchlinski, P. (2007), *Multinational Enterprises and the Law*, Oxford: Oxford University Press.

Mugh, M. (2011), 'Inquiry on Self-interested Foreign Aid: Insights from the ODA-Migrations Link in SSA Countries', *African Journal of Political Science and International Relations*, 5(4), pp. 164–73.

Mullings, R. and Mahabir, A. (2018), 'Growth by Destination: The Role of Trade in Africa's Recent Growth Episode', *World Development*, 102, pp. 243–61.

Naidu, S. and Vickers, B. (2014), 'Regional Regulation of Investments in Africa', in *South Africa, Africa, and International Investment Agreements*, Cape Town: Centre for Conflict Resolution, pp. 26–8.

Narlikar, A. (2004), 'Developing Countries and the WTO', in B. Hocking and S. McGuire (eds), *Trade Politics*, London: Routledge, p. 11.

Narula, R. and Driffield, N. (2011), 'Does FDI Cause Development? The Ambiguity of the Evidence and Why it Matters', *European Journal of Development Research*, 24(1), pp. 1–7.

Narula, R. and Dunning, J. (2000), 'Industrial Development, Globalization and Multinational Enterprises: New Realities for Developing Countries', *Oxford Development Studies*, 28, pp. 141–67.

——— (2018), 'Brilliant Technologies and Brave Entrepreneurs: A New Narrative for African Manufacturing', IZA Discussion Paper No. 11941. Available at: https://doi. org/10.2139/ssrn.3301690

Naudé, W. (2019), 'Manufacturing Optimism in Africa', *Journal of International Affairs*, 72(1), pp. 143–58.

——— (2010), 'Multinational Enterprises, Development and Globalization: Some Clarifications and a Research Agenda', *Oxford Development Studies*, 38(3), pp. 263–87.

Naya, S. F. and Plummer, M. G. (1997), 'Economic Co-operation after 30 Years of ASEAN', in *ASEAN Economic Bulletin*, 14(2). Available at: https://bookshop.iseas. edu.sg/publication/21

Nayyar, G. and Vargas Da Cruz, M. J. (2018), *Developing Countries and Services in the New Industrial Paradigm*, Washington, DC: World Bank. Available at: https://ideas.repec. org/p/wbk/wbrwps/8659.html

Ndumbe, L. N. (2013), 'Unshackling Women Traders: Cross-border Trade of Eru from Cameroon to Nigeria', in P. Brenton, E. Gamberoni and C. Sear (eds), *Women and Trade in Africa: Realizing the Potential*, Washington, DC: World Bank, pp. 43–59. Available at: https://openknowledge.worldbank.org/handle/10986/16629

REFERENCES

Ndung'u, N., Abebe, A. and Ngui, D. (2022), 'The Old Tale of the Manufacturing Sector in Africa: The Story Should Change', *Journal of African Economies*, 31(Supplement 1), pp. i3–i9.

Nelsen, A. (2022), 'European fruit with traces of most toxic pesticides "up 53% in nine years"', *The Guardian*, 24 May. Available at: https://www.theguardian.com/environment/2022/may/24/european-fruit-with-traces-of-most-toxic-pesticides-up-53-in-nine-years

The New Africa Channel (2023), 'Mo Ibrahim Urges African Union to Stop Begging for European Union Funding and Gain Respect', 30 April. Available at: https://www.youtube.com/watch?v=sUQ0cHXUGvA

Newfarmer, R. et al. (2018), *Beyond Manufacturing: Reconsidering Structural Change in Uganda*, Oxford: International Growth Centre. Available at: https://www.theigc.org/wp-content/uploads/2020/02/Newfarmer-et-al-2018-Policy-Note.pdf

Newman, C. et al. (2016), *Made in Africa: Learning to Compete in Industry*, Washington, DC: Brooking Institution Press. Available at: https://library.oapen.org/bitstream/handle/20.500.12657/25778/1004311.pdf?sequence=1&is

Ngepah, N. and Udeagha, M. C. (2018), 'African Regional Trade Agreements and Intra-African Trade', *Journal of Economic Integration*, 33(1), pp. 1176–99.

Nilsson, L. and Davies, E. (2013), 'A Comparative Analysis of EU and US Trade Preferences for the LDCs and the AGOA Beneficiaries', *Development Policy Review*, 38, pp. 613–29.

Njiwa, D., Nthambi, T. and Chirwa, J. (2012), *Reconnaissance Survey Report of Informal Cross Border Trade at STR Implementing Borders of Zambia, Malawi and Zimbabwe*. Lusaka: Common Market for Eastern and Southern Africa. Available at: https://123dok.net/article/zambia-and-malawi-informal-cross-border-trade.q7wk2mjo

Nkrumah, K. (1963), *Africa Must Unite*, London: Heinemann.

——— (1965), *Neo-Colonialism: The Last Stage of Imperialism*, Bedford: Panaf Books.

Nkurunziza, J. D., Tsowou, K. and Cazzaniga, S. (2017), 'Commodity Dependence and Human Development', *African Development Review*, 29(S1), pp. 27–41.

Nolan, P. (1990), *Introduction to Chinese Economy and Its Future: Achievements and Problems of Post-Mao Reform*, Cambridge: Polity Pess and Basil Blackwell.

——— (2001), *China and the Global Economy: National Champions, Industrial Policy, and the Big Business Revolution*, New York: Palgrave.

——— (2003), 'A New Competitive Landscape', *ECR Journal*, 3(1), pp. 17–29.

Noman, A. et al. (eds) (2012), *Good Growth and Governance in Africa: Rethinking Development Strategies*, Oxford: Oxford University Press.

Nshimbi, C., Oloruntoba, S. and Moyo, I. (2018), 'Borders, informal cross-border economies and regional integration in Africa—editorial', *Africa Insight*, 48, pp. 1–2.

Nwuke, K. (2022), 'I confess, I am an AfCFTA sceptic', *The Africa Report*, 15 February. Available at: https://www.theafricareport.com/176253/i-confess-i-am-an-afcfta-sceptic/

Nyabola, N. (2020), *Travelling While Black: Essays Inspired by a Life on the Move*, London: Hurst.

REFERENCES

Nyerere, J.K. (1963), 'A United States of Africa', *Journal of Modern African Studies*, 1, pp. 1–6.

OAU (1991), *Treaty Establishing the African Economic Community*, Addis Ababa: Organisation of African Unity. Available at: https://au.int/en/treaties/treaty-establishing-african-economic-community

O'Carroll, L. (2022), 'Brexit led to 14% fall in UK exports to EU in 2021, trade figures say', *The Guardian*, 30 June. Available at: https://www.theguardian.com/politics/2022/jun/30/brexit-uk-exports-fall-eu-goods-services

OCP (2022), 'OCP AFRICA | Our presence', OCP Africa. Available at: https://www.ocpafrica.com/en/our-presence.

Odijie, M. (2019), 'The Need for Industrial Policy Coordination in the African Continental Free Trade Area', *African Affairs*, 118, pp. 182–93.

Oduntan, G. (2015), 'Africa's border disputes are set to rise—but there are ways to stop them', *The Conversation*, 14 July. Available at: https://theconversation.com/africas-border-disputes-are-set-to-rise-but-there-are-ways-to-stop-them-44264

OECD (2011), *Guidelines for Multinational Enterprises*, Paris: Organisation for Economic Co-operation and Development. Available at: https://www.oecd.org/daf/inv/mne/48004323.pdf

——— (2014), *Migration Policy Debates*, Paris: Organisation for Economic Co-operation and Development. Available at: www.oecd.org/migration

——— (2021), *OECD: Perspectives on Global Development 2021*, Paris: Organisation for Economic Co-operation and Development. Available at: https://doi.org/10.1787/405e4c32-en

OECDStat (2019), *International Trade and Balance of Payments*, Paris: Organisation for Economic Co-operation and Development. Available at: https://stats.oecd.org/

OECD-WTO (2012), 'Trade in Value-added: Concepts, Methodologies and Challenges', Joint note of the OECD and WTO, 15 March. Available at: https://www.biblioteca.fundacionicbc.edu.ar/index.php/Trade_in_Value-Added:_Concepts,_Methodologies_and_Challenges

Ojakol, I. (2021), 'AfCFTA: Africa needs a "one-stop-shop" approach to competition law', *Nile Post*, 4 May. Available at: https://nilepost.co.ug/2021/05/04/afcfta-africa-needs-a-one-stop-shop-approach-to-competition-law/

Olson, M. (1971), *The Logic of Collective Action*, Cambridge, MA: Harvard University Press.

O'Neill, J. (2001), *Building Better Global Economic BRICs*, Goldman Sachs Paper No. 66. Available at: https://www.goldmansachs.com/insights/archive/archive-pdfs/build-better-brics.pdf

O'Neill, J. and Terzi, A. (2014), 'Changing Trade Patterns, Unchanging European and Global Governance', Bruegel Working Paper No. 02. Available at: http://www.bruegel.org/publications/publication-detail/publication/817-changing-trade-patterns-unchanging-european-and-global-governance/

ONS (2022), 'Profitability of UK companies: January to March 2022', Office of

REFERENCES

National Statistics. Available at: https://www.ons.gov.uk/releases/profitabilityo-fukcompaniesjanuarytomarch2022

Onwuamaeze, D. (2021), 'Nigeria: AfCFTA—Dangote group projects $12 billion annual revenue', 6 September. Available at: https://allafrica.com/stories/2021 09060042.html

Oppong-Amoako, W. (2018), *How to Succeed in the African Market—A Guide of the 2020s for Businesspeople and Investors*, Cape Town: Penguin Random House South Africa.

Oqubay, A. (2015), *Made in Africa: Industrial Policy in Ethiopia*, Oxford: Oxford University Press.

Ortiz-Ospina, E. and Beltekian, D. (2018), 'International trade data: why doesn't it add up?', Our World in Data, 5 June. Available at: https://ourworldindata.org/trade-data-sources-discrepancies

Ortiz-Ospina E., Beltekian D. and Roser M. (2018), 'Trade and globalization', Our World in Data Available at: https://ourworldindata.org/trade-and-globalization

Ottaviano, G. I. P., Peri, G. and Wright, G. C. (2018), 'Immigration, Trade and Productivity in Services: Evidence from U.K. Firms', *Journal of International Economics*, 112, pp. 88–108.

Owino, V. (2023), 'Africa getting little of $382bn renewable energy projects cash', *The East African Newspaper*, 12 February. Available at: https://www.theeastafrican.co.ke/tea/business/africa-getting-tiny-drop-of-renewable-energy-funds-4120010

Oxfam International (2002), *Mugged: Poverty in Your Coffee Cup*. Available at: https://s3.amazonaws.com/oxfam-us/www/static/oa3/files/mugged-full-report.pdf

Oxford Martin School (2023), 'Home page', Our World in Data. Available at: https://ourworldindata.org/

Oya, C. (2006), 'The Political Economy of Development Aid as Main Source of Foreign Finance for Poor African Countries: Loss of Policy Space and Possible Alternatives from East Asia', in *International Forum on Comparative Political Economy of Globalization*, Beijing, China [unpublished].

———— (2010), 'Rural Inequality, Wage Employment and Labour Market Formation in Africa: Historical and Micro-level Evidence', International Labour Organization Working Papers 994582213402676. Available at: https://ideas.repec.org/p/ilo/ilowps/994582213402676.html

———— (2011), 'Contract Farming in Sub-Saharan Africa: A Survey of Approaches, Debates and Issues', *Journal of Agrarian Change*, 12(1), pp. 1–33.

Oyejide, T. A. (2000), *Interests and Options of Developing and Least-developed Countries in a New Round of Multilateral Trade Negotiations*, Geneva: United Nations.

———— (2000), *Low-income Developing Countries in the GATT/WTO Framework: The First Fifty Years and Beyond*, The Hague: Kluwer Law International. Available at: https://www.econbiz.de/Record/from-gatt-to-the-wto-the-multilateral-trading-system-in-the-new-millennium/10001473822

————, Collier, P. and Elbadawi, I. (1997), *Regional Integration and Trade Liberalization in Sub Saharan Africa Volume 1: Framework, Issues and Methodological Perspectives*, Basingstoke: Palgrave Macmillan.

REFERENCES

————, Yeo, S. and Elbadawi, I. (1999), *Regional Integration and Trade Liberalization in SubSaharan Africa: Volume 3: Regional Case-Studies*, Basingstoke: Palgrave Mcmillan.

Paez, L. (2016), 'A Continental Free Trade Area: Imperatives for Realizing a Pan-African Market', *Journal of World Trade*, 50(3), pp. 533–62.

PAFTRAC (2022), 'PAFTRAC launches 2022 CEO Trade Survey', African Business, 16 December. Available at: https://african.business/2022/12/trade-investment/paftrac-launches-2022-ceo-trade-survey/

Page, J. and Söderbom, M. (2015), 'Is Small Beautiful? Small Enterprise, Aid and Employment in Africa', *African Development Review*, 27(S1), pp. 44–55.

Pages-Serra, C. (2010), 'The Age of Productivity: Transforming Economies from the Bottom Up', in J. Heckman and C. Pages (eds) (2004), *Law and Employment: Lessons from Latin America and the Caribbean*, Chicago, IL: University of Chicago Press.

Paice, E. (2021), *Youthquake: Why African Demography Should Matter to the World*, New York: Apollo.

Palma, J. G. and Marcel, M. (1989), 'Kaldor on the "Discreet Charm" of the Chilean Bourgeoisie', *Cambridge Journal of Economics*, 13(1), pp. 245–72.

Panagariya, A. (2000), 'Preferential Trade Liberalization: The Traditional Theory and New Developments', *Journal of Economic Literature*, 38(2), pp. 287–331.

Panagariya, A. and Duttagupta, R. (1999), 'The "Gains" from Preferential Trade Liberalization in CGEs: Where from Do the they Come?', in S. Lahiri (ed.), *Regionalism and Globalization: Theory and Practice*. London: Routledge.

PAPSS (2023), 'Connecting Payments. Accelerating Africa's Trade'. Available at: https://papss.com/

Parker, P. (2020), *History of World Trade in Maps*, Glasgow: HarperCollins. Available at: https://www.bookdepository.com/History-World-Trade-Maps-Philip-Parker/9780008409296

Parker, M. (2022), 'Time to tone down hyperbole over AfCFTA?', *African Business*, 31 August. Available at: https://african.business/2022/08/finance-services/time-to-tone-down-hyperbole-over-afcfta/

Perez, C. (2002), 'Technological Revolutions, Paradigm Shifts and Socio-Institutional Change', in E. Reinert (ed.), *Globalization, Economic Development and Inequality: An Alternative Perspective*, Cheltenham: Edward Elgar, pp. 217–42.

Persson, M. and Wilhelmsson, F. (2007), 'Assessing the Effects of EU Trade Preferences for Developing Countries', Lund University Publications, pp. 29–48. Available at: https://lup.lub.lu.se/record/1384847

———— (2015), 'EU Trade Preferences and Export Diversification', *World Economy*, 39(1), pp. 16–53.

Pharatlhatlhe, K. and Vanheukelom, J. (2019), 'Financing the African Union on Mindsets and Money', ECDPM Discussion Paper No. 240. Available at: https://ecdpm.org/wp-content/uploads/DP240-Financing-the-African-Union-on-mindsets-and-money.pdf

Phelps, N. A. (1997), 'Multinationals and European Integration: The Prospects for Welsh Manufacturing Industry', *Environment and Planning A*, 29(9), pp. 1525–41.

REFERENCES

Piermartini, R. and Teh, R. (2005), 'Demystifying Modelling Methods for Trade Policy', World Trade Organization Discussion Paper 10. Available at: https://www.wto.org/english/res_e/booksp_e/discussion_papers10_e.pdf

Piketty, T. (2014), *Capital in the 21st Century*, London: Routledge.

Pilling, D. (2020), 'African countries not ready to implement free trade from January', *Financial Times*, 28 December. Available at: https://www.ft.com/content/ bc612 590-d38e-4d08-a1e1-0e7f5e19be30

————— (2021), 'How Morocco transformed itself into a carmaking hub', *Financial Times*, 11 October. Available at: https://www.ft.com/content/7a8498e5–3fc9–4e90–8dfc-e72d492a8c57

Portes, J. (2021), 'Brexit: The macroeconomic outlook', *UK in a Changing Europe*, 1 March. Available at: https://ukandeu.ac.uk/macroeconomic-outlook-brexit/

Portugal-Perez, A. (2007), 'The Costs of Rules of Origin in Apparel: African preferential exports to the US and to the EU', Paper presented at the ECA African Economic Conference 15–17 November, Addis Ababa, Ethiopia. Available at: https://archive.uneca.org/sites/default/files/uploaded-documents/AEC/2007/alberto_portugal-perez_0.pdf

Prebisch, R. (1950), 'The Economic Development of Latin America and Its Principal Problems', *Economic Bulletin For Latin America*, 7, pp. 1–12.

Prunier, G. and Ficquet, É. (2015), *Understanding Contemporary Ethiopia: Monarchy, Revolution and the Legacy of Meles Zenawi*, London: Hurst.

PWC (2019), *Africa Private Business Survey 2019*. Available at: https://www.pwc.com/gx/en/entrepreneurial-and-private-companies/emea-private-business-survey/pwc-emea-private-business-africa-report-2019.pdf

Qingqing, C. et al. (2011), 'Market Integration in China', World Bank Policy Research Working Paper Series 5630. Available at https://www.researchgate.net/publication/228268092_Market_Integration_in_China

Qumba, M. F. (2020), 'Assessing African Regional Investment Instruments and Investor–State Dispute Settlement', *International and Comparative Law Quarterly*, 70(1), pp. 197–232.

Rabaka, R. (2020), 'Amilcar Cabral, Cabralism, and Pan-Africanism: The Dialectic of Revolutionary Decolonization and Revolutionary Re-Africanization', in R. Rabaka (ed.), *Routledge Handbook of Pan-Africanism*, Abingdon: Routledge, pp. 302–17.

Ramadhan, S. and Otieno, B. (2020), '30,000 graduates join the hunt for jobs', *Standard Media Group*. Available at: https://www.standardmedia.co.ke/kenya/article/200 1353959/30000-graduates-join-the-hunt-for-jobs

Reader, J. (1998), *Africa: A Biography of the Continent*, London: Penguin Books.

Republic of Rwanda Ministry of Trade and Industry (2015), *Domestic Market Recapturing Strategy*, March. Available at: https://rwandatrade.rw/media/2015%20MINICOM%20Domestic%20Markets%20Recapturing%20Strategy.pdf

Riegert, B. (2021), 'The 4 persistent problems dogging the EU', *Deutsche Welle*, 14 September. Available at: https://www.dw.com/en/the-eus-4-persistent-problems-still-dogging-the-bloc/a-59154492

REFERENCES

Roberts, S., Simbanegavi, W. and Vilakazi, T. (2023), 'Cementing Regional Integration or Building Walls? Competition, Cartels and Regional Integration in the Cement Industry in Africa', *The World Economy*, 46, pp. 437–52.

Robertson, C. (2022), *The Time-Travelling Economist: Why Education, Electricity and Fertility Are Key to Escaping Poverty*, London: Palgrave Macmillan.

Robson, P. (1998), *The Economics of International Integration*, 5th edition, London: Routledge.

Rodney, W. (1972), *How Europe Underdeveloped Africa*, London: Verso Books.

Rodrik, D. (1999), 'The New Global Economy and Developing Countries: Making Openness Work. Washington, DC, Overseas Development Council, Policy Essay No. 24, Baltimore, The Johns Hopkins University Press, 1999, x-168 p.', *Études internationales*, 30(4), p. 827.

———— (2008), *One Economics, Many Recipes: Globalization, Institutions, and Economic Growth*, Princeton, NJ: Princeton University Press.

———— (2011), *The Globalization Paradox—Why Global Markets, States and Democracy Can't Co-exist*, Oxford: Oxford University Press.

———— (2012), 'Unconditional Convergence in Manufacturing', *Quarterly Journal of Economics*, 128(1), pp. 165–204.

———— (2015), 'Premature Deindustrialization', National Bureau of Economic Research Working Paper 20935. Available at: https://doi.org/10.3386/w20935

———— (2017), *Straight Talk on Trade: Ideas for a Sane Economy*, Princeton, NJ and Oxford: Princeton University Press.

———— (2018), 'What Do Trade Agreements Really Do?', *Journal of Economic Perspectives*, 32(2), pp. 73–90.

Rodrik, D., Subramanian, A. and Trebbi, F. (2004), 'Institutions Rule: The Primacy of Institutions over Geography and Integration in Economic Development', *Journal of Economic Growth*, 9(2), pp. 131–65.

Roessler P, et al. (2022), 'The Cash Crop Revolution, Colonialism and Economic Reorganization in Africa', *World Development*, 158, article 105934.

Romei, V. and Giles C. (2021), 'Northern Ireland economy has outperformed rest of UK, ONS figures show', *Financial Times*, 29 November. Available at: https://www.ft.com/content/3b5059c4-4ef1-44d1-ae1f-43a875efb7ca

Rose, A. K. (2007), 'Do We Really Know that the WTO Increases Trade? Reply', *American Economic Review*, 97(5), pp. 2019–25.

Rosling, H., Rönnlund, A. R. and Rosling, O. (2018), *Factfulness: Ten Reasons We're Wrong About the World—and Why Things Are Better Than You Think*, London: Sceptre.

Rowden, R. (2015), 'Africa's boom is over', *Foreign Policy*, 31 December. Available at: https://foreignpolicy.com/2015/12/31/africas-boom-is-over/

Roxborough, I. (2009), *Theories of Underdevelopment*, London: Macmillan International Higher Education.

Roxburgh, C. et al. (2010), 'Lions on the move: the progress and potential of African economies', McKinsey Global Institute, 1 June. Available at: https://www.mckinsey.com/featured-insights/middle-east-and-africa/lions-on-the-move

REFERENCES

Rutger, B. (2017), *Utopia for Realists: How We Can Build the Ideal World*, Boston, MA: Little, Brown and Company.

Ruzuhuzwa, K. (2012), *Towards a Common Currency in the East African Community: Issues, Challenges and Prospects*, Kigali: United Nations Economic Commission for Africa. Available at: https://repository.uneca.org/bitstream/handle/10855/22278/Bib-31340.pdf

Sachs, J. D. (2005), *The End of Poverty: Economic Possibilities for our Time*, New York: Penguin Press.

Sachs, J. D. and Warner, A. (1997), 'Sources of Slow Growth in African Economies', *Journal of African Economies*, 6(3), pp. 335–76.

SADC (2023), 'Education & Skills Development', *Southern African Development Community*. Available at: https://www.sadc.int/pillars/education-skills-development

Sanny, J. A.-N. and Patel, J. (2021), 'Beyond borders? Africans prefer self-reliant development but remain skeptical of free trade and open borders', *Afrobarometer*, Dispatch No. 492. Available at: https://www.afrobarometer.org/wp-content/uploads/2021/11/ad492-pap4-africans_prefer_self-reliant_development_skeptical_of_free_trades-afrobarometer_dispatch-bh-19nov21–2.pdf

Santos–Paulino, A. U. (2007), 'Aid and Trade Sustainability under Liberalisation in Least Developed Countries', *World Economy*, 30(6), pp. 972–98.

Santos Silva, J. M. C. and Tenreyro, S. (2006), 'The Log of Gravity', *Review of Economics and Statistics*, 88(4), pp. 641–58.

Sapsford, D. (1985), 'The Statistical Debate on the Net Barter Terms of Trade Between Primary Commodities and Manufactures: A Comment and Some Additional Evidence', *The Economic Journal*, 95(379), p. 781.

Sawyer, A., Jerome, A. and Otobo, E. (2015), *African Development in the 21st Century: Reflection on Adebayo Adedeji's Theories and Contributions*, Trenton, NJ: Africa World Press.

Saygili, M., Peters, R. and Knebel, C. (2018), 'African Continental Free Trade Area: Challenges and Opportunities of Tariff Reductions', UNCTAD Research Paper No. 15. Available at: https://unctad.org/publication/african-continental-free-trade-area-challenges-and-opportunities-tariff-reductions

Schiff, M. (2005), *Brain Gain: Claims about Its Size and Impact on Welfare and Growth Are Greatly Exaggerated*, Washington, DC: World Bank Group. Available at: http://web.worldbank.org/archive/website01589/WEB/IMAGES/MAURICES.PDF

Schiff, M. and Winters, L. A. (eds) (2003), *Regional Integration and Development*, Washington, DC: World Bank. Available at: https://doi.org/10.1596/0–8213–5078–1

Schnepf, R. (2021), 'WTO Doha Round: Implications for U.S. Agriculture', Congressional Research Service Report RS22927. Available at: https://crsreports.congress.gov/product/pdf/RS/RS22927/13

Schreiber, J.-J. S. (1969), *The American Challenge*. New York: Avon.

REFERENCES

Schwartz, H. M. (1994), *States versus Markets*, New York: St Martin's Press.

———— (2018), *States versus Markets*, 4th edition, London: Bloomsbury Academic.

Seers, D. (1979), 'The Birth, Life and Death of Development Economics (Revisiting a Manchester Conference)', *Development and Change*, 10, pp. 707–19.

Selwyn, B. (2018), 'Poverty Chains and Global Capitalism', *Competition & Change*, 23(1), pp. 71–97.

Sender, J. (1999), 'Africa's Economic Performance: Limitations of the Current Consensus', *Journal of Economic Perspectives*, 13(3), pp. 89–114.

Seong, J. et al. (2022), 'Global flows: The ties that bind in an interconnected world', McKinsey, 15 November. Available at: https://www.mckinsey.com/capabilities/strategy-and-corporate-finance/our-insights/global-flows-the-ties-that-bind-in-an-interconnected-world

Seyoum, B. (2007), 'Revealed Comparative Advantage and Competitiveness in Services', *Journal of Economic Studies*, 34(5), pp. 376–88.

Shaxson, N. (2019), *The Finance Curse: How Global Finance Is Making Us All Poorer*, London: Grove Press.

Shepherd, B. (2021), 'How Misleading Is Revealed Comparative Advantage?', Developing Trade Consultants Working Paper DTC-2021–2. Available at: https://developing-trade.com/wp-content/uploads/2021/07/Working-paper-DTC-2021–2.pdf

Shimeles, A. (2018), 'Foresight Africa viewpoint—Understanding the patterns and causes of African migration: Some facts', Brookings Institution Press, 18 January. Available at: https://www.brookings.edu/blog/africa-in-focus/2018/01/18/foresight-africa-viewpoint-understanding-the-patterns-and-causes-of-african-migration-some-facts/

Shingal, A. and Mendez-Parra, M. (2020), 'African Greenfield Investment and the Likely Effect of the African Continental Free Trade Area', Indian Council for Research on International Economic Relations Working Paper 387. Available at: http://www.icrier.org/pdf/Working_Paper_387.pdf

Signé, L. (2017), 'Policy Implementation—A Synthesis of the Study of Policy Implementation and the Causes of Policy Failure', Research Papers & Policy Papers No. 1703. Available at: https://ideas.repec.org/p/ocp/rpaper/pp-1703.html

———— (2020), *Unlocking Africa's Business Potential Trends, Opportunities, Risks, and Strategies*, Washington, DC: Brookings Institution Press. Available at: https://www.brookings.edu/book/unlocking-africas-business-potential/

———— (2021), *Africa's Mining Potential: Trends, Opportunities, Challenges and Strategies*, Salé: Policy Center for the New South. Available at: https://www.africaportal.org/publications/africas-mining-potential-trends-opportunities-challenges-and-strategies/

Singer, H. W. (1950), 'The Distribution of Gains between Investing and Borrowing Countries', *American Economic Review: Milestones and Turning Points in Development Thinking*, 40, pp. 473–85.

REFERENCES

Singh, J., Shreeti, V. and Urdhwareshe, P. (2022), 'The Impact of Bilateral Investment Treaties on FDI Inflows into India: Some Empirical Results', *Foreign Trade Review*, 57(3), pp. 310–23.

Skidelsky, R. (2000), *Volume Three: Fighting for Freedom, 1937–1946*, New York: Viking.

Snyder, E. (1963), 'Foreign Investment Protection: A Reasoned Approach', *Michigan Law Review*, 61(6), p. 1087.

Soubbotina, T. P. (2004), *Beyond Economic Growth An Introduction to Sustainable Development*, Washington, DC: The World Bank. Available at: https://documents1. worldbank.org/curated/en/454041468780615049/pdf/2489402nd0edition0Beyo nd0economic0growth.pdf

South Africa (2015), *Protection of Investment Act 22 of 2015*, 39514. Available at: https:// www.gov.za/documents/protection-investment-act-22-2015-15-dec-2015-0000

Southwood, R. (2022), *Africa 2.0*, Manchester: Manchester University Press.

Spitz, A. (1996), 'Mao and the Rejection of Politics', *Soundings: An Interdisciplinary Journal*, 79(1/2), pp. 221–37.

Spraos, J. (1980), 'The Statistical Debate on the Net Barter Terms of Trade between Primary Commodities and Manufactures', *Economic Journal*, 90(357), pp. 107–28.

Standard Bank (2020a), 'African Markets Revealed'. Available at: https://corporatean-dinvestment.standardbank.com/cib/global/insights/african-markets-revealed

———— (2020b), 'Standard Bank Economy 2020', Available at: https://corporatean-dinvestment.standardbank.com/cib/global/insights/economy-2020

Stein, H. (2001), 'Economic Development and the Anatomy of Crisis in Africa: From Colonialism through Structural Adjustment', Paper presented at the Centre of African Studies, University of Copenhagen, 5 March. Available at: https://teol. ku.dk/cas/publications/publications/occ._papers/stein2001.pdf

Stender, F. et al. (2021), 'The Trade Effects of the Economic Partnership Agreements between the European Union and the African, Caribbean and Pacific Group of States: Early Empirical Insights from Panel Data', *Journal of Common Market Studies*, 59(6), pp 1495–515.

Stephens, B. (2009), *The Amorality of Profit: Transnational Corporations and Human Rights*, London: Routledge.

Stewart, F., Lall, S. and Wangwe, S. (1992), 'Alternative Development Strategies: An Overview', in F. Stewart, S. Lall and S. Wangwe (eds), *Alternative Development Strategies in Sub-Saharan Africa*, London: Palgrave Macmillan, pp. 3–47.

Stiglitz, J. E. and Charlton, A. (2005), *Fair Trade For All: How Trade Can Promote Development*, Oxford: Oxford University Press.

Strachan, M. (2012), 'Paul Krugman: Here's the dirty secret about economic growth', *HuffPost*, 28 December. Available at: https://www.huffpost.com/entry/paul-krugman-future-growt_n_2375040

Streeten, P. (1959), 'Unbalanced Growth', *Oxford Economic Papers*, 11(2), pp. 167–90.

Su, D. and Yao, Y. (2016), 'Manufacturing as the Key Engine of Economic Growth for Middle-income Economies', ADBI Working Paper 573. Available at: https://doi. org/10.2139/ssrn.2784095

REFERENCES

Sun, W. (2013), 'The Productivity of Return Migrants: The Case of China's "Sea Turtles", *IZA J Migration*, 2, article 5. Available at: https://doi.org/10.1186/2193-9039-2-5

Swazan, I. S. and Das, D. (2022), 'Bangladesh's Emergence as a Ready-Made Garment Export Leader: An Examination of the Competitive Advantages of the Garment Industry', *International Journal of Global Business and Competitiveness*, 17, pp. 162–74.

Szirmai, A. (2013), 'Manufacturing and Economic Development', in A. Szirmai, W. Naudé and L. Alcorta (eds), *Pathways to Industrialization in the Twenty-first Century*, Oxford: Oxford University Press, pp. 53–75.

Szirmai, A. and Verspagen, B. (2015), 'Manufacturing and Economic Growth in Developing Countries, 1950–2005', *Structural Change and Economic Dynamics*, 34(C), pp. 46–59.

Tadesse, B. and Fayissa, B. (2008), 'The Impact of African Growth and Opportunity Act (Agoa) on U.S. Imports from Sub-Saharan Africa (SSA)', *Journal of International Development*, 20(7), pp. 920–41.

Tandon, Y. (2015), *Trade is War: The West's War against the World*, New York: OR Books.

Tayo, T. (2023), 'The Road to Africa's Single Market: Progress so Far and Challenges for the Future', Africa Policy Research Institute, 13 March. Available at: https://afripoli.org/the-road-to-africas-single-market-progress-so-far-and-challenges-for-the-future

Teteryatnikova, M. (2008), 'R&D in the Network of International Trade: Multilateral versus Regional Trade Agreements', SSRN Preprint. Available at: https://doi.org/10.2139/ssrn.1344975

Thangavelu, S. M. and Narjoko, D. (2014), 'Human Capital, FTAs and Foreign Direct Investment Flows into ASEAN', *Journal of Asian Economics*, 35(C), pp. 65–76.

Thirlwall, A. P. (2012), 'Balance of Payments Constrained Growth Models: History and Overview', in E. Soukiazis and P. A. Cerqueirain (eds), *Models of Balance of Payments Constrained Growth*, London: Palgrave Macmillan, pp. 11–49.

Thompson, N. and Thompson, S. (2001), 'The Baobab and the Mango Tree: Lessons About Development—African and Asian Contrasts. London: Zed Books (2000). Reviewed by A. F. Robertson', *Journal of Political Ecology*, 8(1). Available at: https://doi.org/10.2458/v8i1.21609

Thomsen, S. E. and Woolcock, S. (1993), *Direct Investment and European Integration: Competition among Firms and Governments*. London: Chatham House Papers.

Timmis, H. (2017), *Formalising Informal Trade in North Africa*, London: Department for International Development.

Titeca, K. (2009), 'The Changing Cross-border Trade Dynamics between North-western Uganda, North-eastern Congo and Southern Sudan', Crisis States Working Paper No. 63: Cities and Fragile States. Available at: chrome-http://eprints.lse.ac.uk/28477/1/WP63.2.pdf

TLDR News EU (2023), 'Europeans Are More Optimistic about the EU: Why?' 23 January. Available at: https://www.youtube.com/watch?v=vELVxyb9W74

REFERENCES

TRALAC (2022), *African Union Reforms*. Available at: https://www.tralac.org/resources/by-region/14704-african-union-reforms.html

Ul Haque, I. (2004), *Commodities under Neoliberalism: The Case of Cocoa*, New York and Geneva: UN. Available at: https://digitallibrary.un.org/record/521291.

UNCTAD (1999), 'Basic Data on the Least Developed Countries', *Least Developed Countries Report*, Geneva: United Nations, pp. 172–214. Available at: https://doi.org/10.18356/99eb1bc3-en

——— (2005), *Transnational Corporations*, 14(3). Available at: https://unctad.org/system/files/official-document/iteiit20059_en.pdf

——— (2013), 'Global Value Chains: Investment and Trade for Development', in *United Nations Conference on Trade and Development (UNCTAD) World Investment Report (WIR)*, Geneva: United Nations, pp. 121–202. Available at: https://doi.org/10.18356/f045c54c-en

——— (2014), *Investor-State Dispute Settlement*, New York and Geneva: United Nations. Available at: https://unctad.org/system/files/official-document/diaeia2013d2_en.pdf.

——— (2017), *World Investment Report Investment and the Digital Economy*, Geneva: United Nations. Available at: https://unctad.org/webflyer/world-investment-report-2017

——— (2018), *Economic Development in Africa Report 2018: Migration for Structural Transformation*, Geneva: United Nations. Available at: https://unctad.org/system/files/official-document/aldcafrica2018_en.pdf

——— (2019), *Economic Development in Africa Report 2019*, Geneva: United Nations. Available at: https://unctad.org/system/files/official-document/aldcafrica2019_en.pdf

——— (2020), *Building and Utilizing Productive Capacities in Africa and the Least Developed Countries: A Holistic and Practical Guide*, Geneva: United Nations Conference on Trade and Development. Available at: https://unctad.org/system/files/official-document/aldcinf2020d1_en.pdf

——— (2021a), *Commodities and Development Report 2021: Escaping from the Commodity Dependence Trap through Technology and Innovation*, Geneva: United Nations. Available at: https://doi.org/10.18356/9789214030461

——— (2021b), *A European Union Carbon Border Adjustment Mechanism: Implications for Developing Countries*, Geneva: United Nations Conference on Trade and Development. Available at: https://unctad.org/system/files/official-document/osginf2021d2_en.pdf

——— (2021c), *Economic Development in Africa Report 2021: Reaping the Potential Benefits of the African Continental Free Trade Area for Inclusive Growth*, Geneva: United Nations Conference on Trade and Development. Available at: https://unctad.org/system/files/official-document/aldcafrica2021_en.pdf

——— (2022a), 'Investment Dispute Settlement Navigator', United Nations Conference on Trade and Development. Available at: https://investmentpolicy.unctad.org/investment-dispute-settlement

REFERENCES

———— (2022b), *World Investment Report: International Tax Reforms and Sustainable Investment*, Geneva: United Nations Conference on Trade and Development. Available at: https://unctad.org/webflyer/world-investment-report-2022

———— (2022c), *Trade and Development Report 2022*, Geneva: United Nations Conference on Trade and Development. Available at: https://unctad.org/tdr2022

———— (2023), 'UN list of least developed countries', United Nations Conference on Trade and Development. Available at: https://unctad.org/topic/least-developed-countries/list

UNCTADStat (2023), 'UNCTADStat database'. Available at: https://unctadstat.unctad.org/

UNDP (1997), *Human Development Report 1997*, New York and London: Oxford University Press. Available at: https://hdr.undp.org/content/human-development-report-1997

———— (2020), *The Futures Report: Making the AfCFTA Work for Women and Youth*. Available at: https://www.undp.org/africa/publications/futures-report-making-afcfta-work-women-and-youth

UNECA (2015), *Economic Report on Africa 2015. Industrializing through Trade*, Addis Ababa: Economic Commission for Africa. Available at: https://hdl.handle.net/10855/22767

———— (2016), *Transformative industrial policy for Africa*, Addis Ababa: Economic Commission for Africa. Available at: https://hdl.handle.net/10855/23015

———— (2018), *ECA—60 Years in Step with African Development*, Addis Ababa: United Nations Economic Commission for Africa. Available at: https://knowledge.uneca.org/eca60/sites/default/files/doc/ECA60Chapter1_en.pdf

———— (2019), *Africa Review Report on Sustainable Consumption and Production*, Addis Ababa: Economic Commission for Africa. Available at: https://archive.uneca.org/sites/default/files/PublicationFiles/africanreviewreport-on-sustainableconsumption.pdf

———— (2020a), *Drivers for Boosting Intra-African Investment Flows towards Africa's Transformation*, Addis Ababa: Economic Commission for Africa. Available at: https://archive.uneca.org/sites/default/files/PublicationFiles/drivers_for_boosting_intra-african_investment_flows_towards_africas_transformation_eng_2020_web_version.pdf

———— (2020b), *Creating a Unified Regional Market: Towards the Implementation of the African Continental Free Trade Area in East Africa*, Kigali: DLVW Creative Ltd. Available at: https://hdl.handle.net/10855/43754

———— (2021), *African Regional Teview of Implementation of the Global Compact for Safe, Orderly and Regular Migration*, Addis Ababa: Economic Commission for Africa. Available at: https://uneca.org/sites/default/files/SROs/North-Africa/gcm2021E2100831.pdf

Urban, K., Jensen, H. G. and Brockmeier, M. (2016), 'How Decoupled Is the Single Farm Payment and Does it Matter for International Trade?' *Food Policy*, 59, pp. 126–38.

REFERENCES

US Department of Commerce (2021), 'Foreign direct investment [FDI]', US Department of Commerce. Available at: https://www.commerce.gov/tags/foreign-direct-investment-fdi

US Foreign Agricultural Service (2023), 'Testimony by USDA Under Secretary for Trade and Foreign Agricultural Affairs Alexis Taylor to Senate Committee on Agriculture, Nutrition, and Forestry', Communications to Congress, 1 February. Available at: https://fas.usda.gov/newsroom/testimony-usda-under-secretary-trade-and-foreign-agricultural-affairs-alexis-taylor-senate

US International Trade Commission (1992), 'Economy-wide Modeling of the Economic Implications of a FTA with Mexico and a NAFTA with Canada and Mexico: Report on Investigation. 332 of the Tariff Act of 1930', USITC Publication 2516, May. Available at: https://www.usitc.gov/publications/332/pub2516.pdf

Usman, Z. and Landry, D. (2021), 'Economic Diversification in Africa: How and Why it Matters', SSRN Preprint. Available at: https://doi.org/10.2139/ssrn.3842228

Utesch-Xiong, F. and Kambhampati, U. (2021), 'Determinants of Chinese Foreign Direct Investment in Africa', *Journal of African Business*, pp. 1–18.

Vanguard Economics (2020), 'Rwanda African Continental Free Trade Area Strategy-Data Presentation from Survey of Likely Trading Businesses to Inform Strategy for AfCFTA for Rwanda', Mimeo, Kigali.

Van der Ven, Colette and Luke, David (2023), 'Africa in the World Trade Organization', in: Luke, David (ed.), *How Africa Trades*, London: LSE Press, pp. 117–140. Available at: https://doi.org/10.31389/lsepress.hat.e

Varas, J. (2017) 'Assessing Bilateral and Multilateral Trade Agreements', American Action Forum, 14 February. Available at: https://www.americanactionforum.org/research/assessing-bilateral-multilateral-trade-agreements/

Vernon, R. (1971), 'Sovereignty at Bay: The Multinational Spread of U. S. Enterprises', *The International Executive*, 13(4), pp. 1–3.

———— (1998), *In the Hurricane's Eye: The Troubled Prospects of Multinational Enterprises*, Cambridge, MA and London: Harvard University Press.

Video remarks of H.E. Mr Alan Kyerematen, Minister of Trade and Industry of Ghana at the webinar 'Implementing the AfCFTA: The Need for Deepening Private Sector Engagement and Commitment' (2021). African Development Bank, UN Industrial Development Organization, International Trade Centre, and World Trade Organization. Available at: https://www.afdb.org/en/news-and-events/events / implementing-afcfta-need-deepening-private-sector-engagement-and-commitment-42144

Von Braun, J. (2008), 'The Food Crisis Isn't Over', *Nature*, 456(7223), p. 701.

Wakabi, M. and Anyanzwa, J. (2018), 'One network area: Roaming charges are back', *The East African*, 14 October. Available at: http://www.theeastafrican.co.ke/business/One-Network-Area-Roaming-charges-are-back/2560-4804088-oh7wsfz/index.html

REFERENCES

Wandera, N. (2023), 'EAC states on the verge of attaining one network area', *People Daily*, 13 January. Available at: https://www.pd.co.ke/news/eac-states-on-the-verge-of-attaining-one-network-area-165426/

Wang, Z. K. and Winters, L. A. (1997), 'Africa's Role in Multilateral Trade Negotiations', World Bank Policy Research Working Paper No. 1846. Available at: https://catalogue.nla.gov.au/Record/406832

Weeks, J. (1996), 'Regional Cooperation and Southern African Development', *Journal of Southern African Studies*, 22(1), pp. 99–117.

WEF (2021), 'Connecting Countries and Cities for Regional Value Chain Integration: Operationalizing the AfCFTA', World Economic Forum White Paper. Available at: https://www3.weforum.org/docs/WEF_Regional_Value_Chain_Integration_Automotive_Case_Study_2021.pdf

——— (2023), AfCFTA: *A New Era for Global Business and Investment in Africa, Insight Report January 2023*, World Economic Forum. Available at: https://www3.weforum.org/docs/WEF_Friends_of_the_Africa_Continental_Free_Trade_Area_2023.pdf

Weisbrot, M. (2015), *Failed: What the 'Experts' Got Wrong about the Global Economy*, Oxford: Oxford University Press.

Weiss, J. (2017), 'Lewis on Industrialisation and Industrial Policy', *Journal of International Development*, 30(1), pp. 61–79. Available at: https://onlinelibrary.wiley.com/toc/10991328/2018/30/1

Wheen, F. (2004), *How Mumbo-Jumbo Conquered the World: A Short History of Modern Delusions*, New York: Harper Perennial.

Whitfield, L. (2009), *The Politics of Aid: African Strategies for Dealing with Donors*, Oxford: Oxford University Press.

Whitfield, L. and Fraser, A. (2010), 'Negotiating Aid: The Structural Conditions Shaping the Negotiating Strategies of African Governments', *International Negotiation*, 15(3), pp. 341–66.

Whitfield, L. et al. (2015), *The Politics of African Industrial Policy: A Comparative Perspective*, Cambridge: Cambridge University Press.

Winters, L. A. (1999), 'Regionalism versus Multilateralism', Policy Research Working Paper. Available at: https://doi.org/10.1596/1813–9450–1687

WITS (2011), 'Sub-Saharan Africa Trade Indicators 2011', *World Integrated Trade Solution*. Available at: https://wits.worldbank.org/CountryProfile/en/Country/SSF/Year/2011

Wolff, E. A. (2020). 'The Global Politics of African Industrial Policy: The Case of the Used Clothing Ban in Kenya, Uganda and Rwanda', *Review of International Political Economy*, 28(5), pp. 1308–31.

Woolfrey, S. (2021), *What Could Have Gone Wrong: African Futures 2030*, Paris: European Union Institute for Security Studies (EUISS). Available at: https://www.jstor.org/stable/pdf/resrep30202.1.pdf

Woolfrey, S. et al. (2021), *African Futures 2030*, Paris: European Union Institute for

REFERENCES

Security Studies (EUISS). Available at: https://www.iss.europa.eu/sites/default/files/EUISSFiles/CP_164.pdf

Woolfrey, S., Apiko, P. and Pharatlhatlhe, K. (2019), 'Nigeria and South Africa: Shaping Prospects for the African Continental Free Trade Area', ECDPM Discussion Paper No. 242. Available at: https://ecdpm.org/publications/nigeria-and-south-africa-shaping-prospects-for-the-african-continental-free-trade-area/

Woolfrey, S. and Byiers, B. (2019), 'The African Continental Free Trade Area and the politics of industrialisation', *ECDPM*, 18 November. Available at: https://ecdpm.org/talking-points/african-continental-free-trade-area-afcfta-politics-industrialisation/

World Bank (1994), *Adjustment in Africa: Reforms, Results, and the Road Ahead. A Policy Research Report*, Washington, DC: World Bank. Available at: https://documents.worldbank.org/en/publication/documents-reports/documentdetail/497781468009320518/adjustment-in-africa-reforms-results-and-the-road-ahead-summary

———— (2000), *Can Africa Claim the 21st Century?* Washington, DC: World Bank. Available at: https://openknowledge.worldbank.org/handle/10986/22962

———— (2013), *Growing Africa: Unlocking the Potential of Agribusiness*, Washington, DC: The World Bank. Available at: https://documents1.worldbank.org/curated/en/189541468007537925/pdf/759720REPLACEM0mmary0pub03011013web.pdf

———— (2016), 'Breaking down barriers: unlocking Africa's potential through vigorous competition policy', 27 July. Available at: https://www.worldbank.org/en/news/feature/2016/07/27/africa-competition

————(2020a), 'Tariff rate, applied, weighted mean, all products (%)', World Bank data. Available at: https://data.worldbank.org/indicator/TM.TAX.MRCH.WM.AR.ZS

———— (2020b), *World Development Report 2020: Trading for Development in the Age of Global Value Chains*, Washington, DC: World Bank. Available at: https://doi.org/10.1596/978-1-4648-1457-0

———— (2020c), *The African Continental Free Trade Area: Economic and Distributional Effects*, Washington, DC: World Bank. Available at: https://www.worldbank.org/en/topic/trade/publication/the-african-continental-free-trade-area

———— (2021a), 'Enterprise Surveys', World Bank. Available at: https://www.enterprisesurveys.org/en/enterprisesurveys

———— (2021b), *From Crisis to Green, Resilient, and Inclusive Recovery*, Washington, DC: World Bank Group. Available at: https://www.worldbank.org/en/about/annual-report

———— (2022a), 'GDP growth (annual %): World Development Indicators', World Bank data. Available at: https://data.worldbank.org/indicator/NY.GDP.MKTP.KD.ZG

———— (2022b), 'World development indicators', World Bank data. Available at: https://databank.worldbank.org/reports.aspx?source=world-development-indicators

———— (2022c), 'Voluntary National Review 2022', UN High-Level Political Forum

REFERENCES

on Sustainable Development. Available at: https://hlpf.un.org/countries/ethiopia/voluntary-national-review-2022

───── (2023), *Global Economic Prospects*, Washington, DC: World Bank Group. Available at: https://openknowledge.worldbank.org/bitstream/handle/10986/38030/GEP-January–2023.pdf

WTO (1991), 'Sector-by-sector information', New York: World Trade Organization. Available at: https://www.wto.org/english/tratop_e/serv_e/serv_sectors_e.htm

───── (1995), 'The 128 countries that had signed GATT by 1994', New York: World Trade Organization. Available at: https://www.wto.org/english/thewto_e/gattmem_e.htm

───── (1999), *United States: July 1999*, New York: World Trade Organization. Available at: https://www.wto.org/english/tratop_e/tpr_e/tp108_e.htm

───── (2012), *World Trade Report 2012 Trade and Public Policies: A Closer Look at Non-Tariff Measures in the 21st Century*, New York: World Trade Organization. Available at: https://doi.org/10.30875/ac42f7b8-en

Wuyts, M. (2005), 'Growth, Poverty Reduction and the Terms of Trade: A Comment on Tanzania', Paper presented at discussion seminar in Dar es Salaam, REPOA, 2 September.

Yang, Y. and Gupta, S. (2005), 'Regional Trade Arrangements in Africa: Past Performance and the Way Forward', IMF Working Paper 05(36). Available at: https://doi.org/10.5089/9781451860559.001

Yasheng., H. (2005), *Selling China: Foreign Direct Investment during the Reform Era*, Cambridge: Cambridge University Press.

Yeats, A. J. (1990), 'On the Accuracy of Economic Observations: Do Sub-Saharan Trade Statistics Mean Anything?' *The World Bank Economic Review*, 4(2), pp. 135–56.

Yeshiwas, T. and Workie, M. (2018), 'Social, Economical and Environmental Issues of Floriculture Sector Development in Ethiopia', *Review of Plant Studies*, 5. Available at: https://doi.org/10.18488/journal.69.2018.51.1.10

Young, C. M. (1994), *The African Colonial State in Comparative Perspective*, New Haven, CT: Yale University Press.

Young, A. (2014), 'Structural Transformation, the Mismeasurement of Productivity Growth, and the Cost Disease of Services', *American Economic Review*, 104(11), pp. 3635–67.

Young, T. (2020), *We Need to Talk about Africa: The Harm We Have Done, and How We Should Help*, London: Oneworld Publications.

Yuan Sun, I. (2017), 'The World's Next Great Manufacturing Center: How Chinese Investment Is Reshaping Africa', *Harvard Business Review*, May–June. Available at: https://hbr.org/2017/05/the-worlds-next-great-manufacturing-center

Yusuf, S. and Nabeshima, K. (2012), *Some Small Countries Do it Better: Rapid Growth and Its Causes in Singapore, Finland, and Ireland*, Washington, DC: World Bank. Available at: https://doi.org/10.1596/978-0-8213-8846-4

REFERENCES

Zeufack, A. G., Kassa, W. and Coulibaly, S. (2022), *Africa in the New Trade Environment: Market Access in Troubled Times*, Washington, DC: World Bank Publications.

Zimbabwe Mail (2018), '"A really big deal"—Strive Masiyiwa comments on AfCFTA agreement', *Zimbabwe Mail*, 17 April. Available at: https://www.thezimbabwemail.com/economic-analysis/a-really-big-deal-strive-masiyiwa-comments-on-afcfta-agreement/

INDEX

INDEX

INDEX

INDEX

independence, 23
Indonesia, 100
industrial employment, 81
industrial partnership agreements
  (IPAs), 281
'industrial policies', 80
industrial tariffs, 105
industrialisation, 81, 83, 89, 165
Inflation Reduction Act (2022),
  279–80
infrastructure deficits, 96
in-kind donations, 51
'intensive margin', 162
Intergovernmental Authority on
  Development (IGAD), 28
international financial institutions
  (IFIs), 40, 47, 216
international markets, 64
international migrants, 223, 226
International Monetary Fund
  (IMF), 38, 86, 216, 317n48
international trade, 179–80, 216
intra-Africa FDI, 183–4, 185–7,
  186f, 191–2
intra-African imports, 168–9
intra-African investment, 187–90,
  190–2
intra-African migrants, 241
intra-African migration, 224–6,
  225f, 226–7
intra-African trade, 20, 31, 208
  economic significance of,
    148–50, 149f
  informal cross-border trade,
    150–2
  intra-regional trade, 142–7,
    143f, 145f, 146–7t
  introduction, 141–2
  as motor of industrialisation and
    development, 161–4, 163f
  recalculation process, 152–3,
    153f

intra-continental exports, 148
intra-European trade, 146
intra-firm transactions, 181
Investment Protocol, 181, 188
IPAs. *See* industrial partnership
  agreements (IPAs)
Italian Somalia, 22

Japan, 70–2, 126–7, 331n48
Jawara, F., 128, 262
Johnson, Boris, 285
Joint Labour Migration
  Programme, 232
Jolly, Richard, 37
Jones, J., 109
Journal of Modern African Studies
  (1970), 36
jua kali workers, 236
Juma, Calestous, 175

Kaname Akmasutu, 71
Kennan, J., 241
Kenya, 20, 28, 88, 107, 110, 277,
  335n31
  employment challenges, 235–6
  movement of border communi-
    ties, 244–5
Kenyans, 235–6
Keynes, John Maynard, 270
Khanna, Parag, 289–90
Kharas, H., 157
Kigali, 1, 4, 229
Kihato, C. W., 225
Klenow, P. J., 162
Kox, H., 183
Krugman, P., 49, 215
Kwa, A., 128, 262

Labour Market Information
  Systems, 232
labour specialisation, 157
Lafarge Zambia, 282–3

411

Pan-Africanism, 10, 23–4, 27,
  33–4, 49–50
Panagariya, A., 203
Peace and Security Council, 229
Pesticide Action Network of
  Europe, 114
pesticides, 114
Peugeot, 196
Pew Research Center, 9
Philips, 287
phosphate, 68, 148, 191, 192
phytosanitary standards, 174
PIDA. *See* Programme for Infrastructure Development in Africa
  (PIDA)
Pierola, M. D., 162
plastics, 166
'plunder agriculture', 65
Poisson Pseudo-Maximum-
  Likelihood (PPML), 204–5,
  338n20
Ponte, S., 122
Portugal, 37, 114
post-primary schooling, 238
poverty, 85, 179, 226, 241–2
Prebisch, Raúl, 62–3
'premature deindustrialisation',
  91
price stability, 65–6
processed goods, 13, 113, 166
Proctor & Gamble, 195
product adaptation, 135
productive activities, 105, 259
productivity dynamics, 90
productivity growth, 90–1
profitability, 66, 189–90, 190f
Programme for Infrastructure
  Development in Africa (PIDA),
  270–1
public health, 221
purchasing power parities (PPPs),
  156

Qiatou, 92

racism, 221
raw materials, 67, 113, 182, 263
Reader, John, 223
RECs. *See* regional economic
  communities (RECs)
redistributive schemes, 50
Refugees and Internally Displaced
  Persons, 231
refugees, 221, 227, 228
regional dimensions, 158
regional economic communities
  (RECs), 19, 48, 144, 206, 247,
  309n33
  contributions to construction of
    continental economy, 291–4
  emergence of, 27–30, 29t
regional integration, 36, 50–1,
  53, 158, 165, 180–3
regional trade agreements (RTAs),
  201–2
Republic of Ireland, 286
research and development (R&D),
  93–4, 159–60, 175, 206, 268
rice, 127, 170–1
robotics, 289
Rockefeller Foundation, 8
Rodrik, D., 49, 58–9, 79, 83, 200,
  315–16n29
Rojas-Romagosa, H., 183
Rowden, R., 81–2
Roxborough, I., 157
RTAs. *See* regional trade agreements (RTAs)
rubber, 63, 68, 166
rubidium, 290
Russia, 100, 157
Rwanda, 1, 109, 129, 151, 163,
  247
  OCP investment in, 192